10

SURGEON'S JOURNEY

BOOKS BY
J. JOHNSTON ABRAHAM

*

THE SURGEON'S LOG
Impressions of the Far East
THE NIGHT NURSE
A Novel of Hospital Life
MY BALKAN LOG
With the Serbs in the First World War
LETTSOM, HIS LIFE AND TIMES
A History of Medical Life in the London of George III
99 WIMPOLE STREET
A Doctor's Digressions
SURGEON'S JOURNEY
Autobiography

*

Under the pseudonym of
JAMES HARPOLE

LEAVES FROM A SURGEON'S CASE-BOOK
The Romance of Medicine
THE WHITE-COATED ARMY
The Fight Against Disease
BEHIND THE SURGEON'S MASK
Life Through a Surgeon's Eyes
A SURGEON'S HERITAGE
The Long Tradition of Healing

*

THE NIGHT NURSE was filmed in
America as *Nora O'Neale* and in
Europe as *Irish Hearts*. The Har-
pole books have been translated into
Dutch, Danish, Norwegian, Swedish,
Finnish, German, Italian, Spanish and
Portuguese.

Bassano

THE AUTHOR

SURGEON'S JOURNEY

THE AUTOBIOGRAPHY OF

J. JOHNSTON ABRAHAM

*

(1876 —   )

HEINEMANN

LONDON   MELBOURNE   TORONTO

William Heinemann Ltd

LONDON   MELBOURNE   TORONTO

CAPE TOWN   AUCKLAND

THE HAGUE

*

First published 1957
Reprinted 1957

Printed in Great Britain
at The Windmill Press
Kingswood, Surrey

CONTENTS

PLATES

TEXT FIGURES

TO

MY WIFE

CHAPTER I

EARLY DAYS

AN EXCITED MAID stared out of a front window on the first floor, holding a very young baby tucked under her right arm. The baby blinked with round unthinking eyes, blew moist bubbles, waggled its head and squirmed; but the girl was too interested in what she was looking at to notice its discomfort.

A noise of confused cheering came from the crowd in the street below. They were all standing, with their backs to her, gazing up at a huge twelve-foot effigy of an officer in seventeenth-century uniform —cocked hat, full-bottomed wig, buff coat and top boots all complete —which had been hoisted to the branch of an oak tree in the church-yard overhanging the main street.

A man, straddled wide-legged below the figure, was beating a big drum hysterically. Suddenly he stopped, and someone ran forward from the crowd with a torch and applied it to the effigy. There was a flicker, and almost at once the whole structure burst into flames.

A deep exultant roar rose from the crowd; they danced and shouted with raucous laughter; the startled baby began to cry; and the noise brought a pink-cheeked young matron running into the room.

"Mary Ann," she cried sharply, "what are you doing with the waen?" (child).

The girl swung round, put her other hand under the baby and faced the mother.

"Nothin', ma'am. I'm watchin' thim burnin' Lundy," she answered defiantly.

The look of anger left the mother's face. She came forward, held out her arms for the baby, and together with the maid stared down on the scene below. The figure was now burning fiercely. The flames rose higher and higher, smoke almost obscuring the outlines. Suddenly something gave way in the framework, and the greater part of the body with the top boots fell blazing in the roadway, leaving only the arms and head suspended, still burning fiercely. Again the crowd let out a triumphant roar and a high, exultant boy's voice cried out:

"No surrender DerryWalls."

Gradually the flames died down, and the crowd began to thin a little. It was a cold, raw evening. Presently the flames from the upper suspended part began to sink lower and lower until they finally went out. The man with the drum then suddenly became active again; two kettledrums joined him; the flute band gathered round him; there was a rattle of the drums, and the flutes took up the old, old marching tune, the tune that drove James II into exile and lost the throne to his descendants forever: 'Lillibullero', better known in Ulster as 'The Protestant Boys'.

The band marched off followed by the remnants of the crowd; and all that was left was a little red glow of ashes in front of the church railings.

"I think we'll put the waen to bed now," said the mother, turning slowly away from the window.

That was my introduction to history and politics in Ulster, for I was that baby in arms; and what the two women and the unthinking child had been looking at was the burning of the effigy of Lundy, the Governor of Derry in 1689, held annually on the 18th day of December in the town of Coleraine in the County of Londonderry in the Province of Ulster. The two women were my mother and my nurse, and the scene was opposite the house in Kingsgate Street, Coleraine, where I had been born about four months previously at two-thirty in the afternoon of August 16th, 1876.

Of course I do not remember that particular burning, but in my boyhood I saw it repeated so many times I feel I do, for Colonel Lundy was our particular historical bogy. We Ulster boys hated him, and the name of Lundy, with an intensity of hatred I now find difficult to recall; and we looked forward to his annual demise in effigy with gloating anticipation.

"And who," you say, "was Lundy? Never heard of him! What had he done to deserve this perennial hate nearly two hundred years later?"

Of course you would not have heard of him if you were not an Ulsterman. His story is over two hundred and fifty years old now, but to us it is still recent history; for the curse of Ireland is our long memory. Lundy was the Military Governor of Londonderry shortly after the Dutchman, William of Orange, drove his father-in-law James II from the throne of England. James was a Papist, he wanted to restore the Papacy in England, so Protestant England would have nothing to do with him. But in Southern Ireland and in Northern Scotland he had a strong following. Only in Ulster, which had been colonised largely by dour Presbyterian Scots and citizens of London, was William's cause favoured. And so when James, the rightful King, landed in Ireland to recover his lost dignities the South rallied to him, but Ulster put herself into a state of defence, having espoused the Williamite cause.

Colonel Lundy was a professional soldier. He had held a commission under Charles II. He had seen foreign service in Tangier. He had actually been appointed Governor of Derry, the great walled city of Ulster, by King James himself; but after James fled from England he had accepted a commission under William, and so the Protestants of Ulster looked upon him as their natural leader.

Instead, however, of defending the frontiers of Ulster, when James's army advanced from Dublin, he withdrew his men from the line of the Erne, allowed the Bann river to be crossed, and failed to defend Coleraine, which had a complete set of fortifications. In this way he permitted Ulster to be overrun by the Jacobite army, withdrawing all his available troops to Derry, the only remaining Williamite stronghold, apart from Enniskillen, in the extreme north-west of the province. Even in Derry he had made no adequate preparations for defence; and when King James with his army and his two French generals finally appeared before the city, early in April, 1689, it was discovered he was secretly treating for its surrender.

At that time Derry was crowded with Protestant refugees drawn by fear from all the surrounding counties. Some remembered as children the massacres of 1641 when the native Irish had murdered thousands of their forebears in their sleep. The story of the Eve of St. Bartholomew was in the thoughts of others; and when it was whispered around that Lundy was going to surrender the city, fear and panic and violent anger

broke out amongst the refugees. Lundy's house was surrounded by a
ferocious mob. They threatened to murder him. His life was saved
only by the exertions of some of the aldermen and clergy; and late
at night he was let down over the wall in disguise and allowed to
escape.

That was how the historic siege which was to last for one hundred
and five days began. This siege, which Macaulay described so vividly,
was unsuccessful. The city was finally relieved by food ships from
England, and the army of King James, decimated by disease, melted
away. But the cost to the beleaguered inhabitants had been terrific.
Ten thousand people died of typhus fever, diphtheria and dysentery,
and the starving garrison had been reduced to eating rats before relief
came.

Little wonder the memory of Lundy remained to be hated. Derry
and Coleraine held him responsible for all the trouble they had been
through. They believed him to have been a traitor. Now in retrospect,
with the calmness of an interval of two hundred and fifty years, we can
see that he was probably only a pessimistic soldier who saw all the points
against the success of the defence and none of those in its favour. And
that appears to have been the opinion of the judges who tried him when
a prisoner at the Tower of London later.

But Ulstermen still burn his effigy every year in Derry on the anniversary of 'The Closing of the Gates' by the apprentice boys of Derry,
December 18th (December 7th, old style), 1688. Whether they do so
also on the same site in Coleraine still, I do not know. Probably not,
for forty years later I stood in that same room and looked across at the
churchyard. The tree on which the effigy was burnt in my childhood
had gone. Nothing but the stump remained. Perhaps they have forgotten Lundy. I hope so, but I doubt it, for it is memories of this sort
that perpetuate the distrust all men of Ulster blood have for men of the
South.

The shadow of the memory of Lundy is responsible for 'The
Border.' I was brought up on this memory. Now, after half a century
of life in London, I still feel it. I know it is irrational but that does not
make it any less powerful; for it has coloured my whole life, and
nothing I can say to myself can alter it.

*

It is interesting to look back to one's earliest recollections. Some people remember nothing before their third or fourth year, and what they remember is generally something irrelevant.

I can fix my earliest memory by the birth of my next brother when I was two-and-a-half years old, because I can remember the garden where the nurse took me to look at a gooseberry bush under which, she explained, they had just found my young brother. It had been raining; it was a very wet bush; and I was glad they had found him and brought him into the nice warm house.

Another dating memory is of the all-pervasive smell of tea at certain times of the week. My father was a tea merchant, and in those days he used to blend the tea himself by hand. It came in big teak chests lined with lead. The chests were opened and tilted on the wooden floor of the mixing room to the right of the hall of the house as you entered. There, with a square-faced shovel, my father did the mixing himself, for it was most important that the blend should not alter. Ulster people are very particular about their tea, and my father's pride was to give them of the very best. He was an expert tea-taster, and in those days he could never delegate the job to anyone else.

We always knew when the mixing was going on, for the aroma of the blended tea pervaded the house. I used often to creep in and watch, fascinated, until I was seized by the petticoats and hauled away. After the tea was blended it was made up into bags—half pound, one pound, up to five pounds—hundreds and hundreds of bags, all done by hand. My father was very expert, but there were so many bags it took him the better part of a week to do them up.

The tea bags were packed into long wooden cases, two of which fitted into a tax-cart—a two-wheeled vehicle rather like a dog-cart. These tax-carts were driven by my father's men all over the counties of Derry and Antrim, carrying our tea to the farmhouses, then remote from the towns; for the roads were bad, locomotion was slow, the parcel post did not function, and the day of the motor-car was still over a quarter of a century away. My father put more and more of these tax-carts on the road as his business grew more successful. The drivers, or 'tea-men' as they were called, were generally farmers' sons, of the yeoman (tenant-farmer) class. They knew the mentality of their customers—whom they could sell to, whom they could trust to pay.

Journeys lasted a week or a fortnight to and from Coleraine; and the tea-men slept and had their meals at certain regular farmhouses on their journey, paying their lodgings in tea.

Often when I was a boy I used to go for a tour around the country with one of these tea-men. It was in that way I learnt to speak the broad Scots of Burns, almost forgotten now. Antrim people, indeed, are probably the only ones who can still read Burns without a glossary, for their accent has not changed as much as that of the people of the Ayrshire coast opposite.

In the small garden in front of our house at Carthall there was a summer-house made from an old stage-coach. It was the last of the mail-coaches that used to run from Coleraine to Ballycastle before the narrow-gauge railway came. When we were good my elder sister and I and my baby brother were allowed as a treat to sit inside; and I have a curiously sharp recollection still that the straps raising the windows were covered with a grey net braid and had fringes at the ends. I do not know how old that coach was when we played in it over seventy years ago; but it might easily have been another sixty years itself then; and if so it linked up with a memory picture of my grandfather, James Morrison of Toberdoney, telling me how he was sitting by the road-side at Deffrick when the mail-coach passed, and the driver told him that "Bony" had been beaten at a place called Waterloo in the Low Countries.

My grandfather was a big lad of eighteen then, for he was born the year before the Irish Rebellion of 1798. He did not remember the Rebellion, but he had heard so much about it as he grew up that it seemed to him he had felt it all. I can still see in memory the old man with his white locks, his withered face, his shaven chin and side whiskers, sitting in his wooden armchair by the great peat fire in the big farm-house kitchen, his thin knuckles shining as he grasped the sides of his armchair with both hands to raise himself stiffly.

"Aye," he said, "I knew all about the Rebellion, laddie. My fether was away with the yeomanry at Coleraine when the mountainy folk surprised us by streamin' from beyont Knocklayde into the Route. They were burnin' the farmhouses, settin' fire to the thatch as they came; and my mither heard they were stickin' pitchforks into the childer; and she was in mortal fear. I was a wee waen at the breast, and she wrapped me in her shawl and up and out of the house and hid herself and me by our lonesomes in the moss (bog). She could see the smoke of the house and the stables burnin'; and the smell of the roasting kye (cattle) came to her on the wind from the sea. She said the smell made her wake wie hunger, for she had no food in her at all, at all. At night she used to slip down and hoke raw turnips for hersel' in the dark o' the moon. She was three days in hidin', and she thocht I was goin' to die, for I was very wake by then."

"And were you all right, Granda? They didn't catch you, did they?" I enquired eagerly.

"Naw, wee son, they did not! The sodgers came, and with them me fether, and the rebels run awa'," he answered. "Six o' their leaders were hangit afterwards, and their heids stuck up on spikes in the Diamond o' Coleraine," he added grimly.

The old man believed that all the rebels had been Roman Catholics. Actually that was not so in Ulster. Most of the notorious "United Irishmen", as they called themselves, were Presbyterians. The leader was Henry Joy McCracken, and it is now known that more than one Presbyterian Meeting House was used to store the rebel arms.

The Reverend James Porter, a distinguished writer and historian, the minister of Greyabbey, was hanged at the gate of his manse. McCracken was hanged in Belfast. The Reverend Robert Gowdie was hanged in Newtownards, and over twenty suspected ministers escaped to America or suffered imprisonment.

This is quite understandable when one remembers how much Dissenters were persecuted in Ulster before the repeal of the Test Acts. Indeed, Ulster Presbyterians had no cause to be loyal to the British Crown in those days. Earlier on in the eighteenth century thousands of them, finding religious persecution so severe, emigrated to New England; and the toughest soldiers in Washington's army were those very Ulstermen or their descendants. That the United Irishmen should have had a strong following amongst Presbyterians is not to be wondered at when one remembers that no Presbyterian in those days could hold a government office or a commission in the army, his marriage service was hardly recognised, and when he died his minister had to read the burial service on the roadside because the rector would not permit it in the graveyard itself.

My grandfather was a stout Presbyterian, but he belonged to a loyalist family and obviously had forgotten the disabilities his faith suffered when he was a baby. This partly accounts for the two violent prejudices which he tried to inculcate into me. I was sitting on a creepie (three-legged) stool beside his armchair, in front of the peat fire in the kitchen, where he always sat, and he put his old gnarled hand on my head.

"Jamie, lad," he said, "never trust a Papist or a Campbell."

"Why, Granda?" I said.

"Because if you do you'll rue it."

Once when I was older I remember repeating to my father these remarks of my grandfather about the Campbells and the Papists. My father came of old Methodist stock in Fermanagh, and had many Roman Catholic friends and even some relatives. He laughed when he heard it, and said:

"That was just like the old man."

"Yes," I said, "I can understand about the Papists, but what about the Campbells?"

"Oh," he said, with a tolerant smile, "your granddad was full of these strange prejudices."

"He was right about the Campbells," said my mother truculently.

For she had had some trouble with my father about that before. He had hired a man named Campbell as a tea-man, and my mother, with some ancestral Scottish prejudice of which she hardly knew the origin, had tried to dissuade him from so doing.

"You'll rue it, William," she said.

Later my father discovered the man was thieving from him and then my mother had the satisfaction of saying:

"I told you so."

It is odd how this prejudice against the Campbells still persists in Scotland. A cousin of mine, Gordon Morrison of Keil in Duror of Appin, owns the land and the little ruined kirk where there is a plaque to the memory of James Stewart of Acharn. Stewart was condemned to death by a judge and jury composed mainly of Campbells, in revenge for the murder of Colin Campbell, though everyone knew he was innocent.

After he was hanged at Ballachulish his friends made the guard drunk, purloined the body, and buried it secretly.

No one knew for years where they laid him; but the nearest sacred soil to his home, Acharn, is the ruined kirkyard on my cousin's land at Keil; and it is generally believed he is buried there.

Tourists come frequently to see the corner where he is reputed to lie; and at the bicentenary of his death in 1952 the Stewarts who gathered at Ballachulish came later to Keil to pay their respects to his last resting place.

It is the story of James Stewart that R. L. Stevenson used in *Kidnapped* and *Catriona*. It happened as long ago as 1752; but even now, I find, two hundred years later, men get hot over the guilt or innocence of Alan Breck, who is said to have fired the fatal shot that killed Colin Campbell, and whom Stevenson made the hero of *Kidnapped*. Such is memory in the Highlands.

Glencoe is not far from Duror. It is a name sacred to the MacDonald clan owing to the massacre perpetrated by the Campbells in February, 1691.

The story of that foul deed must have been but a legend to my grandfather; but I found many years later that it was still an active memory in Scotland.

I was lunching at my club with John Tweed, the sculptor, when we were joined by Ramsay MacDonald, who had recently been elected a member. The conversation drifted round to the kinship of the Scot and the Ulsterman; and to illustrate it I told them in the course of that lunch the story of my grandfather and the Campbells. Ramsay looked at me, and shook his handsome grey head.

"Your grandfather wasn't far out. I can't help feeling the same. Recently I was giving away the prizes at Lossiemouth School, and I said to the girl who got the first prize:

" 'What's your name, lassie?'

" 'Nancy Campbell, sir,' she answered.

"And before I had time to think I heard myself saying, 'Lassie, I'm sorry you havna a better name.'

"She burst into tears, and I felt so ashamed of myself. But I couldn't help saying it all the same."

My grandfather was well over eighty when I first began to get a clear picture of him. He died in 1883 when I was seven years old, but I can picture him quite clearly. He used the broad Scots of his ancestors and said he was the sixth generation from the Plantation in the reign of James I. Morrison is of course a very common name in the west of Scotland and the Isles. It is said that you cannot throw a brick at a policeman in Glasgow without hitting either a Morrison or a Robertson. I have never been in Glasgow, so am not sure about the bricks; but I do know that in the Route, that is, the triangle between Giant's Causeway, Coleraine, Dervock, Mosside and Ballycastle, I have a confusing number of Morrison relatives, besides McAllisters, McConaghies, Cannons, Lyles, Camacs, Hunters and Montgomerys, all cousins once, twice and even three and four times removed.

My great-grandfather, John Morrison, had a large family of sons and daughters all of whom remained and married within a few miles of the old homestead. The difficulty of distinguishing between the various families therefore became very great. My grandfather was known as Cutman Jamie, and his brothers were Lang John, Picket Eddy, Gray Joe, Jack of the Kiln, Daly of Islandrose and Willy of Mosside. And when it is realised that they all had large families one can see the necessity for such nicknames. I gave up trying to unravel all these relationships when a boy, but my mother and my grandmother, with the long pedigree memory of the race, could pick their way quite confidently through the maze.

Children as a rule see more of their mother's relatives than their father's. This was particularly so in my case because my father was a Fermanagh man, travel was slow and expensive seventy years ago, and in consequence I seldom saw any of my Abraham relatives. I have only a faint memory of my father's mother, Sarah Johnston, a terrifying person very proud of being a Johnston of Newtown-Butler. In this connection again I came up against an enormous clan, for there are hundreds of Johnston families along the valley of the Foyle from Derry to Enniskillen, and all of them are related more or less remotely.

She was a big, loud, boisterous woman of the horse-coper, cattle-dealing, squireen class, full of rancour and uncharitableness.

She married my grandfather, James Abraham, in 1844. By all accounts he was a quiet, pious man. He was a linen merchant. Linen was then still woven on handlooms in the cottages all over Ulster, for there were no great factories with power looms such as we see today.

When a weaver had finished his 'web' he brought it to the linen market in the nearest market town, and there merchants like my grandfather bought the long lengths of grey unbleached material. These they sold again to the wholesalers. From the wholesalers the webs were distributed to the bleaching greens all over the country, where the rolls lay month after month on the grass exposed to the Ulster sun, wind and rain, until they became bleached to the snowy white colour demanded by purchasers.

My grandfather Abraham's lot as a linen merchant was a hard one. It was an exposed life, riding in all sorts of weather over execrable roads from one small market town to another, sleeping in rough hotels, eating badly-cooked food.

In his case the almost inevitable happened. He caught a chill, got pneumonia, and died at the age of forty-five, after ten years of married life, leaving his widow with six small children—three boys and three girls. My father, William Abraham, born in 1849, was the youngest of the three sons.

Probably it was lucky that my grandmother Sarah Johnston, thus unexpectedly widowed, was a hard, pushing woman, for anyone soft might easily have gone under. She had a house which she owned and a small farm, and what she could collect from my grandfather's debtors to support her and her six young children. She had no close relatives of my grandfather's to come to her aid. All his brothers had emigrated to Pennsylvania. Only my great-grandfather was left, Alexander Abraham of Aughnacloy, and he was then eighty-three years of age.

Alexander Abraham is the high-spot in my family. He was a very remarkable old man, born at Aughnacloy in 1768 and living until 1873, a hundred and five years. He said his family were originally of Lancashire Quaker stock, and settled in Ireland in the time of William III. Later, however, they came under the influence of John Wesley. My father remembered him well, as he was thirty-four years of age when the old man died. Alexander was the thirteenth and youngest child of his father, who had married three times. He was educated at Armagh Royal School; but during the Rebellion of 1798 he served as a soldier, much to the annoyance of his family, who did not believe in war. I now have the musket he carried, as a memento of that time. It is a great, clumsy flintlock weighing some fifteen pounds. He was 'fugleman' of his company, and after the Rebellion had been squashed he married the sister of his company commander, Captain Levinstone.

This marriage took place at Aughnacloy parish church in 1804, and the young couple settled on a bit of land called Derrameen granted to my great-grandfather for his services in the Rebellion. On this little farm he brought up his family, all of whom emigrated to the United States except my grandfather and one sister who married a Roman Catholic. For this she was ostracised, and she and her husband had to clear out to Canada.

My father told me that my great-grandfather was the only one in the neighbourhood who could write, and that he used to do all the letters for the people around. He also did land-surveying by mensuration as he had been taught that at school. He lived a happy, quiet life—a pious old man with no worldly ambitions whatever towards wealth or position.

One of his elder brothers was the first Methodist minister ordained by John Wesley in Ireland, and there is a tradition that Wesley preached in our old house in Aughnacloy standing on a big wooden chair. Wesley was a tiny little man, and often used to stand on a chair at any meeting he was addressing.

My great-grandfather and my grandfather belonged to a branch of Methodism called Primitive Methodist. These people belonged, in Ireland at any rate, to the Established Church, but they also had their own itinerant preachers, and sometimes their own small chapels where they met on Sundays an hour before the Established Church service, so as not to interfere with it and to be able to attend both services. They maintained that John Wesley had lived and died a member of the Established Church, and that they could do no better than follow his example.

Primitive Methodists ceased to exist in Ireland when my father was a small boy in the seventies of the last century. They amalgamated with the Wesleyan Methodists; but I can still remember one famous preacher, probably the last, the Reverend John Kerr, of whom my father was very fond. He started his ministry as a Primitive Methodist, riding round the country on horseback preaching the gospel from farmhouse to farmhouse. It was a form of ministry that could not survive under modern conditions, and its end was inevitable. In England, however, the Primitive Methodists still remained a separate body until 1932.

It was in this atmosphere of Methodist piety that my father was born and brought up; and it was this atmosphere that largely moulded my own outlook on life until I went to the University. My mother was a Presbyterian, but of course adopted my father's faith when she married.

My father, I can remember, was extremely strict. He would have no work done on Sunday except necessary work. All boots had to be polished the night before, and all cooking that was possible was done on the Saturday. No one ever thought of travelling by train on a Sunday. That was considered immoral, because of course the men who ran the trains had to work on Sunday against their religious convictions. But it was allowable to harness your own horse and trap and drive out to preach in country places. My father, who was what was called a 'local preacher', used often to drive out five or six miles and hold services when a regular clergyman of the church was not available.

No books could be read on Sunday except religious books. Novels were never allowed inside my father's house when I was a small boy.

Sunday was a very long, wearisome day for us children. We used to have 'class meeting' in the morning at ten o'clock. Then we went to morning church. Then we came home to the Sunday dinner. Then we went to Sunday School in the afternoon, came home to tea, and then after that we went to the evening service. No one ever thought of curtailing these services. In the middle of the week in addition there was also a prayer meeting, usually on a Wednesday evening, which when we were older we were supposed to attend.

My father was the main support of the church in our town. For many years he was what is called 'Circuit Steward'. He ran the finances of the church, arranged about the succession of clergymen, and did all the business connected with the administration of the circuit.

The system used in Methodism, where the minister changes every three or four years, makes the clergyman very dependent on his local administrators. He cannot possibly know local conditions, local finance, local customs; and so the Circuit Steward is really the most important lay person in every circuit.

Always the new clergyman was our closest friend. Methodism in Ireland is an intimate family sort of religion. Everyone knows everyone else. The ministers moving about from circuit to circuit have friends all over Ireland, and so when members of any congregation move to another circuit the minister always knows someone who can take care of them and see that they are looked after amongst strangers.

My mother's religion before marriage was something totally different from this. Her people belonged to a very peculiar form of Presbyterianism known as the 'Seceders'. I believe their full title is 'The Original Secession of Seceders'. Their headquarters are in Aberdeen. They had three Meeting Houses in the north of Ireland when I was a boy, and they were the smallest sect of Presbyterians, a little less in number than the 'Covenanters', who were also fairly strong in our area. My grandmother, Ann Hunter, was a 'Covenanter' before she married my grandfather, James Morrison.

The Seceders had their Meeting House about a mile from my grandfather's farm. It was one of those plain, square Presbyterian buildings with absolutely no kind of adornment of any sort—for the House of God to them was a meeting-house only and not a temple. The services to me as a small boy, when I was staying at the farm, were interminably long and wearisome. Farmers from a distance used to drive from miles around to the Meeting House. They drove inside the enclosure, unyoked their horses, and put them in a stable which had about twelve to fifteen stalls behind the Meeting House. Of course the members who lived within two or three miles went there on foot. We always went on foot.

The pews in the Meeting House were of hard wood without any cushions. Everything in the service was arranged to be as different as possible from that of the Church of Rome or the Established Church. We sat down at the psalms. We stood up and turned round and faced the back of the church at the prayers. There was no instrumental music of any kind. That would have been considered a terrible sin. But we had two precentors, a tenor and a bass, who sat in little cubicles underneath the pulpit. The tenor used to strike a tuning fork and get the note. He then led off, and the congregation followed him. I can remember the tenor well. His name was John Colvin. He had a long white beard. He looked exactly like the caricatures one saw of Presbyterian elders in the comic papers of fifty years ago.

The psalms were the only things that were sung. Even paraphrases were not permitted, and hymns were unknown. The minister used to read a chapter from the Bible and then give us a running commentary on that. At first as a small boy I used to think when he had finished this, which lasted well over half an hour, that it was the sermon. But I soon found out my mistake. The sermon followed shortly after, and lasted well over an hour. An hour and a half was nothing unusual. We used to get to the Meeting House about eleven. If we got away between half past two and three we were doing well. Of course people grew very hungry while this long service was going on; and it was not un-usual to see them with their heads fairly well down beneath the back of the pew in front eating oatmeal 'farls' or 'fadge' to satisfy their hunger.

The collection was taken in a peculiar way. The elders appeared, each carrying a pole about ten feet long with a small bag on the end of it. They pushed this pole over the heads of the people to the far end of the pew and then withdrew it gradually towards the aisle. They did the same to the next pew, and so went through the congregation. I have painful memories of being very tired and very sleepy and very glad when these services were over.

Now all this is a thing of the past, and in the Toberdoney Meeting House I believe that today they have a harmonium. If my grand-mother knew there was a 'kist o' whistles' there I think she would turn in her grave. I wonder also how she would feel could she know that the twelve Seceder congregations in Scotland, and the two remaining in Ireland, have now rejoined the main Presbyterian bodies in each country after two hundred years of secession.

Always at holiday times and whenever opportunity permitted, two or three of us children were sent out of the way to the farm in County Antrim, for there were six of us in the family, coming one rapidly after another. And, as if that were not enough for one woman to look after, my mother had also several servants, a number of apprentices, and a good many tea-men to cater for, as my father's business activities kept spreading yearly. He had started originally selling tea to the farming communities in the two counties of Derry and Antrim; but from that, gradually and almost inevitably, he spread his wings into supplying nearly everything a farmer could want—seeds, artificial manures, agricultural implements, coal, iron, groceries, hardware—until eventu-ally he became a sort of farmers' 'William Whiteley'.

The hands in this business were known as apprentices and, as the custom then was, they were indentured three to five years to learn the business. They were paid only a few shillings a week, but they had to be boarded by their employer, and my mother had these young men to look after at the top of the big rambling house in which we lived. Little wonder this harassed young woman, with her big family and all these extra people to cater for, was glad to push her children off to the wide and happy comfort of the big snug farmhouse ten miles away on the road to Ballycastle.

It was a long journey in those days—or so it seemed to a little boy dangling his short legs in a farm cart when one of my uncles came into the market with a load of produce to sell and was returning empty. I can still remember how interminable the time seemed until we came to the familiar cross-roads and reached the hill half-way down which the farmhouse stood. Now it takes fifteen minutes in a motor and the distance seems nothing. Few things surprise people so much when going back to childhood haunts as to find how everything has contracted from what memory recalls.

By the time I was old enough to have any considerable memory my grandfather was dead, and my grandmother, Ann Hunter, was carrying on the farm with two sons and one unmarried daughter. The other son, Robert Morrison, was a medical student at Edinburgh, and I think it was his influence and the stories of medical life and the peeps I had into his anatomy books that settled my fate. Before I was ten I had decided to be a doctor. This is a decision I have never had cause to regret, for medicine is the finest introduction to life that any man, or any woman for that matter, can have. So you can picture me as a small, round-faced little boy running bare-footed over the farm, picking up knowledge of horses and dogs, cats, birds, flowers, cattle, all the things a child learns automatically and unconsciously on a farm.

Everyone smiled good-naturedly over this ambition of mine to be a doctor, and so when an animal died the vet used to let me see the post-mortem. When he bled a horse he showed me how he drove the fleem into the jugular vein in its neck.

One day when I saw a chicken which had a broken leg go flapping round helplessly, and my aunt wanted to have it killed for the pot, I begged her to let me splint it. She laughed and said:

"All right, 'doctor'."

So I put two little sticks, one on either side of the fracture, and bound them to the leg with saddlers' wax-ends. The chicken flapped away on its splinted leg. It couldn't fly up for some time; but it was perching in a month; and I can still remember the pride I felt in this my first surgical success.

"The wee chiel has the healin' touch," said old Molly Taggart, the 'wise woman' who lived in one of our single-roomed 'cottar' houses down the lane, when she heard of it. And, as everyone agreed she had the second sight, that settled it.

She must have been nearly a hundred when I knew her, a little bent woman with a shawl over her shoulders, straggling grey locks, a tanned leather-like face, deep brown eyes and thin claw-like hands. I can still see her in my mind, crouching over the peat fire on the hearth-stone. The floor of the cottage was of baked earth. Beside the fire, on the floor against the wall, she had a straw pallet covered by a patchwork quilt. My grandmother used to send me with 'locks' of tea for her; and sitting on a creepie stool I would listen fascinated while she told me stories about the 'wee folk', and the awful things they could do to you if you offended them. I think most of the neighbours in the town-end were afraid of her.

My grandmother farmed the place with the help of her family, her hired women, and her men servants. There were always two hired men working with my uncles. These men were engaged twice a year at the great hiring-fair at Coleraine in May and in November. Their pay was about twelve to fifteen pounds in the half year, all found. On the hiring-fair day employers and men met and bargained as to the wages. As soon as a bargain was struck the farmer gave the man a shilling, which was called 'earl's money'; and the man then put a little ribbon in his hat which indicated that he was engaged for the next six months and no other would-be employer need bother to speak to him.

In addition to all these people living in the farmhouse and working on the farm there was another class called 'cottars'. A cottar was a married man who had a cottage on the farm for which he gave half or one day's work a week. Each cottar had a bit of vegetable garden, a kailyard, of his own; and he was allowed to 'draw', that is, take sufficient cartloads of peat from the bog to build a stack that gave him fuel for the year. Every farmer had an area of bog of his own, and the time when the peat was being cut and dried was one of the pleasantest of the year.

My grandmother owned about half a dozen cottar houses in a row or 'toonen' (townend), as they called it; and these were situated on either side of a loanin (lane) through the middle of the farm. In this way she was always able to depend on extra labour practically every day. The wives of the cottars and their children, of whom there seemed to be scores, came and helped at all the busy periods such as the hay-making, flax-pulling, corn-cutting or potato-lifting, when extra help was required. I have vivid memories of these barefooted children, all very bright-eyed and healthy, whom my grandmother looked upon as her clan. They had buttermilk and oatmeal from the farm and the mothers had 'locks' of tea from the parlour when they came to see my grandmother. Most of them kept hens or pigs. The children ran about in ragged patched clothes and went to school at Deffrick, about a mile away, in the winter-time to learn reading, writing and arithmetic, which was about the limit of their education.

Seventy years ago every farm had numbers of these children running about, and all the cottar houses were well filled; but now in the same place you will find almost none. The cottar houses are deserted, the thatched roofs have fallen in, the gardens are over-run with weeds and brambles, the white-washed walls are green-stained and cracked. The clean little houses I can remember are just ruins.

What has happened to the people? Well, most of them went to America in the first thirty or forty years of this period, for they kept emigrating in thousands until the quota system was introduced and the United States found itself filling up. By that time our agricultural population had been reduced to a fraction of what it used to be. Looking back on it now I dare say they were over-crowded. I dare say there was little chance of their getting on in life. I dare say many of their descendants are now well-off, comfortable citizens of the United States. But I do not think that their fathers ever were unhappy or even under-fed. I am sure my own memories of them are that everyone was very friendly, everyone was very cheerful. We all ran about together, played together, and the farmers' children and the cottars' children went to the same school without any feeling of social difference, for were we not all descendants of the original Scottish settlers, all of the same blood, all Presbyterians who had the same clannish feeling?

Life was very patriarchal on the big farm as I remember it. And everything centred on the low-roofed kitchen with its glowing peat fire on the wide hearth, over which hung a big pot always boiling, either cooking for the family or preparing food for the cattle. If there was no pot, there was sure to be a griddle (girdle) over the fire, baking hard bread (oatcake) or fadge (potato cake) or soda scones or pancakes or what we children loved most of all—slim cake, a sweet thin scone, a special treat for tea.

Oatcake was of course the staple food cereal used on the farm. Bakers' bread was only an occasional luxury. The oatcake was kneaded out to the proper thickness on a board and then made into a large circular slab eighteen inches in diameter. This was put on the griddle and when it was heated up a little over the fire it was quartered into farles—four farles to each cake. These were baked on the griddle over the fire until they were firm, and then taken carefully off and the next batch substituted. But the baking was not then finished. The farles had to be harned (hardened); and it was here we youngsters were roped in to help. Around the circumference of the peat fire were placed two or three curved props of wood rather like the outer portions of the rim of a cartwheel. These were fitted with little legs to hold them up; and between them and the fire the farles of oatcake were carefully propped so that they could be toasted hard. This gave them a concave shape, made them more brittle; and woe betide the youngster who did not watch carefully and allowed the farles either to burn or to fall into the soft peat ash and get dirty. Well-made oatcake spread with fresh butter and eaten with a mug of new milk was no bad food for a growing child, as the researches of recent years on vitamin content have shown.

Breakfast, I remember, consisted of bacon and egg fried in a pan with fadge (potato cake) or 'meelacrusha.' Fried fadge was good, but we loved meelacrusha best of all. It was oatmeal fried in the hot bacon fat. Before this, however, we had our porridge—'stirabout' as we called it, or 'brochen'—brochen was supposed, I don't know why, to be a vulgar name, and my grandmother rather frowned on the hired men for using it in our presence, when they were having breakfast in the kitchen. The elders had salt with their stirabout, but we, because we were children, were given sugar as a great concession, such softness being beneath the dignity of grown-ups. We had our meals 'ben the house' so as to be out of the way of the work in the kitchen, where all day long something was being cooked for the cattle, the pigs or the poultry.

Always, as I have said, there was a great pot simmering over the open peat fire which roared up the wide chimney and had to be constantly replenished with fresh turves from the 'peetnuick', and logs of fir from the resinous tree trunks found buried in the bogs when the peat was being cut. The big pot was nearly always full of 'dguchrea', a sort of oatmeal gruel which was fed to the young cattle. Or if it wasn't dguchrea it was Indian meal (maize), but this was considered definitely an inferior food. There was a still cheaper sort of cattle food called 'sowans', a gruel made from the husks of oats and any remains that clung to them after milling. My grandmother rather despised sowans. It was only the poor farmers who used them. Now we know these husks contained the Vitamin B that is so essential to good health.

Oatmeal and potatoes in some form or another with buttermilk were really the staple sources of nourishment in those days, and they certainly produced magnificent specimens of men. I can see in my mind the big oatmeal bin in my grandmother's kitchen which stood always to the right of the fireplace. It was filled once or twice a week. And I can remember the old lady, then probably about fifty but incredibly old to us children, standing on the polished tiled floor with her hand on the bin, looking at a beggar woman who had just come in, with a small calico bag, or 'poke', in her hand. This poke was the symbol of the beggar, and it was the rigid custom of the country that the housewife must fill her hand with meal from the bin and put it into the beggar's poke. Neither made any comment. It was a ritual; only the mean farmer's wife begrudged this tribute; for the beggar was also the carrier of news from one farm to another—news of births, deaths, scandals and marriages. And thus her advent was often quite an agreeable break for gossip. It was all part of the freemasonry of life. The beggar departed with her poke, and moved on to the next farm. At the end of a few hours her poke was full of oatmeal, and she had enough food to last her for a week.

There was another kind of beggar, however, 'the gentle beggar', one who had seen better days. The ritual here was different. The gentle beggar was allowed to sit down, was often given a meal or some article of clothing, and when she went away was always given the same courtesy as a cottar's wife—a 'lock' of tea, that is, about two teaspoonsful of tea screwed up in a paper cone.

Tea was the great luxury of the farmer's wife in those days. My father's psychology was sound when he started supplying it direct to them, so that they had not to wait until their next visit to the nearest market town, and therefore possibly run the risk of being without the precious beverage for days or even weeks. His tea was the very best he could obtain. It made his name a household word throughout the two counties of Derry and Antrim, and enabled him later without advertising to sell almost anything the farmer required. It brought him prosperity.

CHAPTER II

*

GROWING UP

I CAN REMEMBER quite well the first story I read. It was *Little Henry and his Bearer: a Tale of the Indian Mutiny*. It opened a new world to me, for we had no books of children's stories or Nursery Rhymes in those days, and no Fairy Tales such as English children are made familiar with in the nursery. My father had an extensive library. He read theology, biography and poetry, but no fiction. I can remember *Barnes on the Acts*, a complete set of Wesley's Journals and Sermons, and copies of Milton, Cowper, Wordsworth and Coleridge in Moxon's editions. There must have been many others, but these I cannot now recollect.

Novels were unknown in our house; and 'Yellow Backs', the two-shilling stiff paper-backed novels found on railway stalls, with lurid illustrations on the covers of half-dressed women being embraced, were considered too wicked even to be mentioned. Religious tracts we were well supplied with and I can remember certain improving little books we were allowed to read, like *Jessica's First Prayer*, and *Christy's Old Organ*. We also had Sunday School prizes of an improving type— *Peter Pengelly, or True as the Clock*, by the Reverend Mark Guy Pearce —and oddly enough books about America like *Peter Cartwright, the Backwoods Preacher* and *From Log Cabin to White House, the Life of President Garfield, Little Women, Good Wives*, and *The Four Girls at Chautauqua*. Why do I remember these names? I do not know, but they gave me an impression of American life that has coloured my outlook ever since.

The word 'novel' was anathema to my father. I remember buying *Waverley* in a paper edition. It was labelled 'Notable Novels. No. 1', and I hid it under my pillow and read it surreptitiously at night.

Later, as the mellowing years came, I was allowed to buy a complete

22

William Abraham, aged 23 (1872)

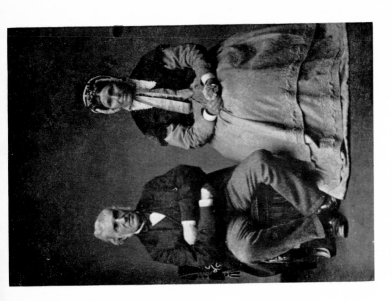

James Morrison, aged 77, and his wife Ann
(*née* Hunter), aged 47 (1874)

The author, Junior Freshman, aged 18 (1894)

Elizabeth Abraham (*née* Morrison), aged 18 (1874)

set of Scott's novels without protest as they came out in paper covers at sixpence each. I bound them myself in six fat volumes. I wonder could I read them now?

But oddly enough it was at my grandmother's farm that I first got introduced to real literature. To this day I cannot think how the curious library I found there originated. None of my uncles read anything except *The Coleraine Chronicle* and *The Witness*, yet there it was— a veritable treasure house to a mind thirsting for the beauty of the written word.

All these books were in what my grandmother called the 'closet'. It is an old English word that has almost dropped out of modern usage, but still survives in Ulster and America. It means a small room off a larger one or off a passage. The closet at Toberdoney was off the passage between the kitchen and the parlour (ben the house). It was a tiny place lined all round the walls with shelves, and having a ladder in the middle that led to the sleeping loft under the thatch above. Its vast importance to me lay in the books on the shelves. They were dusty, dilapidated, uncared for. They had not been disturbed for years. Nobody indeed remembered their existence. Who collected them I never found out. I have an idea it was my grandfather, James Morrison; but he was dead before I was old enough to be interested, and I did not risk asking my grandmother for fear I should be told not to read them. But to whoever collected them and put them there I owe an immense debt of gratitude.

Amongst them were *Sandford and Merton*, *Robinson Crusoe*, and *The Swiss Family Robinson*, Lane's *Arabian Nights*, and a novel by Captain Mayne Reid called *White Gauntlet* that fixed my views of the Civil War for years after. There were two books of American humour: *Texas Siftings* and *On a Mexican Mustang*, written by J. Armoy Knox, who I discovered later was a cousin of my grandfather, and a queer work of American humour entitled *The Adventures of the Elephant Club*. There was an *Almanack* of Benjamin Franklin's, and a *Bell's Elocutionist*. But the greatest find of all was in a lot of battered volumes of Dick's sixpenny classics. Here I discovered two paper-bound volumes that changed my whole outlook on life: the complete poems of Burns and Byron. Imagine the impact of these on the mind of a boy of ten whose reading up to then had been school books and the Bible. It was

B

an open sesame to an enchanted world. They made me drunk with excitement. I used to climb into a sycamore tree across the road in front of the farmhouse. In the tree I had discovered three branches that made a natural armchair; and there I read and read and read, oblivious of the world, until I heard my grandmother's voice growing more and more querulous:

"Wee Jamie, where are you? Sakes alive, where is that wee chiel! Jamie, come in to your dinner."

And then I would slide down from my hidden perch and call out: "Coming, Granny."

Burns was a wonderful discovery. Of course I could talk the broad Scots of County Antrim which was identical with that of Burns. But I had been taught that it was not 'genteel' to talk like that. Only cottar men and farmhands used that sort of language in general conversation. My grandmother and my uncles talked it of course, especially when with the men, because they had to deal with them. But my father, who was a Fermanagh man, talked beautiful English, and sometimes hardly understood what people were saying when they broke into the Doric.

It was therefore a great surprise to me when I first came across 'The Bard' and discovered the beauty of the printed word. It was too wonderful. I learnt 'The Twa Dogs' by heart, laughed over 'Tam O'Shanter', and was secretly pleased, and at the same time shocked, by the 'Address to the Deil'. I felt I dare not quote that to anyone. But I loved it, loved Burns, understood him. The beauty of his lyrics stirred the ancestral blood in me. It was music to my ears. To this day Burns still stirs me as nothing else except the pipes.

Byron was different. He fascinated me in a different way, made me feel worked up. I was afraid of Byron. The narrative poems gave me a shivering excitement I did not understand. I read and read and could not stop. Imagine the excitement of reading 'The Giaour' and 'Beppo' with their reckless stories of illicit love for the first time. Don Juan I felt was very wicked, but I read him breathlessly. And, from those early days in that Ulster farmhouse, "the isles of Greece", that I was not to see until thirty years later, lived clearly in my imagination, so that when I saw the feluccas hauled up on the beach at Salonika with their dark-skinned, ear-ringed, piratical-looking crews, my mind went back abruptly to the sycamore tree and the closet and the dusty volume of Byron on the right-hand side of the third shelf.

Even at ten years of age I was conscious that the characters in *Sandford and Merton* and *The Swiss Family Robinson* were just pegs on which to hang information, but that *Robinson Crusoe* was the real thing—such is the power of genius. *The Arabian Nights* opened a world of enchantment to me which for days made me oblivious of all the ordinary things of life. I lived the adventures over and over again. My prosaic aunt would say:

"What's wrong with the waen?"

She thought I was ill, and wanted to give me castor oil, when she found me mooning about, living in the atmosphere of Baghdad and the great Caliph, Haroun al Raschid. It must have bitten deep into me, for when I wandered round during the First World War in Cairo, and later in Damascus, I felt that I had been there before, that it was oddly familiar to me.

Nearly all my holidays were spent at the farm, where my grandmother spoilt me. I saw the seasons as they came, and ran about barefooted wherever I liked. Both of my uncles were excellent ploughmen and won most of the ploughing matches around. They had great, sleek, powerful horses and the very latest in ploughs; and I was allowed to plod behind the ploughman, watching the brown earth turn like a wave as the share went forward, hearing the ploughman's voice: "Huff-aad-aff, huff-gee" as he steered the straining horses, ignoring the rooks dropping in spirals behind us as we progressed. Then there would be the harrowing, and the drilling or the rolling according to the crop—whether it was oats, or flax, grass, vetches, potatoes, swedes, Aberdeens, or mangel wurzel. We never grew barley, for some reason I cannot remember, and I think we were too far north for wheat. One of our most beautiful sights however in the early summer was the fields of flax, the long light green stems swaying gracefully, topped by vivid blue flowers rippling over the green stems as the gentle summer wind swept across the fields in waves.

Flax in those days was still pulled by hand, for there is no mechanical device as delicate as the human hand for preserving the fibre of the long stalks. When it was pulled it was stacked in sheaves for some time to weather; and then the sheaves were dropped into what we called 'lint dams.' Nearly every farm had its own lint dams, always somewhere close to a burn or running stream so that the dams, about thirty feet long by six feet wide and four feet deep, could be readily filled with water in which the sheaves of flax were immersed. There the sheaves rotted for weeks until the farmer thought that most of the outside of the flax stalk had been eroded away. When he was satisfied that this was so, the sheaves were taken out with pitchforks, opened and spread on the fields on which the flax had been grown.

That is the time not to be in Ulster, for the smell of the rotting flax is something one never forgets. It rises to high heaven and is most unpleasant. The water in which the flax is rotted has to be carefully drained away, for if it is allowed to run into the nearest burn it proves fatal to the fish in the stream. Owners of fishing rights were constantly taking action to restrain careless farmers in my time, and no doubt still are, for human nature has not changed very much in the last half century.

Eventually, however, with sun and rain the smell goes, and the flax is now ready for 'scutching'. The scutching mills when I was a boy were quite small affairs all over the country. They simply teased the greater part of the flax stalk away, leaving only the long fibres that eventually were to be woven into linen. From the scutch mills the farmer collected his bundles of linen fibre, and also the 'tow', that is, all the débris which the teeth of the scutching mill had torn off the fibres. This tow was used rather like cotton wool as a lining for padding quilts or cushions, or something on which to spread a linseed poultice. The bundles of lint were taken by the farmers to the flax market of the nearest town, and there sold after much bargaining to the flax merchants. Formerly the farmers' wives must have spun the threads used in weaving on their spinning wheels, but in my time that had almost disappeared. My grandmother had a wheel, and she could use it; but she found it more economical to send her flax to the market, where it was sold by weight.

Weaving by handloom was quite common when I was a boy. Every weaver had his own handloom in the kitchen of his cottage, and there he would work, throwing his shuttle hour after hour. He always worked the pedals that made the pattern in his stockinged feet, and he never condescended to do any work in the house or garden. That would have roughened his hands, and a man making '1800 linen' needed to have fine, delicate hands without the least roughness.

Weavers were always great talkers, and after they had been at work for a number of years they all got curvature of the spine from stooping over the loom. You could always tell an old weaver in those days by his stoop.

My favourite weaver was James McKay, whose cottage was about half a mile from the farm. I used to sit, fascinated, watching him and listening to his wisecracks, for he was a great wit. A good deal of it was over my head, and I did not understand the guffaws of the elders around.

Then Mrs. McKay would say:

"Whisht, James, a wunther at ye, afore the waen."

And James would reply:

"Och. Hadd yer tongue, wumman. Shure it'll do him no harm."

Milking the cows, night and morning, was a sight that always interested me. There is a warm, comfortable smell about a byre that one never forgets. And cows are great individuals. They will not let certain people milk them at all. They hold their milk in the udders or kick if they feel they are being handled unskilfully. And every cow differs from every other. My grandmother had an old cow for years called Crimmie who bossed all the other cows. If she did not have her way she butted her opponent until she got it. Each cow had her own stall in the byre and went there instinctively. If a new cow appeared in the byre Crimmie taught her her place. When the cows were let out to pasture, Crimmie led them. When they were lowing with full udders to come home in the evening, Crimmie was the first through the gate into the lane. I was very fond of Crimmie. When she grew too old to have a calf, she disappeared. I remember asking for her, and there was a sudden silence. I didn't know why, but I felt sad for days. To console me there came a new puppy, and I forgot.

It was a great privilege to be allowed to go into the big, cool, dim-lit dairy where the milk was poured into shallow circular brown earthenware crocks to allow the cream to rise. That took from twenty-four to forty-eight hours, according to the time of year and the richness of the milk. And then the top was scooped up with a proportion of the milk and poured into the churn. What was left was skim milk, and this was fed to the calves, and given to the servants or cottars if there was any over; for, as was natural on a farm, the calves came first. And excellent food it was, since all that had been removed was the fat, leaving the protein, sugar, calcium, iron and vitamins still remaining in the milk.

Churning the milk to make butter was done by hand in the farm kitchen. It was a tiring job, and anyone handy was roped in to do a turn, or 'gie a brash' as the expression was. You kept pushing the long-handled plunger up and down through the milk, until you feared it would never be finished; and then, when you had almost given up hope, suddenly the butter would begin to separate off and rise to the top, and the churning would be over.

There was a superstition that a woman who was menstruating should not be allowed to churn, for if she did the butter would not separate. This was quite firmly believed in our household.

The milk left after the butter had been removed was called butter-milk, presumably because there was no butter in it. It was a great delicacy to drink when fresh, but it very soon went sour from lactic acid fermentation, and then it was used to make fadge or soda bread or oatmeal farles.

Once a year, in the autumn, the shoemaker came to my grand-mother's farm for about a fortnight, sat in the kitchen and made boots for everyone on the farm. He bought the uppers and the leather for the soles in the nearest market town; and seated near the fire he would work away with his waxed thread, sewing everything together to make sound reliable boots fit to stand up to the hard work of the farm. I used to watch him fascinated while he drew the waxed ends through, until everything was firmly welded; and then out of his little bag would come the hammer and the sparables (small nails) which he would drive into the soles to make them wear longer and hold on slippery ground. These boots were real boots of real leather. You saw them being made, and fitted, and knew that you had the genuine article. Suits of clothes were made in the same manner by the local tailor. He also came for a week or two to make up the material bought by my grandmother for her sons. Everyone had a special suit for the Sabbath Day, and this suit was almost invariably of minister's grey.

The women of the farms, especially the young girls, spent much time with the dressmaker when she came. There were no off-the-peg clothes in those days. Instead there was much discussion of patterns and styles, and comments on the clothes of other girls seen at the Meeting House or a soirée or a dance. Summer comes late in Ulster, and the girls never used to burst into their glory before July 12th, the great Orange Day celebrating the Battle of the Boyne. Then they appeared in what everyone called their 'grandeur'—they pronounced it 'grandther'.

'The Twelfth' is of course the great day in Ulster. It commemorates the Battle of the Boyne, when James II, James of the Fleeing, was defeated by William of Orange (Orange Billy), and the Stuart cause was lost for ever. To us 'The Twelfth' represents the triumph of Protestantism, and the Reformation. In actual practice it has now become a public holiday when 'The Orangemen' parade with flute bands, big drums, banners and great orange sashes in memory of William of Orange who put down 'Pope, Popery and Schism, Brass Farthings and Wooden Shoes'—whatever that means. A week or so before 'The Twelfth' all over the little towns and villages of Ulster you will find great garlands swinging across the roads. They are made of wooden frames, nine feet by three, covered with shavings painted bright orange, and in the centre of most of them is a painting of King William on horseback, and in my day sometimes one of Queen Victoria, with mottoes like 'Our forefathers fought and bled', and names in gold letters like 'Derry, Enniskillen, Aughrim, and the Boyne', commemorating long-forgotten victories—that is, long-forgotten to the English with their short memories, but not to us.

It is true that sometimes we get a bit confused ourselves about the meaning of the great day.

A visitor watching a procession of Orangemen parading past in Belfast, complete with sashes and a big drum which the drummer was battering furiously, once asked a spectator:

"What's it all about?"

The man looked sideways at him, surprised at his ignorance.

"Shure, it's the Twelfth."

The visitor still looked puzzled. "The Twelfth?" he echoed.

"Aye. The Twelfth o' July."

"Yes. Yes. I know the date is the twelfth of July. But what are all these men parading for?"

The Ulsterman was appalled by this ignorance. He looked at the visitor in astonishment, and then he said with icy contempt:

"Och. For God's sake, man, away home wie you, and read yer Bible."

'The Twelfth' came luckily between the sowing and the reaping, and that was the time when the farmer took the opportunity of cutting his winter fuel from the moss (bog). Every farmer had a strip of bog land which belonged to his farm. My grandmother had none on her own land; but she had a patch about a mile away; and one of my most enjoyable tasks was to bring the luncheon basket down to my uncles and their workers when they were cutting and drying the peat. I can see myself, a little chap trudging down the hill, over the bridge that spanned the burn, past the hill of the great neolithic rath of Deffrick, out on to the open bog and down along the heathery path to where my uncle was cutting peat, and hear him say with a laugh:

"What's yer granny gi'en ye for us, Jamie?"

A special kind of spade with a long blade and a side flange (a lye) is used for cutting the oblong block of turf that is the recognised shape for the dried peat. And when it is cut it is quite wet and friable, so it has to be laid out carefully on the heather bank and allowed to dry for several days before it can be handled. It is then up-ended and stacked in little pyramids for some time, and then built up in 'rickles', a criss-cross arrangement that helps to make the peats hard and very dry. After rickling it is stooked in little stacks; and eventually, when the farmer is satisfied it is quite dry, the whole cutting of peat is carted away to the farmyard, and piled up in peat stacks round the house so as to be handy for the women folk.

Embedded in the bog, generally some feet down, one expects to find the trunks of fallen pine trees which must be centuries old. They are a dark red in colour, and full of resin, so they make excellent kindling—in fact the farmer hardly ever uses anything else for kindling. A slither of this log is called a 'split', and it acts as matches to light your pipe or kindle a fire. The log itself is used to keep the fire going in the open hearth all night long. What the farmer could have done without his fir logs in my time, I do not know.

Every farm had its peat stacks, and every cottar was allowed his share which he stacked in the garden behind his cottage. Looking back I think I enjoyed those days in the moss more than anything else. Lying on my back in the warm heather on a hot summer's day, looking up at a sky that seems in memory to be always a cerulean blue, listening to the glad song of the 'laverock', as we called the lark, high up in the heavens, sleepy after a meal of buttered oatcake and hot tea, life had nothing better to offer than the contentment of that moment.

Cutting the hay and then the corn came next after the work in the moss. It was done for most of my young days with the scythe. I can still see the long clean sweep of the bending men, wide-straddled, cutting swathes one behind the other, and the women following, spreading the cut grass evenly on the surface of the field.

Using the scythe was a very skilful job. The angle of the blade to the handle had to be carefully adjusted. The blade had to be swept with a long, beautiful swing close to the ground, but not too close; and woe betide anyone who drove the point of his scythe into the ground.

The sound of the blade being sharpened by the hone was something I associated particularly with the hay harvest. Sometimes we would come across a lark's nest and feel sorrowful as it was destroyed. But it was the persistent cry of the corncrake which I can remember most. It would sound its harsh rattle cry of alarm all day long, retreating before the reapers into the island of standing grain in the centre of the field, and leaving only when its last refuge was laid bare.

My uncles were very skilful with the scythe; but they had to move with the times, and when the reaping machine came they had to accept it, for by then labour was beginning to get scarcer. The men who were left, however, were very angry about this innovation. It could do the work of ten men in half the time, and they felt that their livelihood was in danger. And so we found mysterious bits of iron sticking up in the long grass, slipping between the teeth of the advancing reaper and playing havoc with the serrated blades as they oscillated to and fro. Obviously automation wasn't popular in 1890 either. My uncles used then to get very angry also, because it meant losing a day until they could get new blades from the market town, and because they never could find out who was doing it. They knew it was not their own men or their cottars. They used to go out with shot-guns at night, tearing mad, on the look-out for the silent machine-haters; but luckily they never found anyone, and after a while the trouble ceased.

Later, when the reaper and binder for harvesting oats arrived, all was peace. I can remember, however, how the corn used to be threshed with the flail when I was very young. We had a special barn with a hard earthen floor on which the threshing was done. The sheaves of oats would be opened and spread out on this floor, and then the stalks were beaten with the flail until all the ears were separated from the straw.

The flail consisted of a long wooden pole at the end of which was a shorter stick, the swingle, attached to it by a leather thong. The shorter piece swung loosely, and by raising the longer portion above the head and bringing the shorter one heavily down on the blades of corn on the clay floor, the ears very quickly separated from the stalks. It was hard manual work, and required much muscular energy. When my grandmother decided to buy a threshing machine I feel sure my uncles were more than pleased, for then the work was done mechanically, in a fraction of the time and very much better, without the back-aching exertion required by the flail.

The power that drove the threshing machine was an old mare named Sally. She dragged the long lever working the cog-wheel round and round in a circle, hour after hour, outside the barn; and I can remember how proud and important I felt when I was permitted to march behind her calling out, "Gee, gee, gee," to stir her on her way.

I was even prouder still when, later, I was permitted to feed the sheaves of corn into the teeth of the threshing machine. This went on until my grandmother discovered what was happening; and then there was the devil to pay. My uncle got a tremendous wigging for exposing me to the risk of having my hands caught in the machinery.

"David John, I wunther at ye. Exposin' the waen tae sichen a risk. Hae ye nae sense ava, man! What wud his mither say?"

Threshing usually took place in the winter when the potatoes, turnips and mangolds had been earthed and there were no crops to gather. The corn stacks were in the stackyard, alongside the barn that housed the threshing machine; and when it was decided to do some threshing, we used to collect all the dogs around. They knew what was wanted. They kept rushing and barking around the stacks, eyes bright, ears cocked, as the sheaves of corn were gradually forked down until we came to the lower layers next the ground. Then the excitement became intense, the barking grew more shrill, the dogs circled more wildly. For now the field mice harbouring in the stacks since harvest time were being uncovered. Out they came from their warm nests into the cold winter weather, confused, half-blinded by the unwonted light; and the dogs fell on them furiously. A good Irish terrier could get thirty mice before the rest managed to escape into the bottom of the next rick.

In retrospect it seems cruel now, but I did not think so then. I was sorry in a way for the little mice who ran so helplessly, but I felt, like the farmer, that they were a great destructive source of loss, for they must have eaten tons and tons of oats in any large farm every winter.

Potatoes were stored in the fields in heaps ten to fifteen feet long by three feet broad and three feet high. They were then covered with earth, and a trench dug round the 'clamps', as they were called, to drain off the rain. The only risk they ran was from frost, and occasionally from theft by tramps.

I cannot remember any special harvest-home custom—except one, vaguely, something called a 'Churn'; but in winter-time the women, especially the young ones, had 'Quilting Parties', where they met at one another's farms, and made the patchwork quilts which were once so characteristic of farm bedrooms. This was a time for tea and gossip, ending up with a little hot punch before the girls started on their journey home in the dark of the winter night, each usually accompanied, or as we called it 'convoyed', by some lad who she was quite definitely conscious had an eye on her. The term 'quilting' was carried by Ulster people to the United States, and I believe is still used there in country districts for parties of this nature.

The other great social gathering was the 'Swarry' (soirée). This was always held at the Meeting House or the church and meant tea and buns, followed by 'recitations' and songs, comic or sentimental, by talented amateurs. This form of entertainment gradually faded. Even if it had not, the wireless would have killed it, for the day of the amateur in music, singing and entertainment of this type is quite dead.

Round about Christmas we had a visit from a masked company called 'The Christmas Rhymers'. They came dressed up in grotesque

masks and stalked into the big, warm farmhouse kitchen. One fierce
fellow with a red nose and a huge spiked club particularly frightened
me. He marched fiercely before the others, saying:

> Here come I, Beelzebub,
> And over my shoulder I carry a club;
> And in my hand a frying pan,
> To roast you all as quick as I can.

Beelzebub then fought a fearful duel with a masked man in a green
jacket who carried a big wooden sword. But the man in green was no
match for Beelzebub, for soon he lay defeated on the kitchen floor.

Then in came another figure dressed in black, saying:

> Here come I, old Doctor Stout.
> I can cure the hiccough, the piccough, the
>   palsy, the gout,
> If there's nine devils in I can knock ten out.
> And in my bag I've tonics from Spain,
> Returning to practice in Ireland again.

He bent down over the prostrate man on the floor, producing a
bottle from his bag, and saying:

> Here, man, take a sup from this bottle
> And let it run right down your throttle.

This acted like magic on the fallen man, and he got to his feet, greatly
to my relief.

I don't remember much more, except at the end a small man came
in wearing a black mask with horns. He carried a tin mug in his hand
and went round the audience saying:

> Here come I, Little Devil Doubt,
> With my trousers inside out;
> Money I want, and money I crave.
> If you don't give me money
> I'll sweep you all to your grave.

Round he went, rattling the mug; and at this dire threat everyone paid up.

The first time I saw the Christmas Rhymers I was frightened, and could not understand why everyone was laughing, until Beelzebub took off his mask, and then I saw it was only James Mackintosh, one of our cottars.

What the others appeared like and how they fitted into the performance I cannot now remember. But I looked forward to seeing them around Christmas during all my boyhood days, and I hope they are still going strong.

In retrospect one always thinks that the winters in one's childhood had more snow and more ice, and that the summers were much more sunny than they are today. Anyhow, I have the most pleasant memories of tobogganing down steep slopes, of driving in a one-horse sledge with my uncles and of skating for miles along the River Bann in the depths of one very severe winter when we had ice for two months.

Schoolboy games started with the spring. I believe there is a traditional sequence all over the kingdom, varying a little with climate and latitude. I think our first one was hoops. In Ulster we used hoops made of iron, and kept them running by an iron hook in a wooden handle. Further south I found they used wooden hoops and drove them along with a wooden stick. Spinning-tops came next, and to possess a real boxwood top made one the envy of all the other boys. It had to have a steel spike instead of an iron one to be really first class; and the art of winding the whipcord round the grooved circumference of the top and making the top spin was something one had to acquire and, once acquired, to boast about.   .

Marbles came later on in the year, for it was necessary to have warm weather so that the ground would be dry and one could 'hurkle' down on one's heels and place one's hand on the ground before shooting, with one thumb holding the marble, for the hole, or striking at the other marbles of one's competitors. Marbles had a regular standard of exchange. The lowest was a 'stony', a small grey marble, sometimes painted green. A 'glassy' was a much more valuable one. It was of clear glass with coloured scrolls inside like the old-fashioned paper-weights one sees in antique shops. The most valuable was the 'blood alley', a bit of real marble with streaks of red in veins showing on the surface.

The hop-step-and-jump was very popular; and so was putting the weight, but that was rather for grown-ups. Playing conkers with chestnuts was the craze of the early autumn.

Before the autumn, however, there was the summer season at Portstewart and Portrush, our two seaside resorts which even sixty years ago were very popular. Portstewart was the older and much the more picturesque of the two. It has memories of Maxwell the historian, Charles Lever the novelist, who was once its dispensary doctor, and of Thackeray, who spent a holiday there. But it was deprived of its early advantages over Portrush by the fact that the ground landlord, during the time the railway was being built, objected to its coming to the town, and so it was diverted to Portrush—a handicap from which Portstewart has never recovered. In this the landlord of that time was not alone. The same prejudice against railways then diverted main lines from places like Northampton, Grantham and many other towns and cities in England.

As we grew older my father used to take a house for a month in the summer at Portstewart, and there we six children, of whom I was the second, learnt to bathe and swim and grow up brown and healthy. After this, until the school holidays were over, I managed to get sent back to the farm, where life, in retrospect, was one long summers' day.

We were fortunate in my native town over education, for this was endowed by the Clothworkers' Company of London, to whom James I had granted the town and land around at the time of the Ulster Plantation in 1611. That is why in our municipal shield we blazon the red hand of Ulster together with Wat Tyler's dagger, the arms of the City of London. But Coleraine, which means the Valley of Ferns, is much older than that. It was a stronghold in the neolithic age. The great river, the Bann, runs from Lough Neagh to the sea through the valley. The town is placed athwart the river about four miles from the sea, and there has been a settlement there since before the dawn of written history. It has seen much fighting and much blood, for the river is one of the greatest salmon rivers in Ireland, and the hungry people of the islands in Scotland, which you can see plainly from the river mouth, came over in their coracles and raided it again and again for food.

When I was a small boy I often used to go along to the mouth of the river and prod the sand at the estuary with a stick. I was looking for flint arrowheads. There were hundreds of them, beautifully chipped arrowheads, the finest neolithic specimens I have ever seen. They looked so innocent, so beautiful there, lying in the sunshine, but they represented ferocious battles, a thousand years before the birth of Christ, to capture the salmon-fishing at the ford below the town; and the battles must have swayed to and fro many times for possession of the 'crannog' and this ford. The ford is still there but the crannog is now only a name; for a crannog is a fortified prehistoric village built out into the water, fenced in and surrounded by piles. It served to defend the river ford until well into the Bronze Age. Now there are the remains of a small fort on the site of the crannog, and on the opposite side of the river a great tumulus, or 'rath', an earthen fort put up to defend the river against much more powerful invaders—the Danes—who came in their longboats invading Ulster about A.D. 600.

The battles are but dim legends now. The Danes are no more, but the salmon still come, and between the forts fishermen sometimes capture five hundred in one haul.

The river is tidal to well above the town, and when the tide recedes another ford lies barely a mile upstream. Attached to this there was a legend that a beautiful princess, being pursued and fleeing with her defeated army across the river by night, was drowned accidentally in the confusion of the flight; and the lovely golden torque she wore around her neck was lost in the water. It was just a legend, but about a hundred years ago the torque was found again, after all the centuries between, and the legend suddenly became a reality.

CHAPTER III

TRINITY, DUBLIN

JUST BEFORE my sixteenth birthday the question of what university I should be entered for became important. My doctor uncle had been an Edinburgh graduate; and from him I had heard exciting yarns of student life in 'Auld Reekie'. By this time also I had been allowed to read Sir Walter Scott's novels, and I knew my Burns almost by heart. I was steeped, too, in Scottish history. The skirl of the pipe was to me, and is to me still, the most exciting music in the world. The blood of the Covenanters was in my veins. I knew that the fame of the Edinburgh School of Medicine was international, and felt I should be absolutely at home there. My uncle urged Edinburgh. My father listened to him, and was almost convinced. My mother, how-ever, kept quiet. I knew she had been talking to the Headmaster's wife, and I wondered what the Head had been saying. I knew also that whatever she decided upon my father would agree to in the end.

Then the day of the annual regatta arrived, always a great event on our river; and amongst the crews competing were two from Trinity College, Dublin: an eight and a four, touring the Irish regattas under the guidance of a famous coach, Captain Hetty Ryan. They won both their races, and at the end of the regatta they were gallantly introduced by Captain Ryan to the great local lady who was giving away the prizes. My mother and I, standing near, were looking on.

"That man," she said to me, "has had too much to drink and yet he carries his liquor like a gentleman. I like him, and I like these Trinity boys. They have style. I think we'll send you there."

It seemed an absurd reason. It may just have been her fun. She had a great sense of fun and possibly was pulling my leg, for I learned later that the Head's wife had told her it would be a shame with my love of the classics to send me anywhere except Trinity. But I think all the same that Hetty Ryan helped to persuade her.

My last two years at school therefore were spent—"scorning delights, living laborious days"—over Homer, Demosthenes, Euripides, Virgil, Livy, Cicero and Horace, with some mathematics and French and elementary chemistry thrown in, and English as a school subject completely neglected.

So, at the age of eighteen, I was ready and eager to plunge into the work that was to train me for the career I had been thinking of ever since I was a little boy. All I had been doing up to now was in anticipation of this; and the Head decided I was to sit for the next entrance examination to the University. This was in October, during the first week of Michaelmas term; I knew that on passing it my whole future depended, and I was therefore nervously excited.

It was the first time I had been to Dublin and the beauty of the lovely Georgian city was something I had never seen anything like before, coming from the 'Black North'. Indeed, after all these years, I still think Dublin the loveliest city in the world.

Driving in the jaunting car to my lodgings in Rathmines Road, I passed the great front of Trinity with its statues of Burke and Goldsmith staring stonily at William of Orange mounted on his horse in College Green; and I felt thrilled to think that presently I might soon be as privileged as the black-gowned figures I could see passing in and out of the front gate. So next morning, feeling very shy and self-conscious, I asked my way to the rooms of Dr. Anthony Traill, a rough, bearded, bull-necked man from my own part of the world, who was to be my tutor if I passed my entrance.

Traill was what is known as a 'character'. He was a mathematical Fellow of Trinity who had also qualified as a doctor but had never practised. He was completely ignorant of modern literature; and once when the undergrad paper, paraphrasing Kipling, addressed him on his birthday as, "The old Traill, our own Traill, the Traill that is always new," he was reputed to have said:

"Who is this fellow Kipling? What does he know about me? Never heard of him!"

He had no manners at all, and was totally unlike my idea of a don. Tyrrell, the Professor of Greek, once said of him:

"I am puzzled every time I look at Traill to decide whether he is a buffalo developing into a man, or a man degenerating into a buffalo."

Such was the man who was to be my tutor.

"Ha, you want to be a doctor, do you?" he barked, looking me up and down fiercely.

"Yes, sir," I murmured meekly.

"Well, it's five years' hard work to get qualified, and you've got to take your degree in Arts as well before you get your degree in Medicine. D'ye understand that?"

"Yes, sir," I replied, more meekly.

"All right, come to breakfast in Hall tomorrow at nine a.m. and you'll learn the arrangements then."

"Yes, sir," I answered, now thoroughly intimidated.

Suddenly he smiled—the smile of a grizzly bear struggling to be kind.

"Don't be worried," he said, "your Headmaster says you're a fair classic and not bad at mathematics. You'll be all right."

"Thank you, sir. Is that all, sir?" I murmured, relieved.

"Yes, don't be late tomorrow!"

Next morning found me, well before time, in the great front quadrangle, standing on the steps leading up to the Dining Hall with about a hundred others, all looking very self-conscious, none of whom I knew. The Dining Hall with its long refectory tables and the portraits of past College celebrities on the panelled walls thrilled me. I was too excited to eat much, but I talked to a bright-eyed, copper-haired young man who seemed completely at his ease.

He looked a bit older than most of us, but talked quite pleasantly to me. We discussed poetry. I was keen on Tennyson at the time. He preferred Browning.

I said: "I suppose you are up for Entrance."

He replied: "Well, no, not exactly."

I was therefore taken very much aback when I went in for my viva in Latin two days later to find he was my examiner. I guessed he was quite conscious of my embarrassment by the little smile I saw round his lips; but I don't think I suffered in marks from the encounter. I discovered later I had been up against that astonishing genius, John Bagnell Bury, Professor of Modern History; and I learnt it was one of his little jokes to be taken for an undergraduate by people who did not know him. He was about thirty-three years of age at the time but he looked twenty. Even after he went to Cambridge as Regius Professor eight years later he was still often taken for an undergraduate; and I am told he used to play the same little trick there also.

At the written papers in Examination Hall I sat under a portrait of Queen Elizabeth, our founder, and learned later that this was considered a most unlucky thing to do. No one ever sat under her if he could help it. Happily for my peace of mind I did not know then; but I avoided her in the future.

I do not remember much about the rest of the exam. The celebrated John Pentland Mahaffy passed me in my Greek viva. Mahaffy had been Oscar Wilde's tutor; and it was he who said to Wilde:

"We are too clever for you here, Oscar. You had better transfer to Oxford."

Three days later the ordeal of the Entrance was over, and my tutor told me I was now a member of the University.

"You can cut along to the Medical School now and see the Registrar, Dr. Mackintosh," he said. "The sooner you register the better."

So in the bright autumn sunlight I walked across the College Park to the group of lovely granite buildings that I was to spend most of my working days in for the next five years; and there I entered myself as a medical student.

Dr. Mackintosh was the Professor of Zoology, a tall thin man who looked like a nonconformist clergyman in disguise. Irreverent medical students always talked of him behind his back as 'Tapes', because of his lectures on parasitic worms. As a man he was completely unapproachable. Whilst working for an honours degree in Natural Science later, I never once got inside his reserve in the three years I studied under him. His lectures were concise, admirable for their purpose and completely uninspiring. The big Museum of Comparative Anatomy he controlled was practically wasted. A few curious people came occasionally to see the huge skeleton of Cornelius Mcgraw, the Irish giant, nearly eight feet high, but that was all.

On this my first morning he fixed me with his cold blue eyes.

"I will arrange your lectures in Chemistry and Physics, but you must go yourself to Professor Cunningham in the dissecting-room to pay your Anatomy fees. He can be seen between eleven and one o'clock. Good morning," he said.

I went out feeling I disliked Dr. Mackintosh very much. Then I nerved myself to go to the dissecting-room, expecting something gruesome. The human body is a very intricate piece of mechanism, and no one with any pretence to be a doctor can possibly understand its workings unless he has dissected for himself and seen how the organs, muscles, blood vessels and nerves are arranged. For many centuries this training was prohibited by the Church under the most severe penalties; and monkeys, pigs and cattle had to be used instead. Eventually this proved so dangerous, as well as useless, that criminals were handed over after execution for dissection to the Guilds of Barber-Surgeons in most countries, and accurate anatomical knowledge was thus eventually acquired.

But with the growth of medical schools, and the increase of students, the supply of criminals was insufficient for the demand; and this gave rise in England and Scotland to the 'resurrection men', ghouls who dug up bodies from the shallow graves in the over-crowded cemeteries in the middle of the night after burial, and sold them—no questions asked —to the medical schools before morning. Eventually this became such a public scandal that relatives guarded graves for days, and bodies became scarce once more. The climax was reached finally when it was found that two criminals in Edinburgh, William Burke and William Hare, obtained bodies for sale to one of the schools of anatomy by making their victims drunk and then smothering them with pillows. These cold-blooded murders roused the conscience of the public. Burke was hanged in 1829, and the Anatomy Act was passed soon after, authorising the State to use the bodies of unclaimed persons in the interest of science.

As a boy I'd heard horrible stories about what we called the 'stiffy-lifters', who corresponded in Ireland to these ghouls in Scotland; and so it was with a feeling of morbid curiosity and mild shrinking I walked into the dissecting-room to see the Professor. It was a long, low room lit by windows from the sides and by skylights from above. There were two rows of narrow zinc tables, each with a body in some stage of dissection on it. The room was scrupulously clean and tidy. It smelt strongly of the carbolic with which the bodies were at that time impregnated. Anatomical drawings lined the walls, and beautifully made specimen dissections in glass-covered cabinets were arranged below the charts.

The Professor was standing at his desk at the far end of the dissecting-room. He was a large, powerful, good-looking man, with a fresh complexion, a big prominent nose and a marked Scottish accent—the famous Professor Daniel John Cunningham, F.R.S.

Another student was talking to him before me. His name was Ingram. We both paid the fee, eleven guineas, for the winter course, and the Professor told us when we could start.

I began dissecting a few days later, but there was no sign of Ingram. A month after, however, he again appeared, looking rather thin and white.

"What happened to you, Ingram?" I said. "Why haven't you turned up?"

"I couldn't," he answered. "I was knocked down and gored by a bull that escaped in the South Circular Road the afternoon I paid my fees. I've been in the Adelaide Hospital ever since. I've missed the term I expect."

"Well, yes. You'd never catch up now," I said.

"So I thought," he replied sadly, "and I've come to see the Professor about getting my fees back."

The dissection I was working on was close to the Professor's desk, and I and the other men could hear everything that was said.

Naturally Ingram expected sympathy. But not a bit of it. The Professor looked at him.

"No, Mr. Ingram. No. You cannot have your fees back, but you'll be credited with them for next session." Then he added sternly: "And let me give you a word of advice for the future, Mr. Ingram. Playin' wi' bulls is a verry uncerrtain game."

Poor Ingram, blamed severely for what was not his fault at all! The saying went all round Trinity—"playin' wi' bulls is a verry uncerrtain game."

Coming to Dublin to start life as a medical student was so completely different from all my previous experiences that I can still remember very distinctly details which, if they happened to me today, would be forgotten in a fortnight.

Medical students since the time of Dickens and Albert Smith have always had the reputation of being rather wild. It has been suggested, sardonically, that it is because they know that once they become doctors they must be even more decorous than parsons, and so make the most of it while they can. But, of course, the real reason probably is that their behaviour is the result of coming up against pain and suffering and the gruesome side of life at a time when the only way they can react against it is to rush to the other extreme and hilariously ignore it.

Most of the medical lectures we attended were efficiently conducted. In the arts courses it was not always so. Some were good; some were quite useless. In one tutorial class in mathematics my first lecturer, Freddy Purser, was very learned, very deaf, very short-sighted; and the impulse to make loud derogatory remarks to his face was irresistible. He heard and noticed nothing. Turning his back on us he would draw an elaborate diagram on the board, stop, look at it, stare a moment and, giving no explanation whatever, say: "Well, gentlemen, that is self-evident," and then rub it off the board.

We all nodded vigorously in assent, exclaiming: "Silly old fool! Bally old ass!" etc., and then, quite unconscious of the comedy, he would go on to something even more elaborate. Naturally we learned nothing, and were very pleased with ourselves. But it was just putting off the evil day, for when the shadow of the examinations came, towards the end of the academic year, most of us were driven to a 'grinder' to coach us through.

The lecturer on Chemistry, Emerson Reynolds, was a very distinguished chemist, the discoverer of thiourea, a preparation which was of no importance medically for half a century after its synthesis, but which then suddenly became essential to the successful treatment of toxic goitre (Graves's disease), a condition previously almost incurable apart from operation. Reynolds's lectures were a model of precision. His experiments never went wrong, they were so well prepared. And during them you could almost hear a pin drop. He had complete control of his class.

But not so George Francis Fitzgerald, the Professor of Physics, or Natural Philosophy, as it was called. Here the lecturer was completely incapable of maintaining order. The students let off toy balloons and squibs, stamped with their feet, gave catcalls as and when they liked during the demonstrations. The Professor took no notice whatever. He went on with his experiments, apparently imperturbable.

We did not recognise in 1896 when we saw him jumping from the terrace of the Pavilion in the College Park that he was a pioneer in aviation. His apparatus was a pair of canvas wings on a wooden framework strapped to his shoulders and powered by pedals which he worked with his feet.

A message from Gaffney, his lab. man, that "the Professor will be goin' up the day" would bring crowds to watch. No one quite realised then that nothing without an engine could soar unless it was towed by an aeroplane until well above the ground. The Professor's theories were correct, but he always came down on his hands and knees to a chorus of ironic cheers. We young hooligans did not know that George Francis Fitzgerald was an F.R.S. of international fame. Our treatment of him is a thing I for one am rather ashamed of in retrospect. I am told that the great Lord Kelvin in Glasgow had a similar cross to bear.

There was no rowdiness, however, in Cunningham's Anatomy lectures. Like Emerson Reynolds he was a stern disciplinarian; and he was listened to in complete silence. Actually he was a magnificent lecturer. Every sentence had been worked out beforehand. His demonstrations too were perfect.

The dissecting-room takes up most of the spare time the medical student has after lectures, games and living. Consequently he spends hours there during his first three years, and his mind centres on it unconsciously, since on the knowledge acquired there of the intricacies of the human body all his subsequent training is built.

The 'subjects', as they are called, are laid out straight on narrow stretcher-like zinc tables, and eight students are allocated to each. They have, therefore, to arrange different times so as not to get in each other's way while dissecting. Actually six men can dissect easily.

My first 'part' was a right arm, which I was told it would take two months to dissect. When I got there on my first morning I found the man on the left arm had started, and the head demonstrator was giving him advice. There were two demonstrators, assistants of the Professor, and their job was to supervise the dissections and help the students. So I also listened and did what he told me. Presently he wandered off to some others and we worked away steadily, smoking as we did so.

About an hour later a pleasant fellow came along, asked how we were getting on and began to point out things to us. We smiled gratefully and he sat down, told us some sultry stories and suggested he might just show us one or two points. He did this on Anderson's 'part', the man opposite me. I thought he was a bit slapdash about it, but supposed it was just his manner. Then he borrowed my pouch and helped himself to some of my tobacco. All very friendly. The demonstrator came along shortly after.

"Well, Jones, back again," he said.

"Yes, sir," answered Jones, rather humbly, I thought.

"Up again, I suppose," said the demonstrator, coldly.

"Yes, sir, having another shot."

He melted away after that. I felt something wasn't quite right. A second-year man working at a 'head and neck' at the next table grinned at us.

"Red" (that was the nickname of the head demonstrator, Dr. A. F. Dixon, on account of his hair) "doesn't like Jones very much. He's a chronic! Gets stuck every time. Lazy and too keen on pub-crawling. Bit of a scrounger, too. How much baccy did he get out of you? He has a pipe with a hole in the bowl, and he just 'fills' through it if you don't know the trick."

I looked at my pouch. It was half empty.

"Ha, ha!" said the second-year man, "he's done you!"

It was my first experience of the 'chronic', the man who could not get through his exams, and hung about the medical schools year after year, still trying. The chronic in my time was a nuisance and a great corrupter of innocence. But he is a nuisance no longer, for if he doesn't get through his exams within a definite period, all medical schools now refuse to allow him to continue. Formerly if he had once paid his fees he had a perpetual right to carry on.

One day a benevolent-looking old gentleman of about seventy wandered into the dissecting-room looking for the Professor; and, as he passed, a third-year man working opposite me murmured:

"That's Sammy Haughton. Invented 'the drop', you know."

"Who's he, and what's 'the drop'?" I said, after he had passed.

"He's the Reverend Samuel Haughton, D.D., M.D., D.C.L.,

F.T.C.D., F.R.S.—and a lot more. Used to be Professor of Geology and an opponent of Darwin and Huxley. Wrote books on mathematics before he became a Doctor of Medicine. It was this combination made him think of 'the drop'."

" 'The drop'?" I murmured again.

"Oh. Yes. Sorry! You know murderers used to be hanged by stringing them up and letting them kick and dangle until they suffocated. Sammy couldn't bear this, so he worked out a formula by which the hangman could calculate, after weighing the murderer, from what height his body should be allowed to fall to fracture his neck and kill him instantly. That's 'the drop'. It's a much more merciful way, and that's how it's done now."

I gazed at the old man, fascinated. He looked so gentle. It seemed incongruous. The other man read my thoughts.

"Yes. It does seem an odd thing for a clergyman to have thought of, even though he was a doctor. But it really is much more merciful. The old method was terribly brutal. They kicked for minutes. Benevolent friends used to have to pull on their legs to finish them. It must have been horrible to watch. Sammy changed all that."

I soon found I liked dissecting. Anatomy had a fascination for me. I worked at it and enjoyed it. There is a scientific pleasure in making neat preparations. One forgets one is dealing with the human body. There is also an artistic satisfaction in making a good dissection that stimulates one to work hard. I did work hard, and I was pleased in consequence to find in my second year that I had been appointed a 'prosector', that is, one whose dissections are used by the Professor to lecture upon. As a reward for this I was sometimes asked by the Professor to one of the Saturday morning breakfasts of bacon and eggs given by the Fellows of the Dublin Zoo. These were very pleasant functions, for afterwards we walked round the cages admiring the animals, especially the lion cubs which the Dublin Zoo was then breeding better than any other zoo in Europe. The Professor sometimes brought one of his three sons with him when they were home from school. The eldest said he was going to be a doctor. The second I can remember as a bright-eyed boy in a naval cadet's uniform. The third was a little chap about ten.

All this came back sharply to my mind many years later.

I was standing one day in the entrance hall of my club, waiting for a guest I had invited to lunch, when I heard a voice that sounded vaguely familiar. Looking round I saw a pink-faced, bright-eyed, grey-haired man of about sixty whose appearance was quite unfamiliar to me, talking to the Secretary.

Family resemblance is an odd thing. It can be startlingly reproduced, or it may be something fleeting, seen in a characteristic movement, in an eyebrow, a smile or an intonation of the voice.

"Who is that, Middleton?" I said to the Head Porter.

"That, sir, is Admiral of the Fleet Lord Cunningham, just elected under Rule II."

Then I knew. It was an echo of his father's characteristic voice, a voice I had heard day in, day out, for nearly three years; and my mind flashed back to the dissecting-room in Trinity, and I could hear once again the Professor saying: "Playin' wi' bulls is a verry uncerrtain game, Mr. Ingram."

I realised then I was looking at the victor of the Battle of Matapan, and the previous time I had seen him was at breakfast at the Dublin Zoo fifty years before when he was a middy home on leave. Oddly enough I have talked to him many times since, but never recaptured the particular intonation that registered in my memory that day.

*

But to resume. There are not enough residential rooms in Trinity to accommodate more than half the students, and so for my first year I had to live out. I took rooms, therefore, about a mile and a half from College at 9 Rathmines Road. They were kept by a Miss O'Gorman; and I paid for my lodgings once a week. Every time I did so there was the same comedy.

I would go down into the kitchen on Saturday.

"Good morning, Miss O'Gorman. I've come to pay for my rooms."

Then she would look at me in astonishment.

"But, dochtor dear, ye paid me the other day."

"Oh, no, I didn't, Miss O'Gorman."

"Och, but I'm sure ye did. I couldn't be taking it twice—now could I, doctor jewel? Sure, ye paid me."

At first I tried to argue with her. It was no good. And finally I discovered how to do it. I just left the money on the corner of the kitchen table, and when I had gone she took it. The old dear simply couldn't bear to take money from any of her lodgers. She wanted to treat them all as guests.

My rooms were on the ground floor; the first floor was occupied by a widow and her son; and so we soon got to know one another. Presently I began to feel there was something odd about Terence's habits. His mother told me he had a post as a clerk in the City Hall, but I noticed that he went there only on alternate days; and presently my curiosity overcame me so much that I said to Miss O'Gorman:

"Can you tell me now, Miss O'Gorman, why Mr. Terence goes to his office on Monday, Wednesday and Friday one week and Tuesday, Thursday and Saturday the next?"

She looked at me in mild surprise.

"Sure, what else could he do? Himself and the other young fella has only the one desk between them; and wouldn't it be a botheration for him to go on the other fella's day?"

"But why," I said, still puzzled—"why doesn't each of them have a desk of his own?"

"Och. Sure, how could they? They've only got wan between them, an' them each drawin' full pay for the same job. Mr. Terence's father was well liked in the Corporation, an' when he died, God rest his soul, they had to find a job for Terence."

So Terence duplicated the post to the entire satisfaction of all concerned.

Dublin in those days was not a happy place politically. Under the apparent calm there was seething discontent and fear. Few people now, in England at any rate, remember the Phoenix Park murders; but then the crime was still fresh in people's memories and the horror had not abated even after twelve years. It was such a cold-blooded affair.

Lord Frederick Cavendish, the newly-appointed Chief Secretary for Ireland, had just arrived in Dublin. Next day he was walking in the Phoenix Park near the Vice-Regal Lodge talking to the permanent Under-Secretary, Thomas Henry Burke, when a jaunting car drew up and stopped near them. From it the occupants alighted, and in broad daylight without any provocation attacked and murdered the two unsuspecting men with amputating knives. They then got back into the car and drove away. It was, of course, a political crime.

I knew the whole story—who didn't then! And one day when I was going round Steevens' Hospital, which is the nearest hospital to the Phoenix Park, I was taken into the accident-room to the right of the entrance by D'Arcy, the apothecary. The little man looked at me with beady, gloating eyes. He was rehearsing it all again in his mind.

"Yes. They brought them in to me here, bedad. That's where the bodies lay," he said, pointing to the wooden table. "They were here for five mortal hours before a soul could identify him. Ye see, Lord Frederick Cavendish had been in Dublin only wan day. The house-surgeon then was Tom Myles (later Sir Thomas Myles). Tom had been out and when he came back to the hospital he says to me:

" 'Anything happened, D'Arcy?'

" 'Och, nothin' much,' says I, 'except two b.i.d.'s (brought in deads). That'll be four guineas for you, dochtor, at the inquest.'

"Of course that was before we knew who they were. The Government paid Tom a thousand guineas for givin' evidence at the trial of the murtherers, and he had police protection for ten solid years afther. They stopped it only last year. Not that he needed it, begob. It's a brave fella that would've tackled Tom Myles."

It was said that the double murder was the work of the Fenians, a secret society, largely subsidised from America, seeking to overthrow the British Government by starting a rebellion in Ireland.

An undergraduate doesn't bother much with politics, and a medical student least of all; but indirectly I by chance came into contact with one of the prominent figures concerned with this underground movement. I had become friendly with a student dissecting opposite me. He was a Dubliner and used to ask me occasionally to his parents' home. I suppose his people thought I was lonely and it would be a kindness to a Northerner. Anyhow, they were good to me, and I liked them. There was a kindly atmosphere in their place which reminded me of home. After one particular visit my friend's father presented me with two books he had written. One was called *Daniel in the Critic's Den*, the other *The Coming Prince*. I read them and came to the conclusion, in the cocksure way the very young have, that he must be a bit cracked.

Just about that time 'Major le Caron', the famous spy, died, and the papers were full of his exploits. He was an Englishman belonging to the Secret Service; and somehow he had managed to worm his way into the innermost ring of the Fenian movement in the United States, reporting their movements regularly to the Criminal Investigation Department.

His autobiography and his death let loose all sorts of secrets, the most startling of which was that the tall, ascetic-looking bearded man given to good works whom I knew, whose house I had been visiting, the author of the religious books I had been reading, was no less a person than the head of the Criminal Investigation Department, and it was to him le Caron had been reporting the Fenians', secret proceedings for years. It was amazing. People who knew him could not believe it. No one more unlikely to hold such a post could have been imagined. But it was true! That, of course, was the beautiful cleverness of it. He was entirely unsuspected. The disclosure, naturally, destroyed the value of the secret and, soon after, he and his family left Dublin. Probably his life was not considered safe there any longer, and so he was moved to London to take up a high administrative post at Scotland Yard. I believe he kept on writing more and more religious books. His name was Sir Robert Anderson. He died in 1918.

My contacts with his family ceased when he left Ireland. But the atmosphere in Dublin, the queer feeling of underground hostility that one sensed, remained. When I went home at Christmas I found myself in a different world, but one equally uneasy. People in Ulster, I now discovered, had an exaggerated idea of the hostility of the South towards the North. It was based on fear, a fear of long historical standing, a fear that Gladstone's Home Rule Bill, introduced eight years previously, had brought into renewed activity, a deep fear that they might be handed over to Rome, and, absurd as it may seem, the Inquisition—a fear the brutal Phoenix Park murders had not lessened.

When the Home Rule Bill was defeated they breathed again. But I could well understand this fear, for as a small boy, you will remember, I had been told by my grandfather how he, as an infant in arms, had been hidden by his mother in the bog behind the farm when the rebels burnt it down in '98. Small wonder that as a little lad I believed we should all be murdered in our beds if Home Rule ever came to Ireland.

People talked of the 'Moonlighters' and the 'Fenians' with bated breath. The trouble caused by the Land League and the policy of boy-cotting made them very uneasy. It was all far away in what they always called 'the South', but it was ever-present in their minds.

Our cook said to me after I got home for the first time from Dublin: "An' is it true, Misther James, that ye lived in a Papish house in Dublin?"

"Yes, Mary."

"An' were ye naw feart o' havin' yer throat cut in the night?"

"No, Mary."

She looked at me in wonder. "Man, ye have the quare courage. I wunnther yer mother lets ye."

I thought of my dear Miss O'Gorman and how impossibly absurd such ideas were; but I knew it was useless to explain to our cook. Our fear in Ulster is the fear the Elizabethans had of Spain and the Inquisition, the fear England had in the time of Charles II of the return of Romanism, the fear the Georgians had in the time of the Young Pretender of a Roman Catholic dynasty succeeding to the throne again. It was a fear that seemed reasonable to the Englishman in 1745. What one has to remember is that Ireland has seen civil war three times since 1745, and she is still at the stage England was then. If that is once grasped, the Ulster problem is understood.

When I returned to Dublin in January for the Hilary term, the welcome I got from my landlady, Miss O'Gorman, made all this fear and suspicion seem so utterly absurd.

"Ah, I've got a foine plum puddin' I made for ye, dochtor," she said. "It'll do ye a power of good."

My heart sank when I saw that pudding. It was enormous, made with twenty-eight eggs, and was so stodgy it was quite uneatable. I was in a quandary what to do with it. I hated to hurt the dear old lady's feelings, so I cudgelled my brains until I had an inspiration. I parcelled up a large slice one evening and decided to throw it into the Grand Canal, which was about fifty yards away. I slipped out about eleven in the dark and threw it with a splash into the water, close to the bridge over Rathmines Road. As soon as I had done so a Metropolitan policeman emerged from the shadows on the far side of the bridge and challenged me. I ran for my life. He was on the other side of the canal, and I got away. I learnt next day that the bridges were being watched for fear the Fenians might blow them up. So I had to find a safer way of getting rid of the rest of my Christmas pudding. It took me weeks and weeks to do so, as the pudding appeared regularly for my supper, and a too rapid disappearance would have made the old lady suspicious.

*

At the end of my first year I passed my Arts and Professional exams, creditably but without distinction. I had by then discovered I had a journalistic flair. There was a paper in Dublin called *The Evening Mail* and in an idle moment as a joke I wrote a letter to it entitled 'Should Daughters Have Latch Keys?', signing myself 'Mother of Seven'. It was about the time that the women's movement for equal rights was beginning, and I thought my letter would be topical.

The editor of the paper thought so too and published it. No one took any notice. Rather disappointed, I wrote another, protesting against the mother's view, and signed it 'Revolting Daughter'. They published this also, but again no one took any notice. I then wrote a third, and signed it 'Paterfamilias'. It was a reply to 'Revolting Daughter', pointing out how dangerous her views were, and I followed it up with yet another signed 'Constant Reader'.

I was beginning to get a bit weary of it all by now; but then quite suddenly the thing became alive. People began to write in. They took sides. They abused one another. I sat back and whooped with joy. It went on for weeks.

Dr. Shaw, one of the Senior Fellows of the College, who wrote most of the leaders, heard somehow that I had been responsible for starting the controversy, was very amused, sent for me and told me the editor wanted to see me.

I went. He looked at the callow youth of nineteen, laughed immoderately, shouted with tears in his eyes: "*Mother of Seven!*" and paid me a fiver. It was the first money I had earned with my pen. I gave a wine party on the proceeds.

Years later, a good many years later, when I was writing articles in *Good Housekeeping* for J. Y. McPeake, I told him this story at lunch in the old Savage Club in the Adelphi. As I was talking he smiled, an odd sort of smile, and then he said:

"Yes, it's funny, damn funny, but you don't know how damn funny. I was sub-editor of the paper at that time. I remember it quite well. But I never knew until now it was you."

Another outlet for my scribbling mania began also about that time. A new undergrad paper had just been started. It was called *T.C.D.* and soon I was writing for it also, light verse, little sketches, skits on celebrities. They were, of course, unsigned. I have never since dared to look at the early numbers of this little paper to see what they were like. I suspect they were very jejune. All this, I am afraid, interfered with my real work; but it was an apprenticeship I should otherwise have missed.

The Professor of English Literature at that time was Edward Dowden, the Shakespearean scholar, a grave man with a pointed beard who, if he had worn an Elizabethan ruff round his neck, could have passed for Sir Walter Raleigh. He lectured in a room in the front quadrangle, Parliament Square, a room lined with books from floor to ceiling, piled on chairs and tables, leaving space only for himself and the half-dozen students working under him for an honours degree in Modern Literature.

I knew my way round College by now. I was a Senior Freshman, and I found to my joy that my other lectures allowed me time to attend his also. So I was able to interpose between the classics and the dissecting-room some work on our own superb language under a great master of English.

The men working in the Modern Literature class could not quite make me out. No! I didn't want to study for 'Mods' (an honours degree in Literature). Yes! I intended to try for one in Natural Science instead. No! I hadn't got the time for two courses. Yes! I was a medical student, doing it just for the love of the thing. They thought it was a bit queer; but were quite good-natured and treated me as an intelligent amateur, the sort of superior attitude a doctor takes to a bone-setter.

The lectures that term were on the Restoration dramatists; and at the end the Professor set us a paper on the subject. To the surprise and annoyance of the honours men I won the prize, a sum of money which could be spent on books at the University Booksellers, Hodges and Figgis, then in Grafton Street. I used it to buy medical books. I didn't

Trinity College, Dublin

Arthur Waugh

want to, but medical books are expensive and I felt I was costing my father a lot of money. He laughed when I told him, and said I was not to do it again. So next term, when I won the prize once more, to the increased annoyance of the honours class, I was tempted by Masson's edition of De Quincey, and most of the prize went on that.

Dowden had by now become conscious of me as an individual. We met occasionally in the second-hand booksellers' shops on the Liffey Quays which are such a characteristic of Dublin, reminding me of the stalls on the banks of the Seine behind Notre Dame. Many a time the price of a luncheon went on a book. These books I still have on my shelves. I have forgotten what lunches they represent.

I had now been given rooms in College in a block of buildings known as Rotten Row, which has since been pulled down to make room for the Graduates' Memorial. It was a quaint old panelled set of rooms, very draughty and infested with mice which seemed to be forever running up and down in the hollow walls. In those days there was no electric light anywhere in the College rooms, and of course no baths. We worked with oil lamps and candles. I have often wondered why, in all the long centuries, there has never been a serious fire in the College, considering the wild student orgies that must often have threatened to produce one.

Dowden had by now got in the way of lending me books from his library. Once I had a priceless copy of that beautiful old fifteenth-century ballad 'The Nut Brown Maid'. I was reading it one morning when I suddenly discovered I would be late for an Anatomy lecture, so I left it hurriedly on my table and rushed off. On my return I was horrified to find it had disappeared. I searched frantically, for it was a unique copy of great value. Eventually, with a great sigh of relief, I found it in my waste-paper basket, thrown in there by my 'skip', my college servant, who seeing the old, battered, brown, dog-eared little booklet thought it was of no value. Determined I'd never run such a risk again, I took it back thankfully to Dowden, and told him the story. He smiled his gentle smile, and said it would not have mattered. And I think he really meant it.

It was about this time that a conflict brewing up in my mind became acute. I began to wonder if medicine really was my life work, if I would not be happier as a writer. I was getting more and more

c

absorbed by literature, found I was more interested in competing for The New Shakespeare Society's Prize than one in Biology, and decided if I won the prize I would speak to Dowden about it. I did win it, and so one Sunday afternoon at his house in Donnybrook I talked to him.

He was very kind, very gentle.

"You are the second man doing medicine who has consulted me on this very problem," he said. "Actually your predecessor had taken a Moderatorship in Modern Literature; but in spite of that I gave him the same advice I am now going to give you. It is Charles Lamb's: 'Literature is a very bad crutch, but a very good walking-stick.' So I advise you to do as he did and carry on with medicine. If writing is your bent, medicine is one of the finest trainings for it. Think of Sir Thomas Browne, Vaughan, Locke, Smollett, Huxley—lots of others. If you find you have not the gift, you will still have your profession, and you'll be all the better doctor for your love of letters."

I admit I was bitterly disappointed at the time. I see the wisdom of it now.

"What became of the other man, sir?"

"Oh. He is now a Professor of Pathology. His name, I may tell you, is Almroth Wright. He found that he had chosen his real vocation once he began hospital work. You haven't started hospital yet? No! Then you may find the same. But if you don't, talk to me again."

The name of Almroth Wright meant nothing to me then. It is now, of course, one of world-wide renown. It will go down in medical history with that of Pasteur and Lister and his own pupil Fleming of penicillin fame. Millions of men owed their lives to him in the First and Second World Wars, for, by his inoculation treatment, typhoid— that deadly horror of all previous wars, the horror that slew ten times as many men as the enemy's bullets—has now been shorn of nearly all its terrors.

Sometimes I have wondered idly what would have happened if Sir Almroth Wright had not taken Dowden's advice. Knowing him well, as I came to do in the later years of his life, I think his name might have gone down as that of a great philosopher or a great lawyer, for he had an intellect that soared above technicalities into first principles, and he would have been famous whatever side of his mind he had chosen to cultivate. But, if he had not decided to be a doctor, it is possible that the inestimable benefits vaccine therapy has given to the world would still have been undiscovered; it is more than likely that the great laboratory he built at St. Mary's Hospital would never have been founded; and it is probable, in consequence, that penicillin, which has completely revolutionised surgical treatment throughout the world, would not have been discovered.

CHAPTER IV

HOSPITAL LIFE

ACCEPTING Dowden's advice to carry on, I started hospital in my second year, according to the Dublin custom. Immediately I was happier. I began to see how the preliminary lectures I had been attending—Anatomy, Chemistry, Physics, Botany, Zoology, Histology and Physiology, all a bit wearisome at times except Anatomy, Botany and Zoology—were essential if one was to understand the nature of disease, and the methods of combating the ills that man, and especially woman, has to suffer. I knew I had found my vocation.

Hospital rounds were at nine in the morning, so after a hurried breakfast cooked in my rooms—there were no breakfasts in Hall for undergraduates in my time—I used to sprint across the College Park on my way to Sir Patrick Dun's Hospital to be in time with the rest of the class to meet the Great Man, the Professor of Surgery, in the Front Hall. This was Edward Hallaran Bennett, but we never used that name in conversation, for he was universally known as 'the Boss', no one ever could explain to me why.

He was one of the greatest authorities on fractures then living; was himself the discoverer of 'Bennett's Fracture'; and when X-rays came in, had a supreme contempt for anyone who required their help to make a diagnosis. Certainly surgeons like him of the older school had a wonderful touch, and could feel fractures in a way that is rare now because the practice required to get this delicacy of finger-tips is no longer necessary.

It was a pleasure to do surgical dressings for the Boss. He was a very great gentleman, a repository of surgical lore unequalled by anyone I have since come across. He said he remembered Colles of 'Colles's Fracture' and it is likely he may have, as he was six years old when Colles died. I gained from him an interest in fractures, a commencing love of old medical books, and one life-long fear I have never been able to shake off.

The fear started in this way. A fellow-student of mine when home at Christmas got an accidental gunshot wound in his thigh. He was admitted under the Boss, and I was told to do his dressings. The wound in his thigh was deep but not dangerous, and we were quite happy about him. About a week after admission, however, his temperature went up. I looked at the wound with the nurse. It seemed to me about the same.

"How do you feel, old chap?"

"Pretty well. But there's just one odd thing. I can't swallow as easily as usual."

Ten minutes later I reported this to the house-surgeon, Dr. Gordon Holmes (now Sir Gordon Holmes, F.R.S.), as we were waiting in the Hall entrance for the Boss.

"What's that?" he said sharply. "Why didn't you tell me before?"

"Well, I've only just seen him," I protested, a little nettled.

He looked at his watch. "Hold the Boss up, if you can, until I've seen him too," he said hurriedly.

Together the Boss and Holmes examined him carefully, whilst I and the other dresser hung round. It was obvious something was wrong, but I was too ignorant to understand. The patient now told the Boss that his neck was stiff, and he was getting pains in his legs. The Boss ordered a sedative, made some cheery remark, smiled broadly and went out into the corridor followed by the rest of us. In the corridor the mask fell from his face, and he said grimly:

"Tetanus."

Tetanus is lockjaw, and in those days it meant in ninety per cent of cases a slow horrible death in convulsions, for there was no real treatment for it then. So we watched him helplessly. He lasted for days. We fed him with a nasal tube when his jaw became clenched in the terrible spasms. We gave him morphia to ease him. Towards the end, when the morphia failed, I was deputed sometimes to give him chloroform. It was my first real encounter with inevitable death, and it left an impression on my mind that has never quite gone.

The disease is caused by the tetanus bacillus, an organism which is found abundantly in garden soil, particularly soil that has been manured. And it is a very difficult germ to fight because it is so resistant to boiling and can live for years in soil waiting for a victim. This was burnt vividly into my mind when I was doing bacteriology two years later. The ward in which my fellow-student had died was a small private one of four beds. All the beds had wooden frames, and out of curiosity I took some dust from a crack in the frame of the bed my friend had been nursed in. To my surprise and horror, I grew tetanus bacillus in the tube I had inoculated with this dust. The hospital authorities scrapped the beds at once.

This, and the memory of seeing my fellow-student die in agony, made an indelible impression on me. I have always been terrified of tetanus since, although I know that modern methods have almost killed its deadly power. I appreciate that my attitude is unscientific, but the scar is so deep I cannot help it.

Actually I seem to have been dogged by tetanus all my life. I had to treat a nine-days'-old baby with tetanus as one of my first cases when I became a house-surgeon in London. It survived by a miracle, and I wrote it up under my chief's name. It was my first appearance in the *Lancet*.

A little later I had a man who died of it, from a nail that pierced his foot when crossing Westminster Bridge. I was told by the great Jonathan Hutchinson that one of his sons died of tetanus when he fell down and cut his knees in the garden of Cavendish Square, and when my own little girl fell in our garden and cut her knee badly I remembered this, and was very unhappy for a week. I saw it kill man after man in the Balkans when I was with the Serbian Army in 1914, because we had no antidote to it on the Austrian front.

Of course we had anti-tetanic serum in England as early as 1900; but it was weak and impure, and was often given too late to be of any use. Gradually, however, it became more and more potent, and by 1914, when the First World War started, we were able to use it very successfully. Its use, indeed, in the British Army in Flanders lowered the number of cases of tetanus from nine per thousand to 1.4 in the first three months of the 1914–18 War.

What kills in an acute case is the severe and continued muscle spasms that completely wear out the victim. But now we need no longer depend on morphia and chloroform when some unfortunate person develops the disease. With drugs like Avertin and Nembutal and other preparations we can control the spasms. More dramatic still, we can employ curare, the famous arrow poison of the South American Indians. This secret poison was used by the natives of the Amazon to tip the little arrows which they expelled through a blow-pipe when hunting. Soon after the arrow struck its quarry all the muscles of the wounded animal eventually became paralysed and it died of asphyxia. The composition of the poison was a closely guarded secret of the natives, but samples were eventually brought to Europe by that singular person, Squire Waterton.

It was looked upon for many years as something too deadly to handle. Only limited supplies were obtainable, and these were kept under lock and key in physiological laboratories for experimental purposes. Anyone accidentally puncturing his skin when working with it was in deadly danger, since there was no known antidote. Recently, however, the secret of the composition has been discovered, the drug analysed, and it has been found that carefully attenuated doses can be employed just sufficient to control the spasms of tetanus but not enough to cause death by paralysing the muscles of respiration. Indeed, we now know so much about it and can use it with such safety that it is employed to produce relaxation in ordinary surgical operations, thus greatly diminishing the quantity of anæsthetic required. Science has taken the dread out of curare and made it into a life-saving drug.

We now have got to the stage where we can inoculate to prevent tetanus occurring. This is done for people liable to special risks, such as soldiers, gardeners and agricultural labourers. These can be immunised beforehand by injections of tetanus toxoid, a very attenuated preparation from the actual germ. The Allied armies were thus successfully protected in the Second World War.

All this is common knowledge, but in spite of that, as I have said, I am still terrified of tetanus.

One other bugbear has haunted me: typhoid fever. My dread of it has also lasted all my life, even though Almroth Wright's vaccine has now deprived it of its terrors. If ever I fall ill with obscure abdominal pains and a temperature, I am sure I have typhoid. Such is the power of early impressions.

It started in this way: when I was a fifth-year student not yet qualified, I was appointed to what is called a 'Resident' post at Steevens' Hospital. At this hospital we took in as patients the men of the old Royal Irish Constabulary, a magnificent body of men which was disbanded when the Eire Government took over from the Imperial Parliament.

One morning the ward sister said to me:

"There's a new case in the police ward—admitted last night."

"What's wrong with him, Sister?"

"Not diagnosed yet. Temperature a hundred. He looks awfully ill to me."

I did not think he looked ill when I saw him. But ward sisters are wise people. They have seen so many deaths. So I let her words sink into my mind.

He was a splendid specimen of a man, like most of that famous force. He complained of headache; but I could find little wrong with his heart or lungs. His abdomen was rather tender. He had been ill, he said, for three days or more, but there was no rash on his body, so chicken-pox, scarlet fever and smallpox could be eliminated. The next day passed. No rash yet, so it was not measles. On what was presumably the fifth day there was still no rash. Not typhus, therefore. But the fever was rising. Next morning the visiting physician under whom I was 'Resident' did a round, and I had to read out my notes in front of the class.

He listened, made a few comments and then proceeded to examine the patient—a beautiful bit of work to watch, rapid and complete, the result of years of practice. Afterwards for ten minutes he talked to the class on temperature and its meaning. Then he turned to the house-physician.

"Have you done a Widal test, Wilson?"

"No, sir. I thought it might be too soon."

The Chief nodded. "Perhaps. Best do it after the clinic's over and report to me."

The test was then a new one and depends on the fact that a drop of the blood serum of a patient with typhoid fever clumps a suspension of typhoid germs when looked at under the microscope, whereas the serum of a normal person has no such effect.

Wilson used me as a normal person. He took a few drops of blood from my ear, got rid of the blood corpuscles and tested my serum against some typhoid germs out of a tube in the laboratory. Under the microscope the germs bumped merrily against each other, when I looked down on them, and nothing happened.

"Well, it's clear you've never had it anyway," said Wilson.

Then he did the same with the policeman's blood on another microscope slide.

"Here!" he said, excitedly. "Look at this!"

I did so. The culture of germs that had bobbed round so merrily with my blood serum, when brought in contact with that of the policeman, instead of bobbing round were all still, clumped together in a jelly-like mass on the microscope slide.

"He's got it all right," said Wilson. "Gosh, the Chief will be pleased he's spotted what was wrong so soon. He's seen so many hundreds of similar cases he's got a second sense about them. We wouldn't have been sure without this test for maybe another week, and not even then perhaps."

That was my first typhoid. It has burned into my memory, because next day we had another and another; and every day for weeks they kept coming in. We cleared the ward of general medical cases. It filled up, and presently we had to take over a second ward. By now I knew all about the enlarged spleen and the little pink spots that came on the abdomen, generally round the tenth day. It was obvious we were in for a severe epidemic. One by one the men became delirious. Some got pneumonia, some bled from the bowel, some had perforation, got peritonitis and died. Every morning when I went into the ward I had to record another death. It was horrible—these great big fine men killed by this deadly little germ. There was no drug then that was of any use. Night after night I helped the nurses to blanket-bath the worst cases when the temperature went over 103 degrees Fahrenheit.

The men themselves were beginning to be frightened now. I used to go round smiling cheerfully and talking about a little bronchitis, a bit of a chill, a touch of dysentery. But they knew.

Of course the Home Office had got busy by this time. It was found that all the men infected had been getting their milk supply from one dairy, and the milk there was teeming with typhoid germs, though it was all right when it came from the farm. Someone was infecting the milk, someone in the dairy. The Crown bacteriologist did a Widal on all the people connected with the dairy—twenty-one of them. Twenty were negative. The twenty-first, a dairymaid, clumped the germs even when her blood serum was diluted over a thousand times. She was the culprit evidently. She had infected eighty-six men and twenty-seven of them had died.

"She must have had it recently herself, probably quite mildly," the bacteriologist said. "She's an unconscious manslayer. She's a 'carrier'. She's more dangerous than Jack the Ripper."

*

The years of a medical student's life are very fully occupied. It becomes more and more a question of absorbing thousands of facts; and his horizon gets limited to the next examination looming threateningly ahead.

Two or three external incidents during the period still rise in my memory. One was the parliamentary election after which W. E. Hartpole Lecky, the historian, joined Sir Edward Carson as the second of the members for the University. We had two representatives at Westminster in those palmy days.

Lecky was a long, lanky man getting on in years, and did not in the least relish fighting a contested election. To the undergrads, however, it was a golden opportunity for a rag; and one of my most vivid memories is the sight of Lecky being wheeled in a wheelbarrow up Grafton Street, the Bond Street of Dublin, one afternoon by a riotous group of students, his long legs sticking over the front of the barrow, with the *élite* of Dublin looking on, slightly puzzled but rather amused. He was nearly sixty at the time, must have hated it, and probably was in some danger of being injured; but looking back on it now I remember he showed no sign of discomposure whatever.

Later, when he came over to make a speech at a meeting of the Historical Society, founded by the great Edmund Burke when he was an undergrad, I helped to chair him through the front Quad. By this time he was a familiar figure in Parliament, and a well-known caricaturist of the period, F. C. Gould, for some reason always represented him as wearing very short trousers with elastic-sided boots.

I thought he really did wear elastic-sided boots, so when we were chairing him I got in closer, and tried to drag one boot off to keep as a trophy. It wouldn't come, so I had a good look and, to my horror, found he was wearing laced boots. Conscience-stricken, feeling I must have hurt him, I wrote a letter of apology next day; and like the great gentleman he was, he answered most courteously, said he quite understood and would write and complain to Mr. Gould of the *Westminster Gazette*, for obviously it was his fault, not mine.

Another event that sticks in my mind was the visit of Queen Victoria to Dublin during the Boer War. She was an old lady, then in her eighty-first year, very small, very bent, dressed in black. But she disembarked at Kingstown and drove in an open carriage the six miles to Dublin through a cheering mob, bowing the whole time. It seemed to me in those days a superhuman feat for an old lady of eighty to perform; and, as a nearly-qualified doctor, I was wondering how it was possible. I was lucky enough to have a seat on a stand inside the railing of Trinity next the Provost's house, looking on to College Green. The street is very narrow there, and I could look down into the carriage as it passed only a few feet away.

Then I saw how it was done. Her seat in the carriage balanced on a pivot on each side, and a footman seated behind her rocked it gently backwards and forwards with his foot on a pedal. All she had to do was very slowly move her head from side to side. All the bowing was done by the tilt of the pedal. None the less it must have been very tiring to the wonderful old lady; but she was determined to go through with it.

Actually it was also a very courageous thing to do. The Boer War was not popular in Ireland. There was a persistent rumour, firmly believed by the underworld of Dublin, that the elusive war leader, De Wet, was in reality Charles Stewart Parnell, who hadn't died at all but had slipped off to South Africa in disguise, leaving a dummy body to be buried in his coffin at Glasnevin cemetery. Recruiting for the war was not going well; but as Lord Roberts was very popular as Commander-in-Chief in Ireland it was thought that, if the Queen went over as well, enlistment in the Irish regiments would be stimulated.

That night there was rioting in Dublin; and the Trinity undergraduates, armed with sticks, came frequently to blows with the hostile mob.

One young medical student, John Askins, said to me next morning: "Och, it was the gran' time we had last night. I was fightin' for an hour an' I was dressin' cut heads at Mercer's Hospital for the next two; an' the owld dear will niver know I was doin' it for her."

He said this in a heartfelt tone of regret I still remember. Nearly twenty years later, I met him in London at a Service dinner. He was then a Lieutenant-Colonel, R.A.M.C., and I reminded him of the incident. He said he had forgotten it.

Askins was an amusing dare-devil, but, like many others not too studious, he made an excellent doctor after he qualified.

I remember, as our names both began with 'A', we were generally examined in vivas close to each other. Once I came out from a Physiology viva and he followed me. He had not done well and he knew it.

"How did you do, John?" I asked.

John looked at me solemnly. "He asked me a question. I answered it. He fainted away," he said. "He asked me a second question. I answered that too. He menstruated twice."

I was just about to laugh outright when, to our horror, the examiner, Professor John Malet Purser, came out of the laboratory door. Obviously he must have heard us.

"Not quite as bad as that, Mr. Askins, not quite," he said, as we both bolted down the steps.

The South African war dragged on. The first flush of patriotic fervour was over. The airy belief in a speedy successful campaign finishing in three months had been shattered by the failures of Buller, Methuen and Gatacre. The gloom of that time was like nothing I can remember except what we felt after the fall of France and Dunkirk in 1940.

Lord Roberts's post as Commander-in-Chief in Ireland was an honorary one given to a retired warrior; and he lived, appropriately, at Kilmainham Hospital, the Irish equivalent of the Chelsea Hospital for Pensioners. The hospital was close to Island Bridge, where the University Boat Club owned a stretch of land on the right bank of the Liffey, which we used as a tow-path.

Lord Roberts had been given special permission to use this tow-path, and most of us were accustomed to the little figure in tweeds and riding breeches watching us in training. He looked like a jockey, but we all knew who he was. One coach, however, when cycling along training his crew, nearly came into collision with him and, not recognising him at once and being rather ragged in temper, began "What the hell . . ." etc. etc. etc., before he could stop. It needed some diplomacy on the part of the Captain of the Boat Club to smooth the matter over, especially with Lady Roberts; but soon all was well, and the little man resumed his walks along the tow-path.

Then suddenly he appeared no longer on his daily walk, and the next thing we heard was that he had been appointed C.-in-C. in South Africa to supersede Buller; and that he had insisted on having Kitchener of Khartoum as his Chief of Staff.

'Bobs of Kandahar' was a name to conjure with in those days. His book *Forty-One Years in India* (1897) had been a great success; Kipling had made his fame world-wide in the *Barrack Room Ballads*. Kitchener, too, was a successful general. He had annihilated the Mahdi's army at Omdurman two years previously. The combination promised well. Immediately our spirits rose and recruiting was stimulated. There was no conscription in those days, and this rise in public confidence was therefore essential.

So Roberts went out and the war suddenly became popular. Success followed success. The tide of victory rolled on; and we who were waiting to qualify began to think we would be too late to join up.

CHAPTER V

*

LONDON

SIX MONTHS after the Queen's visit I obtained my medical degree. It is a very momentous and solemn period in a young doctor's life. For five or six years he has thought of nothing further ahead than the hurdle of the next examination. Then suddenly he clears the final obstacle, the last lap is over and, somewhat breathless, he finds he need never sit for another examination again. At first there is an intense feeling of relief, a weight off the back, an unaccustomed leisure—all very pleasant. I do not know how long this lasts in normal times, but in the middle of a war when you are counting every day, hoping to have qualified in time, it hardly lasts at all.

Immediately I qualified I wanted to volunteer. I went to one of my chiefs for advice. He was a man I had the utmost confidence in.

He nodded gravely when I put the question to him.

"So you want to volunteer, do you?" he said. "I'd have said 'Yes, certainly,' to you a year ago when we were in a bad way. But not now. Ladysmith, Kimberley and Mafeking have been relieved. Pretoria's been occupied. Kruger has fled to Europe. Roberts is coming home. The real fighting is over, and Kitchener has been left to clear up the mess. They're putting the Boer women into concentration camps and, if I know anything, that means typhoid. You wouldn't like it. They call people like you 'civil surgeons' and make you take any dull medical job that is going in some rotten base camp. You want to be a real surgeon, don't you? The Army is riddled with typhoid—you don't like typhoid, do you? It's killing five times as many men as the Boers. The Medical Service is a disgrace to this country. It's the fault of the War Office. It's always treated its doctors like dirt, and as a consequence it has got the doctors it deserves—a lot of incompetent asses. We do not want any of our good men to go

68

into the Medical Service. We're going to boycott it until we get proper recognition of our value."

This was an eye-opener to me. I knew nothing of the struggle that was then going on to get decent recognition, definite rank, disciplinary powers, adequate pay and reasonable opportunities for scientific work in the Medical Services; nor how Treves and others had been fighting an antediluvian War Office to get these things done, in order to make a career in the recently formed R.A.M.C. more attractive. Looking back on it now it seems impossible there should have been so much opposition to such obvious reforms as were suggested, but there was.

I did not volunteer.

Then one day the Professor of Botany, Dr. Percival Wright, the uncle of (Sir) Almroth Wright, sent for me.

"The post of Physician to the King of Siam is vacant," he said. "It's an odd sort of job—semi-political. The King of Siam has three European doctors: a Frenchman, a German and an Englishman. He has little faith in Western medicine, but when the native doctors fail he calls on one or other of the Europeans—sometimes all three—so as not to appear to favour one country more than another. So far the English doctor has always been an Irishman, and the appointment has been ours. There'll be very little to do, but it opens great opportunities. We've always offered it to a Natural Science Moderator. Would you like the post? You are a good botanist, you know your zoology. Siam is an almost virgin country from the natural history angle. You would be able to collect many hitherto unknown plants, reptiles, birds, mammals. I have been asked to find a suitable person. What do you think?"

I was startled. This was something I'd never bargained for. He saw my hesitation. "You needn't decide for a fortnight. I suppose you are going home for Christmas? Turn it over in your mind and let me know."

At first I was attracted by the thought, for I was keen on natural history at the time. But Siam! It was very far away. The more I thought of it, the less I liked it; and I did want to be a surgeon. When I was at home I wrote to the professor and refused. I have often wondered since what would have happened to me if I had taken the post. I think I should have liked it, for the call of the East was very persistent in the 1900s. We were all Kipling mad. We read him avidly. I myself was completely under his spell.

Kipling was the greatest recruiting officer the Indian Civil Service, the Indian Army and the Indian Medical Service ever had. I decided that what I wanted was a commission in the Indian Medical Service, for at that time it was a truly scientific body of men whose work provided illimitable opportunities for surgery and research amongst the teeming millions of Hindustan.

Entrance to this Service was eagerly sought after at that time by candidates from all the medical schools in the United Kingdom, in striking contrast with the state of the Army Medical Service; and in consequence there was much competition for the number of medical commissions offered.

I felt, however, that my knowledge was still inadequate for the examination, and decided to take a job in Dublin which would allow me to do post-graduate work. So, a month after qualifying, I became medical officer in a private asylum, Farnham House, on the North Side. The salary was low, one hundred pounds a year, all found; but the work was not onerous, and I could attend classes in Bacteriology and Pathology and go round the hospitals looking at interesting cases. I found I could also amuse myself and keep fit by coaching crews at Island Bridge for regattas in the coming summer. This chance recreation and not the work I was doing in the labs, curiously enough, was the means of settling my future life.

One day I got a copy of the regulations applying to the Indian Medical Service and learnt something that was like a bombshell to me: my eyesight was not up to the standard required. I knew I could satisfy the examiners on the physical side, for I was fighting fit; but if they wanted they could legitimately exclude me on vision.

I went and saw a retired Director-General of the I.M.S., and he explained:

"You see, it's like this, my boy, your first job might be on the Afghan frontier, and a man wearing glasses just doesn't fit into the picture. If he loses his glasses he is useless."

At that time first-class eyesight was essential for all the Services. Senior officers, when their sight was failing, were allowed to wear monocles; but the lower ranks, emphatically no. It was only later in the 1914–18 War, when we came across the spectacled German, and found him just as tough a fighter as ourselves, that the rule was altered.

I think this was the most bitter disappointment of my young life. I wanted so keenly to go East, and when I found it was impossible I felt I was just wasting my time remaining longer in Ireland. I became very restless. My job at the asylum, which I had looked upon as merely a halting point until I went up for the I.M.S., suddenly became wearisome. I wanted to get away. Anywhere out of Dublin.

It was June. I was lounging one day in a deck-chair on the balcony of the Boat Club; and at the psychological moment the Captain came along, sank into a chair beside me and said:

"Abe! What about going over to Henley in medical charge of the crew entered for the Ladies Plate?"

A minute before I had been in the doldrums. But this—this was an idea. My spirits rose rapidly. I jumped at it.

"Just the thing. I can have a look round, see what is going, and if nothing better turns up, go out after all as a civil surgeon to South Africa!"

For the war was still hanging on, and Kitchener with his drives and block-houses was finding it more difficult than he expected to force the surrender of the elusive Boer.

The Trinity crew, which had been coached by R. C. Lehmann, the famous Leander oarsman, had gone over in advance and I arrived at Euston towards the end of June, 1901. I had arranged to room with a friend coaching for the Indian Civil Service, and we had lodgings behind Westbourne Grove, close to Wren's grinding school in Powis Square, then famous for its success in getting men into the higher Civil Service.

It must have been over three miles from Euston to my lodgings, but when I arrived there I found two men, rather breathless, had been running the whole way behind my four-wheeler, just in the hope of earning a tip carrying my heavy trunk up to the fourth floor. They looked so exhausted, probably from undernourishment, I gave them each a shilling. It was a big tip for those days, and they were embarrassingly grateful. Looking back on this I can see it meant there must have been desperate unemployment in London for men to hang around Euston on the off-chance of such precarious earnings. At the time it did not strike me as pitiful, which shows how little one thinks.

Those were the days of General Booth's 'Darkest England' when we talked complacently of the 'Submerged Tenth' and 'The Great Unwashed'. There were many hungry bellies in the golden days of Queen Victoria's reign to which people now look back so longingly. We forget the black spots and remember only that in those days England was the acknowledged leader of the world in wealth and power, and we boasted that the sun never set on the Queen's dominions.

Henley in the 1900s was a microcosm of the wealth of England. I can still remember the beauty and luxury of those days. The rows and rows of gorgeous houseboats, white and gold, green, yellow, blue, scarlet, with their roof gardens of flaming geraniums, nasturtiums or other flowering plants, that lined the course. The bright billowy dresses of the ladies, gaudy parasols, the big picture hats, the blazers, the boaters, the club ties—each recognisable to the initiated. The long lazy days in punts or Canadian canoes. It was a picture of the undisputed acceptance of wealth in an assured world in violent contrast to the scenes of squalor and unemployment I half-consciously knew existed.

Wimbledon was a humble affair in those days. It did not compete with the five great social sporting events of the year: Ascot, the Oxford and Cambridge match at Lord's, the Eton and Harrow that followed, Henley, and finally Goodwood to end the season.

I found my crew in great fettle. They were extraordinarily quick off the mark, had a pretty style, a good length and were being favourably written up in the sporting papers. I had to watch their diet, however, as they were inclined to indulge in unsuitable dishes, put before them by an enthusiastic landlady whose idea was to feed them up.

They won each heat to the semi-final, which was against Eton. We were all exceedingly excited. I thought I had got them through without any mishap, and was rather pleased with myself. Then stroke got cramp in the night. He said he was better in the morning, and the Captain, Mr. Lehmann and I decided to let him row. They lost by a canvas. Probably they would have lost anyway. It was the luck of the game. They went back to Dublin and I started looking for a job.

Searching through the advertisements in the *Lancet* I saw one for a house-surgeon at the West London Hospital.

'Just the thing for me,' I thought. So I called on the Secretary, got a list of the medical staff, the address of the President, William Bird, and finally those of the members of the House Committee, made up of a bank manager, a house agent, an auctioneer and some local tradesmen, on each of whom I was expected to call. All this preliminary work rather daunted me, specially when one of the medical staff said:

"Would a London man get such a post in Dublin?"

"No, I don't think so," I answered, truthfully.

"Well, then. Why do you apply here?" he said sharply.

"Because, sir, London is more than London, it is the capital of the Empire," I retorted.

He smiled thoughtfully at that. "I see your point," he said, and I felt encouraged.

It was a very tiresome job going round, particularly for someone who didn't know his London. The doctors were all right. They treated me courteously. They had to work with whoever was appointed, so naturally they wanted to see the applicants. But why should laymen want to see the candidates? What difference could it possibly make to them? I felt humiliated interviewing, metaphorically cap in hand, an auctioneer, who obviously did not want to see me, but would have been annoyed and voted against me had I not called. It made me resentful, and I am happy to say it is a custom that soon after passed out of fashion in all London hospitals, and has now died completely under the National Health Service.

There were two consulting surgeons to the hospital, William Bird and (Sir) Alfred Cooper. They had retired from the active staff of the hospital, but I was told I should do a courtesy call, especially on William Bird, whose father had founded the hospital.

The story about William Bird was that his father, George Bird, was a very successful Hammersmith builder; and that he had founded the hospital for his son because William had been unsuccessful first of all in getting on the staff of St. George's Hospital, and later on to that of St. Mary's Hospital, although George, the father, had built St. Mary's without any guarantee that he would be paid for his work.

Bird, when I called to see him, was a very old man. He lived in a gloomy mansion, Bute House, in Brook Green, Hammersmith, which his father had built; and I had great difficulty in getting to see him. For some reason he was being guarded against visitors; and only on the second attempt was I admitted. He was in bed in a night-cap, and I was not allowed to see him alone—I never fathomed why. He was quite pleasant and wished me success. I left him heartened, little guessing I was to pull his last tooth six months later.

(Sir) Alfred Cooper lived at 9 Henrietta Street, Cavendish Square, a beautiful Adam house before it was altered for the worse. I did not know what an intimately important house it was to become to me twenty years later when it was in other hands.

Alfred Cooper was then at his zenith. He had an immense consulting practice; he had married a sister of the Duke of Fife; and was an intimate friend of Edward, soon to be crowned Edward VII.

He saw me in the drawing-room on the first floor and was most kind and courteous. Again I felt heartened by the interview, although he said he no longer went to the hospital committees. A charming boy of about ten was playing on the carpet. I could not have known then what I know now, that I was looking at one who was to become later a distinguished historian and novelist, and our Ambassador in Paris. Still less could I have known that fifty years later I would be writing this autobiography with my feet on the carpet on which he was then playing.

I spent about a week canvassing the two committees, gradually becoming more and more depressed, especially when I was told, in confidence, by the one Trinity man on the staff, that I had not the slightest chance of getting the post.

He was so sorry for me that he said:

"Doing anything on Saturday night? No? Well, come and dine with me at the Savage Club. It's in Adelphi Terrace, just off the Strand. Seven p.m. and don't dress."

There for me started the enchantment of London. The wit, the brilliancy, the music, the comic turns, the famous names went to my head like fiery wine. I was completely carried away. I had been in some doubt before. I decided that night that I would stick it, that London was my Mecca, that in due course I too, if possible, would become a member of this famous club. It might mean, it probably would mean, years of hard work, disappointments, set-backs, but I decided it would be worth it.

Obviously my difficulty was to find a footing, especially against men who had qualified in London, knew the ropes and had their chiefs to recommend them. I felt if I could get one hospital appointment and make good there, I might eventually reach the goal so many desired, so few attained: Harley Street.

I finished interviewing people about three days before the date the appointment was to be made; and so I decided I would pay a courtesy call on the house-men, just to see what sort of fellows they were. Apparently this was an unusual thing to do, and it made a favourable impression. Most of them were Bart's men, and they told me that practically no one but a Bart's man had any chance of getting on the house. None the less they were all very pleasant. I liked them. One house-surgeon drew me aside as I was leaving.

"I wonder, would you mind giving me your address?" he said. "I'm applying for another hospital. I'm not too happy here. I don't get on with my Chief."

A little surprised, I gave it to him.

The great day came. I was interviewed by the General Committee, and asked a few perfunctory questions that made me feel sure they had no real interest in me. My suspicions were correct; I did not get the job; and I went back in deep gloom to my rooms.

Three days later I had a wire.

"Can you come to the hospital. Urgent." It was signed "Harold Stiff". It was from the H.S. who had asked for my address. I took a hansom straight away.

"I've just had a frightful row with my Chief and asked him if I might resign," he said. "I told him you were keen on the job and would jump at it. He said he remembered you, and told me to ask you to call on him. If he likes you he said he might take you on. If not I shall have to continue here for another three months."

"What's wrong with him?" I queried.

"Well. He's very deaf. He's a bit mad. He's hard to get on with. But he is a first-class surgeon."

"I'll see him," I said.

I did, I liked him, he liked me and I got the job. To my surprise I found I then became senior house-surgeon, for my Chief, C. B. Keetley, was the senior surgeon and I took precedence over all the others.

The Dublin custom of having fifth-year men as 'Residents' before qualification was now, I found, enormously valuable to me. None of my fellow-house-men had held a resident post before qualifying and, though theoretically sound and full of book learning, they were not yet good practical men. But they were an excellent set of fellows; we all got on remarkably well together; and very soon I found them asking my opinion on some cases they had admitted. Generally nothing much depended on this; but once it turned out to be very important.

The senior house-physician said to me casually one day:

"I've just taken in a beautiful case of pustular eczema. Like to see it?"

I have always been interested in skin diseases, so we went along to one of the medical wards and there in the middle bed of one row was the patient.

I looked at him. I was startled.

"He's got smallpox," I said quietly, so quietly that no one else in the ward would hear.

"Good God! No! I don't believe it!" exclaimed the H.P.

"Well. I've seen a good many cases. It's not uncommon in Dublin. Have you ever seen a case?"

"No. We don't get them in London," he admitted.

"Well. You will soon. You tell me this man's a postman! It'll be all over Hammersmith, if I'm right. He'll have spread it everywhere."

Of course there was a tremendous rumpus about it. The Medical Registrar was called. He thought I was right, but was not quite sure. The Medical Officer of Health for Hammersmith was summoned. He said I was right. That settled it. The ward was isolated and I vaccinated all the occupants. In the next week two or three more cases came to the hospital. It was the beginning of the smallpox epidemic of 1902 in Kensington and Hammersmith. All the house-men on duty had become wise to it by now; and we just admitted the patients to the Casualty Room inside the main door of the hospital, signed them up, notified the Medical Officer of Health, and had them carried off by ambulance to the Fever Hospital.

The Sanitary Inspector's people then came along, sealed up the Casualty Room and fumigated it with sulphur. When this kept occurring every day or so, we got bored. It was a nuisance having the room where we saw minor accidents being constantly put out of action this way. It was also, we knew, practically useless; so I said to Brown, the Head Porter:

"See here, Brown! You can spot these people coming up the steps. Don't take them in to Casualty. Hold them up outside in the hall, or even on the steps, and send for the M.O. on duty."

Brown smiled a wise smile. He was an old hand at guessing which department a patient was likely to want.

"I'll see to it, sir," he said.

It was warm autumn weather. The victims used to walk up the steps to the front door of the hospital near Hammersmith Broadway covered with spots on their faces; Brown would take one look at them, ring the casualty bell, and the H.P. on duty, warned, would come down, sign the form and send for the ambulance.

"We needn't have the Casualty Room fumigated any more. No contagious cases are being admitted in future, Brown," I said.

"No, sir. Certainly not, sir. I'll inform the Sanitary Inspector, sir."

My reputation rose. It was decided that all the nurses who had been in contact with the first case should be vaccinated; and I, as senior H.S., was told to do it.

Several of the nurses asked to have it done on a leg so as not to have a scar on the arm. This seemed very fair to me, and I agreed. Several days later, however, when I was doing dressings in one of my surgical wards the junior H.P. looked in and grinned at me.

"You're for it," he said. "Ma's looking for your blood. She's coming along now to see you."

It was my first interview with that Olympian dignitary, the Matron —large, fiftyish, imposing, very full-bosomed, looking like a very big pouter-pigeon.

"I understand, Mr.—er—Abraham, that you have been vaccinating some of my nurses on their legs," she said severely.

"Yes, Matron."

"Well. Four of them have had to go off duty owing to swelling and pain. Most inconvenient, most inconvenient," she said.

"Och, sure, a rest'll do them a power o' good, Matron," said I, assuming an exaggerated Dublin accent.

I could see the horrified eyes of the Sister goggling in the background, and the little pro. behind her turning scarlet with suppressed emotion. The Matron, like the great Queen, was not amused. She stared at me.

"Most inconvenient and—may I say so—improper, Mr.—er— Abraham. Please do not do it again," she said, and sailed away like a great square-rigged ship, fully conscious of her dignity.

*

The hospital was a very busy one and whoever was on casualty duty always had a heavy day. The public-houses did not close till twelve-thirty a.m.; and I soon found it was unwise to go to bed before one-thirty on my twenty-four-hour duty day. The drunks and incapables, cut heads and fractures collected by the police had a way of appearing about one a.m. Also I made the discovery every doctor soon makes that the ordinary sober citizen has a habit of developing some complaint, putting up with it all day, getting panicky in the middle of the night and rushing with it to hospital in the small hours. Sometimes it was important, sometimes not. But always one had to make sure, for to miss anything serious might mean a tragedy.

I remembered one hectic night. It was Christmas Eve and I was in charge. My duty, when a serious accident or emergency too important for a house-surgeon to deal with occurred, was to call up the assistant-surgeon on duty for the week. A man was brought in, and I diagnosed a depressed fracture of the vault of the skull. Nobody really wanted such a casualty, particularly on Christmas Eve, and I knew Mr. L. A. Bidwell, the surgeon on duty, was having a party for his children in Wimpole Street. Still, I had to ring him up.

"You're sure of your diagnosis?" he said sharply.

"Yes, sir, I think so, sir."

"All right, I'll come," he said, reluctantly.

When he came he confirmed the diagnosis and we proceeded to trephine. In the middle of the operation I had another call downstairs. When I came back I said rather diffidently:

"I've got another depressed fracture, sir."

"Oh, no," he said, "not two! Not likely!"

"Sorry, sir. 'Fraid so."

"All right, this one's finished. Get the other up, and we'll look at him."

The man was brought in and Bidwell ran his fingers over the scalp.

"You're right," he said. "Well, I suppose we must do him. It's half-past eleven and I want to get home."

Bidwell was a surgeon with beautiful skilful hands. It was a pleasure to watch and assist him. We started again, and were getting on swimmingly until I had another call downstairs. When I came back I couldn't look at him. The theatre sister was helping, and he was busy raising the last segment of bone.

He looked up. "Well," he said sharply, "wash up again and help me finish."

As I hesitated he added peevishly:

"What are you waiting for?"

"Sorry, sir, but I've got a third depressed fracture just come in," I answered meekly.

"Hell!" he burst out. "Blast it, you don't mean it. It's impossible. Never heard of such a thing."

"Nor I, sir. But it isn't my fault they're celebrating," I murmured.

"Well, you'll darn well have to do it yourself," he said.

"May I, sir? You really mean it? May I?" I exclaimed eagerly. It was something I had never yet dared hope for.

Suddenly he laughed. The peevishness left him.

"Get him up," he said. "I'll help you do it."

That was my first life-saving brain operation. I've done a good many depressed fractures since, but I've never had more than one in one day, not even during the two great wars that have occurred in my active surgical life. It was just one of those queer things that happen against all the laws of probability.

My salary at the hospital was nothing-per-annum, plus full board and free quarters. I had to pay my own laundry bill, a not inconsiderable item. Twice a week I was on casualty duty night and day, and I was allowed a half-day off once a fortnight. It seems incredible now that anyone should be expected to accept such terms. But we did. The work was so good, and the training so excellent, that it was thought worthwhile.

My Chief, C. B. Keetley, was one of London's characters. He was a very brilliant surgeon, but because of his deafness it was assumed he would not be able to lecture students, and so he had been passed over at his own hospital, St. Bartholomew's. For some reason I was able to make him hear, speaking quite softly; and I saw that his irritability was really superficial. Actually, though short-tempered, he was very lovable. His great weakness was that he had no idea of time and was completely unbusinesslike. To anyone with an orderly mind he was a heart-break. But I loved him, and I developed a great respect for his work. He was like a father to me.

Keetley knew I was having no salary and, according to the custom then, whenever he had a private case he asked me to assist him. For this I got two guineas—when he remembered to pay me. He had a large following amongst the Kensington doctors, and I soon learnt 'who was who' there. Sometimes he would arrive an hour after the time fixed for operation. The doctors were used to that. Sometimes he forgot entirely and did not turn up at all, or arrived next day. That *did* annoy them. I had a bit of soothing to do on such occasions. But always he was forgiven.

When it came to fees he was equally erratic. Frequently he forgot to charge at all. A good many of his patients were 'Brother Savages'. He never took a fee from any of them, and many a free theatre ticket came to me in consequence. Buffalo Bill, I remember, had a great 'Wild West' show at Olympia at that time. One of his women riders fractured her thigh, and I made the acquaintance of the great man when he came to see her in the hospital. George Edwardes was a friend and patient of Keetley's, and I had the run of the Gaiety.

Occasionally Keetley would get mad with me over something. Soon, however, his anger would blow over, and half-shamefacedly he would then say:

"Come and dine with me at the Savage Club on Saturday night."

It was his way of saying 'I'm sorry'. I came almost to look forward to a rumpus, for the Savage Club Saturday nights in those days were a delight to me.

Even then the old Shakespearean actor, the great E. J. O'Dell, had become a legend. His tall figure, grey beard, broad-brimmed hat and cape of many folds were famous. His arrogant condescension was accepted as 'just O'Dell'. Keetley told me he never paid for anything in the Club, and no one knew where he lived. Sometimes on a Saturday evening he would be persuaded to sing in a high cracked voice, 'The Harvest Home', or recite what he said were extracts from *The Two Gentlemen of Verona*. He was the last great Bohemian.

Looking at celebrities produces a feeling of awe and excited privilege in the young. I remember on different occasions staring at the bearded Henty who wrote boys' stories, Henry Irving, Pinero with bushy eyebrows, Franklin Clive the singer, Luke Fildes who painted 'The Doctor', and felt I was amongst the immortals. Everyone knew Keetley, and was kind in consequence to the young house-surgeon. One of the kindest was Phil May, the *Punch* artist, then at the height of his fame. He had a large bulbous red nose, the result of much conviviality; and I once helped Keetley to scarify it with a fine tenotome, scratching long, thin lines down the middle and sides just enough to draw blood, the object being to reduce its size and render it less conspicuous. I don't think Phil minded his bibulous appearance much. J. J. Shannon at that time had painted a portrait of him and also one of Sir Thomas Dewar of whisky fame. Phil suggested they should be hung side by side at the Academy, the one of Dewar labelled 'Cause', that of Phil, 'Effect'.

In spite of my chronic impecunious condition life was very pleasant in those early years. The work was hard, but it was excellent training. Keetley was absolutely in the front rank. His special interest was orthopædic surgery—the surgery of bone deformity. He was the first person to describe the condition known as 'coxa vara'. Once a week we had what he called his 'plaster afternoon', when he fitted patients who had deformities of the spine into special jackets of poroplastic or actual plaster of Paris. They loved him. He was so gentle with them. When operating he was extraordinarily deft and quick—almost too quick. I had to guard my fingers from his knife.

Operating-tables, such as we now take for granted, were unknown then. A pillow was placed under a patient's head and the surgeon operated on him as he lay flat on his back. Keetley had a questing mind. One day in the theatre, half-way through an operation, he got dissatisfied with the position of the patient and insisted, to the great annoyance of the anæsthetist, on having his lower end lifted up. To do so he sent for a chair and some cushions out of the Residents' sitting-room. We stood by helplessly while he experimented, placing the chair on the operating-table, covering it with a carbolic sheet and hanging the unconscious patient's legs over the top of it, producing what we now call the 'Trendelenburg' position, a position unthought-of then but now universally used. This improvised arrangement looked ramshackle and rather mad to me; but he did a very successful lower abdominal operation easily which would otherwise have been most difficult and taken a great deal longer. Actually he was ten years in front of his time, for all the elaborate tilting arrangements which are commonplace today were unheard-of then.

Keetley had complete confidence in his own judgment and skill. He disliked having any other consultant looking on at one of his operations. Once Howard Marsh, a surgeon at St. Bartholomew's and a great exponent of rest in tuberculous joints, came to one of our operations. He had been asked to be present by anxious relatives. Keetley was of the opposite school. He believed in operating on tuberculosis. He was extremely expert as a surgeon. Marsh was known not to be. The two men disliked each other. The case was a child with a tuberculous knee. Marsh said to me in a loud whisper, knowing that Keetley was deaf:

"What's he going to do?"

"An excision," I said.

"All wrong," said Marsh.

Keetley, hearing nothing and taking no notice, commenced. During the operation a pair of forceps fell on the floor. Marsh picked them up and offered them to Keetley. This was too much. Keetley pushed his hand violently away with his elbow. Neither said anything. We finished tensely and I went off with my Chief.

"Marsh," he said, "can't understand the germ theory, and his only idea of treatment for T.B. is rest."

I have often thought of that remark since, for both men were right, both wrong.

Marsh, though a poor surgeon, was a very charming man. He ended as Professor of Surgery at Cambridge, and Master of Downing College. His son, Eddie Marsh, was a famous social figure in the reigns of four Kings: Edward VII, George V, Edward VIII and George VI. Like his father, he, too, had great charm.

Keetley, deaf, short-tempered, maliciously witty, a fine draughts-
man, a beautiful operator, just missed fame. I loved him with all his
faults. But if there is any moral here it is that charm wins every
time.

CHAPTER VI

CORONERS AND LOCUMS

MY FIRST HOUSE-SURGEONCY passed quickly and happily, and in addition I picked up a great deal of useful general information. For instance, the earliest legal problems the young house-surgeon comes in contact with are usually those connected with the Coroner's Court.

When casualties are brought into hospital dead, or when they die shortly after admission, the M.O. on duty who admitted them has to notify the Coroner; and the Coroner then decides whether or not an inquest is necessary.

Generally in London the Coroner is a doctor as well as a lawyer and so can appreciate both aspects of a case. Our Coroner at that time was a lawyer only, unfortunately, and the house-men often got into trouble with him in consequence. I had been warned of this.

"He's a difficult old chap. He'll try to browbeat you. But if you stick to your guns he has to give in, for, not being a doctor, he doesn't really know."

One night I was on duty and a man was brought in by the police, unconscious and smelling heavily of drink.

"We'd like you to examine him, Doctor, just to make sure he has no injury, before we take him to the cells."

I did so and was not satisfied.

"I think, Officer, I'll take him in for the night. I don't feel happy about him."

"Very well, sir. Thank you. Good night, sir," and the police clumped off.

It was lucky I did take him in, for he died in the night. Next morning I learnt there was some story of a quarrel and a fight in a public-house—he had been found lying on the foot-path outside. I could not be sure of the cause of death, so naturally I asked for a post-mortem.

This the Coroner refused, so I went to the inquest considerably annoyed. In the witness-box I was asked the cause of death.

"Well, sir, it might be due to one of several causes: for instance, a stroke or a fractured skull, or even narcotic poisoning. If it was a stroke it's nobody's fault. If it was a fracture, someone may be guilty of manslaughter. I'm afraid I can't say without a post-mortem."

That got him.

"Very well, then," he said, acidly, "I'll adjourn the inquest for twenty-four hours to allow you to do a post-mortem."

"But I'm not permitted by my hospital to do post-mortems, sir," I said.

At this he got red in the face.

"If I order you to do a post-mortem you must do it," he exclaimed angrily.

I had been coached by the Registrar how to circumvent this and I answered:

"Yes, sir. But a house-surgeon, who has to help at operations, doesn't like to carry possible infection from post-mortems to a living body. It might be fatal. But, of course, if you order me . . ."

I could see a wave of antagonism spreading over the faces of the people in court. Here was a brutal person in authority ordering a defenceless young doctor to do something he had no right to do.

The reporter in the corner was scribbling away, and I could visualise the headlines, *Coroner orders doctor to take dangerous risk*, appearing in the local paper next week. So, too, could the Coroner. He stared at me, and I felt suddenly sorry for him.

"One of the house-physicians, of course, could do it for me, sir. That would be quite safe," I said.

He grasped at that, with relief.

"Very well, Doctor. The inquest is adjourned until the result of the post-mortem is known."

I never had any further trouble with that Coroner. I got to know him personally later and found him most likeable; but neither of us ever referred to our first encounter.

My house-surgeoncy at the West London gave me the necessary start. I knew that I would be able now to apply for other posts with some prospect of success; and I got several. But institutional work is hard, one gets stale and tired, and there is a limit to the number of appointments one can usefully hold. So, after about another eighteen months, I did what most young doctors did in those days: I took a series of locums. A locum tenens is a doctor who does holiday duties for other doctors. Generally he is young and looking for some place to settle. Nowadays his fee would be fifteen to twenty guineas a week; but in those days he was paid three guineas all found and the railway fare both ways.

It was a pleasant way of seeing England and, for a young man like me who had been working hard in hospitals, a most agreeable change. The work was seldom strenuous. The doctor who owned the practice usually timed his holiday when he was slack. And a locum's post hardly ever lasted more than two or three weeks; so there was constant variety.

My memory of those locums is now rather hazy. But one sticks out clearly in my mind. I had been doing work mainly in the Home Counties; and returning to London after one I called at the Medical Bureau supplying locum tenens like me.

The agent through whom I got my engagements looked up from his desk and said:

"How'd you like to do a locum in a Welsh mining village for a change, Doctor? These locums are not popular but there's an extra guinea a week, and it isn't really necessary to speak Welsh."

Evidently he had had some difficulty in filling this particular post, and I felt he rather wanted me to take it. He had given me several good locums, so I was quite willing to help.

"Right, I'll take it," I said.

Changing trains at Pontypridd I travelled up the Rhondda Valley through mining town after mining town, each gloomier, blacker, more dismal than the previous one. It was a land that seemed torn open by some fearsome monster. Slowly but steadily my spirits sank, and I was heartily regretting my choice when I arrived in the dusk of evening at Mardy, the last village apparently in this desolate country.

As I stepped out on to the platform a man addressed me in the singsong Welsh accent I had been hearing since Newport. I agreed that I was the new doctor.

"We'll walk to Dr. Griffiths's house. It's not far; and Evan Jones here will carry your baggage," he said.

The doctor's house in an English village is usually a largish red-brick Georgian affair covered with Virginia creeper in the High Street, with whitened doorstep and a brass plate that shines resplendently in the sunlight. It is unmistakeable by day and had, in the early 1900s, a little red light shining through the fanlight over the front door by night.

But Dr. Griffiths's house was not like that. It was just a superior workman's cottage with a front parlour and a kitchen, two bedrooms and a bathroom. There was a large surgery alongside, with the usual waiting-room and dispensary.

I learned that Dr. Griffiths was very seriously ill and I was there to help the assistants. The doctor kept no accounts. He was paid three-pence in the pound per week from each miner's wage packet; and as there was no other industry and everyone depended on the miners, he attended the rest of the community free—it wasn't worth his while bothering about accounts. He and his two assistants visited, doctored and dispensed for the entire village. It was hard work, for there was a lot of sickness, many accidents and a prolific birthrate. But the people were very lovable. It's many years since I saw the back of Mardy, but my affection for the miner, my respect for him, my admiration for his courage have remained undiminished.

On my first morning I was given a list of people to see. I looked at it.

"But," I said, "this is just a list of streets and houses, not people."

Dr. Jones, the chief assistant, laughed.

"Yes. It's the only list that'd be any use to you. The patients' names don't matter. They're either Evans or Jones or Thomas or Griffiths or Edwards. Simple, isn't it?"

So I went round on foot knocking at the numbers and explaining I was the new doctor. Sometimes the woman of the house had no English, and had to get her husband on night shift out of bed. One woman banged the door violently in my face and would not let me in.

"She took you for a Johnny Fortnight," explained Dr. Jones, after-wards. "They're travelling bagmen hawking round, tempting women

D

with cheap jewellery, lace, ribbons, which they sell them on the instalment plan. They call once a fortnight for the money, and sometimes this call is anything but welcome."

Dr. Jones and I took alternate weeks to do the midwifery. In my midwifery week I slept over the Temperance Cafe; and I found I was called out every night, sometimes twice in the night. It was very warm weather and I used to walk down the village street just in my pyjamas (unknown as night-attire to the miners), carrying the doctor's little black bag that held the midwifery forceps, the carbolic and the extract of ergot. We put forceps on to every case in those days as soon as a certain stage in labour was reached. I used to give the chloroform myself and then apply the forceps when the patient was well under the anæsthetic. Looking back on this now I wonder how I had the nerve to do it. But at the time it seemed quite simple, and nothing ever went wrong.

The sanitation of the place must have been very primitive. A week after I arrived an epidemic of infantile diarrhoea started. No sooner did that wane than we had an outbreak of measles amongst the children. Nearly all the babies got pneumonia and most of those under two years died. It was heartbreaking. I used to fall into bed completely exhausted, and sleep like a log when it wasn't my week to do the confinements.

I suppose the general unhappiness made everyone irritable, for suddenly, for no reason I could understand, there was a flare-up and a strike at the mine. Everything came to a standstill. The miners lounged round the street corners looking lost, or got in the way of the women in the kitchen and were made to feel horribly out of place. No one had any money. The doctor's weekly cheque ceased, the grocers and butchers had to give credit.

I wanted to know what it was all about from both sides; but I was the miners' employee and I could not talk to the manager without raising suspicion.

There were six sorts of nonconformist chapels in the town, nobody was doing any work and consequently services were held every evening in each, with much singing. Then a famous preacher came down from North Wales and began to deliver fiery sermons about the wrath to come, in one of the chapels. People began to crowd in. The singing increased, fervour rose, and all at once we were in the grip of a religious revival. I had heard of these revivals. They fascinated me. People went round with the light of love in their eyes, tempers dissolved into kindliness, a feeling of peace spread, the strike was settled, and the miners returned eagerly to work, full of good will towards all men.

Meanwhile great happenings were going on in London. The South African War had ended at last. The Coronation of the new King Edward VII had been fixed. We had begun to get used to 'God Save the King' instead of 'God Save the Queen'; and *Punch* made a joke of all the K.C.s now being 'ex-Q.C.s'. Even down in our remote village we prepared to celebrate.

Then out of the blue came the news of the King's illness and the sudden operation for appendicitis by Sir Frederick Treves two days before the date of the Coronation. Everyone was upset and disappointed, and all preparations for celebrating the Coronation were stopped. In the afternoon Jones and I were busy in the dispensary, making up the medicines that we had ordered on the morning round, when we heard the sound of a heavy detonation.

Jones laid down the bottle he was filling and looked at me grimly. "The mine. An explosion. God! What bad luck!"

He grabbed the emergency bag of instruments and dressings always kept ready.

"Come on," he said.

We both rushed out into the street, but already others were before us: pale, wild-eyed women thinking of their men, children running, night-shift men struggling into coats—all making for the pit-head.

When Jones and I got there the crowd before us had stopped and to our surprise were shouting abusively at some six or eight young men standing about, looking sheepish and half angry.

"Whatever is the matter!" Dr. Jones exclaimed in Welsh.

There was a torrent of replies which meant nothing to me.

"What's it all about?" I said, completely puzzled.

Jones scowled, then laughed. "These bloody young fools were determined to celebrate, Coronation or no Coronation, and they've just let off ten detonators at the pit-head. That's what's the matter."

The relief everyone felt that there was no explosion had now turned to anger against the perpetrators. Lumps of coal began to fly, and they had to make a run for it. But the end was not yet. All down the valley the sound had travelled and produced the same idea. Ambulance after ambulance came rolling into Mardy from Aberdare and beyond. It took some explanation to satisfy these eager volunteers it was not our fault, that it was only a senseless prank of some unthinking young men. They, too, departed baulked and angry at being deprived of the excitement of a catastrophe. Meanwhile Jones and I had gone back to our dispensary to carry on.

It was on the very next day I had my first call to an accident in the mine itself.

I was fitted with a suit of dungarees, and given a Davy lamp after I had been searched to see I had no matches on me. Then I went down in the grimy cage with the manager, hundreds of feet, until we struck the pit bottom. We then stepped into a coal wagon which ran on rails drawn by a pit pony for about a mile or so through the old disused cutting. It was a long, dusty, black tunnel, high at first, gradually getting lower and lower until it just cleared our heads.

"We get out here," said the manager.

And then we walked, stooping, for what seemed to me an interminable distance, guided by the light of our Davy lamps. Line after line of timber pit-props on either side and above us came into the feeble light as we went along, crouching. My back was getting very tired.

"Have we much farther to go, Mr. Phillips?" I said.

"Not far now, Doctor. We're near the coal-face. There's been a fall on the man, Evan Davis, and we're afraid he's fractured something, so we want you to get him out. I know how easy it is to make a simple fracture into a compound."

There was not room for two men to get at him at the same time, so I had a look first. His head and arms and the upper part of his body were clear. The fall from the roof had been behind him as he was working on the coal-face. Obviously he had gone on cutting coal without putting up props to support the roof behind him as he followed the seam. Foolishly he had trusted the roof to hold, and the rubble had fallen on his back.

I injected a hypodermic of morphia into his moist, grimy leg covered with coal dust. It was very hot. He lay there quietly like a dumb animal. The light from the Davy lamp was feeble but I could now see better as I had become more accustomed to the darkness.

"Get the stuff off him without moving him," I said, wriggling back. "By the time you've got it off the morphia will have worked and I can see what's wrong."

It seemed a long time waiting before they cleared the fall, there was so little room to move, and it was so dark and so hot down there.

"Now, Doctor!" the manager said at last.

I put my hands gently over him. Clearly the left thigh bone was broken, but I wasn't sure about his spine. I fastened his legs together and helped to slip the stretcher under. It was wonderful to see the skill of those men working in the confined space. My back felt awful, but they moved quite easily. We got him on the stretcher and worked back to where we could stand erect.

Eventually we got him to the pit-head. The gentle way these rough-looking chaps carried him was most touching. When I was able to examine him properly I found he was paralysed from the navel downwards. His spine was fractured, and he would never be able to earn the bread to keep his family again. It wasn't easy telling this to his wife afterwards.

All this happened of course many years ago, but still when I hear comfortable people abusing the miners, talking about their exorbitant demands for extra wages, shorter hours, more amenities, complaining of absenteeism, I wish they had to spend an hour in a mine helping to release a man from under a fall. I think if they did so they would have more understanding.

I left the valley with a deep respect and affection for the miners, but I should have hated to practise permanently amongst them. Social life was non-existent apart from the chapel gatherings. The doctor could not be friendly with an owner or a manager without creating suspicion of his trustworthiness. There was nothing to read, nothing to do, nothing to see. Dr. Griffiths, who owned the practice, earned over £2,000 a year, and that at a time when income tax was a shilling in the pound. I never saw him. He was away with a mental breakdown. But I was told he was a kindly man, a good accident surgeon. The people loved him. His wife said to me pathetically just before I left:

"We came here with the intention of doing about ten years' work, saving all we could to buy a practice in some pleasant seaside town like Aberystwyth, where I come from. We have been here over twenty years, and we are fit for nothing else now. We shall die here. I am glad we had no children. What sort of companionship would they have had here? It isn't that my husband didn't love the work and the people. It's that mentally, he says, he's completely atrophied. No doctor should be allowed to stay more than five years in a place like this."

*

CHAPTER VII

DIVERS EXPERIENCES

WHEN I GOT BACK TO LONDON I went to see Keetley. He pointed to a chair opposite in his consulting-room.

"Well," he said, "how do you feel about things? You've been doing locums for months. Would you like to go into general practice or do you still want to be a surgeon?"

"A surgeon, sir."

He looked at me with his kindly blue eyes, a little sadly.

"I don't want to discourage you, but it's a very hard grind. If you want to be a consultant you'll have to take the Fellowship of the College of Surgeons. It's the most difficult surgical exam in the world. You'll have to begin again as a student with Anatomy and Physiology before they'll let you sit for the surgical part. It'll take you about three years all told, with luck. When you do surmount that you'll have to get on to a hospital staff, for you cannot be a surgeon without a hospital. Even after you get a hospital you'll have to wait for doctors to find you out and send you work. It means years of waiting. It means you can't afford to marry. D'ye think it's worth it? Sometimes I feel I'd have been happier in my uncle's practice in Lincolnshire, and yet I've had a fairly successful life."

I listened to all this, completely unconvinced. I thought the old man was just a bit tired. He did get weary at times. So I said:

"I still think I want to be a surgeon, sir."

He looked thoughtfully at me. "Right. Well, then: I'll take you on as my assistant and you can start at once revising my book, *The Index of Surgery*. It will be good practice for you, reading the journals and bringing it up-to-date."

This was an extraordinarily generous offer of his. It was more, much more, than I had dared to hope for. It gave me the run of the hospital.

This was now very valuable, for with his far-seeing mind he had recently started a Post-Graduate Medical School there—the first in the country—to encourage doctors in practice to rub up their medicine and surgery. No one had thought of the idea before, and it is largely due to Keetley that London now is the best post-graduate centre in the Empire. I knew this post-graduate idea had been fermenting in his mind for years and I was eager to help. I had seen how rusty even good men could become in general practice. So I looked at him with gratitude and said:

"Thank you so much, sir. I'll do everything I can to justify your confidence."

This sounds a little pompous now, but it was the way we talked fifty years ago.

And that started a collaboration that was to end only with his death.

I had a facility for writing, so besides working at Anatomy and advanced Physiology for the Primary Fellowship, I started revising his *Index of Surgery*; but unfortunately I never finished it because he kept revising what I'd done and the book was never completed. It was known, however, that I was doing it, and another surgeon asked me to write a book on *Diseases of the Throat and Nose* for him.

"But I don't know anything about diseases of the throat and nose," I said.

"No, of course you don't, but I do. I give you the headings, you read up the standard books and write up the text for my headings. I criticise your script and we'll get it done. I haven't the time; you have; and it's a hundred and fifty in your pocket."

"Done," I said, and it was done.

The book went through three editions in the next seven years, and we were both satisfied. All this was very useful experience to me in those days; it helped me to tabulate things in my mind so that I found I could read an article in one of the scientific journals, concentrate the facts down, and submit the abstract as a leaderette, either to the *Lancet* or the *British Medical Journal*. Sometimes these little articles were accepted, sometimes not; but combining all these ways I managed to live whilst reading for the Primary part of the Fellowship.

No one expects to pass this at the first attempt. It is a test of endurance as well as knowledge, and I was no luckier than most. I learnt a lot, however, from this first attempt, not only about what was required but also about the examiners and how one should approach them.

All the same it was rather a weary job starting over again, and I approached the next attempt less light-heartedly. The ordeal lasted for days. I hardly knew how to carry on. I was convinced I had failed, and on the way to hearing the results I felt so sick I had to turn into a side-street and vomit.

The examinees were huddled into one room at the College of Surgeons, and when we were all assembled an attendant called us out one by one. Through the open doorway we could watch the victims answer and go down the stairs. As each passed, a clerk from the office standing on the half-landing told him his fate. It was a horrible ordeal. I saw the shoulders of the man who was called in front of me sag suddenly.

'Poor devil, he's stuck,' I thought.

Then it was my turn. I felt stoical by now. I knew I was pipped.

"Your name?" said the clerk.

I gave it.

"I'm pleased to say you've passed, sir," he said.

I could scarcely believe my ears. "You're quite sure?" I said.

The clerk smiled woodenly. "*Quite* sure, sir."

I rushed to the telegraph office in the Strand and wired home: "Passed."

My feeling of relief and exhilaration lasted for about a week. Then an intense lassitude followed. I felt tired and depressed, nothing seemed to matter, life appeared to have lost its savour. I also developed a troublesome cough which I could not shake off. I found I had lost weight, and immediately imagined the worst. In these days an X-ray of my chest would have settled the matter; but at that early stage in radiology such a thing had not been thought of. I got a friend to examine my chest. He was worried and sent me to a well-known specialist. The great man asked me what I had been doing, how I had been living. Then he examined me.

"Well, sir, what do you think?" I said, anxiously.

"I can't find anything much wrong," he assured me, cautiously. "There are a few creps at the apex; but, in view of what you tell me of your family history, I think you should knock off work for six months and get out of London."

This was a facer.

"Six months!" I said, in dismay. "I can't afford to lose six months, sir; I want to start reading for the Final Fellowship, straight away."

"Well," he answered grimly, "you have my opinion. It's for you to decide."

I went to my rooms like a beaten dog.

It was Wilson, the pathologist, who came to my rescue. We shared a top flat where he kept guinea-pigs in a pen on the roof; and when I told him the verdict of the Brompton Hospital physician, and said I couldn't see how I could afford to lie off for all that time, he answered:

"Ass! What you want is a ship. See the world at someone else's expense, and come back bursting."

It took me three weeks to find a ship, and I was told she would be sailing for Yokohama within another fortnight. She was a large comfortable 10,000 ton cargo boat bound for Egypt, Malaya and the Far East, without passengers but with a mixed crew of British sailors and Chinese firemen. These totalled twelve officers and about one hundred and twenty men; and I realised that I was to be responsible for their health and safety for the next six months, often in unaccustomed waters where other help in an emergency would not be available. I had a feeling of exhilaration that this should be so, for it was my first post where I had to depend entirely on my own judgment and training.

Ships of this sort had to carry an official set of surgical instruments as laid down by the Board of Trade; and I found I was expected, legally, to provide these out of my salary. I looked at the list. It may have been up-to-date in the time of Nelson, but I could see at once it would be comparatively useless. All this, of course, has been altered since. I am writing of the early 1900s, you will remember.

'I can't buy this rubbish,' I said to myself.

So I made enquiries and found I could hire a set from a firm in the Strand which specialised in supplying them for a small fee, on condition they were returned intact at the end of the voyage. They were just dud sets, made for show, not for use. None of the knives would cut, and the other tools were nearly as bad; but they looked all right and would pass any non-medical eye. So I hired them. But for my peace of mind, and the probable safety of the crew, I made up a set of my own that I could rely on.

I joined the ship at Birkenhead the night before we sailed. My steward unpacked my kit and said the 'Old Man' (the Captain) had not arrived so I wouldn't see him before morning.

In my cabin there was a big cupboard fitted to hold drugs. These, I found, were well chosen. I checked them before we sailed as on them I knew I should have to depend entirely at times.

Looking back on it now, I appreciate how extraordinarily lucky I was in my shipmates. The Old Man was exactly like John Bull in naval uniform. He had learnt his seamanship in sail and had a supreme contempt for steamboat sailors. He was a big man with a gargantuan appetite, a magnificent sailor with a complete contempt for all foreigners—Dutch (by which he meant German), Dago, Nigger or Chink.

The chief engineer was a fellow-Ulsterman. We made friends at once. The others all fitted in comfortably. The deck crew were mainly Welsh, the firemen Cantonese Chinamen who talked a most astonishing pidgin-English when I had to interview and treat them.

For someone who had previously never been out of the British Isles it was a stimulating experience. I developed an intense pride in the might of the British Empire. Its flag flew in every port. I learnt to appreciate the honesty of the Chinaman and formed a dislike for the Japanese that made my views unpopular in those days, when the Japs were our allies. I saw and admired the wonderful colonising work of the Dutch in Java. Wherever I went I visited hospitals and talked to doctors. I learnt about strange tropical diseases at first hand; and all the time I was getting fitter and fitter. I completely lost my apprehensions.

Six months later I was back in London, very brown, very fit, a stone heavier. I felt as if I had been away for years. I had absorbed so much, seen so much, been so far.

When I got out at Aldgate Station to go down to the London Hospital, the old lady selling flowers outside was sitting in exactly the same position. Nothing seemed to have changed. A man I knew slightly said to me as I was hanging up my hat in the cloakroom:

"Haven't seen you about lately. Been out of town?"

"Yes," I answered.

*

Getting through the Primary Fellowship was like clearing a five-barred gate. Getting through the Final Fellowship, I was told, was like clearing a double dyke with a brook on the far side, without splashing. That, I was given to understand, was the experience of others. So I began to look round for some job which would give me temporary security and time to read as well.

In the *Lancet* I found an advertisement for a Resident Medical Officer at the London Lock Hospital for Women, Harrow Road. I knew nothing whatever of this hospital, so I thought I'd take a bus, and have a look at it to see what it was like.

The conductor said he'd come up and call me when I got there.

"Here ye are, sir. Lock Bridge. The 'orspital's just beyond. Ye get down 'ere."

From the top of the bus I could see a large mid-Victorian building with several wings, approached by a carriage drive with a porter's lodge at the entrance. Inside the grounds there was a chapel and a parsonage; and beyond these the actual hospital with a garden extending down to the Regent's Canal. I could see a tennis court under the trees and that the grounds were a blaze of flowers.

'Looks comfortable to me,' I thought.

The next day I saw the secretary, got details of the post and the names of the staff on whom to call.

When I went up the Harrow Road that sunny afternoon I hadn't the least idea I was starting an association of over forty years, and that in this apparently casual way my whole life was being settled for me. If I had suspected it I would probably have turned back. But are we ever free agents? I wonder!

As you may guess, I got the post.

They paid me a hundred a year, all found. I had three mornings and three afternoons free to work at the London Hospital, and a fifth-year medical student from St. Mary's Hospital to act as my assistant. He helped to do the treatments and any emergency dispensing and was on duty when I was out.

We each had a bedroom and a sitting-room, and we shared the dining-room. There was actually also a spare room where we could put up a guest for week-ends, if we wished. It was a casual, very pleasant sort of place—no rules, no restrictions—as long as you played the game and did your work. I was happy there.

A hundred a year in those days before the First World War was equal to four hundred and fifty pounds now. You could be a 'man about town' on it. Dressed in tails and a white tie, with a sovereign-purse on your watch-chain, and a sovereign or two in it, the world was yours.

A three-course dinner at Pinoli's in Wardour Street cost one-and-six; at Frascati's it was half-a-crown. At the Pavilion you could hear Dan Leno and Malcolm Scott. At the Oxford, Marie Lloyd. My old Chief, Keetley, still took me frequently to the Saturday night dinners at the Savage Club, in the Adelphi. There I could hear the best music, see the best cartoons, and laugh at the best comic turns in London.

Life was good.

My first clinical assistant was a cricketer with the good cricketing name of Hobbs. He played for Hampstead, and had as fellow-players Frank Reynolds and James Thorpe, the *Punch* artists. Often after a match they would come along to dinner with us.

Hobbs was extremely good-looking. Thorpe used to draw posters for Wills's Gold Flake. In spite of himself he found himself always drawing Hobbs. We used to chip both of them. Occasionally the artists invited us to an evening at what I think was called the London Sketch Club. We dined on bare wooden tables set on trestles, and the menu was always boiled beef and carrots with beer. After dinner we went round, looked at the sketches, and the artists ragged one another good-humouredly.

Hobbs left the hospital after he qualified; and my next clinical assistant was Campbell William de Morgan. I guessed he was some-how important from his name, and found I was correct. He was a grandson of Augustus de Morgan, F.R.S., the very famous and quarrel-some Professor of Mathematics of University College. He was also a grand-nephew of Campbell de Morgan, F.R.S., the cancer specialist of 'de Morgan's spots', surgeon to the Middlesex Hospital. And finally he was a nephew of William de Morgan who had suddenly become famous as a novelist by his book *Joseph Vance*.

William de Morgan was a great dear. He was one of the Pre-Raphaelite Brotherhood, a tall benevolent figure, blue-eyed, gentle, stooping. His sudden fame startled him. He could never quite believe it.

Young de Morgan, his nephew, adored him, and heartily disliked his wife. She had been a Miss Stirling and made quite a comfortable living by painting replicas of saints in Italian churches, for sale to English Roman Catholic chapels. So that replicas of this sort could not be passed off as originals, it was a regulation of the Italian Government that they had to be painted two-thirds size.

William de Morgan, her husband, was considered an artistic failure. He made stained-glass windows and pottery in Chelsea, neither of which sold until after he became famous as a writer. And Mrs. de Morgan, who meanwhile earned the bread and butter, kept him well under restraint in consequence. It was rather pathetic, and young de Morgan and his sister resented it very much. She patronised them and thought little of him. Then suddenly his first book became a huge success. It was published by William Heinemann, who had a flair for discovering genius. Miss Louisa Callender, who was at that time secretary to William Heinemann, told me the story of this first book, *Joseph Vance*, years later. It was written in de Morgan's own handwriting, five hundred thousand words long, and he brought it in a cab to Heinemann's office in Bedford Street, Strand. This was next door to the Post Office, and from the Post Office de Morgan borrowed a barrow. Into this he piled the manuscript, which he wheeled into Heinemann's office and dumped down before William. Probably no one in London but William would have looked at it. But he never missed a chance. He read it, saw its possibilities, made de Morgan reduce it by one-half and published it. That was the beginning of de Morgan's career as a novelist. More books followed: *Alice-for-Short, Somehow Good, It Never Can Happen Again*, etc.

Once he became famous, people wanted to meet de Morgan. They were not interested in his prosaic wife, and to her annoyance she was gradually pushed into the background. They lived in a quaint old house in the Vale, Chelsea, a little cul-de-sac of several houses, most of which were occupied by artists.

William used to come up to the hospital to have dinner with us occasionally. He was writing a novel at the time in which a woman of the prostitute class was a character; and young de Morgan and I supplied him with a certain amount of local colour. I read the book when it came out. It was called *An Affair of Dishonour*.

One other memory of him remains. While his nephew was with me the Vale was scheduled for demolition; and those who had houses in it decided to give a farewell party, to which young de Morgan and I were asked. They labelled the invitations 'Vale', the double meaning of which struck us as clever. What I remember most was a bevy of young girls swarming round William and Henry Holliday, the painter of the well-known picture 'Dante and Beatrice at the Bridge'. They all seemed to have long swan necks like that of Rossetti's wife, Elizabeth Eleanor Siddal—the Pre-Raphaelite neck Rossetti painted in 'Monna Vanna'. It struck my medical mind as odd. Did all these girls really have goitres, or was it just one of those things? Women are so plastic that they can imitate anything. Were these girls modelling themselves on Monna Vanna? I wondered.

At that time we had two pathologists at the hospital: Alexander Fleming, who afterwards became world-famous as the discoverer of penicillin, and Gilbert Hare. Hare was a son of Sir John Hare, the well-known Edwardian actor-manager, and the old man had insisted on Gilbert following in his footsteps. Gilbert was a born actor but he hated the stage. He acted only when compelled. Somehow he got away from parental control at one time sufficiently to qualify as a doctor in Germany. But his degree was of no legal value in England, so he could not practise on it. What he did was to take a post like that of pathologist or bacteriologist, which luckily did not then require medical qualifications. And that is how it came about that he was working with us when I joined the hospital. His salary was £150 a year, which of course was quite inadequate for 'Bertie'; so every now and then, when he got really hard up and couldn't borrow any more from his friends, he accepted a part in a play at £100 a week. Sometimes he played with his father, sometimes with Gerald du Maurier, for they were bosom friends, and Gerald was always willing to find him a part, since he was, as I have said, a first-rate actor.

*

It was during my time as R.M.O. at the Lock Hospital that two great discoveries were made about syphilis. This disease had been introduced by Columbus's men after the discovery of America in 1492, and it had swept like a scourge through an unprotected Europe hitherto unacquainted with it, killing and mutilating. But gradually in the next four hundred years it had become less virulent, and under the influence of mercury it could now be fairly well controlled. The cause of the disease, however, was still unknown.

Bacteriology had become a science in late Victorian days. Koch had proved that tuberculosis was due to a bacillus in 1882; and every now and again someone claimed that he had discovered the germ of syphilis. But every time this statement proved erroneous.

And then one day we read that two Germans, Schaudinn and Hoffmann, claimed that at last they had actually found it. The reason, they said, it had never been discovered before was that it did not stain like other germs with aniline dyes, and so was invisible under the microscope. They stated, however, that if a slide was prepared from a sore, flooded with Indian ink, allowed to dry and then put under the microscope, the white germs could be seen quite easily against the background of Indian ink. Of course we were sceptical. We simply didn't believe it. But we did stain slides of the discharge from the patients' sores, and every time we did so there was a queer corkscrew translucent organism showing up clearly against the dark background of the Indian ink under the microscope. We were seeing for the first time the 'Treponema pallidum'. I can still remember the thrill of it. It was no longer possible to doubt. This was it.

A year later came the discovery of the 'Wassermann reaction'. This was a blood test. People who had active signs of syphilis gave a positive reaction. But, still more important, people who had no signs or symptoms could still give this special reaction, proving they had had syphilis years before and were now *latent* syphilitics.

It was a new and startling test of the utmost importance. I had very good reasons to remember this soon after it was established. A little girl of eight was brought into the hospital with active syphilis. A soldier, home on leave, who was stopping with her parents was suspected of having infected her. There is a queer superstition that if anyone has a venereal disease and makes contact with a virgin he can transfer the disease and get cured himself. This was what was suspected in the case of the little girl. The soldier had been arrested and he was in Brixton prison. But unfortunately when the prison doctor came to examine him he could find no sore, no rash, no evidence of syphilis.

The man denied the accusation; the case against him, though strong, was purely circumstantial; and it was felt a jury might not convict. Talking it over with the Home Office expert who came to see the little girl at the hospital, I told him about the new test.

"Could I go down to Brixton and take a sample of the prisoner's blood?" I asked.

"Yes, of course, if the prisoner does not object."

The man was surly and cocky but not suspicious. He made no objection. I felt, a bit uneasily, that I was taking advantage of his ignorance. But I said to myself it worked both ways: if the Wassermann blood test was negative the case against him would fail. If it was positive and the judge accepted it, he would be convicted. It was fifty-fifty either way.

So I took a sample of blood from his arm with a syringe and Bertie Hare did the test at the hospital.

It was positive. Hare could not give evidence, as his qualification was German and not recognised in England, so I had to go into the witness-box. My evidence added to that of the other witnesses carried conviction, and the man got seven years.

It was the first time this test had been used in evidence in an English court, and the Home Office was very pleased. They wrote and asked me what my fee was. This worried me a lot. The usual fee a house-surgeon then got on giving evidence was two guineas. I felt it was not enough for this unique case. So, greatly daring, I asked for twenty. To my surprise and delight they paid it without a murmur. And when you think what twenty guineas could buy before the First World War you can imagine my joy. Bertie Hare and I celebrated.

We had a dinner, regardless, at Scott's. I remember we started with a dozen oysters followed by a porterhouse steak. I didn't know till then that I had become allergic to oysters. I know now. I was violently sick after that dinner. I have never been able to eat oysters since.

For six months after the Wassermann test came out I was the most popular young medical man in London. Pathologists made much of me. One of the ingredients in the test was an extract of the pulped liver of a dead syphilitic baby; and there were more dead syphilitic babies born at Harrow Road Hospital at that time than anywhere else in London. So I was constantly being courted, invited out and asked diplomatically, when well-oiled, could I, would I, spare a bit of syphilitic liver, just enough to do one or two tests? If I could . . . All this was very pleasant. I basked in it. And then, unexpectedly, someone discovered that an extract of ox heart was just as good for the test as syphilitic liver. This was unfortunate for me. My stock slumped to zero immediately, and I was just an ordinary M.O. again, not worth fussing about. It was a lesson in humility I have tried never to forget.

One evening it suddenly occurred to me that all this experience with new tests, new diagnostic methods, ought not to be wasted. Although I was working for the Fellowship of the Royal College of Surgeons I felt there was no reason why I should not produce a thesis and if possible take my M.D. on it.

So I wrote the subject up under the title 'Recent Advances in the Diagnosis and Treatment of Syphilis', and with some trepidation offered it to my old University. I got a notice summoning me to read it before the Regius Professor of Medicine, Dr. James Little. There were two other candidates. We all appeared before the old gentleman together, but as we were taken alphabetically I read my thesis first. The old man listened with some interest and when I had finished he said:

"I accept your thesis, Doctor. Can I have it for the *Dublin Journal of Medical Science?*"

I knew he edited this journal at the time, and I was immensely flattered.

"Yes, of course, sir," I said.

The next candidate then stepped into my place. He held a huge document in his hands, and looking over his shoulder I could see it was full of elaborate drawings of sewers and sanitary equipment. Slowly he started to read. The old man listened casually with bent head for about three minutes. Then he looked up and said:

"Stop, Doctor, stop! I can see you agree with me that W.C.s are useful things to have about the house. I pass you."

That was all. I cannot remember what happened to the third man;

but we three duly appeared at the next 'Commencements' a few days later, and were each duly admitted M.D. by the Chancellor, Lord Iveagh. I think, however, the author of the thesis on W.C.s must have felt he had cast his pearls before an unappreciative audience.

The Final Fellowship examination a few months later was not such a pleasant memory. I failed to satisfy the examiners. They caught me out on a subject I was hazy about. That was just my luck. The subjects are so numerous it is not possible to be up to examination standard in all of them.

Actually, also, I had not been able to keep up my work at the London and the Lock at the same time, and attendance at the London had had to be curtailed. There wasn't time for both.

It was after the results came out that the tall Canadian who had just been successful said to me:

"I'm going back to Toronto, and I want to find someone who'll take on my job before I leave."

"You did it while you were doing the Fellowship, didn't you?" I asked. "What's it like? Would it suit me? I can resign my hospital in a month, if necessary."

"I wonder if you'd care for it," he said. "It's with a doctor who runs a Shilling Surgery at King's Cross. I take the surgery for two evenings a week, seven to nine p.m., and do the night calls. I have all day to myself, and every evening except Tuesday and Friday. I can get to the London by Underground in twenty minutes. I live in rooms over the Surgery. There is a housekeeper who is quite a good cook. I'm off to Toronto as soon as I can get away. It might suit you if you don't mind night midwifery."

CHAPTER VIII

THE SHILLING SURGERY

THE CALEDONIAN ROAD is close to King's Cross. The doctor's Surgery was about one hundred yards from the Underground Railway and therefore handy for Aldgate Station and the London Hospital. I looked at the Surgery. It was most uninviting—a drab, two-storeyed house in bad need of repair, with a butcher's shop on one side and a poulterer's on the other. The Surgery had a shop window, the glass front painted black, with 'Surgery', in what had once been large gold lettering, indicating its use.

There was a private door with a broken bell-pull on the left side, and a second door opening into the waiting-room on the right, over which a bell rang as you pushed it to enter. The butcher's shop had an open front where slabs of dark-looking beef and mutton—fly-infested in the warm weather—were exposed, each slab labelled with its price. The red-faced butcher with his blue-striped apron was inside chopping up joints on a wooden bench multi-marked by years of chopping.

The poulterer's next door had packing cases of eggs exposed on the pavement. I noted the labels: New-laid Eggs 2/- a dozen, Fresh Eggs 1/6, Eggs Guaranteed 1/-, and finally, and ominously, Eggs 4d. a dozen.

I looked inside the bleak waiting-room. It was empty and I felt very dubious about the whole venture. I decided finally, however, to see the doctor and judge if I could work with him.

So next day I called by appointment to see Dr. McFee, and I liked him at once. His Scots accent warmed me. He might have come from the County Antrim. He wore the morning coat, stiff shirt, collar and cuffs, and striped trousers then essential in a professional man. His silk hat lay upturned on his desk. I gathered that his practice lay all around, and he worked it on foot or by tram. His surgery hours were ten till

twelve in the morning and seven till nine in the evening, and he paid
visits during the rest of the day.

He was a bachelor, I discovered, and after his surgery hours were
over he retired to Hampstead, where his sister kept house for him, and
their hobby was music—he played the 'cello, she the violin.

I learnt these things gradually, for I had agreed to take on the job.
This was all, of course, before the days of panel practice, and long
before the National Health Service had been thought of. He was what
was called in those days a 'club doctor'. He had 'Oddfellows',
'Buffaloes' and 'Foresters', clubs of working men who paid, I think,
about six shillings a year per member. These were treated free, and
had certificates when they were ill. Everyone else who came to the
Surgery was charged a shilling, and for this they were given advice
and a bottle of medicine.

Once a week he made up his medicines in large Winchester quart
bottles. These were concentrated mixtures. One ounce was all that
was required for an eight-ounce bottle of medicine. The rest came
from the dispensary tap. He had six standard prescriptions: a cough
mixture, a heart tonic, one for dyspepsia, one for rheumatism, a
purgative and one for diarrhoea. Those, and a few standard pills like
Blaud's, made up his pharmacopoeia.

And always in every prescription there was sacch. ust. That was
essential, I was told. The patients expected it. If sacch. ust. wasn't in
their medicine they did not think they were getting value for their
shilling.

Sacch. ust. is abbreviated Latin for saccharum ustum: burnt sugar.
It made a clear mixture look as if it contained something definite, and
it sweetened the bitter ones. Sometimes if there was nothing whatever
wrong with a patient they had sacch. ust. and tap water only, for they
had to have something for their shilling—advice was of no importance
compared with the bottle of medicine.

I learnt a lot about human nature from Dr. McFee. He was really
a very good doctor. His patients trusted him. He knew all about their
social background and family history. His stethoscope and a clinical
thermometer told him all he wanted to know about their physical
condition. If a case was obviously surgical he sent it to University
College Hospital or the Royal Free. Fevers he sent to the London

Fever Hospital. Ordinary medical cases he looked after himself with the aid of patients' relatives to do the nursing. Looking back on it now I think he made a very good job of it.

When I took possession, I found I had a sitting-room overlooking the street and a bedroom behind. The housekeeper cooked my breakfast, and I lunched at the hospital and dined at an Italian restaurant down the road. The housekeeper's husband was a retired Army pensioner, a big hefty man who never did any work. His wife said that when he walked fifty yards he got such severe cramp in his legs he had to give up. At the time I thought he was just bone lazy. I think now I was probably unfair to him. We didn't know much about thromboangiitis obliterans fifty years ago.

So for over a year I led a strange double life. During the day I was studying disease at a great research centre with all the paraphernalia for scientific investigation at my disposal. I talked to men of international fame. I met the best brains in the surgical world of England, America and the Continent, either at the hospital or some other teaching school, or at the College of Surgeons. I had as fellow-students the pick of the younger generation of coming surgeons. I saw every imaginable complication the human body is liable to suffer from. And then in the evening, reading my books, I could hear the tinkle of the Surgery bell as patients came in to see Dr. McFee, and I knew each of them would get something out of one of the six Winchester quart bottles.

On the two nights I took the surgery, I did the same; and strangely enough I soon found I did not feel my treatment was inadequate. There was seldom anything of any importance wrong—generally just coughs, rheumatism, anæmia. The diagnosis was easy, the treatment simple. The work of a general practitioner, I began to think, did not seem to require any of the expert knowledge I was acquiring so assiduously.

And then, every now and again, something would happen; and if it had not been for my expert knowledge I'd have missed it. A man came in complaining of pain in the back. He'd been treated for months elsewhere for rheumatism. I noticed something that made me examine him more carefully. He had tuberculosis of the spine and a commencing psoas abscess. Another man came complaining of constipation. It was really intestinal obstruction from cancer of the colon requiring immediate operation. A woman sat in the chair opposite me. She said her periods had started again, much to her surprise, and wanted something to stop them. She had a commencing cancer of the womb. That was the sort of thing that made it seem worth while to go on training my clinical sense.

When I started my two evening surgeries a week, I used to get ten to twelve patients a night. Gradually it increased until I was getting twenty. That meant I was earning £2 a week for my chief at a shilling a head; and I calculated that he must be making £500 a year from the Surgery alone, and £1,000 more from visiting. With income tax what it was, and things at the price then prevalent, £1,500 a year was a very comfortable income.

Midwiferies came my way occasionally. I liked them. I had been trained at the Rotunda, Dublin, and no complication came to me as a surprise. Occasionally I was called in by a worried husband when the young medical student from the Royal Free doing her 'Midder' on the 'district' got flurried, and the extern from her hospital was not available in the emergency.

On Saturday nights it was almost impossible to work at my books. There was pandemonium all along the road. The butchers and greengrocers on either side had stalls in front of their shops, and were selling off their wares by a sort of Dutch auction. The sound of raucous voices calling "Buy, buy, buy, buy, buy", was so incessant I couldn't work.

Then I would drop everything and forget the world in a novel. In the drab life I was leading I think that kept me normal. There was a Boots Library at the King's Cross pharmacy, and the girl in charge used to keep any new books she thought I'd like under the counter until I came in. I never knew her name but I've always been grateful to her. If she's still alive and happens to read this I'd like her to know how much she lightened my days.

Occasionally I would drop into the Lock Hospital at Dean Street to see Gilbert Hare, who was then working in the laboratory with a Dutchman named de Korté. One day he said to me:

"Abe, I'm broke. I'll have to go on the stage again."

And the next thing I heard was that he was working with Mrs.

Brown-Potter at the Savoy in a play about Madame du Barry, the mistress of Louis XV, who was guillotined in 1793.

It was a part that suited Mrs. Brown-Potter, who liked to represent famous historical women of great beauty; but the play failed because her manager embezzled a large sum of money, and she became bankrupt.

It was a blow that would have demoralised most women, but not Cora Urquhart Brown-Potter. She wasn't a red-head for nothing. She did what was an unheard-of thing for a famous actress in those days: she went on the music halls in a sketch entitled 'The Murder of Rizzio', which lasted for half an hour, sandwiched between singers, comedians, acrobatic displays and performing animals. Mrs. Brown-Potter was Mary, Queen of Scots, Gilbert Hare was Darnley, her jealous husband, and Esmé Percy was the unfortunate Rizzio.

The music hall audiences of those days had probably never heard of Mrs. Brown-Potter; but the little one-act play was intensely dramatic; she was a lovely woman; had an excellent supporting cast; and the venture was a great success. She was able to save the house she had just bought at Staines from the wreck and clear herself from the bankruptcy court.

The success of 'The Murder of Rizzio' suggested that it might be expanded into a play, and (Sir) Kennedy Cox, the author, was persuaded to try. Eventually it was written, named *Mary, Queen of Scots*, and produced at the King's Theatre, Hammersmith.

Mrs. Brown-Potter played her original part as Mary. Esmé Percy, very young and eager, very French, was Rizzio; Bertie Hare played Bothwell; and a very good-looking young actor, Godfrey Tearle, made his first London appearance as Darnley. Forty years later I reminded him of this in the cubby-hole sacred to members of the Garrick Club. Slowly it came back to him and he too remembered.

Cora's mother, Mrs. Urquhart, a lovely silver-haired, stately old lady with a beautiful Southern accent, lived in the house at Staines, and Cora dashed down at week-ends with her friends to see her. It was Gilbert Hare who introduced me into this unexpected and exciting new world. All the week I lived in the drab surroundings of the Caledonian Road, dealing with drab people in squalid back streets. On Sunday morning I took the train from Paddington to West

Drayton, changed, got out at Staines and walked to the Old Bridge House just behind the 'Swan', a minute from the river.

It was a gracious house in gracious surroundings. The front was of warm sun-baked Elizabethan brick. Someone in the eighteenth century had added a Georgian wing behind. There was a deep walled garden at the back with a spreading lawn seen from the french windows of the drawing-room, and some oak trees at the far end.

Mrs. Brown-Potter had discovered the oak beams in the Elizabethan part, hidden by lath and plaster in Georgian times, and had had them uncovered again. There was a definite theatrical look about these ground-floor rooms in front with their red-tiled, very polished floors, angled iron-work fireplaces and leaded screens. It was all very spick and span and sparkling in the Elizabethan part, and all soft and cushiony and brocady in the Georgian. The effect was, I am sure, intentionally startling.

Mrs. Brown-Potter was famous in those days. People knew where she lived, and on Sundays used to stare through the front windows. The high wall running alongside the house had a small green door opening into the garden; and curious people would frequently open it and gaze inside, to the annoyance of anyone sitting out at tea on the lawn. Apart from locking the door there seemed no way of stopping this, until one Sunday I had an inspiration. I suggested to Mrs. Brown-Potter she should have a notice I had thought of painted on the door. This was:

"Beware of the LYCOPODIUM."

She did, and it had a most surprisingly deterrent effect. People thought it was some sort of fierce, wild animal, probably a poisonous snake. Actually it is a powder used for coating pills, but I banked on no one knowing this except a doctor or a chemist.

My memory of those days is that it was always sunshine, though I'm quite sure it could not have been. Long lazy days punting upstream, coming back to exotic meals, for Cora had cosmopolitan tastes and was herself an excellent cook; odd and exciting people coming to call. Any distinguished American passing through London felt it was his duty to do so. I remember Owen Wister, who wrote *The Virginian*, a tall, shy man with a beautiful voice, and Colonel Colt, the son of the revolver king.

Edith Craig, Ellen Terry's daughter, came occasionally but I do not think she was welcome. Edith Evans on the other hand was greatly liked. She was young, enthusiastic and bubbling with life. Sometimes an Indian prince or a foreign ambassador would drop in, sometimes a famous actor. It was all very exciting to me—such a contrast to the Shilling Surgery.

One week-end a young American girl from the Deep South practically gate-crashed on us. She had come over to sing the negro songs which were later called spirituals. She sang them in a deep, throaty voice in the garden after tea, and we were all spellbound. It was a new experience to me, though of course to Mrs. Brown-Potter, born in New Orleans, they were familiar. The girl was pathetically anxious for help to get going. I said if she told me about them I'd write something she could say by way of introduction from the platform before she began to sing.

I did write it, but I don't know if she ever made good—probably not. She may have been too soon, before her time, and it required the real negro voice to put these spirituals over.

I think those happy week-ends at Staines helped to keep me from giving up my ambition of becoming a consulting surgeon. Towards Friday I would begin to feel weary. Then would come the week-end. Life suddenly lightened and I used to start work again on Monday at the London full of the joy of effort. Mrs. Brown-Potter was very good to me. Looking back I have often wondered why she bothered over anyone like me when there were so many much more interesting people anxious for her smile.

Life wasn't too easy. When I was not at the London I was working in the College of Surgeons Library or Museum. When I read something I thought interesting I used to write a short synopsis of it and send it, as I have said before, to the *Lancet* or the *British Medical Journal*. Sometimes it would be accepted as an annotation in one or the other and I would get a small fee. Often when one refused it the other took it.

It was about this time also that I wrote my first novel. Like most first novels it was more or less autobiographical as it was built round hospital life. When it was complete I found it had run to 180,000 words, and I gaily sent it off to T. Fisher Unwin, a publisher in the

Adelphi who made a speciality of producing authors' first novels. I thought it was really good. I was quite confident he would be delighted to have it.

I don't know whether he read it or not, but he returned it to me with a covering note saying that if I cut it down to 90,000 and paid him £80 he would be pleased to publish it at my expense. At first I was very angry. Then I felt sick. Then a wave of depression swept over me, and I threw the MS. into the bottom of my big leather travelling trunk. And there it remained for years before I looked at it again. I know now he was quite right. It was much too long, much too clotted with technical detail, and no doubt quite unsaleable. But at the time I felt the bottom had fallen out of my world.

It was a year before I attempted any more writing. And then I started on a play. Probably my association at that time with actors and the theatre put this idea into my head.

It was to be a costume play based on the life and adventures of Charles Brandon, Duke of Suffolk, who married the sister of Henry VIII. The subject was an excellent one, dramatic and colourful. But costume plays, I was told, were no longer popular and I never completed the play. I suspect it was very amateurish, but looking back on it now I feel I had struck on a good subject as it has since been used twice in the last twenty years.

I was a year at the Caledonian Road before I had another try for the Fellowship. The written papers seemed not too bad, but I felt I could have done better and wasn't very happy about the way I had tackled some of the questions. Next came the long-drawn agony of the practical examination, which lasts about a week. I was dreading this part more than the papers. But in the operative surgery I was given the third stage of the subclavian artery to tie. I could have cried with joy. It was a gift. For in the Paddington Infirmary next door to the Lock Hospital I had made friends with the pathologist; and whenever he was doing a post-mortem he allowed me to tie the main arteries. I had tied the subclavian twenty-eight times in the last two years. The examiner strolled away after telling me what to do. Five or six minutes later he came back. I was standing waiting for him.

"Well," he said, "what about it?"

"I've done it, sir."

"Hm." His eyebrows lifted. "You've been damn quick about it. Let's see," he said, a little sceptically.

He took the forceps and scalpel from me and turned back the edges of the incision. Then he looked at my ligature and made sure I hadn't tied a branch of the brachial plexus instead of the artery. Then he just grunted and said:

"Yes, it's all right."

After that I was 'on the pig's back'. I felt the stars in their courses were with me. In the clinical examination I was shown case after case to diagnose. By some curious bit of fortune four of them were old syphilitics. I couldn't have missed them. They were just up my street. Luck was certainly with me. I was getting things I knew.

My elation lasted until the last day, when the candidates assembled at the College of Surgeons to hear the result. We were herded into a room, as we had been at the Primary, and then called out one by one. As each candidate was summoned, he was confronted by a clerk from the office who had a list in his hand. If he had passed he was told to go straight on into the library. If he had failed he went down the stairs into the cold world outside.

I saw the man whose name was called out in front of me go to the clerk, listen, and then walk slowly down.

'Poor devil,' I thought, sympathetically.

It was my turn next. In spite of my previous optimism I felt my heart beat faster. The clerk looked at me, asked my name, looked at the list and then said:

"I congratulate you, sir. You're through."

I bounded across the passage into the library, a weight as of a thousand tons off my shoulders. There was one other man before me in the long, quiet, book-lined room. We had the place to ourselves. I had never seen him before. I never knew his name. I've never seen him since. But solemnly we joined hands and waltzed the whole length of the room, up and back, arriving just a little breathless as the door of the Council Room opened and we were beckoned to appear before the President and Council. There we were solemnly admitted, signed the Roll, took the Obligation and became Fellows of the Royal College of Surgeons of England.

It was the end of a struggle, the beginning of another, for now a whole new world of opportunity was possible and had to be faced. I sent a telegram to my people and went back to the Caledonian Road, for it was my evening to do the surgery.

This was an anticlimax.

I should have been celebrating, but I had made no arrangements, as I did not dare anticipate getting through. So I carried on almost automatically. It was a dull evening—nothing of any interest. At eight p.m. I looked into the stuffy waiting-room. It was empty but I could not close before nine, so I strolled to the door and looked out into the Caledonian Road for a breath of air.

It was then it happened.

A cab drew up at the door and a man in his working clothes tumbled out, doubled up with pain.

"Doctor," he said, "I'm afraid I'm dying. I felt so bad I had to take a cab from King's Cross."

When a working man takes a cab for a hundred yards he must be bad, so I got him into the Surgery and listened very carefully to his story. It seemed he had been having bouts of indigestion, and was getting on all right until this sudden violent pain attacked him on his way home. The story was so typical that after a quick examination I came to the conclusion he must have a duodenal ulcer which had just perforated. That meant hospital and an urgent operation. So I wrote a chit to the R.M.O. at the Royal Free giving the diagnosis, and sent him on at once in another cab. A few patients trickled in later and I went on with the evening surgery.

At nine p.m. I rang up the R.M.O. at the hospital to ask when the operation was likely to take place, as I wanted to be present.

A casual voice, which I did not recognise, replied that they had taken him in, but that Mr. Berry, the surgeon under whom he had been admitted, would not be doing a round until the next afternoon.

"But he's an emergency! He's a perforated duodenal! He should be done tonight," I protested.

"Oh, you think so? Sorry, I'm afraid I do not agree. Good night," came the voice, and the phone clicked off.

I was inarticulate with rage. I sat down and began to think. This would not do. The man's chances of recovery would be greatly diminished if nothing was done until next day. He might even die.

Obviously the old R.M.O. had gone, and I was dealing with a recently appointed one who was treating me, a newly-elected Fellow of the College, as a fussy G.P. getting rid of an awkward case. This would not have happened with the previous R.M.O. I had sent him an ectopic, an acute appendix and a volvulus during the last few months, and he accepted my diagnosis. But this one of course did not.

I felt I must act rapidly. The man, he said, was under Mr. Berry. I knew Mr. Berry, and decided I must get on to him. When I did so he was not a bit pleased. He was having a bridge party, but he listened to me.

"Look here," he stuttered, "I suspect you may be right. We've got a new man. I'll go round to the hospital, as if on my way home, and ask if anything of interest has come in. The R.M.O. will probably be a bit worried in spite of what you tell me about his attitude. I'll see the case and decide. But I'm afraid I can't ask you to come along. Mustn't let my new R.M.O. down."

"That's all right for me, sir. Thank you so much," I said.

Two hours later he rang up. His voice was now very friendly.

"You were quite right. I think we got him in time; and, as you may guess, I have a rather chastened R.M.O. He's learnt something he won't forget."

CHAPTER IX

MY FIRST BOOK

WHEN A YOUNG MAN gets his Fellowship today he can step almost at once into a Registrar's post worth £850 to £965 a year under the National Health Service. It was vastly different in my time. There were no posts like that then available. We had to accept anything we could get, often with no salary or a mere honorarium attached. We hung round the hospitals. We took little jobs in pathological laboratories or anatomy rooms. We coached men for their finals, and applied for every possible job advertised in the medical journals. How anyone without a private income ever managed to survive in those days I cannot now quite remember.

My father had given me an expensive education and, as soon as I qualified, we agreed I should stand on my own feet. He had told me several times he was willing to buy me a practice and leave me that much less in his will; and he could not understand why I wanted to try the hard way and become a consultant—for one cannot buy a consultant practice.

At this time, however, I had three friends, all thinking of taking the same risk. They were living at the Hampden Club behind King's Cross, and we four often used to go down to Epping to play golf on the public course there. We hired for a shilling each the red jackets that were then obligatory, and during the rounds we talked constantly about the future. All four of us decided to take the plunge together.

Two were Irishmen like myself: Henry MacCormac, afterwards Dermatologist to the Middlesex Hospital, and John Swift Joly, eventually Senior Surgeon to St. Peter's Hospital, Covent Garden. The third was a Scot, Jock Gillespie, later Senior Surgeon to the Prince of Wales Hospital, Tottenham.

Greatly daring, I went round the agents looking for a consulting-

room in the Harley Street area. I didn't know at the time, but I was
seeing the last of an era. For the period when nearly every consultant
lived in his own house and his was the only brass plate adorning the
front door was nearly over. The change had been coming slowly, and
it was getting noticeable when I began to practise.

I was offered a room I thought I could afford at 79 Wimpole Street,
and was flattered to discover later that the house had formerly belonged
to the great Charles Murchison, M.D., F.R.S., whose work on
Continued Fevers is still a classic.

I said good-bye to the Caledonian Road and took the plunge.

At the end of a year I had paid my rent. Some of the money came
from patients of Keetley's who could not afford his fees. Others came
from doctors for whom I had done locums. Some came from 'ghosting'
the new edition of *Diseases of the Throat and Nose*. One way and
another I managed to get through.

And then a tragedy happened: Keetley died suddenly of coronary
thrombosis, and my best friend and supporter was gone.

No one remembers Keetley now, but he founded the West London
Medico-Chirurgical Society, a Society which still flourishes; and with
the aid of Leonard Bidwell he started the Post-Graduate Medical
School. In addition he originated the idea of the Territorial Medical
Service after seeing how comparatively useless civilian surgeons, un-
trained in administration and discipline, were at the beginning of the
South African War. What an enormous difference that made in the
First World War! His early death at the age of sixty-one deprived me
of my surgical father. I missed him intensely.

*

The disappointment over the rejection of my novel of hospital life
damped my literary enthusiasm for well over a year; but later some
journalistic success reawakened my desire to write, and I started on a
book about my voyage as a ship's surgeon in the Far East, writing
whenever work got slack, leaving it aside when I was busy professionally. I had recently been appointed Surgical Registrar to the Harrow
Road Hospital and did some of the writing there.

At last after about a year it was completed and, greatly daring, I
bought a typewriter and typed it all myself. When it was finished,

I packed it up in brown paper and posted it at a small local post office near the Lock Bridge to one of London's leading publishers. It came back in three weeks with a polite note of refusal. Nothing daunted, I re-parcelled it and posted it to another publisher. It came back in a month with no comment whatever. That made me feel angry. At least they might have been polite about it, I thought. After all, a publisher owes his livelihood to authors. I posted it again to yet another publisher. I got a letter back asking if I had any photographs that would illustrate it. This was encouraging. I sent the photos. Nothing happened for some months and then the typescript and photos came back again. It was heart-breaking.

By now I had become self-conscious about posting it, time and again, from the same little post office in the Harrow Road. I thought the woman behind the counter was laughing at me. Of course that was complete nonsense. I knew it was nonsense, but I posted it next time in the old post office in Vere Street that has now disappeared.

It was on the morning after the ninth refusal that I decided to give up the struggle. I nearly threw the dog-eared script into the fire. But that afternoon I happened to go down to St. Peter's Hospital, Henrietta Street, Covent Garden, where my friend Swift Joly was R.M.O.; and, looking out of the house-surgeon's sitting-room, which was then in the front of the hospital, I saw the name 'Chapman & Hall, Ltd.' on a building across the way.

'Dickens's publishers,' I thought. 'I'll try them, and if they fail me I'll give it up.'

So once more the battered script with the first three or four pages re-typed was parcelled up and posted. I expected to hear nothing for a month as usual, so I arranged to do some work for a friend in the North of England.

I was completely taken by surprise, therefore, when I got a letter a week later, sent on from London with 'Chapman & Hall' in bold letters on the back of the envelope.

Eagerly I tore it open. I could scarcely believe my eyes. They wanted it! It seemed too good to be true after the weary, weary months of refusal.

What had happened was that Arthur Waugh, the father of Alec and Evelyn Waugh, who was then the managing director, saw it on his desk the day it arrived, opened it, read a bit and liked it. That night he took it home and read it. Next day he wrote offering me terms.

He was cautiously optimistic, as a publisher should be, for no one really knows how a book will go. Only the public can answer that. But he had hopes of my book and naturally I shared them.

I had called it *The Cruise of the Clytemnestra*. He said that was an impossible title and renamed it *The Surgeon's Log*.

Well, it came out; and I waited nervously for the reviews. To my amazement they were astonishingly good. John Masefield started the ball rolling with a splendid selling notice in the *Manchester Guardian*. The *Daily Telegraph* gave it two columns. Other papers were equally laudatory. It was published on September 5th, 1911.

Suddenly and quite unexpectedly it became a best-seller on both sides of the Atlantic. Review after review praised it. No one was more surprised than I. It had run into six editions before June, 1912. Then it settled down steadily, selling quietly all the time; and it has been doing this ever since. It has appeared in all sorts of guises, for it is now approaching its half-millionth copy and in its thirtieth edition. I've never quite been able to understand why it has been such a success. It shows, however, how fallible publishers, who ought to know, can be.

Suddenly I had become a personality and the sun shone on me. I was not carried away, however, by the success of the book. I remembered Dowden's advice given fifteen years before and continued to concentrate on my professional work.

But one success leads to another. If you're lucky, you're lucky. I applied for the post of Assistant Surgeon to what is now the Princess Beatrice Hospital, Earl's Court, and I was elected. That gave me the opening I required. I had six surgical beds which I could fill from my own out-patients; and I could also take cases sent up to me from practitioners in the country whom I knew and who trusted me with their surgical work.

Life became very pleasant. I allowed the royalties to pile up and carried on as usual.

One result of my success that pleased me more than most was being elected to the Savage Club, where my old Chief, Keetley, had been such a prominent member. The Club was then in the Adelphi and its gracious Adam rooms overlooking the Embankment were a haven of rest to me in those days. From the Club windows I could watch, pipe in mouth, the moving panorama of the river, and look across to the huddled houses dominated by the great Shot Tower and the Red Lion Brewery on the Surrey side.

Often when I was tired after hospital on a summer evening I would go there, and sit at an open window listening to the distant music of the band in the Embankment Gardens, feeling the weariness gradually slipping away.

There was one picture there which used to make me feel happy. It was by Joseph Harker, and it depicted a long, sunny valley looking down to the sea. I don't know why I loved it so. Perhaps because it was so peaceful.

Of course once my first book proved a success I was approached by several of the publishers who had failed to see its potentialities; and one well-known literary agent, Pinker, wrote wanting to market my future work. I had no future work and told him so. Then one day Arthur Waugh said to me:

"You know, your name is worth something now. Have you nothing you could offer us?"

"Well," I said, "I've got an old novel I wrote some years ago. I don't think it's any good. I'll have a look at it, if you like. But I don't want to be known as a novelist. It would ruin my practice."

Medical etiquette was much stricter then than now. Doctors whose names were mentioned in the lay press were open to the suspicion of advertising; and it was customary to see in the *Lancet* or the *British Medical Journal* every now and then a note disclaiming any such notice, saying it appeared entirely without the knowledge or permission of the writer. I was afraid of this happening to me, especially at the beginning of my career.

But all the same I had a look at the discarded novel. It was bad, disjointed, overwritten, bogged down with technicalities. Little wonder T. Fisher Unwin—whose office in the Adelphi I passed every time I went to the Club—little wonder he had turned it down. But there were good things in it. I thought it had possibilities. I read it through again, cut, reshaped, rewrote and finally took it to Waugh.

He read it and said there was a story in it—the story of a life the public knew nothing about: the life of the nurses and the students and the junior medical officers of a big general hospital. It was a new back-ground.

I called it *Concerning Fitzgerald*. Waugh told me point-blank I had not the slightest idea of how to invent a selling title. Mine, he said, was useless. It should be called *The Night Nurse*. And *The Night Nurse* it was called.

I think the title sold the book. At any rate it rapidly went through six impressions and was banned by the matrons of all the London hospitals, except Guy's. Of course every nurse naturally, therefore, wanted to read it; and it was hidden beneath pillows away from the eyes of sisters and read surreptitiously at night.

It was said to be a bad, sordid book that no nurse should be seen reading. It was very wicked, very disgraceful, a caricature of the real life led by nurses. I dipped into it again the other day, and I could not for the life of me see what all the fuss had been about. Compared with the present-day novel it was like reading *Cranford*. The conversation, too, seemed to me to be quite impossible. No one ever could have talked like that. I hardly recognised it. But I suppose we must have talked like that before the First World War.

I did not publish it under my own name, hampered, I suppose now, by some scruples of medical etiquette, a fear of publicity that might hurt my growing practice. It was entitled 'By the Author of *The Surgeon's Log*'. But, of course, lots of people knew, and it got round that I was giving up practice and making up my mind to devote myself to writing.

Actually I was very worried. I had had two striking successes as a writer, but the public had shown no great desire to rush for my aid as a surgeon.

Then came two flattering surprises. I had a letter from the editor of *Who's Who* asking for particulars of my life and career for the 1914 edition. *Who's Who* in those days was a slim volume. It was said that the privileged people who were admitted to its pages were chosen personally by old Mr. Black, the proprietor, who came to his office in Soho Square every morning on a Bayswater bus. And it didn't matter who you were: if Mr. Black didn't want you in *Who's Who* you weren't in *Who's Who*. This often caused a lot of trouble to users and much heartburning to important people, for if one looked for details of a peer or a Member of Parliament, musician, painter or writer, they might not be there. Naturally I was very flattered and supplied the necessary details, as I have done now for over forty years.

The next surprise was when another well-known literary agent approached me with a tempting offer if I would allow him to handle all my future work. I went to see him.

"If you will put yourself in my hands, I will guarantee you two thousand pounds a year," he said.

"But I couldn't earn all that money and carry on my practice," I replied.

"No, of course not. You'd have to give up your practice," he said, in a tone of surprise.

That brought me up sharply.

"No," I said, "I can't agree to that. I love my job as a doctor too much."

He smiled at me.

"Take your time. Think it over," he said smoothly.

I went home to my rooms, very soberly. I thought it over; his offer was very tempting, but finally I wrote rejecting it. As soon as I'd done so I began to wonder if I had not been foolish. And again I thought of Dowden, and was sure I hadn't.

Arthur Waugh left me alone for six months and then suggested I should write another novel for him.

"What about one on the subject of women doctors? It would be very topical with all these suffragette women stirring up trouble," he said. "We might call it *The Lady Doctor*. I feel that would be a wonderful follow-up title to *The Night Nurse*."

Of course it was a gold-medal idea. I could see that; and I was greatly tempted again. I could do it almost without thinking. I knew all about it. It would be easy. But would it be wise? I felt I was slipping.

So I decided to take a holiday at sea and think it over. It was June, and I thought I'd like to have a look at the Panama Canal, which had just been opened to traffic.

So I went down, arrayed in top hat and morning coat, as was then the custom, to Elders and Fyffe's, the banana people; and I boldly asked for a ship to the West Indies.

I suppose they must have looked me up in the Medical Directory. I never heard; but the managing director, Roger Ackerley, a large, hearty man, asked me to call on him a few days later.

"We can offer you one of our best ships, *The Bayano*," he said. "I'm sending my son Peter as a passenger this trip. I have told the Captain that he and the Doctor are to kick my boy round the deck every morning for the good of his soul. Will you take it on?"

"Done," I said, and three weeks later I was at sea, once again a ship's surgeon.

It was like old times. We had two passengers on the outward voyage. One was a girl going out to be married, and my first surgical operation in this ship was to bore the lobules of her ears so that she could wear the ear-rings sent home as a present by her future husband. The other passenger was a Scottish sugar planter, a man of few words.

It was all very peaceful and the intimacy that I remembered of old came back to me. The Captain and I duly chased young Peter round the deck after breakfast. It was good exercise. The Mate, the Chief, the Old Man and I yarned to each other to our hearts' content. It was all very pleasant. But the ship was in water ballast. That is to say, she had no cargo. She was going out empty, stabilised only by the water in her tanks. And she rolled and rolled alarmingly, as much as forty-five degrees at times, going across the Western Ocean. The officers and crew took it for granted.

"It'll be all right on the voyage home," the Chief said. "The hold will be full up with bananas and she'll be as steady as a rock."

After ten days crossing the Western Ocean, windy, wet and boisterous, we entered the Caribbean Sea between San Domingo and Puerto Rico. Immediately peace and tropical sunshine surrounded us, and I began really to enjoy myself.

As a schoolboy I had been fascinated by tales of the Spanish Main, after I had accidentally picked up a copy of the first edition of Dampier's *Voyages* which somehow had found its way on to Johnny Templeton's second-hand bookstall in my remote native town; and my head was full of later reading about Morgan and Blackbeard, Captain Kidd and Sharp. I remembered also Dr. Dover of 'Dover's powder', and his buccaneering experiences before he settled down to become a respectable London physician. I thought of doubloons and pieces of eight, of Hawkins and the beginning of the Slave Trade, of the sack of Cartagena, of Nombre de Dios and the galleons waiting to carry the gold, jewels and silver of Peru to Philip II of Spain; and of how Drake and his tough companions had captured the mule train carrying the great treasure across the Isthmus from Panama.

We were bound for Colon at the western entrance to the Panama Canal and I had arranged to write a description of it for Dr. Squire Sprigge of the *Lancet*. This would have been most interesting medically, and very topical if I had been able to do it, for the construction of the Canal was a great medical rather than an engineering triumph. But when I got back home it was the end of July, 1914, and, like everyone else, I was soon thinking of other things.

Ferdinand de Lesseps, after his success in constructing the Suez Canal, had become so famous that when he offered to build a canal across the Isthmus of Darien, and so connect the Atlantic with the Pacific Ocean, he got all the millions he demanded from his countrymen. But he had forgotten one thing. The West Indies had been saturated for centuries with malaria and yellow fever, particularly yellow fever; and people going out there had a habit of dying. The Spaniards who were born there were 'salted'. Those who had not died in childhood survived, and were immune.

Time and again from the reign of great Elizabeth I onwards the English had tried to colonise; but always the yellow fever had defeated them, and the Spaniard remained in possession of the mainland.

De Lesseps tried to cut a way across the Isthmus. Twenty thousand men died of yellow fever working for him. Many thousands more were invalided home. The Panama Canal Company failed. The works were abandoned. Rusty machinery lay all along the route from Colon to Panama, and de Lesseps died broken-hearted. At Port Said* there is a great statue of him pointing to the canal he made successfully. At Colon there should be a memorial to Jesse Lazear.

Who was Jesse Lazear?

Lazear was a doctor, who served in the American Army in the Cuban War of 1898, and in that war had seen thousands of nice, white American boys die of yellow fever, although the sanitary authorities had cleaned up the unspeakable filth of Havana.

* The Egyptians blew up this statue in December 1956.

Obviously sanitation didn't stop yellow fever. Three things were known about it: frost checked it, one attack made the survivor immune, and it was impossible to inoculate any laboratory animal with it. The only real way to find out, therefore, was to experiment on human beings. But the men of the American Army had seen 'Yellow Jack', as Nelson's sailors called it, and they had seen the awful headache, the prostration, the intense jaundice that had given it its name, the abdominal cramp and the horrible black vomit that meant death was near.

The doctors, therefore, felt they had no right to ask for volunteers from laymen. So two surgeons of the U.S. Army Medical Corps decided to experiment on themselves. They had a suspicion it was carried by mosquitoes, because Ronald Ross had proved this for malaria in India.

These two surgeons, Carroll and Lazear, allowed themselves to be bitten by captured mosquitoes that had been seen to suck the blood of yellow fever patients.

Four days later they were both seized with violent headache, shivering and a rise of temperature. That was it. Mosquitoes obviously did carry the disease. For days they lay tossing, delirious and unconscious. Then Carroll began to recover, but Lazear started the dreadful vomit and, in spite of everything they could do, he died.

Volunteers from the troops were now asked for. Thirteen responded to the offer of three hundred dollars a head. Some allowed themselves to be bitten by infected mosquitoes. All of these got yellow fever, but luckily none died. Some slept for weeks amongst yellow fever cases, wrapped in blankets from the patients who had died. They all remained healthy, so it wasn't contagious.

By a series of experiments it was found that one special mosquito, 'Aedes Aegypti', alone carried the disease. Clothes or contact with other patients did not carry it—only the bite of an infected mosquito. All one had to do, therefore, was to clear the breeding places of the mosquito and protect oneself by mosquito-netting from being bitten.

It was this knowledge that armed Dr. William C. Gorgas when the Americans took over the de Lesseps derelict canal. He was given complete sanitary control, and in eighteen months yellow fever, which had slain its many thousands in the four centuries of European occupation, was conquered.

Gorgas drained the stagnant water or oiled it and so prevented mosquito breeding. He housed all the employees in mosquito-proof houses. Anyone found with yellow fever was isolated in a mosquito-proof hospital so that he could not infect more mosquitoes. In this way the vicious circle was broken—yellow fever patient infecting mosquito—infected mosquito infecting healthy victim with yellow fever—yellow fever victim infecting mosquito, and so on, and so on.

Gorgas stamped out yellow fever and the work of excavation went on steadily until the Canal was finished. It was this Canal I had come out to see.

Colon at the Caribbean end of the Canal is not an impressive place, though combined with Christobal it perpetuates the memory of Christopher Colombus. We anchored inside the breakwater, and immediately the heat of the tropics fell upon us.

The Canal Zone, administered by the United States, is ten miles wide, and Christobal in the Zone at the entrance to the Canal is just inside the breakwater. We approached it across the bay of Porto Bello, where Drake found his last resting place, past the ruins of the city sacked by Sir Henry Morgan in the days when he was a pirate, and before he found grace and favour in the eyes of Charles II.

We discovered when we got to Colon that the Canal was temporarily blocked. There had been trouble with the lock gates where they opened into Gatun Lake, and there had been a fall of earth at the Culebra cut. Ships were not going through, and we could see nothing of the working of the Canal in consequence. At that time Colon was one long street of Spanish villas and prefabricated houses that looked like meat safes—just frames with fine wire netting and four-leaved doors swinging on a central pivot to prevent mosquitoes getting inside.

Panamanians did not love the occupying troops. American soldiers armed with rifles and fixed bayonets stood guard over the entrance to the Canal. I took a photo of one nice lad on sentry duty and promised to send a copy to his mother somewhere in Kentucky. She never got it, for when it was developed I had lost the address he gave me.

The Republic of Panama was a political invention of Theodore Roosevelt. When his Government wanted to take over the Canal, the Republic of Colombia was not co-operative. So, unofficially of course, the party not in power in Colombia was furnished with rifles and so was able to stage a successful revolt. They then founded the Republic of Panama, and in gratitude leased the land on either side of the Canal to the United States. It was thus possible to go ahead, clean up the place, clear the area of mosquitoes carrying yellow fever and finish the Canal. Everything was for the best in the best of all possible worlds. The Americans opened a new world route of immense importance and brought great prosperity to a diseased and poverty-stricken country. But to their surprise they found themselves in consequence very unpopular. It is an experience we British have had so often that we have come to expect it.

*

We unloaded some machinery destined for sugar plantations; and now began to take on passengers. Some came from Panama itself, a few came over from Jamaica. But most of them were from Peru or Chile. Eventually we had, in all, about thirty. The peace of the decks was gone; and I began to have to earn my living.

Colon was just an incidental stopping place. The passengers were also incidental. Our real object was to carry bananas to Bristol; and for this we had to go three hundred miles north to Puerto Limon in Costa Rica. Here we berthed, and within a few hours were loading feverishly. The bananas came alongside in open railway wagons piled high with bright green bunches, each bunch carrying about one hundred and twenty bananas. From the wagons these were swung up to the deck on an endless chain of metal buckets running all the time; and from the deck they were slung into the holds, where each bunch was hung separately on a hook. The handling was so skilfully done that there was almost no bruising. I stood on the deck, fascinated, watching the great, green bunches moving upwards on the chain of buckets, and then disappearing into the holds.

After I'd looked on for some time I went ashore and walked leisurely along the white, shingly beach beneath the palm trees. The sea was of a marvellous ultra-marine. The water, smooth as a millpond, lapped lazily along the shore. Great white land crabs, two or three feet across, scuttled away as I walked. They looked horrible. I felt they lived on dead bodies.

I came back to the ship and talked to some of the passengers at lunch. There was one beautiful, bronzed Spanish girl from Bilbao with her father, a youngish widow with a very white daughter from Jamaica, two hard-bitten women of uncertain age from Chile, a British Consul and his wife, a fat little widow with an eight-year-old son, and several mining engineers from Peru—men who talked about nitre or the Pearson Company and lived mainly in the bar.

After the siesta, during which everyone slept and all work ceased on the ship, we had tea. I wandered round the deck taking stock of the passengers. All of them seemed in the pink of condition, all very lively and talkative. Already they were beginning to pair off as people do on board ship.

In the evening the lights ashore beckoned. The Chief, young Peter Ackerley and I presently found ourselves in a café near the beach. A woman was dancing a slow, rhythmic, sinuous dance, flicking castanets in long, tapered fingers. Swarthy men, hawk-nosed, black-haired, with big brown smouldering eyes watched her. A little orchestra played Latin-American music. It was all curiously erotic. We were sipping a mixture of grenadine and rum. The heat was terrific in spite of the breeze that comes at sunset. Everyone was smoking either long cigars or some brand of cigarette that looked cheap and nasty. Then two men started to quarrel, eyes flashed, fierce gesticulations, excited jactitating speech followed. Soon others joined in. The row was spreading but the woman danced on. I saw the flash of a knife.

"Come on," said the Chief. "Let's get."

It was very quiet outside. The air was clean and lovely. We strolled back in the moonlight towards the ship, our shadows very black against the white, dusty street.

I found a message waiting me. The widow's little son had a temperature. Would I please go down to her cabin to see him. I took his temperature. The thermometer registered 104 degrees, but the boy had no rash, so I gave him quinine on the off-chance that it might be malaria.

*

Our Company was a subsidiary of an American one, 'The Great White Line'. You've got to know the Caribbean to understand what 'The Great White Line' means.

'The Great White Line' at that time practically owned Central America. If 'The Great White Line' approved of you, all was well. If not, 'The Great White Line' eliminated you. That was in 1914. It may be different now.

Costa Rica then lived by the export of bananas. I was taken to see one of the huge estates owned by the Company. It had its own railway, which was two hundred and forty miles long. The railway twisted and turned, turned and twisted round the enormous estate of terraced hills and deep valleys, collecting bananas, transporting equipment, carrying the estate employees, who seemed all to be Jamaican negroes, bringing round supervisors—experts in banana cultivation.

This estate had its own canteens, its own grocery, hardware and clothing stores, the contents of which it sold to its employees, in this way recovering much of the wages paid.

The negroes were inveterate gamblers. Every time one of them won anything in the State Lottery he had a tooth extracted and a golden one put in its place. One fortunate fellow gave me a complete, dazzling, golden smile. Every tooth visible was gold.

It took us hours going round the estate before we got back to the station on the Government line that ran up to San José, the capital. 'The Great White Line' at that time owned the railway. I came to the conclusion that it would be most unwise to quarrel with 'The Great White Line'.

When the ship was fully loaded, the hatches were battened down and the refrigerating plant began to pump cold air around the holds. The bananas came in green, and they were kept green by refrigeration. It would never have done to let them ripen and go rotten on the ten-day voyage to Bristol. Every morning, therefore, the Mate and I went down into the holds and took the temperature of the bananas, to see that all was well. That was part of the medical work I did whilst in the Caribbean.

The lady passengers laughed and flirted with the officers, played deck games, gossiped. The men from Peru propped up the bar. The plump little widow, whose boy had now recovered, made a dead set at the

Chief Engineer. He was terrified and used to take refuge with me whenever possible.

Each day after we had taken the temperature of the bananas, the Mate brought up a bunch and hung it in one of the deck-houses to ripen. This seemed a harmless sort of thing to do. The bananas, however, often had snakes and enormous spiders hidden in the bunches when they were shipped. They had become comatose and stiff under the refrigeration; but when a bunch was brought on deck they had a habit of coming to life again and scuttling about the decks, to the consternation of the women passengers. I suspected that this was an amusement purposely engineered by the ship's officers. They must have known it was bound to happen every voyage.

We were all bright and cheerful, full of life—until we got out into the Western Ocean again; and then suddenly the cold struck us. The decks immediately became empty of passengers; and I was going round treating shivering, chattering patients running temperatures. All these sun-baked people had endemic malaria, and the sudden cold spell brought it out in them as soon as we left the tropics. I was very busy for nearly a week before they recovered.

As we approached England we began to get wireless messages: "Keep temperature steady." "Allow temperature to rise to seventy degrees." "Keep at seventy degrees." These had nothing to do with me or my passengers but with the bananas. If there was a glut in the market the bananas were kept green. If there was a shortage they were allowed to approach to yellow so that they would be saleable as soon as we reached port. Apparently we were betwixt and between.

One advantage of refrigeration was that we could always have beautiful cold iced beer. That, however, brought me my one and only bit of surgical work during the voyage.

The Second Engineer, carrying a bottle to his cabin from the hold, tripped and fell. The bottle broke and gave him a deep gash across the front of his wrist, severing the tendons that moved his fingers, and cutting the median nerve that gave them motion and sensation.

It was just before dinner. I was called hurriedly from the deck, went below to his cabin, and bound the wound temporarily. It was important, however, to try to join the ends of the cut tendons, and especially those of the median nerve, as soon as possible. So I arranged to operate next morning.

We did it in a store-room below the promenade deck. The Chief Steward gave the anæsthetic, and I started. The passengers, of course, had not been told anything about the accident, and did not know what was happening below deck. But to this day I can still remember while I was searching for the ends of the tendons, and making sure I really had got the cut ends of the median nerve, someone was singing a popular song of the period; and the chorus, taken up by a dozen voices, came down clearly to me:

Joshua, Joshua,
Sweeter than lemon squash you are,
Yes, by gosh you are,
Joshu', Joshua.

It's a song one doesn't often hear now, but occasionally I do; and when I do it brings everything back to me: the bad light in which we had to operate, the sweltering heat, the amateur anæsthetist I had to watch all the time, and the Third Mate, a very plucky fellow who nearly fainted, helping me.

Eventually to my great relief we got it done and carried the patient back to his bunk to sleep off the anæsthetic.

We berthed in Bristol towards the end of July, 1914, and none of us had the faintest inkling that it was the end of an era. We scattered all over England promising to write to one another, a promise seldom kept after steamboat friendships, almost impossible as it turned out for us.

*

CHAPTER X

WAR AND SERBIA, 1914

ON THE DAY war was declared I was a cripple in Bath, with a violent attack of sciatica all down my right side. It was damnable. I had been punting on the river at Staines the Sunday after my return and I thought I had got overheated and so started the sciatica.

I suppose the diagnosis now would be that I probably had slipped a disc from the unusual exercise, coming soft from the tropics. Maybe. Anyhow I was a cripple in the Francis Hotel for the first fourteen days of the war; and I could feel that the old ladies with rheumatoid arthritis, watching me limp along, were thinking I was scrimshanking, trying to avoid joining up; for posters of Kitchener stared me in the face everywhere, pointing with an exaggerated hand, saying: "*Your King and Country Need You,*"

Old Dr. Thompson of Bath made a good job of me. To his and my delight I was back in London in a fortnight.

Next day I made for the War Office and was directed to A.M.D.1, if I remember aright. This I found was a small office; and, to my surprise, sitting at the desk was one of my old house-surgeons in captain's uniform.

We greeted each other warmly.

"What can I do for you, sir?" he said.

"I want to join up," I answered, cheerfully.

He looked at me with obvious embarrassment.

"Well, sir, that's really rather difficult. You see, sir, you're a bit old for us. You are over thirty, and we really only want young newly-qualified men to do dressings in the front line. We don't need Fellows of the College. You're too heavy guns for us. The war will be over by Christmas."

That was the sort of thing they were saying in the War Office at the end of August, 1914. I was very angry and very deflated, and I went to my rooms intensely depressed. Nobody wanted me with a war on. I was too old. I tried to work, but everything seemed flat and unprofitable. Nothing interested me except the news; and the news wasn't too good in spite of censorship. Days passed, and I grew more and more restless.

Then one afternoon someone said to me:

"Never mind the damn silly War Office. Why don't you go to the Red Cross and St. John people?"

I did, and I was referred at once to Sir Frederick Treves, from whom I had a very different reception.

"We're wanting surgeons badly in Belgium, Abraham. Souttar— you know Souttar—is there now. Would you care to go to Antwerp?"

"Delighted," I answered.

"Right. Well, come tomorrow and we'll fix you up."

Next day he said:

"Antwerp has fallen, as you know. What about Ostend or Dunkirk?"

"Anywhere, Sir Frederick."

Ostend and Dunkirk fell just as it was arranged for me to go over. The Germans were sweeping across the Low Countries. The dream of a war over by Christmas was fading. I saw Treves again.

"Would you care to go to Serbia?" he said gravely. "We are fixing up a mission going out in a troopship in a few days. It will be very rough campaigning, and we can only send men of first-class physique. Could you get ready in five days?"

"Certainly," I said.

And in five days I was at Southampton on board the troopship, having settled my affairs, got leave of absence from my hospitals, and arranged for a colleague to look after my practice.

Our unit was called 'The First British Red Cross Serbian Mission', and consisted of six medical officers and twelve St. John's Ambulance orderlies. The troopship had two Territorial regiments already on board, bound for India, and six hundred officers of the Indian Army, from generals to subalterns, hurriedly recalled from home leave by the unexpected outbreak of the war. We had been dumped on them at the last moment with instructions that we were to be disembarked at Malta; and as the ship was already overcrowded we were not welcome.

We had been told in London:

"It won't be possible to give you cabins. I'm afraid you'll have to sleep rough in the holds. No one under the rank of major will have a cabin; you will dine of course with the officers, but everyone will have to queue for baths."

To an old ship-surgeon like me this sounded most unpromising. We had not been told the name of the ship for security reasons, but when we got there Dr. Banks, one of our number with whom I had struck up an immediate friendship, suddenly exclaimed:

"Why, I was surgeon on this boat two voyages ago! Let's see the Chief Steward."

We did so and were received with open arms.

"Don't say a word," he warned us. "The billeting officer knows nothing about ships. I have a spare cabin with two bunks and a private bathroom next to mine. They're yours."

And ours they were.

We watched the generals, colonels, majors queueing unhappily for everything, and smiled secretly.

We dined with the officers, but our Red Cross uniforms were a great trouble at first as the stripes on our arms nearly resembled those of a lieutenant-colonel, and the troops kept saluting us, to our embarrassment, in a puzzled way until it got found we were mere civilians. Then to our relief they ceased abruptly.

We travelled with lights out for fear of submarines all the way to Malta. Actually if anything had happened to us the Indian Army would have lost most of its staff. But nothing did.

They dumped us at Malta and we said good-bye to them without regret.

The prevailing colour in Malta is chrome yellow. The great forts of the Knights of St. John built to defend Malta from the Turk, the Hostels of the Knights and the Cathedral of St. John are all built of Eocene sandstone.

The streets of Valletta, going up from the harbour, are like flights of steps until one gets to the plain above. There the great, paved squares have large round knobs scattered symmetrically over their surfaces. These knobs are plugs covering the entrances to granaries which the Knights of Malta provided against possible sieges in bygone days.

Everywhere one goes the Maltese goat is ubiquitous. When a Maltese housewife wants milk she hails a goatherd and he milks a goat on her doorstep. Formerly the Garrison and the Navy did the same until Sir David Bruce of the R.A.M.C. discovered that this goats' milk carried the germ causing the Malta fever which most newcomers suffered from after arrival. One attack, as a rule, produces immunity for life, so the Maltese take no notice, they've all had it as children. But the Garrison and the Navy and their wives and children are in a different category; and now care is taken that their milk is pasteurised before they drink it.

There were several Territorial regiments in Malta when we arrived, and I knew some of the officers. We were honorary members of the mess which was in the *auberge* of the German Knights of St. John. There I made a *faux pas*: I asked the Maltese head of the British Order of St. John's Ambulance, a captain in the Maltese Artillery, to lunch at the mess. This was embarrassing as the Maltese were not at that time welcome guests. However, he was very pleased, I liked him, he liked me, and I arranged for him to post a pound of tobacco once a month to me in Serbia. It was lucky I did, for it was the only tobacco I got all the time I was there.

We had to wait at Malta until we were picked up by a *Messageries Maritimes* boat going to Athens, Salonika and Dedeagatch. The shops in Malta are excellent. I bought myself a good Kodak which proved extremely useful afterwards. I think we were a week there before we were able to leave.

Eventually we did so. The boat was very French. The Chief Steward slept in the only bathroom. It was used also in the day as a dark-room for developing photos. Banks and I slept in a cabin next the bathroom. Every morning a steward would look in cheerfully and we would call out *"De l'eau chaude"*, and he would grin and repeat, *"De l'eau chaude"* and bring us our hot water.

There were two other Englishmen besides us in the saloon. One was a Consul who kept all the French in good humour. He laughed and joked in excellent French, but with an accent *très Britannique* according to the ship's Captain.

The other was 'our Mr. Brown', a traveller in cotton goods from Manchester who came aboard at Malta. He came up the gangway in civilian clothes; and, just to show how civilian he was, he had with him two kitbags with Royal Navy stamped all over them. He and I used to walk up and down the deck together for exercise. I am a bad walker, I never can keep step with anyone; but I soon noticed that 'our Mr. Brown' always kept in step with me. No matter how I stepped, long or short, stumbled or stopped, it didn't matter, 'our Mr. Brown' was always in step.

Our first port of call was Athens; and, saturated as I was in the classics, I loved every moment of it. We landed at the Piræus and I took the tram from there to Athens. It ran through a flat plain covered with olive groves. Twenty-five years later, I was there again just before the Second World War, and when I landed at the Piræus I found, to my surprise, the entire area between it and Athens covered with houses.

Athens, the Athens of Pericles, is a small place. I had seen so many photos of its classical architecture that I was able to wander around by myself quite happily. I remember particularly how I felt coming down from the Acropolis, saturated with the calm, white loveliness of the Parthenon, at peace with the world. And it was most unfortunate, therefore, that across my path should come at that moment a tweed-clad fellow, the back of whose close-cropped brachycephalic head melted into a roll of red fat behind his ears. He glared at my uniform, stepped to one side and spat on the ground. This struck me as unnecessarily offensive; and I made rude remarks about his simian ancestry. I felt better after that, but it disturbed the happy feeling I had had that the world was on our side in this war. There were actually people who did not like us; who really felt savage about us.

When I rejoined the ship I found that the happy family feeling had gone. We had taken on Greeks, Bulgars, Rumanians, Jews, nondescript Levantines bound for Salonika, and an American 'drummer', that is, a commercial traveller, bound for Dedeagatch in Turkey.

The 'drummer' was actually a German spy. He fastened on us and spent most of the time between Athens and Salonika trying to find out if we were what we said we were. On this account he entirely overlooked 'our Mr. Brown', who got away unnoticed at Salonika and proved a frightful nuisance to the Austrians on the Danube that winter —for 'our Mr. Brown' was an expert on explosives.

Half-way to Salonika a mysterious delay occurred in the middle of the night. We slowed down off one of the Greek isles, another ship appeared, the donkey engines of the two ships began to work, and curious clanking noises could be heard. We were not encouraged to go on deck, but we learnt later that the other ship was Bulgarian. It was loaded with railway lines from Krupps ostensibly for Dedeagatch, and these had been transferred to us for use in Serbia. The Bulgars were not yet in the war, and our patrols in the Channel could not stop their ships. How much Krupps knew of these happenings was anybody's guess.

Next morning we woke to a sunlit, dimpling sea. We were in the Gulf of Salonika. Land lay on either side and ahead. To starboard were the blue hills of the Chalcidice; to port the mountains of Macedonia with the great peak of high Olympus, sacred to Zeus, dazzling white, immaculate, dominating all.

In front, getting clearer and clearer as we approached, lay Salonika, an irregular quadrilateral mosaic of black and white and terracotta, with curious long needle-like streaks of white, amid the reds and blacks, that presently proved to be the slender minarets of the many domed mosques scattered throughout the city.

As we came nearer we could see the masts of hundreds of feluccas anchored along the low seafront, except to the left where a modern breakwater sheltered steamships flying every flag except those of Germany and Austria.

All along this front were the palatial façades of hotels, restaurants, banks and other public buildings, past which electric trams ran to and fro.

This was Salonika, the ancient Thessalonika of the Greeks, the scene of the missionary efforts of St. Paul, the siege-torn city held in turn by Romans, Byzantines, Saracens, Normans, Venetians, captured by the Turks as long ago as A.D. 1430 and torn from them by the victorious Greeks only eighteen months before our arrival.

We berthed in the duty-free port at seven a.m. and were met by the Serbian Consul and also by the British Vice-Consul, who, to my surprise and pleasure, turned out to be an old schoolmate of mine. Our path was thus smoothed through the Greek Customs, and our heavy baggage taken to the station, consigned to Ghevgeli, the Serbian

frontier town. Against advice, however, we clung to our personal
luggage. This was lucky as our hospital equipment was lost for a fortnight. We found out afterwards that the Greek porters had been bribed
by Austrian agents to lose it, suspecting it might be war stores. It was
found eventually at Monastir.

Salonika was full of foreign agents, for Greece was neutral. So we
had Austrian, German, French, Italian and British all watching each
other. The place swarmed with Greek soldiers, as the army had just
been mobilised. Many of the men had been to America and talked
English. They were very cheerful, and quite sure Greece would come
in on the side of the Allies almost immediately.

We breakfasted at the Olympus Palace Hotel; and I watched with
interest the cosmopolitan crowd in the gay restaurant. Greek officers
in khaki uniform, resplendent with gold epaulettes and big curving
swords, were particularly prominent. It was all very bright and cheerful. We six medical officers, very hungry, ate our breakfasts and
watched. We were also very hungry for news, as the close-down at
Malta had been almost complete and we had heard nothing for three
weeks.

Salonika on the other hand had all the news, and fresh editions of the
papers were coming out hourly. Benbow, our Australian, first of all
got hold of a French journal, *Le Nouveau Siècle*, and his face grew longer
and longer. The news was all about great German victories on the
Marne. Banks by then had found another paper, *L'Opinion*. It presented the cause of the Allies in the most roseate colours. The Germans
were at their last gasp according to it. Holmes from Manchester had
ferreted out yet another journal, *L'Indépendent*. It too was optimistic
on our side but not so roseate as *L'Opinion*. Of course we discovered
afterwards that all three papers were heavily subsidised, and that the
Austrians especially were spending money like water to keep the
Greeks from joining us.

We found it would be twenty-four hours before we could proceed
north, so Benbow, Holmes and I wandered round, sightseeing. Salonika,
like every ancient city still flourishing, is a palimpsest of history; and
in spite of its electric trams we felt the persistent note was still Oriental.
This was mainly due to the constant panorama presented by the
kaleidoscopic passers-by—fezzed Turks, white-capped Albanians,

Cretans with enormous baggy trousers, tall white-kilted Greek mountaineers with whiskered shoes, solemn Greek priests, Jewish rabbis, piratical-looking dark-skinned sailors—gold-ear-ringed with gaudy handkerchiefs tied round their heads—bringing cargoes of fish, squids, sponges from the Isles, which they were unloading from the feluccas along the seafront.

The very new and the old jostled each other everywhere. We wandered into a wide street with tram-lines and mean houses. No street could have been more ordinary. And then suddenly we came on a crumbling, weather-beaten arch stretching over it, supported by square columns carved in three tiers of worn bas-reliefs in marble, representing Roman legionaries marching in triumph.

We stared at it solemnly.

A little Greek clerk who was passing turned his head.

"*C'est l'Arc de Triomphe d'Alexandre le Grand,*" he said.

Benbow drew a deep breath.

"Gee," he said, "this is some arch! Why, it's B.C.!"

And then it dawned on me. This commonplace street with its rattling trams and mean tumbledown houses was the 'Via Egnatia', the great Roman road running from Constantinople across Macedonia to the Adriatic, built to connect the two capitals of the Roman Empire; and the arch we were looking at was the Arch of Constantine over the Calamerian Gate.

Under it, grim Roman centurions had led their legionaries to battle against the barbarian. It had seen the gorgeous processions of Byzantine Emperors. Fierce hook-nosed Saracens had stormed through it in triumph, scimitar in hand. It had looked down on the armed hosts of the Crusaders. The Norman Knights of Boniface, Marquess of Montferrat, King of Thessalonika, had kept watch and ward within its portals. Captains of the Republic of Venice had defended it in armour against the Infidel. Finally the Crescent had triumphed over the Cross, and for five hundred years it had slumbered under the shadow of the Padishah. For five hundred years it had heard the silver call of the muezzin from the corbelled gallery of the minaret adjoining.

Constant reiteration of this call had blotted out all memory of the pale-faced Nazarene. It seemed as though its slumber would last for ever.

And then suddenly, little more than a year before we stood looking at it, the slumber of centuries had been broken by the sharp staccato of the machine-gun. A miracle had happened. The immemorial Turk had vanished. The voice of the muezzin had ceased to call the faithful to prayer. The Cross once more had triumphed.

We found that most of the mosques had now been closed, and those that had been churches before the time of the Moslem, notably St. Sophia and St. Demetrius, had been reconsecrated. We wandered into the Church of St. Demetrius. It had been a mosque for centuries, but the Turks had been so casual in its conversion that they had simply whitewashed over the wonderful Byzantine mosaics of the Saviour in gold and green and blue which have now once again been given to the light of day. They had also respected the tomb of the Saint and his reputedly miracle-working body in its stone sarcophagus at the entrance to the church.

The body of the Saint is said to exude a miraculous oil. This oil is reputed to cure almost every affliction that flesh is heir to; and pilgrims have always flocked to it, even in modern times. The tomb had been carefully looked after by a dervish of the Mevlevi order, and the holy lamp kept lit; but when we saw it it was again in charge of a Greek monk.

The tomb is in a dark little side chapel to the left of the entrance, and the devotees, mostly women in black, came in quietly, bought a taper from the monk, lit it, stuck it in a niche, murmured their prayers, and then as quietly slipped away.

We too left quietly.

That afternoon we got back just in time for the great social function of the day: five o'clock tea, to the strains of an orchestra, the frou-frou of skirts, the gold and silver and blue of uniforms, the sound of gay voices, tea-cups, clinking spurs, tapping swords. Deft waiters crossed and recrossed the view. There was much stately bowing and kissing of ladies' hands, sidelong glances under heavy lashes, gesticulating, laughter and more laughter.

I saw a man looking at me whose face I recognised.

"How d'ye do," I said, casually.

"Fairish, thank you, fairish," he answered, and sat down beside me, after ordering tea.

I knew he was a brother Savage. I guessed he was a war corres-
pondent, but I didn't know his name nor he mine.

Naturally I asked him to dine with us that evening. We were due
to leave next morning early. We were supposed to be going to Nish,
the war-time capital. But when the Serbian Consul came in after
dinner he said we had been posted to Uskub (Skoplje).

That worried us.

"Are you sure there will be enough work for us at Skoplje?" we
asked.

The Consul shrugged his shoulders mournfully:

"Work! There will be too much work. The Serbian doctors are
too few. Our good friends the Russians cannot help. Sirs, there is
work everywhere in Serbia."

My friend from the Savage Club murmured quietly to me:

"Poor devil. He doesn't say so, but the Austrians may be in Nish by
now. The news is very bad. There is talk of moving the Government
to Skoplje; and if you get there you'll be in the thick of it."

"If we get there?"

"Yes. A nice harmless old gentleman with a German accent, probably an Austrian agent, confided to me this afternoon that the Bulgars
were going to cut the line tonight to isolate the Serbs from Salonika.
Of course it's only a boast. If he really knew he wouldn't tell me. But
the Serbs are very short of ammunition. The French are sending up
quantities from here, but if the line is cut it's 'Good-bye Serbie'."

"But the Bulgars are not at war with the Serbs!" I exclaimed.

"The Komitadji are. You'll learn all about the Komitadji if you get
through."

Well. We did get through. We were met at Skoplje and billeted in
an Austrian nunnery, near the station, of which the gentle-eyed nuns
had been dispossessed two months previously. They were warm, comfortable quarters, and we spent the next six months there happily until
the calamity fell on us.

Skoplje was on the main line from Belgrade to Salonika, and the
wounded kept pouring back on us. The only real military hospital
was in the Citadel, a huge old Turkish fort overlooking the Vardar, the
great river that flows southward to Salonika and the sea.

On our first day we went to see the military hospital. In it was a most efficient Serbian medical officer. He was operating at great speed in a large out-patient department, surrounded by wounded, extracting bullets and pieces of shrapnel without any anæsthetic. We asked him why. He looked at us with lifted eyebrows.

"I haven't time for anæsthetics," he said, in halting German.

We soon found that this was true. Every day thousands of walking sick and wounded poured into the town. Every day train-loads left for Veles, Ghevgeli and Monastir; and every day more train-loads arrived. No one was kept whose temperature was under 104 degrees Fahrenheit unless he was a compound fracture or obviously dying. The position was desperate.

The Serbs were retreating daily, fighting back savagely. But they were outnumbered, they were short of artillery, guns, ammunition, and their one arsenal at Kraguievatz was threatened with capture. Things looked very black.

We had been sent out by Sir Frederick Treves as an Advanced Dressing Station. The Serbs wanted us to run a hospital instead. And what they offered us were three great buildings, formerly tobacco warehouses. The largest, No. 1 Hospital, had three floors holding six hundred patients. There was no medical staff except one Russian woman doctor, no inside sanitary arrangements, no water laid on, no operating theatre. A few feeble electric lights dimly illuminated each floor, and all the heating was by wood-burning stoves. The hospital was full, three patients to two beds. The men lay in their dirty field uniforms with their foul dressings unchanged for days. They were looked after by untrained 'sestras' and 'bolnitchers' (male orderlies). Not a window was open. The smell was appalling.

No. 2 and No. 3 Hospitals had no lighting at all, and were filled with sick Austrian prisoners of war lying on straw, unattended. The Serbs were asking us—six doctors and twelve St. John's Ambulance orderlies—to run these three hospitals having more in-patients than the London.

We said we couldn't do it.

Banks and I went up to the top floor of No. 1 Hospital to reconnoitre. There we found the little red-haired Russian woman doctor, Dr. Kadish, doing dressings at a series of trestle tables. She said she started at nine each morning and worked until the light was too bad to carry on. She had been doing this alone for two months. That was too much for us.

We buckled to and helped her, and that settled it. We took on the impossible task, and we took her on as well.

She was a wonderful little woman, and without her I realise we never could have carried on, for she spoke Serbian, Russian, German, French and English equally fluently; she had the heart of a lion, and the infinite tenderness of a woman for the sick and suffering. She had been terrified that we would not want her, and pathetically relieved when we made her one of us. She stuck to us all through the horrible time that came later; she nearly died in our service; we fought for her life, and saved it. She is dead now, but none of us still alive will ever forget Esther Kadish.

At first there was no time to go round the hospitals. Patients came to the dressing-tables or were carried there. If they did not come again we presumed they had died. For every day as we went into No. 1 Hospital we could see ten to twenty bodies laid out on stretchers, each wrapped in a blanket with a candle burning at his head. They were men from Northern Serbia with no one to mourn them, simply numbers on a casualty list.

The pressure of work was so great we hardly had time to think. Once I opened a huge abscess in a man's armpit, but in doing so, unfortunately, I also opened an arteriovenous aneurysm behind it which spurted blood violently in my face. I plugged the big cavity hastily with iodoform gauze, stopped the hæmorrhage, bandaged the man up, sent him away on his stretcher and started on the next case. Next day he was not brought again, so I was quite sure he had died. A fortnight later he was once more brought to the table. No dressing had been done in the interval. I loosened the stinking bandages very, very gingerly. Nothing happened. There was a good granulating wound, obviously healing.

I said to the Little Red Woman:

"Why is it that some patients come on stretchers daily and some, like this man, not for a fortnight?"

She flared up angrily.

"It is the bolnitchers. If they do not get tips from the patients they will not bring them. And so they die. It is awful."

I was shocked, but could do nothing, for no supervision was possible until we could start hospital rounds. And every time we thought we could start these rounds a fresh train-load of walking-wounded would be dumped on us from the front. The men poured in daily and the numbers never seemed to lessen, for as soon as they had a night's rest lying in the straw in their billets in disused mosques, gymnasia and school buildings, they were sent on south and new train-loads arrived from the north.

It seemed unending, and it went on for six weeks. Then suddenly it lessened; and we were able to do rounds at last and pay bed visits.

We heard the Serbs had gained an immense victory and had captured 90,000 Austrian prisoners; but we had been so plugged with propaganda we didn't believe it. It was true all the same. There had been a great victory. Whole Czech regiments had deserted the Austrians and marched over to the Serbs, complete with regimental bands and equipment. Luckily we did not know then what those ninety thousand prisoners were also bringing us; and we were happy.

We had managed to get a theatre going; we were able to visit our patients in their beds. We had learnt enough Serbian to be able to ask simple questions; and we were now able to do some major surgery. It was mainly amputations for septic compound fractures, and ligaturing arteries for secondary hæmorrhage. I never thought when I was doing operative surgery for the Fellowship that I should have to use any of the set operations except on the rarest occasions. For the surgery we were doing was the surgery of the Napoleonic Wars. We were ligaturing subclavians or brachials or femorals, popliteals or posterior tibial arteries, or doing the classical amputations we had learnt out of books.

Amongst the Austrian prisoners recently captured were a large number of trained medical orderlies, infinitely better than the ignorant bolnitchers we had been depending on. Many of them were Czechs, for the Czechs were then Austrian citizens; a good many had been to the United States and could speak American English. Some two hundred were allotted to us. They were disciplined men and made excellent orderlies. We gave our St. John's orderlies sergeant's rank and allotted twenty men to each. And so we really got going. Christmas came. Everyone went about cheerfully saying "Christ is born, Christ is born", after the Serbian manner.

At the turn of the year the work suddenly slackened. The fighting had died down. The Austrian defeat had been even greater than we had guessed. We were now able to examine and treat our cases with something resembling deliberation. We actually could operate at our leisure.

There was quite a lot of relapsing fever in the hospital, but we just had to ignore that. Some of the orderlies got it and recovered completely. One of the medical officers unfortunately got three attacks one after the other, and we had to send him home. But when our unit began to get diphtheria and smallpox it became more serious. Still we were not alarmed. We could cope with these also.

And then we began to hear disquieting rumours about mysterious illnesses amongst the prisoners. Still nothing happened in our hospital to worry us.

Then one day I had an Austrian sergeant brought up for dressing on whom I had done a double amputation the day before. When my orderly took off the dressing I saw something—something that filled me with horror. It was a rash. I knew that rash. I'd seen it in Connemara. The rumour was true. There was typhus fever in the P.O.W. camp. I had been told there were twenty cases already at the Polymesis —the fever hospital in the town. But the Serbs call relapsing fever 'teephoose', and typhoid 'teephoose', and typhus 'teephoose', so deliberately I had shut my eyes and banked on this ambiguity.

My patient had typhus, and he was in my hospital. I knew there must be hundreds of contacts already from him in our overcrowded wards. I knew also that fifty per cent of our patients would get it and twenty-five per cent would probably die. It was clear our unit could hardly hope to escape and almost certainly some of us would die.

We stopped operating. And then the trouble fell on us. My own special orderly, Edwardes, whom I particularly liked because he was so kind, so gentle with the patients, so absolutely dependable—Edwardes got it. We isolated him in the gate-house of the nunnery where we were quartered. We put a special orderly on to him. We did everything we could, with our chief physician in charge and Banks in consultation. He lived for seventeen days; he ought to have pulled through but he did not.

The Serbs gave him a military funeral, complete with band playing

the dead march, and a salvo over the open grave. The Serb Commandant made a funeral oration over him which the Little Red
Woman said was beautiful. I wept like a child.

He was the first.

More followed until out of the original twelve orderlies we were
down to eight. The doctors began next. The first was Benbow, one
of our physicians. When he became delirious he was full of the most
dangerous delusions, hid a Kruger pistol under his pillow and tried to
use it. Holmes got it next. This was almost inevitable. He was our
chief physician. He too became delirious. He thought his head was
coming off, and somehow managed to get a heavy chain and padlock
from somewhere, which he hung round his neck to keep it on.

We borrowed Sister Fry, a nurse from the Lady Paget Mission. She
was an old friend of mine from West London Hospital days, who
volunteered to come to us in our extremity. It was a most courageous
thing to do, for we were naturally treated as pariahs. Then the Little
Red Woman got infected and refused blankly to come into our
quarters to be nursed. We pointed out to her that our quarters were
already infected and carried her in by force. Then she broke down and
wept with relief. More orderlies got it. We put them in tents in the
garden of the nunnery. I think that saved three from death.

All attempts by military and civil authorities to conceal the cause
of the spreading epidemic had now been stopped. Up to this time
they had refused to acknowledge the cause; but by now everyone knew
we were in the throes of an immense epidemic of typhus.

Historically it is a disease that has always swept over Europe in the
wake of war, killing millions more than fire and sword. We knew
there was no way of avoiding it. Typhus, the scourge of the Middle
Ages, the decimator of Germany in the Thirty Years War, the enemy
that helped frost and dysentery to annihilate Napoleon's army in the
retreat from Moscow, the enemy that practically finished the Crimean
War, the Morbus Hungaricus that always lurks in the Balkans, had
fallen upon us.

It is a disease we never see in England now. But it was rampant in
the eighteenth century; and the memory of its devastating power is
perpetuated in the custom still prevalent at the Old Bailey, where the
Judge of Assize is presented at the beginning of each session with a

bunch of sweet-smelling herbs—now only a ceremony but one which was supposed to protect his predecessors from the fever carried into the Court by the wretched prisoners in the time of the early Georges.

The Austrian prisoners amongst whom it started died in thousands. From them it spread to the civil population. The hospitals filled. Nurses and doctors caught it and died. People died unattended in their homes. They died in the trains fleeing South. They died in the streets of the towns. It is said that over a million people were infected.

Presently Banks and I were left with five orderlies. The number of victims was still great but the death-rate was falling a little.

We had stopped operating now for some time, and were able to discharge such of our surgical cases as had recovered and escaped infection.

Banks and I were therefore idle. So I transformed myself into a physician; and, after much bickering, was given the Military Cadet Barracks to run as a typhus hospital, with a hundred Austrian orderlies to do the nursing. This was a great improvement on my tobacco factory hospital. Sister Fry came as matron and she and I worked together.

Banks remained at our old hospital looking after the surgical cases that still had the disease. He also took care of our doctors, Benbow, Holmes and the Little Red Woman, all of them, luckily, recovering.

At this juncture a London consultant, Dr. R. O. Moon, Physician to the National Hospital for Heart Diseases, arrived in Skoplje, and he came to see me, full of enthusiasm. He was a man of about fifty with a smartly trimmed grey beard; and I told him at his age I did not think he should risk treating typhus. This annoyed him extremely as he was a man of very Spartan habits who never wore an overcoat, winter or summer, and prided himself on his physical fitness. So he went away in high dudgeon and offered his services to the Serb authorities. They promptly gave him the Polymesis Hospital, where the two previous doctors, both Greeks, had died of typhus.

He took over. It was an extremely brave thing to do at his age. Three weeks later, however, I was called to see him. He was delirious and did not recognise me. I took him into my hospital and looked after him. Eventually he recovered, but his memory from fourteen days after his arrival in Skoplje until well into convalescence was completely blank, and when we met in London years later he could not remember me.

I found indeed this was characteristic of the disease—an almost total amnesia covering the period of the attack. Dr. Holmes, Dr. Benbow, and several of the orderlies could not remember quite a lot of queer things I told them they had done.

The only doctors of our unit now working were Banks and myself, and we were both tired and depressed. Any day we knew the rash might come out on us. We used to smear our bodies with a mixture of 'Vaseline' and paraffin oil to keep the lice off us; and to this I attribute the fact that we both came through unscathed. For, though we did not know it then, the disease is carried by lice.

But by this time I began to feel I could not go on much longer. In the hope that I might get help from our No. 2 Red Cross Mission, which had been posted to Vernjatskabanya, I took three days off, travelled to Nish and got through to our unit and the James Berry Mission. But they could not let me have any nurses or any of the hospital equipment I so badly needed. The work they were doing fully occupied them.

I came back to my Barracks Hospital still more depressed and carried on. In the meantime, however, the Lady Paget Mission, which was also working in Skoplje, had decided to tackle typhus because there was no surgery left to do. Lady Paget herself took over another barracks across the campus from us, turned half the staff into a typhus-fighting unit and busied herself getting her barracks scrubbed out and disinfected. Just when she was ready to start, however, she too got typhus and came into my hospital.

It was now the end of February, and the almond trees came out in blossom. Spring was with us, and with spring quite suddenly the number of admissions began to decline, less and less arrived, and we actually had a few spare beds.

The epidemic was declining, and we ceased to be overworked.

Holmes and the Little Red Woman were convalescing and developing enormous appetites. So too was Benbow, the first victim amongst the doctors. They all came up to my windswept hospital to recuperate. We felt happier.

But of course we were all very tired. I had come out to Serbia

Elliott and Fry

The author, Senior Captain Serbian Army (1914-15)

General Sir Edmund Allenby, G.C.M.G., K.C.B.

weighing twelve stone. I found I was now only 8 st. 4 lb. and could not eat. I asked Banks, who had little to do, to take over from me for a few days, and began to think. It was the first time for months I'd been able to do so.

As it happened, a fresh unit from the Serbian Relief Fund in London had just arrived, full of enthusiasm, very eager to be of use, and they offered to take on our work. I suppose they saw we were about done and pretty useless. It was obvious, moreover, the epidemic was petering out. I knew that none of our doctors who had had typhus would be fit for any hard work for months. Our contract with the Red Cross was up, but I understood they would extend it if we wished. So I put it to the five orderlies, out of the original twelve of our unit, who were left. They all said they wanted to go home. None of them wished to sign on again. The unit as a driving force was dead. The men were tired. We were all tired. So I handed over thankfully to the Serbian Relief Fund and made arrangements to leave.

A lot of people came to see us off. I could not sleep in the *wagon-lit*. I could not believe it was all over. At the frontier a smart Serbian officer came in to see me. He was very spick and span, very bright and cheery.

"Will you come back to Serbie?" he asked, politely.

"Perhaps," I answered, "next year."

"Ah. A year's time. It will be all over then. In two months the Russians will be in Buda Pesth."

How little he knew. How little I knew. How little anyone knew. For that conversation was in March, 1915.

*

Fourteen days later we were in London; and I went to report to Sir Frederick Treves at the Combined Headquarters of the British Red Cross and the Order of St. John of Jerusalem. He listened with amazement to my story, for nothing of the epidemic had been allowed to pass the censorship because the Serbs feared they might be invaded if it was known they were so defenceless.

Treves stared at me as I talked. When I had finished he said:

"This is most important. The D.G. (Director-General Army Medical Service) must hear of it."

F

So I repeated the whole grim story to Sir Alfred Keogh at the War Office. He listened intently, cross-examined me closely and then sent a message which brought a Staff Colonel into the room.

Again I went over the same story to the three quiet men, who sat gazing at me, thin, drawn and weary in my battered Red Cross uniform.

I did not know then that I was repeating my story to Kitchener's Military Secretary. But in 1919, when it was all over, Treves told me that the War Office had almost decided to send an expeditionary force up from Salonika into Serbia, and might have done so if it had not been for the epidemic. But the risk was too great. If they had, it is possible the Bulgars would not have come in on the German side, the Germans then would not have been able to go to the aid of the Turks, Gallipoli would have been unnecessary and the campaigns in Mesopotamia and Palestine radically altered—another example of how disease can change the course of history.

*

CHAPTER XI

LONDON AND THE R.A.M.C.

A MONTH AFTER I GOT HOME I joined the R.A.M.C. There was no question now of not wanting the services of people like me. Kitchener had told the optimists very bluntly that it would be a four-year war; and the sobering experience of the retreat from Mons, the fighting on the Marne and the Ypres salient had underlined his prophecy.

I was now a Lieutenant, R.A.M.C., a two-pipper liable to be sent anywhere at home or overseas, as and when required. My duty and the duty of people like me was to report every morning at ten a.m. to the Adjutant at Queen Alexandra's Military Hospital, Millbank, London S.W.1.

Our names were called out, we answered, and then we were dismissed with an injunction to report again at ten a.m. next day. All this was new to me and seemed silly. It wasn't, of course. We were a pool of able-bodied men passed as fit for foreign service, available on twenty-four hours' notice for posting anywhere the British Army required us. And each day some of us were taken out of the pool and sent abroad to France, Malta, Egypt, East Africa, Mesopotamia, India, anywhere. Nothing happened to me for a month. And then one day I was sent for by Colonel Pilcher, the Professor of Military Surgery and the chief surgeon at Millbank. He asked me what were the ribbons I was wearing. I told him they were Serbian. I didn't know then I had no right to wear them without War Office permission; but nobody had bothered about me, and my ignorance was my protection.

It brought me, however, to Colonel Pilcher's notice and he gave me some work to do in the wards. And thus began a friendship that lasted all our lives. I think Pilcher must have judged me fairly shrewdly. I wasn't really fit. I was jumpy. I wasn't reliable for major surgery. I had been through too much. So he nursed me back into competence. I did nothing but dressings for at least two months. He gave me odd jobs to do: visiting convalescent homes run by society ladies in their country houses, going down to Woolwich to pass surgical instruments for use in the Army, examining men who had been recommended for commissions. After that he allowed me to operate. I was given charge of the Officers' Block. That got me into trouble. Some of the patients were Guardsmen or high staff officers, and when their relatives came to question me anxiously about them they used to look rather surprisedly at my two-pip sleeve. That hadn't bothered me, but it did them. They thought their sons, brothers, nephews were being looked after by a raw junior officer, and began to demand consultations with Harley Street. That did not annoy me. Actually in this way I met several of the great men of the profession whom I hadn't previously known. The greatest of these was Sir Robert Jones, who made the War Office adopt Thomas's splint for compound fractured femurs and thus reduced the mortality from this calamity from eighty to twenty per cent. Sir Robert was a delight. He had that wonderful combination, greatness with humility.

Another such was Robert Scot Skirving, the grand old man of Sydney, N.S.W. He and I successfully extracted a bullet out of a man's heart. It is a story I have told elsewhere, and its success was then a four-day wonder until the victim died of pneumonia and robbed us of victory.

Often, doing my rounds, when I heard someone complaining, I used to pinch myself to make sure I was seeing what I was seeing, the contrast with what I had so recently been experiencing was so unbelievable: clean linen, clean bandages, clean bodies, the long spacious wards with polished floors, windows that opened, temperature charts, diet sheets and nurses—real nurses—all the things I had taken for granted before the war and had since almost forgotten still existed.

One evening a big convoy arrived from France. Amongst the patients was a sergeant with multiple shrapnel wounds. At Millbank we had an elaborate X-ray plant which took photos of the bullets and showed exactly where they were. So next day, with the patient under an anæsthetic, I looked at the X-ray in the theatre, made my incisions, inserted a telephone probe that made a bell ring when it touched metal, and extracted the shrapnel bullets. When I had finished, I had a mental flashback to Skoplje and my unbelievably septic hospital, where I used to feel for the bullets with my fingers and cut them out, ten, fifteen, twenty times a day, without any anæsthetic at all.

One evening a patient was admitted to the Officers' Wing of whom even the sister seemed to be in awe. He was put in my charge and I was given special instructions concerning him.

"What's the fuss about? He's only a colonel. You didn't make so much ado about General X. last week," I said.

"Ah, yes. But this is one of the Military Secretaries," I was told.

Before he left he said to me:

"Why are you only a lieutenant?"

"Well," I said, "we all join as lieutenants, no matter who we are. We're paid twenty-four shillings a day, and, if we behave ourselves, I'm told we're made captains after a year. I've only been three months in the Service."

A week later Colonel Pilcher sent for me.

"You've been promoted captain," he said. "It's in the Orders for the Day. I think it's the doing of the Military Secretary. But," he added dryly, "you don't get any more pay. You're still on twenty-four shillings a day."

I laughed at this, but I was pleased all the same. I went to my tailor and had the sleeves of my uniform altered, for in 1915 we wore the badges of our rank on the sleeves like the Navy. It was the fact that this made officers conspicuous and exposed them to sharpshooters, with dire results in France, which forced the later alteration to shoulder badges only.

The hospital had been named after Queen Alexandra, and the Queen Mother, therefore, always took a special interest in the place. Every now and then we would get a message that she and the Princess Victoria intended to pay us a visit. The old lady was rather deaf, and somehow it was noted that I could make her hear without shouting; so it became the rule that, no matter what I was doing, if the Queen came I was to be there with the Commandant to take her round.

Once a week I was orderly officer and had to sleep in the hospital at Millbank. It was the period of the Zeppelin raids, which then seemed so devastating, but now, with our later and grimmer experiences, appear so trivial. When a raid was on, the orderly officer had to go as quickly as possible to the Horse Guards Parade Headquarters of the G.O.C., London Area, to the little room just inside the gate to the left from Whitehall, where the Duke of Wellington used to have his office.

Nothing ever did happen at the Horse Guards, but on one of these raids, when the guns were going and I was on duty, the General's wife rang me up on the phone to ask me to make sure the General was wearing his underpants. His language when I had the temerity to repeat the order was unprintable.

Month after month passed. Men came to Millbank, reported for a week or so, and then disappeared into the blue; but I was still there. By now I had completely recovered from the nightmare of Serbia. I had been made a surgical specialist and given complete freedom by Colonel Pilcher. And I was quite happy, except when occasionally I went out in mufti and some giggling young girl handed me a white feather. But after a while I got restless. I began to wonder why I was not being sent abroad when obviously I was available for foreign service. So one day I tackled the Adjutant, Major Owen.

"Oh," he said, in an aggrieved tone, "I thought you knew. Every time your name comes to the top of the roster, and you're due to go, the Colonel says he can't spare you and tells me to put you to the bottom again. You remember he got you promoted captain when you'd been only three months in the Service. He said you were the only officer he had with first-hand knowledge of war surgery. And, of course, that is true, for none of the fellows we get here have yet seen active service. That promotion of yours was quite irregular. I don't think the War House will stand his interference much longer."

And in this he was quite right. The War Office didn't. On May 11th, 1916, in spite of my Colonel's protests, I was detailed for duty in Egypt as surgical specialist to a stationary hospital. But to placate my Colonel, and to the great annoyance of the Adjutant, I was promoted major.

"It's preposterous," said the Adjutant. "Here you are, a field officer with just one year's service—the same rank as myself after fifteen years of it. Can't think how you've done it."

"Bribery and corruption, Major," I explained.

He laughed. "Oh, go to blazes!"

So I said farewell to Millbank, reported at Aldershot, had lodgings for three or four days in a house run by a sergeant's wife, and then found myself on a hospital ship at Portsmouth, outward bound for Alexandria.

We were sailing under sealed orders not to be known until we reached Egypt; but an R.A.M.C. corporal returning to his unit, which was stationed at Port Said, told us we were the 24th Stationary Hospital. I paid no heed to this. It seemed too absurd that he should know when our Colonel, who was travelling with us, did not know. But he was right, as it turned out. We were the 24th Stationary Hospital. The grape-vine had worked, and the elaborate security arrangements, futile and unnecessary anyhow, had failed.

We were under the command of Lieutenant-Colonel E. D. Powell, R.A.M.C., a regular officer. We had one Territorial medical officer as Adjutant. The rest were temporary officers; and the personnel, 120 rank and file, made up the complement.

The ship was returning to Egypt to bring back more sick and wounded, so we were travelling light, carrying nurses, other medical officers and some Army Chaplains—all people protected theoretically by the Geneva Convention. All the same we travelled with dimmed lights, and with paravanes in the water swinging wide from our bows to push off floating mines should we encounter them.

We didn't. Our journey was quite uneventful; and I can now remember nothing much except a trivial comment made by one of the chaplains about me. It's odd what unimportant things one does remember after forty years. I had a rather beautiful silk dressing-gown which I wore going to and from the bathroom.

One morning as I was returning I overheard one of the padres say:

"Look at the Major! Fancy anyone going to a war front with a thing like that. He can't know anything about war conditions."

A few days later I gave a talk on Serbia and typhus in the saloon. I could see the padre's face getting redder and redder, for he knew I had overheard him.

But he was a good fellow. He came and apologised to me next morning.

"I'm sorry, Major. I should have remembered St. Matthew, Chapter Seven: 'Judge not, that ye be not judged,' " he said.

CHAPTER XII

EGYPT AND THE SINAI DESERT

WE PASSED MALTA without calling, and arrived at Alexandria on May 28th, 1916. There, for the first time, I felt we were part of the machinery of war. We landed under the instructions of the M.L.O. The Colonel took the head of the column, we lined up behind him. Sergeant-Major Debney barked out the words of command, and we marched along the cobbles of the landing-stage to the railway station, where the R.T.O. took charge of us. We were ordered to the transit camp at Sidi Bishra, which is on the coast of the Mediterranean about five miles from Alexandria, near the bay of Aboukir, where Nelson defeated the French fleet in 1798 and in consequence Napoleon's dream of carving for himself an Empire in the East faded away.

I have unhappy memories of Sidi Bishra. The catering was in the hands of Alexandrine Greeks, and we all got the common complaint, 'Gippy tummy', a type of acute diarrhoea, which newcomers to Egypt seemed to get with monotonous regularity. It was probably not the fault of the caterers, but we blamed it on them, and were most unhappy for the next two days.

Just when we were beginning to think life worth living again, however, and had begun to explore Alexandria and join bathing parties in the warm Mediterranean, we were suddenly ordered to entrain at Sidi Gaber for Moascar.

I remember nothing of that journey except seeing a lonely little graveyard, with white tombstones surrounded by iron railings, in the middle of the desert as we approached the Suez Canal. This was the burial ground of the men who fell at the battle of Tel el Kebir in 1882, when Sir Garnet Wolseley defeated Arabi Pasha's army and we took the Khedive and Egypt under our protection. This lonely graveyard struck me as pathetic. None of the men with me knew anything about the battle. Actually it was no credit to me that I did. My family had some distant connection with General Gordon, and I had been brought up on the story of Egypt and the Sudan.

Eventually we arrived at Moascar, a military camp just outside Ismailia on the west of the Sweetwater Canal. It was a deadly place. We found we were taking over from No. 1 New Zealand Stationary Hospital, which had been detailed for service in France. It was a 400-stretcher-bedded tented hospital, well laid out, but very primitive in its comforts. Its great merit to us, however, was that it had adopted sanitation by incineration instead of the horrible trench latrine. We carried on this technique, and later proved its immense value all through the campaign in Sinai and Palestine.

All around us were tented transit camps where whole brigades marched in, stayed a few days and marched out again, leaving their tents standing for the next arrivals to use.

At night under the Egyptian moon a band outside some Brigade H.Q. would play 'God Save the King', and we near-by in our mess tent would stand up. Then another brigade band and perhaps yet another would start up and we'd stand again. Eventually the Colonel said:

"Stand up for the first we hear, but not after."

We did that but we always felt a bit guilty about it.

The only permanent camp was that of the Second Australian Light Horse, which lay between us and the Sweetwater Canal. So, apart from casuals, all our patients came from them. They were a wild lot. Their chief term of endearment was to call each other "bastard". They offered to lend us horses to ride and, when two of us accepted innocently, the men stood round to watch us mount. I hadn't ridden a horse for years, and thought I'd struck a cyclone. Actually it was a buck-jumper and I was shot unceremoniously over its head. So too was McDonald. The troopers standing round hooted with laughter, and it suddenly dawned on us it was a plant. That was enough for me but not for McDonald.

He tried again and got thrown again, twice. That turned their laughter to admiration of his pluck. They gave us peaceable mounts ever after.

But they were really grand fellows. I have no grouse against the

Second Australian Light Horse. Once I admitted one of their officers for a minor operation. His batman came to see me and asked if he might nurse his officer. I said:

"No. It is quite against regulations. Patients can be nursed only by R.A.M.C. trained orderlies."

He looked at me pathetically. He was an oldish man; he hesitated a moment, and then said:

"Please, Major, he's my son. I joined up only to look after him. Can I?"

That got me. To think of anyone joining up as a private to look after his officer son was too much. I broke all the regulations and said:

"Yes. Under the circumstances you certainly can!"

All around our hospital for miles and miles right to the limit of the horizon westwards there was nothing but sand and sand and yet more sand. But to the east we could see a mile away the palm trees, the green foliage and the white houses of Ismailia. We were connected with it by a track made of railway sleepers which led to a bridge over the Sweetwater Canal, and so into the town. Out in the desert were about a dozen dummy planes to deceive the enemy should they fly over. To the south-east of our camp was Lake Timsah, one of the Bitter Lakes through which the Suez Canal runs.

For over two months we sweltered in the heat doing practically nothing. But for me it turned out to be one of the most valuable training periods of my life.

At Millbank I had learnt nothing about soldiering. I had dodged the parade outside the hospital, where every morning at ten a.m. recruits were drilled. I might just as well have been a civilian coming in daily. But here it was a different matter. Our Adjutant had had to be invalided home. There was no one to take his place, so, as second in command, I had to learn about drill, discipline, pay and promotion; I had to run the canteen, sit as chairman of invaliding boards, take kit inspections, all the routine work that devolves on an officer of field rank. Feeling horribly ignorant I read doggedly through King's Regulations, that inestimable collection of wise information on everything military.

I had practically no surgery to do. It was a wonderful opportunity to educate myself, which proved of immense value to me later.

My Colonel was efficient but lazy. He gave me a free hand, and when I got bogged and asked his advice he was always most helpful. He knew all the ropes and all the snags. For some reason, however, he had a horror of inspections by superior officers and, whenever we were visited by 'brass hats', pushed me forward to take them round.

I thus met Sir Archibald Murray, the G.O.C., General Altham of the Levant Base, and our own D.M.S., Surgeon-General Maher.

When Murray inspected the hospital I took him round the wards. He picked up the temperature sheet of one patient.

"I see," he said, with a cold, sarcastic smile, "you don't keep your charts very up-to-date. This is the fifteenth of the month. You've charted him to the tenth only."

I looked at the chart he handed me.

"Sorry, sir. It's the tenth day of the disease, not the date of the month," I answered.

He made no further comment, but he did not apologise. That's why he failed to get the devotion from his Army that Allenby obtained so easily.

Major-General Altham came round later to inspect. A few days before, I had operated on a case of acute cholecystitis (gall bladder inflammation). This patient was the first real case I'd had since Millbank. He was a big, fat sergeant and the heat was so great in the tent that we operated with nothing on, naked except for our surgical gowns. We had no female nurses then.

The operation was a complete success, and I was rather proud of it. But when I took Altham to see him and told him I'd done it he was very angry.

"You had no right to do such an operation in the field. He should have been sent back to Cairo," he said.

Of course, theoretically, he was right. I recognised that later. But I had not then grasped this from the military standpoint, and so I was much deflated. The fact that he probably would have died if I'd sent him on didn't matter to Altham. It was the principle.

General Maher, the D.M.S., did not trouble to do a formal inspection; but on his way back from Advanced G.H.Q. to Cairo he paid us a courtesy call. Our Colonel was much more afraid of him than of the G.O.C. He pushed me forward to entertain him.

"He's another Irishman. You handle him," he said.

Maher was a tall, lanky man with a tired, humorous face. I liked him straight away.

When he heard my name, he said:

"Oh, yes. I know about you. Pilcher wrote to me. Let me see. Didn't you write *The Night Nurse*?"

"Yes, sir, one of my sins, for which I hope to be forgiven!" I answered.

*

It was at this time that I learnt the inestimable value of good N.C.O.s. Our Company Sergeant-Major, Debney, was a particularly competent one. As I have mentioned, we were tented for 400 trestle beds. The hospital was well laid out, but the tents were showing signs of needing repair.

All around us was the tentage of the transit camps, often empty for weeks. As a consequence we could see collapsed tents lying on the sand, every now and again, quite close.

One morning when the Sergeant-Major and I were doing an inspection round, he said:

"There's a marquee down on the sand over there, sir. That won't do it any good. Don't you think we ought to pick it up 'for Ordnance'?"

I looked at him. His face was solemn. He didn't bat an eyelid.

"Hm, yes, Sergeant-Major. An excellent idea," I said, equally solemnly.

So we rescued it, and put it up temporarily to keep the canvas from deteriorating.

A few days later we rescued another. Then we began to look out for special tents that ought to be rescued when they fell.

And then later still we used to slip out at night and slacken guy ropes, to find to our surprise in the morning that some particular E.P.I.P. or other special tent had fallen in the night and ought to be rescued.

In this way by the end of July, 1916, we had tentage to cover another 800; and with the extra trestle beds we were able to obtain from Ordnance we brought our capacity up to 1,200.

The Colonel must have known all about this, but said nothing.

*

Sanitation in the desert was looked after by a then newly-devised Army unit, a 'Sanitary Section'. This was a Territorial idea, adopted by the Regular Army only in 1914. It consisted of an officer, generally a doctor, some N.C.O.s and men, with Egyptian Labour Corps personnel attached. The unit saw to the sanitary arrangements of any new camp, instructed the camp sanitary squad how to carry on and then left them to it, returning only to inspect when there was trouble.

No transport arrangements in Egypt had been made at first for the officer commanding one of these Sanitary Sections. He had no horse, no motor of his own. It was a hot, tiresome job plodding through desert sand in the blazing sun, inspecting camps and criticising the sanitary arrangements, often to the annoyance of the O.C., who thought he was being interfered with.

One day a tired and very weary sanitary officer came to see me, reporting sick. He was, I should think, well over forty. He looked done.

"What's your name?" I said.

"Eastes," he answered.

"Not Eastes of Eastes's Laboratory?"

"Yes, that's me," he said, surprised.

"Well, I'm damned! I live next door to you in New Cavendish Street, and it's the first time I've ever set eyes on you. What do they mean giving you a job any sanitary inspector could do?"

"It was all right," he answered, "until my heart began to give. I'm afraid I can't go on."

I took him into the Officers' Ward, sent him to bed, and then examined him. His heart was fibrillating.

"Would you like me to Board you, and send you home?"

He looked at me eagerly. "Could you?"

"Of course I can. You're a sick man, and anyhow you're wasted here in such an elementary job."

So I Boarded him.

Eastes was a well-known pathologist who had a private laboratory in the Harley Street area which did tests for the patients of consultants.

And Eastes did not forget me. After the war, when I got back, anything he could send to me, he did. We remained friends until his death, years later.

Punctuated by little episodes like this that I remember, life went on monotonously.

We sweltered uncomfortably in the heat until we found it was a good thing to take everything off and sleep in our tents from two to four p.m. each afternoon. There was only one water point in the camp. We made friends with the Sappers and got this altered. Our bully beef melted in the hot tins and was quite horrible until we had ice sent to us daily from Port Said as medical stores.

Gradually we began to make ourselves more and more comfortable.

War seemed very far away. There was fighting going on in the Western Desert against the Senussi; but the Turk on the borders of Palestine, far away across the Sinai Desert, seemed too distant to be any danger. The land between Port Said and Kantara had been flooded on the east side by breaching the Canal bank. We had a bridge-head further south of revetted trenches and barbed wire ten miles out, also on the east side of the Canal. It was especially strong opposite Ismailia where the Turks had failed to cross in February, 1915. And this was considered sufficient to keep raiding parties from trying to block the Canal. No one expected the Turk to try to cross the Sinai Desert again, as he had done so disastrously fifteen months previously, when he thought the Egyptians would rise in revolt as soon as his troops reached the Canal.

That then was the state of affairs when one day we were lounging round in the mess tent having our usual elevenses, which meant tea and tea and still more tea—and you've got to soldier in the desert to know how delectable tea really is. It was August 4th, 1916, and nothing, absolutely nothing, seemed to be happening.

Suddenly the Staff-Sergeant appeared at the mess tent door, and came straight to the Colonel.

"Message, sir, from G.H.Q., Ismailia."

The Colonel took it.

"Great Scot!" he exclaimed, after he had glanced through it hurriedly, "the Turks attacked at Romani yesterday and we're to take in one thousand wounded from Kantara West. They're coming by train forthwith."

That woke us up with a vengeance. Suddenly we were all cheerful. There was work to do.

Kress von Kressenstein, the German Commander-in-Chief, had tried again. The Turk was on his toes after Townshend's surrender at Kut in Mesopotamia, and he was making for Ismailia and the Canal once more.

We were all very excited as the first train-load of several hundred weary men was dumped on us. Many of them were walking-wounded. Most were just men utterly worn out by marching and fighting in the exhausting heat over a terrain of soft sand, where troops could not move more than a mile an hour. They were dead weary, and all we had to do was put them to bed and give them cold drinks.

In the middle of the hustle the D.M.S., General Maher, arrived with his A.D.M.S., Colonel Keble. They were very, very worried, for General Maher had taken up command only two months before.

"We didn't anticipate this," he said. "What are we going to do? You're a four-hundred-bedded unit. You'll have at least a thousand more casualties coming in."

My Colonel looked cautiously at me.

"Sir," I said to the General, "we can accommodate twelve hundred comfortably and fifteen hundred at a push. We've got tentage for them all."

He stared at me incredulously and swung round to the Colonel. The Colonel nodded. Relief broke over the General's face. Suddenly he laughed and smacked his hand on his thigh.

"You have, have you! I won't ask how you've done it. If I did I'd probably have to court-martial the lot of you," he said.

He never mentioned it again, but he never forgot. We had saved his reputation for preparedness.

*

War surgery is not like surgery in civil life. It comes in bursts of intensive activity with periods of extreme quietude. Our war with the Turks was what we called a 'gentleman's war', such as the old regular British Army was used to, and liked. We made an attack on an average every three months. If we won we advanced. If not we tried again three months later, and we had no disastrous retreats or defeats.

After Romani I can remember little for some months except that we made the hospital more and more comfortable. Occasionally one or other of us got off on week-end leave to Cairo, putting up at Shepheard's, from whose balcony one could see the multi-coloured life of the East—for Cairo, not Baghdad is the real home of the Arabian Nights.

Every time we stopped at Shepheard's we were told we must write in the hotel register our names, rank, unit and location. This we did religiously until it was discovered that it gave the enemy spy system complete and accurate information about all the units in the Canal Zone. It was supposed to be a check on unofficial leave, and was just one of those stupidities of the official mind. The lists went weekly from Port Said to Cyprus, from where they were easily smuggled across to the enemy in Asia Minor. It was a year before this was found out and stopped.

Oily gentlemen, too, used to come down from Cairo for a bit, visiting messes and offering the mess-presidents whisky, wine, tinned fruits, and things of that sort, more cheaply than they could buy them officially. That too had to be stopped after we had fallen for it for some time.

It was difficult for us to realise quite a bit that the Egyptians didn't in the least love us, as we fondly imagined. We thought because we'd done so much for them they must. It was just our innocence.

To keep our unit amused I started a journal which we called *The Sandy Chronicle*. It ran for three months before we got too busy to continue.

Ismailia was only a mile away and there were still many French employees of the Suez Canal Company there, with their wives and children living in the town. Once I was called in by the French doctor, M. Camboulin, to see a lady with appendicitis whom he had been treating with ice packs, until she developed an iliac abscess. The request came through G.H.Q., and I was told to go in uniform wearing a sword. Accordingly I borrowed a sword and so went, duly armed. When I appeared M. le Docteur Camboulin looked at me quizzically and suggested with a twinkle that the sword was obviously "*pour défendre ma vertu contre la nourrice"* as it could not be of any possible use for operating purposes. He was a charming old gentleman, thirty years behind the times; but we got on well together, especially when the patient recovered after the operation.

For the benefit of the employees on the Canal Zone, the Suez Canal Company had established an excellent French Club looking out on Lake Timsah, and we were made honorary members whilst stationed in Moascar. It was very pleasant of an evening when the day's work was done, and the cool breeze blew from the lake, to sit in the open in a basket chair at a little glass-topped table, and go through an excellent menu with a bottle of wine at one's elbow, listening to a British military band playing Sullivan's music from the stand in the centre. It made war seem far off.

But of course it wasn't. Into this calm burst activity. We had orders to move in October, 1916, to Kantara on the east bank of the Canal about twenty miles from Port Said. Kantara was the place where the railway which General Murray was building across the desert began. It obviously was going to be a focal point where sick and wounded would collect, and needed much greater hospital accommodation than the 26th Casualty Clearing Station already there could provide.

The Colonel sent for me.

"I want you," he said, "to go with the advance party to Kantara, pick the site for our hospital, arrange the layout, and get on to the Works Department about hutting as quickly as you can. Report progress."

This was a lovely job. It made me not regret leaving all the work I'd done coping with the snags at Moascar, improvising improvements, learning how to extract things from Ordnance, the Army Service Corps and the Sappers.

Kantara was a small camp, vastly different from the huge base camp of 120,000 men it ultimately expanded to. The only buildings, then, were the Suez Canal offices, the old headquarters of the Sinai police, and the hangar of the aerodrome. I could choose, therefore, where I liked, so I chose a section of sand parallel and close to the railway. That meant no long carry over sand with stretcher cases when the ambulance trains arrived. Actually there were no ambulance trains, but we knew they were coming.

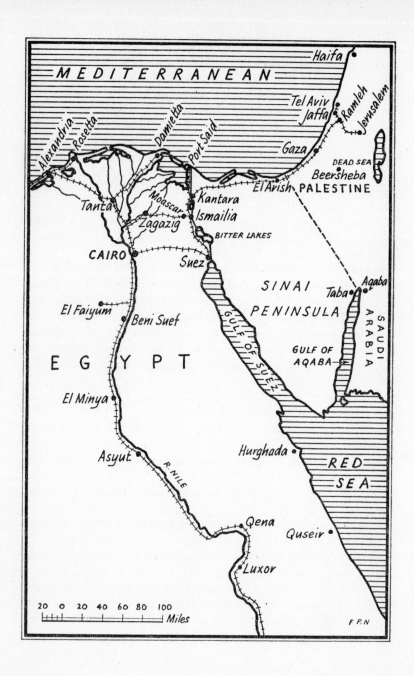

With the help of a prismatic compass, the Sergeant-Major and I laid out and pegged our site; and when the Works Department came to set up the huts for storage, the kitchens, X-ray, bacteriological laboratories, bath huts, canteen, and so on, we were only about two degrees out.

We knew all the things that were wrong with our layout of tents at Moascar, and we were thus able to plan the new 24th Stationary Hospital so that it proved to be a model for all the other hospitals we helped to build up the line in the next two years.

In November, 1916, we moved in. A month later the first two emergency hospital trains were working, and we were taking in the sick and wounded from up the line. For there was always skirmishing going on, and we had many casualties also from the effects of heat and sand and flies. Our job was to feed them, make them as comfortable as possible, and then transport them over the Canal to hospital trains waiting at the Egyptian State Railway, Kantara West, to take them to Cairo, Alexandria and perhaps with luck home to 'blighty'. It was a worthwhile job. We were really busy all the time; we had a first-rate set of N.C.O.s and men and were a very happy unit.

Some genius had just invented the wire road. This was made of two six-feet-wide rolls of rabbit-wire netting laid on the sand and pegged down to make a twelve-foot track. On this we could run an ambulance car. It was an immense improvement on the sand-carts, with slats of wood chained to the iron tyres, drawn by mules, or the camel cacolets we previously had been using. Somehow, I cannot remember how, or when, or who suggested it to us, we suddenly thought:

'Why not use wire-netting all through the hospital to make good level ward floors and paths throughout the whole area?'

We did, and the amount of ankle weariness it saved was unbelievable. I wish I knew whose brain first thought of it: for, once thought of, it was so obvious.

The one thing we were short of was water. In this we were restricted to a gallon a day per person for all purposes. That meant for cooking and drinking as well as shaving and washing. Of course it was inadequate, but water was very precious, for all our supply had to be brought from the Nile, seventy miles away. This came via the Sweetwater Canal from Cairo across to Ismailia; and from there a branch ran alongside the Suez Canal to Port Said at one end and Suez at the other, supplying both cities as well as Ismailia with water. It was called the Sweetwater Canal to distinguish it from the Suez Canal proper, and was of course on the west bank of the Suez Canal. We, however, were on the east bank, so the water intended for use at Kantara and by the troops beyond had to be pumped across below the Canal.

From Kantara, the R.E. Railway Companies were laying a twelve-inch pipe-line to carry this precious water across the Sinai Desert towards Palestine. At the same time they were constructing a standard gauge railway. When we pitched the tents of the 24th Stationary Hospital the railway had got a little beyond Romani. It grew slowly, about fifteen miles a month. And all the while the railhead, as it slowly crept across the desert, was being attacked by German aircraft and skirmishing patrols of the enemy Camel Corps.

It was hard, dangerous work, and every day there were casualties. The railway advanced faster than the water supply, so the men working on the line had to be supplied with water by camel convoy, each camel carrying two small metal tanks called 'fanati', one strapped on each side.

The heat and the flies and the scarcity of water made the troops very susceptible to injury. A scratch from barbed wire on an arm or leg soon became an ulcer that would not heal. It was what we came to call a 'desert sore', and nothing seemed to do it any good except evacuation to Egypt, where fresh food, vegetables and clean dressings rapidly produced a cure.

Life settled into a routine. G.H.Q. had moved back to Cairo after the battle of Romani. It was a bad move from the military standpoint. Brass hats living in luxury in Cairo soon began to forget. Nothing happened.

I had collected together and built up a specially comfortable set of tents as quarters for sick and wounded officers. They actually had real beds, and the men using them certainly earned them. But, anticipating that we should be inspected from time to time by some of the V.I.P.s, I felt it would be politic to set aside some E.P.I.P. tents also for them, complete with beds and electric light.

Sir Courtauld Thomson, the British Red Cross Commissioner, I remember, was one of our most welcome visitors; and I was very glad we could make him comfortable. For immediately afterwards when he went up the line he was so distressed to find the conditions so different by contrast, he told me on his return, that any Red Cross comforts he could supply we should get. That promise proved of immense value to me later when I needed his help badly. It must have saved many hundreds of lives.

It was lucky, however, that we had no visitors in March, 1917, for one morning after an intolerably hot night the sky became overcast, a hot wind blew from the south-west and the whole horizon was blotted out with driving sand. Sand in the air, sand in the tents, sand in the food, sand in one's uniform, sand everywhere, blowing continuously. It was like a furnace. We sweated and got caked with it. We swallowed it. We felt gritty in our eyes. We got irritable with each other, lost our tempers, behaved like children.

It was the 'khamsin', the hot wind blowing from the desert at this time every year, carrying tons and tons of sand on its journey. No one could do any work. It lasted nearly three days, and when we began to get about again we found some overthrown tents buried two and three feet in sand. It made me understand why the Sphinx was two-thirds under sand, and why temples and tombs were continually being discovered by Egyptologists and dug up from twenty to thirty feet underground.

By now, indeed, several of us had become bitten by the story of this ancient civilisation. The land our camp was situated in had once been part of the delta of the Nile before the mouth at Pelusium got silted up and the fertile soil reverted to desert. It is said to have been Goshen, where the Jews dwelt in captivity, and where they built the city of Pithom for Rameses II. Certainly round our camp all one had to do was to take a spade and begin to dig. In this way one unearthed bits of pottery, mostly handles of water jars, almost anywhere, and every now and again a collection of the blue beads called 'mummy beads', so frequently found in Egypt.

*

All the temporary medical officers like myself were on a yearly contract for foreign service, and this terminated early in 1917. Four of our officers had decided to resign. It was clear that none of us who remained could expect home-leave like officers in France, and we were all a little unsettled.

Things were comparatively quiet, however, over Christmas 1916, and I thought that it would be a good time to ask for leave to visit the temples in upper Egypt situated on or near the banks of the Nile. I therefore sent in my application, knowing home-leave was impossible. I chose as my companion Lieutenant C. E. O. Wood, R.E., who had been most helpful to us at Moascar. He was an ideal comrade for such an outing. Those who have read *The Seven Pillars of Wisdom* will remember he was afterwards with Lawrence of Arabia in the raids on the Mecca railway which proved so troublesome to the Turks.

On the morning after our arrival in Cairo we were sitting on the verandah at Shepheard's, revelling in the unaccustomed luxury of a leisurely breakfast, beautifully cooked and served with all the etceteras of civilisation.

"What about seeing Cairo and the Pyramids before we go south?" I said.

Wood agreed. He always agreed. That was one of his best points.

In the street below, at that time, there were generally a number of men standing about, looking up at the verandah, waiting to act as dragomans. One man smiled at me. We liked the look of him, so we took him on.

His name, he said, was George. He was a Copt. He took us round all the sights: the Citadel, the great mosques, the University of Al Azhar. But in addition we saw what the tourist seldom sees: the Coptic Christian churches hidden away obscurely so as not to tempt trouble in a Moslem world.

We were so pleased with him we engaged him next day to take us to see the Sphinx, the Pyramids, and then on to Sakkarah and back again to Shepheard's.

At the Pyramids we hired camels for the journey across the desert to Sakkarah. We were wearing spurs, and the owner of the camels was very loth to let us ride with them on. Now, when I look at my photograph taken at the Sphinx, I think how perfectly awful I must have appeared with spurs. It was ignorance, pure ignorance, as Dr. Johnson said to the lady who criticised a wrong explanation in his dictionary.

It was my first camel ride, and I found it easy for the ten miles or so to the famous Step Pyramid—much older than the great Pyramids of Gizeh, near Cairo. Here was the still more famous mausoleum, recently discovered, where the sacred bulls of Apis were buried. While we were looking in at them I heard an unmistakable English voice talking loudly and authoritatively, a voice that I came to know very well later.

"Who's that?" I said.

George, our dragoman, enquired discreetly. It was Captain Bahr (now Sir Philip Manson-Bahr), the famous expert on tropical diseases. I did not know then, nor could I have guessed, how closely we would work together in Palestine later.

After Sakkarah, Wood and I rode on to Badrashên, the railway station that would bring us back to Cairo. We gave up our camels there and boarded the train. We then made for a first-class carriage, but were hastily stopped by the guard, who ushered us back into another where two black-bearded, obviously important gentlemen with sporting guns were already sitting quietly. They scowled at us; for inadvertently we had tried to get into a carriage filled with the ladies of their harems. Clearly we were not welcome in either carriage.

Back in Cairo we had a talk with George. We told him we wanted to go up the Nile as far as the first cataract, but we would not have time to go on as far as Khartoum. He offered to take the whole responsibility off our shoulders and suggested we go by train to Luxor, then to Aswan. At Aswan he would hire a dahabiya for us, provision it, cook for us and take us back to Cairo, floating down the Nile at our leisure, stopping at temples on the way, sleeping on shore or on the boat as we wished. The idea appealed to us, and we agreed. The trains of the Egyptian State Railway are comfortable. There were no tourists, of course, as war was on; and at the Luxor Hotel there were only a few nurses on leave from Cairo.

My memory of Luxor and Karnak is vague, but I was impressed by the way so many wonderful buildings had got covered up with sand for twenty to sixty feet. It made me appreciate the power of the khamsin when buildings were neglected. Across the Nile by boat from Luxor is the Valley of the Kings. We did the journey riding up the Valley on donkeys. The great tomb of Tut-ankh-Amen with its many treasures had not then been discovered by Lord Carnarvon, but we saw enough to realise what immense riches must have been buried with these kings and queens whose tombs had been sacrilegiously broken into by robbers in later centuries for the gold and jewels they contained. Aswan and the first cataract ended our journey south.

The Temples in Philae were uncovered then, and we were glad to know they had been completely underpinned for safety, since they are covered with water when the dam is full. What I remember most vividly, however, was seeing a granite obelisk lying on its side in a quarry nearly ready for transport. It was identical with Cleopatra's Needle, formerly at Alexandria, now on the Thames Embankment. The ancient Egyptians used to cut their obelisks in this quarry at Aswan, manhandle them to the river and then send them down the Nile by raft to lower Egypt. It was most interesting to us to see the quarry from which Cleopatra's Needle, so called, had been hewn in the reign of Thothmes III, 1600 years B.C.

At Aswan we boarded our craft and drifted slowly down the Nile. We took on board enough food and, in particular, bottled Evian water to see us through. For the water of the Nile is infested by the cercaria of that dread disease 'Bilharzia hæmatobia', which makes the victim pass bloody urine, and must have been endemic in Egypt for millennia, since the eggs of the worm that causes it have been found in the mummified kidneys of the Pharaohs. I had already seen its effect on some of our troops who had been foolish enough to bathe in the Sweetwater Canal, strictly against orders. We weren't having any.

We drifted slowly down the river by day, stopped at temples near the bank, tied up at night, and gradually worked north. My memory now is of a haze of temples, but I can still remember one distinctly: it was at Denderah. And the reason I remember is that it was there we saw the sculptured portrait of Cleopatra as the goddess Hathor; and alongside it another of Cæsarion, her son by Julius Cæsar.

It was just a lazy, gentle, idyllic, floating journey with occasional landings—the sort of holiday we needed. I left Wood at Ismailia and arrived back, bright and smiling, at Kantara again, satisfied, ready to tackle another year in the desert Neither of us knew of the troubles that were coming to us. Soon afterwards Wood was posted to Aqaba, where later, as I have mentioned, he got caught up reluctantly in the whirlwinds caused by Lawrence and the Arabs. He was a quiet little man, not physically fit owing to a head wound suffered in France, but keen on his job as a constructional engineer; and it must have been very much against the grain for him to work with such a dynamic person as Lawrence, slipping down in the dark to blow up railway bridges on the line to Mecca with gelignite.

Nor did I know it was the last holiday I'd have till the war was over, that in a few months my time at the hospital would be finished, and I would be hustled into a world completely new to me.

CHAPTER XIII

*

DEFEAT AT GAZA

ALL THROUGH THE AUTUMN MONTHS the railway had been pushing forward from Kantara towards the Holy Land. The policy of defending the Canal from attack had been altered to that of driving the Turk out of Palestine. The pipe-line followed the railway, and the Imperial Camel Corps and the Anzac Mounted Division, patrolling the desert, kept the enemy at bay. It was a weary, monotonous time for the advancing infantry holding the line. The Turks were garrisoning El Arish, the town on the seashore at the end of the Wadi El Arish (the River of Egypt), which was the ancient boundary between Palestine and Egypt. Here the desert ends, there is good water and the start of arable land.

By this time I had come to the conclusion that the war might go on interminably, and so I wrote to my bankers to say I wished to give up my consulting-rooms at 79 Wimpole Street. It seemed foolish to go on paying rent when there appeared to be no visible end to the war.

My landlord was very decent about it. He offered to take half fees, but even that did not tempt me. I felt the war would go on for years, and prepared my mind to accept the consequences.

All along the route from Kantara towards Palestine there were at that time little stations, now forgotten, with names such as Ogratina, Bir el Abd, Bir el Mazar, where pumps had been erected to force the pipe-line water on. And at railhead and these stations a few medical personnel belonging to Field Ambulances or Casualty Clearing Stations were posted to load up the hospital trains, supply sanitary equipment and generally supervise things.

One day my Colonel sent for me. "I have orders from the D.M.S.," he said, "to send you up the line to Advanced G.H.Q. to collaborate with Major Bagshawe, D.A.D.M.S., G.H.Q., over the comfort of troops at intermediate stations."

"I suppose that means we're preparing to attack," I said.

"Probably," he answered.

So Bagshawe and I worked out a scheme for storing and supplying the medical comforts which Sir Courtauld Thomson gave us, ensuring that hot coffee or tea, blankets and emergency medical treatment would be available at any of these stations for sick or walking-wounded sent down in open railway trucks, after our one hospital train had been filled with serious cases. We actually had two hospital trains, but could use only one at a time—a bad arrangement, but inevitable until we doubled the line, for rations and ammunition had to take precedence over everything else.

When we advanced against El Arish the Turks evacuated it. But at Rafa, the former border town between Egypt and Palestine, and at Magdaba, they fought savagely and we captured these places only after considerable loss. We took in at our hospital 130 wounded from Magdaba, and 350 from the Rafa fight.

This tested out our arrangements *en route* for the contemplated attack on Gaza, and we found they held good. Everything was now set for the attack.

We were all excited about Gaza. Gaza, the city of the Philistines, that mysterious race who were such a thorn in the flesh to the Israelites. Gaza, and the story of Samson and Delilah. Gaza the famous fortress, the southern defence of Palestine, besieged by Alexander the Great, Pompey, Napoleon.

Looking at it later, with its tangle of cactus hedges six to ten feet high all around, I wondered how any troops could possibly have captured it. One of its natural defences was the Wadi Guzze six miles to the south. This was a steep ravine with vertical banks thirty to forty feet high in the dry season, and in its bed little pools of water which in the rainy season could become a raging torrent.

The Turks might have defended the Wadi but they didn't. They retreated instead to Gaza and dug themselves in among the cactus hedges, on the heights of Ali Muntar, and on Samson's ridge, where, tradition says, stood the Temple of Dagon, the pillars of which the blinded giant pulled down on the heads of his gloating enemies.

Ali Muntar is the traditional site east of Gaza to which Samson carried the gate of the city. People don't read the Bible as they used to, so I will quote:

> Then went Samson to Gaza, and saw there an harlot, and went in unto her. And it was told the Gazites, saying, Samson is come hither. And they compassed him in, and laid wait for him all night in the gate of the city, and were quiet all the night, saying, In the morning, when it is day, we shall kill him. And Samson lay till midnight, and arose at midnight, and took the doors of the gate of the city, and the two posts, and went away with them, bar and all, and put them upon his shoulders, and carried them up to the top of an hill that is before Hebron. (Judges xvi, 1–3).

Later I stood on this hill and looked towards Hebron.

Our great trouble in the battles for Gaza was keeping the troops supplied with water until they could capture the place. This required about 600,000 gallons a day. Every military commander from Thothmes III to General Allenby knew that the capture of Gaza was essential on account of this absence of water on the route from Egypt. Gaza is the gateway to Palestine; Pompey and Napoleon each had to capture it before they could advance further.

Gaza itself with its fifteen or twenty wells had ample supplies of water. Our pipe-line was miles behind, and we could only supply water for twenty-four hours to the men and horses. So it meant a quick victory or failure. The plan of attack in the first battle of Gaza, March 26th, 1917, was simple: the infantry were to advance against the trenches and the guns on the heights, the cavalry were to swing round behind the city, attack in the rear, and hold off Turkish reinforcements coming from the lines of communication. It had to be captured before sunset. Kress von Kressenstein actually thought it had been. The German Commandant of Gaza, Major Tiller, blew up his wireless station, thinking all was over. Our cavalry had got into the streets. And then water and ammunition began to fail. There was some bad intercom staff work and we withdrew. .

I can now disclose a curious medical fact. Mounted troops actually got into Gaza, and, in emulating Samson, three of them got gonorrhoea. As there was no chance of acquiring this in the desert and as none of them had been on leave in Egypt, we were satisfied they really had been inside Gaza.

I heard a number of reasons advanced in various messes afterwards for the withdrawal. The main one was that Murray was too far back to keep control. That was where he differed from Allenby. But no one personally really was to blame.

As is inevitable in a defeat, the sick and wounded came piling back. The Field Ambulances cleared them to the 26th Casualty Clearing Station and the 2nd Australian Stationary Hospital, both of which were at El Arish; and they sent most of the sick and wounded back to us at the 24th Stationary Hospital, Kantara, by hospital train and in the open trucks of the supply trains. It was a bad show. We never knew how many were killed, but there were 2,480 wounded, 1,930 of whom passed through our hands at Kantara between March 27th and April 2nd.

We worked in shifts night and day to clear them safely into Egypt, and I learnt a lot about how not to clear a battle front. It is perhaps inevitable, and unfair in a way, that the people who see and profit later by the mistakes of those before them should get all the credit. They probably would have made the same mistakes themselves had they not seen those of their predecessors. I saw all the mistakes, all the unnecessary suffering, all the stupidity of the official mind, and I was hopping mad. But I profited by it later. I knew where the snags were, and avoided them when I was in control.

The Turks, who never expected to hold Gaza, were so elated at their success that they counter-attacked and poured thousands of reinforcements into it, determined to hold the place. Immediately they began to dig trenches east of Ali Muntar and consolidated the positions which we were to know only too well for weary months later: the Tank Redoubt, the Atawineh Redoubt, the Hareira and the Sheria defences. These stretched out across-country towards Beersheba. There was now no chance of turning the position with cavalry unless the infantry broke through. The second battle of Gaza was therefore conducted as a frontal attack—the mentality of the Somme. It started on April 17th and ended in complete failure on the 19th. Six thousand five hundred sick and wounded men came down the line, most of them to Kantara, where we were the only hospital able to receive them, treat them and evacuate them to Egypt.

The more serious cases came in the two hospital trains. The lighter cases came in the open trucks of the supply trains. They were provided with mattresses and pillows, blankets and tarpaulins, and should have been not too uncomfortable. The journey started in the morning in hot sunshine, and ended at Kantara generally about midnight, when we took them in by the light of flare lamps. By then it was very cold —the desert air at night can be very chilly—and we found to our horror that a number of them were dead, cold and frozen because the blankets and tarpaulins with which they had been issued had been commandeered *en route* by an ordnance officer short of stores who thought they did not need blankets and tarpaulins in hot, open trucks. It was a stupid, unimaginative thing to do. We raised hell and it did not happen again.

For us it was a nightmare time. Captain Neve and I were the operating surgeons. In one spell we each worked for forty-eight hours. I slept thirty-six hours solidly afterwards. I can remember little detail now; it was all so hurried; we hadn't time to think. But odd things stick in one's memory. An officer came down the line with a bullet embedded in his neck. No one in the Field Ambulance or C.C.S. had risked taking it out because it had entered in front of the sternomastoid muscle, gone behind it, and the point projected at the back of the muscle. It was lying, therefore, obviously on top of the carotid artery, and vibrated gently with the pulsations of the great vessel. Neve and I looked at it. We could see both ends. What would happen if we tried to take it out? Would we have a sudden, uncontrollable hæmorrhage? Obviously it could not be left, so we tackled it.

Neve put his thumb on the artery below to compress it against the sixth cervical and I caught the butt-end of the bullet very gingerly with a bullet forceps. Very slowly and gently I eased it back, twisting it slightly. It came, and there was not a drop of blood. We each drew a long breath.

"That's that," said Neve, "very tricky, what!"

Of course it was really nothing—just a curiosity of surgery. That's why I remember it. All the hard work, the rapid operations, the monotonous dressings and re-dressings have now been completely forgotten.

What I remember most was the sudden flatness that came over us once the rush of sick and wounded had ended. The sacrifice of so much young life had been in vain. We all felt that something must be wrong with the Higher Command. We lost confidence in our leadership. The 'Cairo' generals who were more familiar with Groppi's tea-shop than the front line came in for scathing criticism. It was all probably most unfair, but people like us living in the desert, who had only a couple of days very occasionally away from the sweat and sand and flies and general discomfort, rather grudged those continuously enjoying 'the fleshpots of Egypt'.

Certain episodes in the flat period between the second and third battles of Gaza come back to me.

So far I have said nothing about the Egyptian Labour Corps, that vast organisation of native labour which supplied the manpower for railway construction, camp building, dump handling, camel transport, water transport, all and any sort of manual work the Army required from men accustomed to tropical conditions. There must have been many, many thousands of these men working for us, and many thousand camels surrendered to us, not too willingly. The men worked in gangs handled by native ghafirs controlled by European officers who could speak Arabic. Anyone who could speak or learn Arabic could apply for a commission; and as soon as the supply from Europeans who had lived in Egypt became exhausted, British N.C.O.s working with these gangs who picked up enough Arabic to make themselves understood began to apply for E.L.C. commissions. They could do so if recommended by the O.C. of their unit. One particularly bright corporal in our hospital whose father was a nonconformist parson asked me if he could apply to be examined. I agreed. The Colonel agreed. He was examined, he passed and at once became a Second-Lieutenant, E.L.C. We will call him Lieutenant Brown.

I saw him soon after in his neat, new uniform and congratulated him. Three months later I saw him again. He had been celebrating in Cairo, and arrived back at Kantara on his way up the line to rejoin his unit. But instead he became ill on the train and had been admitted to our hospital. When I saw him he had a temperature of 103 degrees Fahrenheit and was delirious. As I bent over him he half recognised me.

"He touched my eyes, Major. He touched my eyes. He told me that then I could see with my eyes closed."

"Who touched your eyes?"

"The magician in Cairo. He did it with a silver probe. Oh, my God, I can't close my eyes now. Fifi, why did you let him touch my eyes, Fifi?"

The orderly looked at me.

"He's been calling out for Fifi, sir, some girl I suppose in Cairo, off and on for the last hour."

Frankly, I was puzzled. It wasn't any of the usual fevers. I ordered a sedative and said I'd see him later on my evening round. When I did so he was asleep. Next morning after the effects of the sedative had worked off he was talking wildly about Fifi, about his eyes, about the fact that though he closed his eyes he still could see through his lids. He tossed and turned, and babbled. And then quite suddenly and unexpectedly he died.

I didn't know what to register as the cause of death. P.U.O. (pyrexia of unknown origin) is the Army refuge in cases of this sort. So Captain O'Connor, our pathologist, said he'd do a post-mortem, and he went to see the body in the mortuary tent. Presently I had an excited message from him to come at once.

"Look," he said, "there!"

I looked. In the inner corner of the white of each eye there was a black mark the size of a pin-head.

"Good God! He wasn't as dotty as we thought," I said. "You'd better take a photo of this. His eyes have been interfered with."

O'Connor took that photo. Three hours later he took another. By then the black spot was as big as a pea. Three hours later it covered the inner half of each eye. Three hours after that both whites were completely black—a queer, shivery thing to look at.

"This is murder," said O'Connor, and I agreed.

At the post-mortem we could find nothing abnormal. The eyes had not been punctured. There was no evidence of injury of any kind except the odd black spots that had started where he said his eyes had been touched and had spread till they covered the whole conjunctivæ.

We reported to 'Intelligence' but they could find nothing. Fifi is a name prostitutes in Cairo use frequently. There is no doubt he had been murdered. Officers of the E.L.C. were particularly obnoxious at

Camel cacolet carrying stretcher wounded (1916)

Camel cacolet carrying walking wounded (1916)

Lieut.-Col. J. Johnston Abraham, D.S.O., A.D.M.S. Palestine Lines of Communication (1917-19)

that time to Egyptians, as the Labour Corps was practically con-scripted. It was the old hated *corvée* back again. There was intensive bitterness about it, for we took their camels, we took their donkeys, we took their fodder, we took their men. Village life was disrupted by our demands. Little wonder the E.L.C. was hated.

How was he killed? I don't know. There is a poison, 'Ouabin', used in Tanganyika to tip arrows, which is very deadly. And in Egypt there are indigenous plants, varieties of Adenium and Orginea, which can kill in two hours if injected or swallowed. It took twenty-four hours to kill Second-Lieutenant Brown, E.L.C., by merely touching his eyes without penetration.

Another memory is of a medical officer who had been a missionary before the war. Because he was a good Arabic speaker he had been put in charge of one of our Egyptian hospitals in the front line; and from there he had been sent down to Kantara with fever. When I saw him in the admission tent, I knew that fever: it was my old enemy, typhus.

I told the Colonel, and we isolated the patient in a bell tent in our isolation hospital behind the lines, under the care of Lieutenant H. North, one of our officers. Two orderlies were detailed to look after him with instructions that he was never to be left alone, as typhus patients are liable to become delirious and get out of bed.

At seven a.m. next morning I was summoned hurriedly to his bed-side. He lay there smiling.

The orderly uncovered his chest, and I saw a wound one and a half inches long between his third and fourth rib on the left side. Air was bubbling out of the wound as he breathed.

"Who did this?" I said.

"I did," he answered, smiling at me.

"Why?"

"Because I am not fit to live. I have shown cowardice in the face of the enemy," he answered.

"That's nonsense," I protested, "what have you done?"

"I've pushed a penknife into my heart," he answered, quite calmly. "It's inside now."

This seemed so fantastic, I doubted it. So we put him on a stretcher and took him to the X-ray hut. There, sure enough, when we

G

developed the plate was the shadow of an army knife, butt-end down-wards, lying inside the chest behind his heart, resting on the diaphragm. Obviously to leave it would be fatal. But to operate on a man with typhus fever and a temperature of 104 degrees!

I sat in the mess tent after breakfast, thinking. No one could help me much with advice. I was the surgical expert. The Colonel was a regular and looked at it purely from the administrative standpoint. It was found that at the time it happened the patient had been left un-attended between the night and day shifts for ten minutes; and he therefore put the two orderlies under arrest for failing to relieve each other properly. He then announced that if the officer survived he would have him court-martialled for attempted suicide. That appeared to satisfy him, and there he considered his job ended. It was now up to me to carry on.

This was the second time I had had to decide upon operating on a chest to remove a foreign body. The first had been at Millbank Military Hospital with Dr. Scot Skirving of Sydney, N.S.W. Then we removed a bullet from the wall of a patient's heart, but he died of pneumonia four days later. The chances of recovery in this second case were, I thought, probably worse.

I talked it over with Captain Neve, my surgical assistant.

"Well," he said, "he may die if you operate, but he's sure to die either of typhus or the knife if you don't."

I knew he was right but hated to admit it.

"It's easy for you to say so," I said peevishly.

"Sorry, old chap," he answered disarmingly; and my momentary irritation passed.

*

Well, we did it. I opened up the chest and watched the lung collapse. I hoped I would find the knife lying behind it; but I could not be sure as our field X-ray was not good enough to tell us if it was there, or if it was inside the pericardium.

I put my gloved hand behind the lung. It was not there.

Neve told me afterwards I turned very white then.

"How is he?" I said to the anæsthetist.

"Quite chirpy," he answered. "Carry on, sir."

"We'll have to open the pericardium," I said to Neve.

"Yes," he answered, "but it is odd I can't see any sign of a puncture or a wound in it."

"Neither can I, but here goes."

I made an incision in the pericardium—the bag inside which the heart lies concealed, like an apple inside a paper bag—and there again for the second time in my life I saw a naked heart beating before my eyes. Very gently I retracted the edges of the incision. Nothing. I put my fingers slowly round behind the heart, lifting it forward. It felt like a bird fluttering beneath my hand. Still nothing. Then my middle finger touched something pointed—the blade.

"Got it!" I exclaimed with a gasp of relief.

It came out quite easily, an ordinary brown-handled one-bladed service knife.

"Good egg!" said Neve.

Surgeons did not see beating hearts in those days. We didn't operate on them deliberately for another thirty years, so it was a great adventure.

He stood the operation well and for the next seven days we were hopeful. But his temperature never fell, and on the eighth day he died of typhus.

It cast a gloom over us for several days. Odd, because we had all seen so many deaths in the previous six months. He was a Highlander and we buried him with full military honours, a piper, convalescing in the hospital, playing 'The Flowers of the Forest'. As I walked behind the coffin to our graveyard out in the desert, I was wondering what I should write to his old people in a far-off manse in Scotland about their only son.

Yet a third memory before my whole world changed completely: a big, heavy sergeant was rushed into hospital one afternoon when we were all half asleep. I was summoned to see him and found he had a transverse cut right across his abdomen ten inches long, and his bowels held up by a bloodstained towel were showing.

I looked at the wound.

"That was done by a nigger," I said, "I remember seeing one in Costa Rica. They do it with a razor. Who is this fellow?"

"He's a sergeant warder from the military prison. He was attacked by a prisoner, a man of the British West Indian Regiment. It *was* done with a razor," replied the officer who brought him in.

Well, we sewed him up and he recovered. But at the court martial the negro was condemned to be shot at dawn; and I found it was part of my unpleasant duty as a field officer to be present with the Assistant Provost Marshal to certify the death.

The day of execution came. I can remember every detail of that morning still. Daylight comes rapidly in the tropics. At a quarter to six it is quite dark. At six the sun rises. At six-fifteen it is clear morning. We started in the darkness to drive across the desert sand in a battered old Ford—my Quartermaster in front with the driver, the Baptist Chaplain and myself behind. None of us spoke during the entire journey. The A.P.M., the prisoner and the firing-party had marched in front to the place of execution, the mud wall of a disused rifle range alongside the Suez Canal. We got there just before dawn. The prisoner was standing close to the wall, a magnificent bronze Hercules, clad in a pair of khaki shorts only, his hands fastened behind his back. The firing-party, men from a Labour Battalion, stood huddled some twenty feet away. Their faces looked white and drawn in the gathering light. I glanced at my little Quartermaster. His face, usually ruddy, was blanched. I turned towards the A.P.M. He was nervously fingering his revolver. We were all in a state of extreme tension. Then I looked at the prisoner. The light was now coming up from the East. It glistened on his bronze skin and the whites of his eyes, and I was startled to see there was a smile of beatitude on his face. His white teeth sparkled. He was completely at ease.

The Baptist Chaplain went over to him. They conversed in quiet tones for a minute. The man's eyes seemed to glow with an inner joy.

The A.P.M. standing beside me stamped his feet, for the dawn was chilly and he was getting more and more edgy. Still the prisoner and the padre talked quietly. I watched them, fascinated. At length the chaplain stepped back. He nodded towards our group. 'That means he's ready,' I thought. Someone was whispering behind me to the A.P.M. It was the N.C.O. in charge of the firing-party. The A.P.M. turned to me.

"He says, Major, that the men are afraid they mayn't kill him at the first volley, and they'd like you to mark where his heart is. Do you mind?"

Evidently my Quartermaster had been told of this beforehand, for he straight away produced a roll of sticking-plaster and a pair of scissors.

Together, then, we walked up to the prisoner, and with strips of plaster I marked a star the size of my palm on his chest. It stood out clearly on his dark skin in the brightening morn. Once I looked up at the man. His brown eyes were gazing at me, soft as a gazelle's.

Finally I stepped back, and someone produced a handkerchief to blindfold him.

"May I die with my eyes open?" he said in the educated tones so surprising to those who do not know the West Indian negro.

"Better not," I said gently.

"All right, Doctor," he answered submissively; and they slipped it over.

A few seconds later the quick word of command rang out; then came the volley; and then the great, beautiful body crumpled and suddenly fell. It didn't seem real, somehow. The A.P.M. and I ran forward.

"Is he dead?" he gasped, drawing his revolver, for his gruesome duty was to finish the job if the rifle fire had failed, and he was not as accustomed to death as I. We turned the body over, and I looked at the chest with the holes in it.

"Quite dead," I answered.

The chaplain and I got into the Ford again. The Quartermaster slipped in beside the driver, and we drove back to camp. It was now broad daylight. No one spoke until we passed a gang of coolies putting up wire fencing. That broke the spell. I turned to the padre.

"The courage of the man! I was surprised," I said.

The padre looked at me. "You needn't have been. I have never known anyone so ready to meet his Maker," he answered quietly.

And then it was all clear to me. The padre had been with him almost hourly during the previous week. He had repented of his sins, and believed he had been forgiven. He was ready therefore to face his God, "fortified by the rites of Holy Church".

It was an episode I can never forget.

*

All this time we were being kept in happy ignorance of what was going on in France on the Western Front. We knew nothing of the failure of the French offensive in Champagne and the murderous pressure on our men. All the bulletins issued to us were so optimistic. But during the months following Gaza II we were gradually being depleted of British troops. They were being sent to France to strengthen the front there, and we began to hear of Indian units coming to take their place.

Soon administrative changes became noticeable. The war with the Senussi in the Western Desert was over, and more men and materials became available to us.

At the 24th Stationary Hospital we were joined by some medical officers who replaced those going home. Major John Mackenzie was the most important of these. This might have created some little difficulty, as it gave us two majors; but 'honest John' was all right. We got on well together. He was not a surgeon, so he took over the medical wards.

The next thing we heard was that the title of 'Eastern Force', as we were called, was being done away with, and troops and medical units from Kantara to railhead were now to come under a new command, 'Lines of Communication', with its headquarters at Kantara, under Brigadier-General Edward Broadbent, a nephew of the famous Victorian doctor, Sir William Broadbent.

"That means," said our Colonel ruefully, "we'll have the A.D.M.S. on our doorstep." (A.D.M.S. means Assistant Director of Medical Services.)

Sure enough, a few days later we were called upon and inspected by the new A.D.M.S., Colonel Sexton, accompanied by Captain J. H. Wood, his D.A.D.M.S. They said they were billeted in the Canal Company office, where they had their own mess; and our Colonel sighed with relief when he heard this, as he feared they might have attached themselves to us. All these details turned out to be of vital importance to me afterwards, though I didn't know it at the time. I took them round the wards, and the only comment of the A.D.M.S.

was that he hoped our arrangements to prevent fire were adequate, as the tents seemed rather close together.

He was quite right, but I was disappointed that he hadn't commented favourably on our operating theatre, our X-ray department, our electric light plant and our sick officers' quarters—all of which I was particularly proud of.

Soon things began to happen. The Colonel sent for me one morning.

"I have an order from the D.M.S. You are to report to him at Cairo forthwith."

"Does he give any reason, sir?"

"None whatever," he answered.

So I went up, rather puzzled. When I got to his office he cross-examined me over my impressions of the evacuation of sick and wounded at the two battles of Gaza. I told him straight out what I thought. He nodded occasionally. Colonel Keble, his A.D.M.S., chipped in.

"So you think Kantara is a bottle-neck, Major?"

"Yes, sir. You should have two stationary hospitals there, to take in patients on alternate days. No hospital can do it continuously. We are overcrowded and overworked."

The D.M.S. nodded.

"Well," he said, "we're giving you another hospital at Kantara. Will you lay it out for us on the same lines as your own?"

I went back and told my Colonel.

So for a week I talked to Major Lister of the Works Department, and we pegged the site and arranged the layout of the permanent huts.

It was called the 44th Stationary Hospital, and Major Mackenzie was taken from our hospital to command it. That meant promotion to lieutenant-colonel.

We sent a blueprint of the layout to the D.M.S., and he came down to see the unit. He was very affable. We fixed him up comfortably, and after dinner in the mess tent he talked. Soon our watchful Colonel relaxed: obviously there was no sinister intent in the visit. The idea of having twin hospitals side by side to relieve each other seemed to have struck the D.M.S., for he said to me:

"We are going to put up the 43rd and 45th Stationary Hospitals together at Masaid, just short of El Arish. They'll take the first shock of the next offensive, and then they'll pass them on to you. We're using your plan of the 44th for them. As soon as they are completed I want you to go up and inspect them and report to me."

All this was pleasant in a way, but I got the impression somehow that I was being used and yet overlooked. Some of our officers had said I should have been given the 44th Stationary instead of Mackenzie. I hadn't thought that, but I had hoped for some sort of recognition.

In June, 1917, we learnt that Sir Archibald Murray had been recalled home and was being succeeded by General Sir Edmund Allenby. None of us was surprised. Murray was essentially an office wallah, in contradistinction to Allenby, who was a front line soldier.

It was Murray's foresight and imagination that was responsible for the railway across the desert, and the magnificent idea of carrying the waters of the Nile from Egypt to Palestine.

He bridged the desert. But in Cairo he lost touch with his fighting troops, and to that was due his failure as a Commander-in-Chief. Allenby reaped where Murray sowed, and, like the great man he was, he acknowledged this fully in his despatch in June, 1919.

He was like a breath of fresh air in a sultry room. He came in like a whirlwind.

The first thing he did was to inspect the front line and get to know his officers. The next was to move G.H.Q. from Cairo to Kelab, just behind the front. Allenby had no use for the Continental Hotel and the ornamental gentlemen who used to pass the buck there. His presence in the front line acted like a tonic. The men saw him, 'big bull Allenby', going round the trenches, talking to junior officers, inspecting the lie of the land. A wave of optimism took the place of the depression that had fallen on us after Gaza II. Confidence in the leadership came back.

*

One day I got another message to report to the D.M.S. at Cairo, where he still was. He asked me in his message to stop the night at his flat.

There were four of us at dinner: the D.M.S., Colonel Keble the

A.D.M.S., G.H.Q., Major Bridges the D.A.D.M.S., and myself. They were all, of course, regular soldiers with many years' service. I was a temporary officer who had been in the Army a little over two years. I wasn't even a Territorial.

Over the port the General looked at me and said abruptly:

"Abraham, I'm going to make you A.D.M.S., L. of C."

I stared at him in astonishment. I had never thought of such a thing. To be put on Allenby's staff and give orders to people like my own Colonel. I choked over my port.

"Sir," I said, "d'ye think I could do it?"

"If I didn't think so, I wouldn't offer it to you," he answered. "I've thought it all out carefully. You will succeed Colonel Sexton at Kantara, and you will have Captain Wood as your D.A.D.M.S. He'll initiate you into office work."

I slept very badly that night. It was such an earthquake suggestion to me. In the morning I returned to my hospital under orders not to say anything to anybody about the appointment. My Colonel was curious. He thought, he told me later, I was being offered command of a hospital, but he made no comments, and he never suspected what really was going to happen.

CHAPTER XIV

ALLENBY AND JERUSALEM

ON SEPTEMBER 5TH, 1917, I was gazetted A.D.M.S., Palestine Lines of Communication. When it appeared in General Orders my Colonel said:

"Good God!"

And I felt like agreeing with him, for the idea of a temporary officer, of two years' service, not even a Territorial, being put in medical command of Lines of Communication in a war area over the heads of regular lieutenant-colonels, some with over twenty years' service, was unthinkable. It had never happened before, and I doubt if it has ever happened since.

I left my hospital and my surgical work with regret. I knew I had an immense job before me; for the next advance, I was told as a top secret, would be in two months' time and I had to get ready for it. Luckily I had learnt from Gaza I and Gaza II what not to do.

I moved my kit to my headquarters next day. Captain J. H. Wood received me very politely. I had seen him twice before, when he accompanied my predecessor Colonel Sexton on inspection, and I felt we would get on together. He had a very bright smile.

Our quarters were in a building overlooking the Canal itself. It was comfortable, cool, especially built for the climate. My office was a large room with a very high ceiling from which some twenty to thirty huge black bats hung motionless all day long, sallying out through the open casements at dusk.

There were three people in the mess: myself, Captain Wood, my D.A.D.M.S., and Captain Briercliffe (now Sir Rupert Briercliffe, C.M.G.), who was in charge of the water-testing laboratory which examined and certified the safety of the pipe-line on which the supply of water to the entire Expeditionary Force depended. He had a

Bisharin servant who was an excellent cook, and to whom he talked in Arabic. We were most comfortable—cool by day, warm by night, quite different from tent life, where it is hot by day and surprisingly cold by night.

Wood and I got down to work.

I found I had five Stationary Hospitals in my command, four Advanced Depots Medical Stores, two Casualty Clearing Stations, two Egyptian hospitals for the Labour Corps, four hospital trains, a Bacteriological Laboratory, two hospital steamboats based on Kantara on the Canal, to carry casualties to Port Said or Suez, and a fleet of ambulances also based on Kantara. In addition I had the Scottish Horse Field Ambulance up the line, a type of unit not usually found in an L. of C., but one which proved invaluable to me. When I wanted some odd job done to my satisfaction without supervision I gave it to the Scottish Horse Field Ambulance. They were a grand lot, officered mostly from the Edinburgh Royal Infirmary and Aberdeen.

One of the first things I ached to attack was the disposition and use of the hospital trains. No one knew at what hour a train would arrive at Kantara, night or day. No one knew in advance even what day a train might be expected, or how many sick and wounded it would have on board. Ration trains and ammunition trains had to run of necessity daily. If a hospital train was coming down the line and a ration train going up, the hospital train had to be pushed into a siding. It might lie there for hours. That was just too bad, but it could not be helped—food and ammunition must take precedence.

My D.A.D.M.S., Captain Wood, said one train at Kantara hadn't been up the line for three weeks, and, when they tried to move it, it stuck. Each train had a staff of one medical officer and six to ten R.A.M.C. other ranks. Their trains would be sometimes immobile for weeks at a time and then rushed to death. This was most demoralising.

I asked for an appointment with the A.D.R.T. (Assistant Director of Railway Transport), Lieutenant-Colonel Percy Bruce.

"Your trains," he said, "are a bloody nuisance. They are the plague of my life. They're always in the way."

"I know, Colonel," I replied, "I know they're in the way. What I want you to do is to run them for me to a definite timetable so that they won t be such a nuisance. If you can give me a schedule time so that I can get my cases into hospital in daylight, I'll guarantee to run one train a day. The wastage at the front averages a hundred and fifty a day, so I can do that. I'll see these are not held up in the Casualty Clearing Stations or the Field Ambulances along the line."

"Give you a definite timetable? Great God, Colonel, there's nothing I'd like better! You shall have it. It'll save us an infinity of trouble."

So that was that. It was as easy as that. The railway people were delighted. The hospital trains ran to time. Each train had its scheduled journey. A train arrived every evening and the 24th and 44th Stationary Hospitals took in on alternate days.

The patients came daily without fuss. Previously we used to know when an attack was imminent because the front line units cleared themselves. The enemy ground intelligence on the Canal were quick to guess this also. Now the change had been made, it was so simple; the wonder was, no one had thought of it before. Where I scored, of course, was in that I'd seen the muddle, suffered from it, and thought out how it could be remedied.

The headquarters staff of the Lines of Communication had its officers' mess in the Sinai Police H.Q., and there we met in conference daily under General Eddy Broadbent. And there I learnt how an army staff works, and what an A.A.G., an A.Q.M.G., an A.D.O.S., and all the other letters of the alphabet meant.

I had to learn fast, for we had only two months to prepare, and I knew most of my hospitals were still under-equipped and under-staffed. If it hadn't been for Captain Wood I couldn't have done it. But he was a first-class officer. He had been a Medical Officer of Health in peace-time, and routine work came easily to him. He gave me time to think. One morning I had a surprise. General Maher wrote that he was retiring and Colonel Keble was taking over as D.M.S. until the War Office appointed someone to the post. I wondered how I'd get on with the new Chief.

A few days later Keble sent for me, all smiles.

"I want you, Abraham," he said, "to go up the line to Advanced G.H.Q., at Kelab, talk to Major Bagshawe, see the O.C.'s. units, get a general idea of the front, and report back to me."

I was glad of the opportunity. I had no less than ten regular lieutenant-colonels, including my own Colonel, now taking orders from me, and I had felt rather nervous about it. I needn't have. They were all loyal to me—all except one. I felt his antagonism from the first day. He queried everything he could, and Wood and I had to watch our step, for he knew all the ropes and all the pitfalls. Unfortunately also he was in a key position at railhead.

At G.H.Q. I questioned Bagshawe about him.

"Yes," he said, "he's a good officer but a disappointed man. He just can't get on with people. He keeps blotting his copy. You'll have to watch him. Of course he resents you being pushed over his head. He said to me, 'Who the hell is he anyway? Just a bloody temporary officer!' Actually we're all a bit surprised about you! Can't blame us, can you?" he added genially.

"I'll go and see him and have it out with him," I said.

Bagshawe grinned. "Well, you're both Irishmen. You're from the North. He's from the South. I'd like to be there. It would be fun."

I drove over to see him by appointment. He received me ceremoniously with all his officers lined up. I wasn't yet used to that, but I said nothing.

I could see, however, that his C.C.S. was beautifully laid out, and I said so. At lunch he relaxed a little. In his tent afterwards I came to the point. I explained that I had been pushed into my job, that I knew it was going to be difficult, that I had to depend on regulars like him to keep me straight.

He listened to me grimly.

I added that I gathered he had not been very well treated, and that his merits had somehow been overlooked. I hinted there was a ribbon he ought to have had and that, as far as I was concerned, I'd see he was not forgotten.

Of course it was bribery and corruption, but he had done his job well and had been disappointed because he had had no recognition for it. That had made him bitter. He knew also that any possible award he could now hope to get would have to be through my office, and he saw himself at the mercy of someone who to him was just a civilian. It all looked very bleak. Now I was offering him a chance, an unexpected chance. He stared at me.

"I mean it," I said. "Let's shake hands on it."

We got on famously after that. There was nothing he wouldn't do to help me. All he had wanted was that little bit of coloured ribbon and the order it carried, intrinsically worth about two days' pay, but representing something that meant recognition of work well and truly done over many years.

He got it six months later, and no one was more pleased than I. It made him happy. It made me happy too. Until he died he used to write to me every Christmas, a charming letter telling me of his doings.

*

To make intelligent arrangements for prospective casualties before the third battle of Gaza, I made a tour of the front in a rickety Ford—the only cars we found of use for that sort of work in Palestine were Fords and Rolls-Royces. The Turkish front ran in an almost straight line for twenty miles from Gaza to Beersheba. Gaza was practically impregnable to frontal attack, Beersheba well defended by trenches; and between the two places the Turks had three strongly defended points. It was a most formidable position to attack. Allenby's plan was to appear to repeat the frontal attack on Gaza, but to make the real attack on Beersheba, capture it and then let loose the cavalry, swinging them round behind the Turkish lines.

To do this it was necessary to deceive the Turks by making a strong bombardment from land and sea, augmented by infantry attacks on Gaza for three or four days before the real attack on Beersheba began; and to make surprise possible we had to conceal the fact that we were concentrating no less than 47,000 infantry, 30,000 transport camels, and 11,000 mounted men within striking distance of Beersheba.

Nothing gives strategic plans away to an enemy so much as provision for casualties. So my orders were to erect and open three new Casualty Clearing Stations, each of 1,000 stretcher beds, between dusk and dawn on zero day, as close as possible to Beersheba, at a place called Imara. I said to Colonel Keble, the acting D.M.S., that I couldn't do it. It was physically impossible. He said those were Allenby's orders. I would have 600 Egyptian Labour Corps men attached temporarily to each Casualty Clearing Station to help me, and it just had to be done.

The three Casualty Clearing Stations—35th, 65th, and 75th—were stored in dumps at Rafa, twenty miles from Gaza, and I went to see them. My orders were not to say anything about their destination or what their job would be. I found that their mess tents only had been erected; and the tentage and equipment of the three C.C.S.s, piled neatly all round, were unopened. I made sure that the inventory of stores was complete for each unit, and I had talks with the three Commanding Officers. One was Colonel MacDougall, actually 'The Mac-Dougall'. The second I cannot now remember. The name of the third was Cooke, a very bright, energetic young Captain, R.A.M.C., Acting Lieutenant-Colonel.

'This is my man,' I thought. So I said to him:

"Colonel, I want you to put up your C.C.S. of one thousand beds complete, as quickly as you can, let the other C.O.s inspect it, and let me know when it is up."

It took him seven days. I went along to see it. It was neatly laid out. I praised it, as a good show, and then said:

"Take it down, Cooke, and let me know when it is down."

He looked at me, but said nothing. Two days later he reported that it was all down. I telephoned him:

"Thank you, Colonel. Put it up again and let me know when it is up."

He did it in four days.

I rang him up and said:

"Splendid, take it down again."

"Very good, sir," he answered, but I felt he must think I was mad by now. I ignored that, and told him to put it up again. He put it up in two days and reported. I thanked him.

"Take it down again, please, Colonel, and await orders."

He said: "Very good, sir."

By now, however, I gathered that there was a rumour in Rafa that the A.D.M.S. had gone completely dotty. I didn't blame them. It was hard, hot, tiresome work and they must have hated it, and me. But two days before zero we moved the three Casualty Clearing Stations with all their equipment to Imara, dumped everything laid out ready for erection on the sand, covered the tents with more sand and waited for the word 'Go'.

A few enemy planes came over reconnoitring, but saw nothing.

The railway track for three miles behind was covered with sand. We were just a small dump in the desert, harmless, innocuous.

I can remember the night seventy-two hours before zero still very distinctly. There was an almost full moon. I was the guest of the 60th Division, and we had a concert by 'The Roosters'. The men sat out in the open listening intently, and very quiet. I remember that one of the songs was:

> Sing that simple little melody
> Which my mother used to sing.

It set me wondering how many of them would be alive in three days and how many mothers would mourn. We were attacking across fifteen miles of waterless country; and if we did not capture Beersheba and its wells by surprise within twenty-four hours after the attack began, we would not be able to carry on and the attack would be another failure because our water supply would then have run out. It seemed so impossible a task to the Turks that they had discounted the idea of attack by more than a few thousand men.

*

For three days before zero we could hear the guns battering at Gaza. Obviously the Turks thought that was the major point of attack. At sunset on zero night I gave the order and watched the tents of the three Casualty Clearing Stations go up. The men worked all night by the moon. At five a.m. all the 3,000 beds were up under cover. It was a grand bit of work.

"Now I understand, sir," said Colonel Cooke. "We couldn't have done it without all that preliminary practice."

Attached to our three C.C.S.s were the Immobile Sections of the Divisional Field Ambulances of the 20th Corps. They acted as reception stations for us.

The attack began on October 31st, 1917, at four a.m. The full moon set at three a.m. We could hear the guns starting in the distance. I had been around all night watching the tents go up, been along to the advanced reception station at six a.m. to get the list of the first wounded coming in, talked on the field telephone to the D.D.M.S. 20th Corps,

Colonel Luce, and satisfied myself that everything was going smoothly. So I thought: 'Now is the time to snatch some sleep,' and I went to my tent.

I was just falling off when I heard a loud, young voice outside, saying: "God, the battle's started and the bloody A.D.M.S. is asleep!"

It was an excitable young officer from one of the Field Ambulances who did not know where my tent was and had been told I had turned in.

By the evening, Australian cavalry galloping furiously had captured the town, and the enemy had been taken so by surprise that they had not had time to destroy more than two of the fifteen wells, so the horses could water.

Our main trouble in breaking the Gaza–Beersheba line was recognised to be the lack of water. The Turks had abundance at Gaza and Beersheba, and a fair supply at the strong-points in between. We on the contrary were dependent on the pipe-line from Egypt, which ended fifteen miles from Beersheba. This had been a little augmented by cisterns at Shellal on the Wadi Guzze, where water was found by well-sinking. But the land between Beersheba and the Wadi Guzze was barren and waterless at that time of the year, and it was this terrain we had to fight over. Probably it had always been so. I looked up Samson's experiences when fighting the Philistines in the same area:

> The spirit of the Lord came mightily upon him . . . and his bands loosed from off his hands. And he found a new jawbone of an ass, and put forth his hand, and took it, and slew a thousand men therewith . . .

The story, as I read it, crystallises memories of many sporadic raids by Israelite tribesmen sweeping down from the bare Judean Hills on the Philistines of the fertile plain of Sharon. Samson was a legendary tribal leader around whom such stories concentrate. In one of these raids he heavily defeated the Philistines but did not penetrate into Gaza. Consequently the water supply failed him and his men as it nearly failed us. In the words of the Bible, "he was sore athirst, and called on the Lord, and said, Thou hast given this great deliverance into the hand of thy servant: and now shall I die for thirst . . ." Whereupon a miracle happened, for, following the jawbone which he had cast away, and which had almost certainly fallen into the Wadi Guzze, he found water, as we found it thousands of years later.

To supply the 58,000 troops we needed 400,000 gallons of water a day. This was carried by the 30,000 transport camels in twin fanati. Aware of the water difficulty, our men had been specially trained beforehand to march at night, star-guided, and to exist on two pints of water a day. On the night of the attack on Beersheba each man, therefore, had two water-bottles sufficient for one day. But unfortunately on zero day the dreaded khamsin blew hot air and blinding dust, and consumption of water rose heavily. The worst affected were the 'Gyppos' (Egyptian Labour Corps). They suffered intensely from thirst, and kept crying out incessantly for 'moya' (water). Many of the camel drivers also suffered from night blindness, and had to hang on to their camels to prevent themselves from getting lost.

The cavalry, instead of being able to gallop ahead after Beersheba had been captured, and so get behind the enemy's lines of communication and capture the whole Seventh Army as Allenby had hoped, had to come back each day to Beersheba to water their horses. There were not nearly enough wells at Beersheba for this big army; and the infantry, trudging wearily, pack-laden, through soft, black cotton soil with the dust coating their sweating faces until they were black, had to fight not only the enemy but also the intense thirst.

At every place they captured as they advanced from Beersheba towards Gaza, they found hundreds of wounded Turks from the disorganised retreating enemy lying unattended, crying pitifully for 'moya'. One Turkish officer offered an R.A.M.C. corporal all the money he had for a drink of water. A Field Ambulance sergeant wrote afterwards to his Colonel, T. B. Layton:

"The water question, like the flies, was always with us. How often we longed for a drink yet dare not touch our water-bottles! For one thing, it was strictly against orders and, for another, our common sense told us to keep what we had until we knew we could replenish the stock. It was a terrific temptation."

One brigade was so tortured by thirst that after they had captured Sheria, between Gaza and Beersheba, they raided the wells there, not knowing how slender was the thread between success and failure.

Hundreds of men fell out exhausted on the march, and the Field

Ambulance, moving a hundred yards behind, picked them up and passed them back to us at Imara, where we watered them and fed them and passed them on. War isn't all a matter of bugle calls and bayonet charges.

I went into Beersheba the morning after it was captured, to take over the enemy hospital. I was stopped outside by a very irate cavalry general who wanted to know what the hell I meant by wanting to go in there.

"Not on your life," he said, "not till we've cleared it of their booby-traps. Some of my fellows got hurt there last night."

"Who's that?" I enquired, when he was out of earshot.

"That's Chetwode. He's like a bear with a sore head. Take no notice. He's tearing mad because he can't get his horses watered fast enough to pursue the enemy and cut across their retreat."

When I did take over the hospital, the main stores I found were twelve dozen bottles of sweet champagne, a huge supply of '606' for the treatment of syphilis, and the equipment of the Ophthalmic Hospital in Jerusalem, belonging to the Order of St. John, which the Turks had commandeered.

All day for several days the wounded and the dead-beats came in, mainly in camel cacolets, for wheeled transport was next to impossible. But they were quite different in spirit from the casualties of Gaza I and II. Then they were a defeated army, depressed and gloomy. Now they were all bright and cheerful in spite of their wounds. They had been fighting a successful battle. We got them into hospital, and next day they were on the train bound for Egypt. Indeed, half of the first 1,200 wounded who passed through Imara were in hospital in Cairo thirty-six hours after the capture of Beersheba. It was a record.

At Imara I grew to like and admire 'The MacDougall', twenty-ninth hereditary chief of the clan. He was a shy man, difficult to know, and anyone less like a famous highland chieftain it would be hard to imagine.

His father, the twenty-eighth chief, had been a Surgeon-General, serving most of his time in India, seeing little of his Scottish home. MacDougall had been educated at Clifton and, though he qualified at Edinburgh, he had one of the most pronounced 'Oxford' accents I ever came across. I doubt if he really understood broad Scots such as I had been familiar with all my life; and I found it very difficult to imagine him as a kilted chief leading his men to battle as his ancestors must have done time and time again in the troubled history of Scotland. But there was no doubt about his competence as a medical officer. His C.C.S. was a model, and the fact that, though a regular colonel, he had to take orders from me, a temporary lieutenant-colonel, never seemed to worry him. It was just an accident of the job.

For a week after the capture of Beersheba we were taking in the wounded from the fighting along the line of fortifications between it and Gaza. In all we accounted for 4,400 sick and wounded whom we sent down to Egypt before we closed down.

Meanwhile on the extreme left of our line the 21st Corps had been closing in on Gaza itself, and on November 9th the Turks, seeing their front had been turned, evacuated the place, and we entered nine months after our first attack. By now the enemy were in full retreat, fighting fierce rearguard actions as they retired through Philistia. And, as they retreated Allenby moved G.H.Q. forward. He had no use for Murray's methods.

Before the third battle of Gaza he had moved G.H.Q. from Cairo to Kelab near Rafa; but now this was too far back for him. Similarly our Lines of Communications H.Q., which was at Kantara on the Suez Canal, had also become too far back; so we were ordered to keep ourselves in readiness to move forward from the Canal and take over the G.H.Q. camp at Kelab as soon as G.H.Q. moved into Palestine.

As our troops advanced, the broad gauge railway from Egypt was pushed forward behind them over the Wadi Guzze to Gaza and beyond. And as the railway lengthened so did the Lines of Communication, for they automatically extended from railhead to the Base.

*

The medical units in front of us were the Field Ambulances. Our most advanced units in the Lines of Communication were the Casualty Clearing Stations.

All this time we were expecting the rainy season to start, when the so-called roads would become impassable quagmires. The 'former rains' of the Bible were due on November 1st, the 'latter rains' not till January; and we had to press the enemy hard while the going was good if we were to capture Jerusalem, which Lloyd George had been promised as a Christmas present to cheer the British people.

It did start to rain early in November, but the tracks were fairly firm for the first two weeks, and motor-ambulances could run. As the troops advanced, pushing the Turks before them, our medical arrangements were that the Immobile Sections of the Field Ambulances should stop at convenient sites, whilst the Mobile Sections went on with the advancing troops, sending back their casualties to the Immobile Sections. Then, as railhead advanced, we of the L. of C. pushed forward a C.C.S. to take over from the Immobile Sections; and they moved on again to another site behind the advancing army, remaining there, collecting sick and wounded, until we and the railway overtook them once more. In this way we kept pushing the L. of C. onwards to take over from G.H.Q. There was thus officially a Casualty Clearing Station at railhead ready always to receive the sick and wounded, and send them back by ambulance train to the nearest Stationary Hospital, or even at times to the Base. My administration, therefore, began theoretically with the Casualty Clearing Stations; but I liked to keep in touch with the Immobile Sections of the Field Ambulances.

One day I was motoring up to one of these Sections at Beit Hanun when my car bumped over a big cylinder in the middle of the track over which lorries and ambulances were passing hourly.

"What's that?" I said to my driver.

"Oh, that, sir. That's a shell from one of our naval guns shelling Gaza that didn't go off."

"How long has it been here?"

" 'Bout a fortnight."

"And is no one arranging to take it away?"

"Not as I knows, sir."

It was still there a month later.

*

When the rains came heavily the chaos produced was instantaneous. I was up well in advance of the L. of C. inspecting the 75th Division's temporary C.C.S. at a place called 'Junction Station' on the old Turkish narrow gauge railway between Jaffa and Jerusalem. The bridges over the Wadi El Arish and the Wadi Guzze had been washed away, and the new railway we were building had been dislocated in places; the so-called roads through Philistia were deep mud; and no wheeled transport was possible. This cut me off completely from my own H.Q. At the temporary C.C.S., actually a Field Ambulance, we could take in sick and wounded from the front all right, because there was a fairly good metalled road connecting 'Junction Station' with both Jaffa and Jerusalem, and our men were fighting in the Judaean hills along this road. But we could not evacuate the wounded when we got them.

To add to our trouble, the Germans had recently sent out some new planes, faster than ours; and, with German precision, one used to come over at nine-forty-five each evening and machine-gun us. We knew exactly when it would arrive. At nine-thirty a sort of silence fell on the mess. At nine-forty I felt I'd rather be outside, and I would go into the open. At nine-forty-five over it came. We could see the pilot plainly. He came down quite low, sprayed the C.C.S. and then boomed on. Occasionally we found holes in the canvas of the mess tent.

None of us blamed the German Air Force for these nightly visitations. 'Junction Station' was one of the most important strategic points in the advance. By capturing it we had cut the old Turkish narrow gauge railway between Jaffa and Jerusalem, and divided the supply line between the Seventh and Eighth Turkish Armies. Supplies came up to us by train from Egypt only as far as Gaza, where the new military broad gauge railway ended. Beyond that they came by lorry, and there were great dumps of military stores and ammunition all round the C.C.S. Little wonder the Germans gunned the place hoping to set these dumps on fire.

We, too, had considered it most important when it was in Turkish hands, and a raiding party of Sappers had been sent up to see if they could demolish the bridge over the Wadi just outside the station on the Jaffa side, and so disrupt the line to both Jerusalem and Gaza. Greatly daring, they managed to get there and blow up the bridge; only to find out later, to their annoyance, that the Turks had already evacuated the place, and this had been unnecessary. When our troops got there, the yawning chasm our over-enthusiastic Sappers had made had become a confounded nuisance, because we had to restore it, and bridging material was almost unobtainable.

It was the inelasticity of the German mind that finally finished the nightly raiding. The pilot came too regularly to time. One evening he arrived as usual, but we had just had some Bristols a few days before, and one of them was waiting for him. There was a brief exchange and we were troubled no longer.

But a worse enemy than the raiding was the rain. It kept pouring night and day. Men who had been sweltering in the heat were now marching north through quagmires, soaking wet, shivering in the thin khaki uniform and shorts they had been wearing in the Sinai Desert.

The temporary bridges over the Wadi El Arish and the Wadi Guzze had again been swept away by raging torrents. The railway lines sagged. The so-called roads became impassable to wheeled traffic. Evacuation by ambulance became impossible.

The troops, however, were now well through Philistia and across the Jaffa–Jerusalem road. They could send their sick and wounded back to us at 'Junction Station' easily; but, as I have said, we could not evacuate them. They piled up on us. Soon we began to run short of rations, and we had to ask the Field Ambulances to hold their casualties. At length we were compelled to open the emergency stores, and eventually we were down to thirty-six hours' supplies. Our plight, of course, was known. Five hundred camels were assembled hastily at Gaza, and the 30th Field Ambulance battled through the rain and mud to us by forced marches just as our food ran out. Some hundred camels died on the road, but the rest got through. And were we glad to see them!

Luckily there is a short interval between the 'former' and the 'latter' rains, and in this interval we got the sick and wounded back over the reconstructed railway.

Presently we heard that Ludd had been captured and the two Turkish armies had now been cut off by road as well as rail from one another by our men straddling the Jaffa–Jerusalem road. Ludd is the Lydda of the Crusades. It is also the scene of the martyrdom of St. George of England. When I went to the Chapel there, later, I was shown the great toe of the Saint, a holy relic preserved in a glass case, revered equally by Christian and Moslem. It looked no different from any other old man's rheumatoid-arthritic toe.

Jaffa was the next important place captured, and I placed the 77th

C.C.S. there. That meant that the L. of C. had now been extended fifty miles in three weeks.

All the next week we were breathlessly waiting for the news that Jerusalem had been captured, but fighting in the Judaean hills was a slow affair compared with fighting in Philistia: our first attempt failed. Then we heard that Nebi Samuel (The Mountain of the prophet Samuel) had been captured. This was the mountain-top from which one could see Jerusalem, sitting like a jewel amongst its surrounding hills. Richard Cœur de Lion is traditionally supposed to have stood on the top of Nebi Samuel, looked at the city and wept because he could not hope to enter it.

The problem was to capture the city without bombardment, for in it were the sacred places of three great religions—Jewish, Christian and Moslem—and it was essential to avoid damaging any of the sacred sites. This could only be done by capturing the enemy positions in the south between Bethlehem and the city, cutting across those to the north and advancing steadily from the Nebi Samuel heights in the west. And this is what was done. We heard on December 9th that an officer of the 60th Division saw a group of black-robed men with a white flag coming out from the city. It was the Mayor of Jerusalem offering the keys. And it was to Major-General Sir John Shea of the 60th Division that the formal surrender was made.

Thus very quietly, very simply, the sacred city which had been under the domination of the Turks for four hundred years was finally torn from their grasp. I can still remember the thrill of exultation this produced in us all. It was a thrill that reverberated all round the world. From the military standpoint it was not of great importance, but psychologically it was an immense victory.

General Allenby entered the city two days later by the Jaffa Gate. He walked in quietly on foot in his simple khaki field uniform. It was a superbly calculated gesture, in violent contrast to the entry of Kaiser Wilhelm when he too entered Jerusalem years before. Then a portion of the wall had to be levelled for him, and he rode in proudly on horseback, surrounded by a staff resplendent in gold and red and blue. The world read of both, and remembered.

As soon as the news that the city had been captured was flashed back, everyone at the Base wanted to visit it on any plausible excuse. The last stand by the Turkish army had been a fierce rearguard action on the Mount of Olives; and it was thought, rather unwisely, that the city was now safe from further fighting.

We had pushed the 66th C.C.S. forward to cope with the wounded. It was located in one of the numerous religious buildings, known to be bug-infested, and it was overcrowded with casualties owing to the weather hold-up. That gave someone in Cairo a bright idea, and a plausible excuse. The D.M.S. was bombarded with messages. The weather had improved, and on my way back to Gaza one morning I was passing a group of men repairing the wire road when I saw four ambulances approaching.

"Look!" one of the men shouted in an incredulous voice. "Look, women!"

It was a bevy of nursing sisters on the way up to the 66th C.C.S., looking very, very neat, very feminine to our eyes—eyes that had not seen a European woman for twelve to eighteen months. To those tired, wet men in sloppy uniform these girls looked like angels.

Unless one has lived in the desert for two years seeing nothing feminine except an occasional ragged Bedouin woman selling oranges, it is hard to visualise how excitedly the eyes of these men, sex-starved for many months, gazed fascinated on them. Not only were they white women but they were ministering angels going forward to hardship and possibly danger, to look after their comrades. It was an immense thrill.

They crowded round the cars almost reverently. Even I, who very much doubted the advisability of allowing women so near the front so soon, felt a pleasurable glow.

They told me they had been promised Christmas in Jerusalem, and I wondered who had put pressure on the D.M.S. to allow it. Actually they were too soon for safety. The Turks tried to recapture the city two days after Christmas, and fighting within five miles of the Damascus Gate went on for four days until the attack, designed by Marshal von Falkenhayn to recapture the city and restore the prestige of the Moslem world so badly shaken by our success, had failed. But it was touch-and-go for twenty-four hours.

As a result of the failure of this counter-attack, however, the 20th Corps drove the Turk well out of range of the city; and the 21st Corps at the other end of the line advanced eight miles and drove the enemy clear of artillery fire at Jaffa. This gave us elbow room and made the harbour and the prospective railway safe. The line was thus made secure all along the front; but we had overrun our communications and we could not advance any farther till these had been improved. Both armies settled down for the cold, bitter winter, each to consolidate its position.

Jerusalem itself was in a horrible, filthy, insanitary mess. The Turks had done nothing about cleaning it up for months. Rubbish and excreta were all over the place, particularly all round outside the walls and in the Valley of Hinnom. So we sent the 115th Sanitary Section forward at the request of the D.D.M.S., 20th Corps, to clean up. The Section was under the command of a bright young officer, Captain McDowall, who is now Professor of Physiology at King's College, London. He made a splendid job of it. I wonder if he remembers.

One of our main troubles was the lack of winter clothing. We had been fighting in tropical kit for two years in the desert, and none of us had any garments suitable for the winter in Palestine. We heard that the winter clothing sent out had been torpedoed on the way. There was a feeling, too, that it was unsafe to billet troops in houses, as these were liable to harbour typhus. Many of the hostels and monasteries were, we knew, bug-infested and so the order was to keep to tents. But when I went to inspect the 77th C.C.S. at Jaffa I found that the empty houses in the Jewish colony near-by at Tel Aviv were considered safe, so I was billeted for a few days in one which apparently had belonged to a dentist. Idly opening a drawer in a writing bureau I found a three-year-old invitation card to a wedding reception at Frascati's in Oxford Street. It gave me an odd, warm, intimate home feeling—it was so unexpected. The family had evidently been hurriedly evacuated, because I also found in my bedroom the woollen undergarments of the lady of the house. She must have been of ample proportions in different directions from mine for they were too big for me. But I was thankful for them all the same. I hope she forgave me on her return for taking the liberty of commandeering them. They saved my life in the cold, wintry weather of 1917-18 in the season of the 'latter rain'.

*

Soon after we took Jerusalem the D.M.S. sent for me.

"I have to send in my lists for awards," he said, "and I want to recommend you for a D.S.O., or would you rather have C.M.G.?"

I thought quickly. "I'd prefer a D.S.O., sir. Any civilian might get a C.M.G."

He laughed. "I see. You think of yourself, quite rightly, as a soldier now."

"Yes, I suppose I do, sir. I hadn't thought of it really like that before."

"Well, I will recommend you for a D.S.O. It'll show you have been under fire when you're a civilian again," he added with a twinkle.

And a D.S.O. it was. I was very pleased. I hadn't thought of any award when doing the job, but it was nice to write home about.

*

Returning to my headquarters at Kantara on the Canal, after being in the front line in the cold and rain for so long, was like going back into another world. It was chilly at night, but by day it was still round about 100 degrees Fahrenheit in the shade, and rain was unheard of. Working from Kantara, however, was now obviously much too far back; and we were delighted to learn we would be given the headquarters of the G.H.Q. at Kelab as soon as Allenby moved forward again.

The L. of C. now extended from Kantara to Jaffa and Jerusalem. From railhead to El Arish we treated our sick and wounded in eight C.C.S.s. Each C.C.S. had a military laboratory and an Egyptian hospital attached to it. From El Arish to the Canal we had five Stationary Hospitals. After that the men passed out of our domain into Egypt. My job was indeed getting bigger and bigger; and it was with a sigh of relief on my part that in the spring of 1918 we moved from Kantara and took over the camp at Kelab, south of Gaza, vacated by G.H.Q.

It was in a bare tract of country, just a series of huts and tents surrounded by barbed wire, and with a guard commanded by Lieutenant Albert Rutherston, who had changed the original spelling of his name, and was the younger artist brother of Sir William Rothenstein. 'Our Albert', as we came to call him affectionately, for he was a very lovable

person, stayed with us until the end of the war, and kept up a friendship with most of us to the time of his death. What he would have
done at Kelab if we had been attacked by Bedouin I cannot imagine.
But we never were.

It was very pleasant and very quiet at Kelab (which I believe means
the Place of Dogs). Reconnoitring enemy planes came over and
photographed us occasionally. They didn't get much information from
these reconnaissances, however. We were still described as G.H.Q. on
documents captured six months later, and our guard of British West
Indians was labelled Soudanese Troops.

We worked hard because we were told General Allenby intended to
make another advance in March. I was given a Staff Captain, H. S.
Crichton Starkey (later Group Captain Starkey, R.A.F.), to assist my
D.A.D.M.S., Captain J. H. Wood, and help cope with all the new
units that were coming into the L. of C.

The nearest native village was Khan Yunus. We could see the huddle
of huts and the slender minaret of the mosque; but the village was out
of bounds to all, both officers and other ranks. General Broadbent,
however, had a Bisharin Egyptian servant, who used to sneak away to
the village whenever he could. That shouldn't have mattered. But it
did.

One day I was called in to see the General. He looked ill, lying in
his tent. I started to examine him and stopped abruptly.

"What's wrong?" he said.

"Sir, you've got typhus fever," I answered.

"Colonel, I couldn't. How d'ye know? How could I get typhus?"

"Sorry, sir. It is typhus. I've seen hundreds in Serbia. I bet it's that
goddam man of yours. He's brought it from the native village."

I had to send him to the 36th Stationary Hospital which we had
placed in Gaza. Luckily he recovered completely and returned to us
before the great advance. Later when he was General Sir Edward
Broadbent we often talked over old times either at the 'Senior' or the
Athenæum.

CHAPTER XV

THE FINAL FIGHT

OUR PLANS for a spring offensive were now beginning to shape. I had two more Stationary Hospitals allotted to me at Gaza. The great Base Depot Medical Stores, holding a million pounds' worth of equipment, drugs and dressings, had been moved from Alexandria to Kantara and was now under me also; and a lovely white enamelled hospital train, No. 40, able to carry 600 patients, fitted with all the latest equipment, had come out from England. It was so precious I kept it at Kantara and never allowed it nearer the front than Gaza. In addition I had four other hospital trains, and two special ones for Egyptian Labour Corps sick and wounded, and for prisoners of war.

We heard that the Cabinet had sent out a very important hush-hush General to talk over plans for the offensive with Allenby, whose headquarters were now at Bir Salem, two miles from Ramleh on the Jaffa-Jerusalem road.

There was a good wire road from our L. of C. H.Q. to Ramleh which passed round a very conspicuous high, white, square medieval tower, 'The Crusader's Tower', surrounded by a broken wall. This was just outside Ramleh. I was travelling sedately on this wire road in my Ford to G.H.Q. to see the D.M.S., and had just got to the tower when a Rolls-Royce driven at tremendous speed swung round the corner and came dead at me. Both drivers swerved away from each other, the big car missed me and shot on to the soft powdery soil. My car banged gently into the wall surrounding the tower; and when I looked across I saw a figure in General's uniform, with rows and rows of ribbons, and could hear him swearing violently. That was my first and only meeting with General Smuts.

He had been sent out by Lloyd George to plan the prospective spring offensive with Allenby; but he left Palestine shortly afterwards, for all our plans for another advance had had to be scrapped. The reason was the German spring offensive against the Fifth and Third Armies which nearly broke through on the Western Front. This decisively stopped all idea of sending reinforcements to us. Instead the War Office began to deplete us of some more of our seasoned troops. Two complete divisions left us in March, nine Yeomanry regiments and nine battalions of infantry followed in April, and fourteen more battalions of infantry in May.

In their place we were informed we would be given two Indian divisions and some Indian cavalry. That meant a complete reorientation of my hospitals. I was now told I had to arrange for Indian troops with all their caste distinctions, special kitchens for certain castes—Hindoos and Mohammedans, Sikhs and Gurkhas. If the shadow of one man fell across the kitchen of another of a different caste, the food was unclean. And then there were the sweepers, the untouchables—I knew nothing about how to tackle all these difficulties, and it was obvious that most of the work I had done would have to be undone.

In addition, the presence of our army in territory recently occupied by the enemy, and the threatened addition of Indian troops, gave us two new major problems to tackle. In Sinai we had had desert sores, mainly diphtheritic, a few cases of typhus, some bacillary dysentery and one or two scares about cholera. In Palestine with the advent of Indian troops we would have amœbic dysentery added. But what was even more important was that Palestine was a highly malarious country, and the Turks had done nothing about it—or almost nothing. When we captured a German hospital later at Tul Keram, one of the medical experts there was a famous Professor of Tropical Medicine who had been lent by Berlin. I can see him now, a shambling, short-sighted, oldish man with thick glasses, who was pathetically grateful for being captured, and wanted to get home. He told me that for months he had been afraid of his life when inspecting in the front line, for the Turkish soldiers used to take pot-shots at German officers who came there.

Naturally nothing had been done to clear the malarious wadis and marshes behind the recent Turkish front. And now we had captured their terrain we soon began to find this out. Cases of P.U.O. (pyrexia of unknown origin) began to be rather frequent. But as we had no method of diagnosing the real condition in the front line, they all had to be evacuated to the Base. This worried me and I asked the D.M.S. for help. He sent me Major P. Manson-Bahr, R.A.M.C.

Manson-Bahr came, made an inspection of the fronts and reported to me, making certain suggestions which I referred to the D.M.S. These were obviously excellent, and we put them into force at once.

Hundreds of Egyptian Labour Corps men in consequence were placed at our disposal. The marshes were drained and oiled to prevent the mosquito larvæ developing. Small streams were canalised to prevent stagnant water collecting; and in this way we tried to make the occupied territory safe for troops. But of course we could not protect everyone from malaria. So Major Manson-Bahr worked out a scheme which he submitted to me. I approved this and the D.M.S. adopted it.

It was to form what we called 'Malaria Diagnosis Stations'. Seven medical officers and sixteen orderlies were sent down to Deir Seneid for a short course of training, and two malaria stations were allotted to each Corps. Each station had two bell tents, an E.P.I.P. tent, tables, lamps, two microscopes and the necessary slides and stains. Everything could be carried in a G.S. wagon. So, when a casualty from one of the divisions came into a Field Ambulance with a temperature, a blood slide was examined for the malaria parasite and, if it was found, he was treated at the Field Ambulance and returned to his unit quite quickly. This scheme was co-ordinated and controlled by Manson-Bahr from a central laboratory at Ludd. It turned out to be a brilliant success, saving many hundreds of men from months of invalidism.

One rather comic example of anti-malarial over-enthusiasm occurred near Jaffa. The cisterns of water in the orange groves were found to be swarming with goldfish. Some interfering person had these taken out of the cisterns, and the cisterns were then oiled with paraffin to kill mosquito larvæ. This caused great annoyance to the owners of the orange groves, who didn't like the oiling and had had the goldfish put in originally on purpose because they ate the larvæ of the mosquito. When I learnt this, I had to send down to Cairo for a tank full of minnows to placate the owners, replace the evicted goldfish and so keep down the mosquitoes.

The broad gauge railway which superseded the narrow Turkish one had now been extended up to Ludd; and in consequence our L. of C. headquarters had been transferred from Kelab to Ramleh, two miles from G.H.Q. and a few miles behind Ludd. Ramleh is a village on the Jaffa-Jerusalem road of some 7,000 inhabitants. It was out of bounds to troops for fear of typhus. We were quartered in the Franciscan Monastery, which was said to be on the site of the birthplace of Joseph of Arimathea. It was a fine stone building with great thick walls; and my office in it was extremely cool and comfortable. The monks had been evacuated by the Turks many months before; but the place had not been looted. There was a blue and gold chapel with the most ornate priestly vestments, heavy with gold embroidery, that I have ever seen—drawer after drawer full of them, all neatly folded up awaiting the return of their owners. Attached to the Monastery was a press for the extraction of olive oil. This was run by the monks for the benefit of the neighbourhood, as extensive olive groves surrounded the village. The Monastery had a flat roof on which I often used to sit in the cool of the evening watching the multitudinous life of the villagers.

About fifty yards away from the Monastery there was a white-washed building reputed to be situated over the tomb of Esau. It had been a Christian church in the time of the Crusaders, but it was now a mosque; and from its tall square minaret each night as I lay in my tent in the almond grove near-by, I could hear the muezzin chant in a clear tenor voice his call to the faithful to prayer.

The mosque stood on the edge of the Jaffa-Jerusalem road, and all traffic had to pass close to it. Each day on the dusty roadside in front of the mosque a picturesque scarlet-turbaned figure, bronze-faced, with a straggling grey beard falling over his long, loose, cotton jebbah of faded blue, used to sit squatting. In front of him was a pyramid of oranges which he replenished from a basket at his side; and as the traffic passed him his long lean fingers manipulated the oranges. We got used to him. He was there for months. I sometimes bought oranges from him. And then one day he disappeared. His pyramid of oranges had been a code with which he transmitted messages of troop movements to enemy spies passing along the road. I was sorry when I learnt we had had to shoot him.

*

General Hospital, Deir-el-Belah, Palestine (1918)

Inspection of prisoners of war, Ludd, Palestine (1918)

The author's wife Lilian (*née* Francis)

Nowhere in the world is the difference between the rainy and the dry season seen more distinctly than in Palestine. We had spent a miserable cold winter, mud everywhere, transport dislocated, troops unhappy in tropical kit.

And then came the spring, and in the words of the Song of Songs:

> Lo, the winter is passed, the rain is over and gone; the flowers appear on the earth; the time of the singing of birds is come, and the voice of the turtle is heard in our land.

The porous, limestone soil absorbed the surface rain; the wadis changed from raging torrents to streams; the so-called roads became passable to wheeled traffic; and I was at last able to get round to inspect my hospitals and Casualty Clearing Stations, from railhead to the Base.

At this time, while our trained and seasoned troops were being quietly moved back to the Western Front to help to counteract the German spring offensive, a new headache was sprung upon me. I had had a magnificent body of R.A.M.C. orderlies up to Christmas. Then suddenly I had instructions to release as many of these able-bodied men as possible for transfer to the infantry. In their place they gave me Class B men as stretcher-bearers and general duty orderlies; and these poor old chaps just could not stand up to the heavy work. It was probably necessary, but most disconcerting.

My own batman went. I said good-bye to him. I never expected to hear from him again. But I did. In 1920 he was living at High Wycombe, and I sent him on some things he had left in my charge for his wife in case he was killed.

Travelling by car through Philistia to inspect my hospitals, C.C.S.s and Field Laboratories was now a pleasure. Everywhere the land was blue with flowering Iris Palestina. The sun shone. It was warm. The foothills of the Shephelah on the left were bright with asphodel and anemones. The blue mountains of Judaea now seemed friendly as I looked across towards Hebron. Gath, a city of the Philistines, was a mound nestling at the entrance of the Wadi Burshein; Askalon, a Crusaders' ruin, on the edge of the blue Mediterranean. Gaza itself was a battered mass still almost deserted. I felt filled with biblical history.

H

My first stop was at Deir Seneid, where I had to settle a point of discipline between the O.C. of the C.C.S. and Captain Arthur Davies, the O.C. of one of our Field Laboratories. I came down heavily in favour of Davies and the laboratory.

At Gaza I now had three Stationary Hospitals, and after a considerable fight I had been able to persuade the railway people to build a special hospital siding for them because my Class B men couldn't carry loaded stretchers across the sand.

There I found my hospital siding was working and our beautiful white shining No. 40 hospital train busy evacuating sick and wounded. In it I travelled in great comfort to Kantara, where I stopped at my old hospital, the 24th Stationary. The Canal Zone had now been added to my area, as if it wasn't big enough already; and I had to inspect the 26th Stationary Hospital at Ismailia and two Indian General Hospitals at Suez.

On Lake Timsah at Ismailia there was a gunboat with a medical officer whose name sounded familiar. I met him at the French Club; and to my surprise recognised a well-known surgeon who had suggested in April, 1914, that I should join the R.N.V.R.

He stared at me in astonishment.

"I hear," he said, "that you're the A.D.M.S., L. of C."

"Yes," I answered.

"Well," he said, "it's lucky you didn't join us. I'm still a lieutenant-commander. God, what a bit of luck for you, and what an escape!"

At Ismailia also I met the Principal Medical Officer appointed to the Royal Flying Corps in Egypt. No one knew what sort of a uniform was correct for him, and he wore something between that of an admiral and a general. It looked odd. The Flying Corps then had no medical officers of their own, so I had to look after them as well.

At Suez I found I was also supposed to control hospital ships going to India. Actually these ships were being used to bring Indian hospital personnel and equipment to Egypt. All this was very hush-hush, and even I had been told only a week previously. The medical officers at Suez hospitals seemed to spend most of their time on the golf course, which was quite good except that it had not a single blade of grass on the whole of it. I cannot now remember anything more about them. They were out of the stream of casualties—just waiting. That is one of the unavoidable wastages of war. You've got to be ready even if you're never used.

This run to Suez, though I didn't know it, was the end of my slack period until the war was over. For now the change from British to Combined British and Indian Hospitals and Casualty Clearing Stations fell upon us.

To replace the seasoned divisions transferred to France, we had the two Indian divisions from Mesopotamia that had been promised us; and four of our remaining British divisions were converted into composite divisions, British and Indian. That meant Stationary and General Hospitals for Indians and Combined Clearing Stations with Indian bearers and sweepers.

The Indian Government, with its usual parsimony, sent these medical units short of officers, and still more short of stores. It was a headache. The D.D.M.S., Indian troops at G.H.Q., a charming little man who was more famous as a jockey than as a doctor, was not of much help to us; and I was at my wits' end, when the D.M.S. phoned me that he was giving me a D.A.D.M.S. (Indian Troops) to help with the administration.

"He is a Major David Munro, I.M.S., who has been acting as a surgical specialist at the new Indian hospital at Masaid. He was D.A.D.M.S. (Sanitation) at Basra, and I think you'll like him."

That was how David (afterwards Air Vice-Marshal Sir David Munro, K.C.B.) came into my life, and remained my friend for all the years that followed. In his autobiography, *It Passed Too Quickly*, he described in some detail his impressions of our time together at Ramleh.

My British D.A.D.M.S., as I said before, was Captain Crichton Starkey. His main job was to look after the evacuation of sick and wounded from the front line in Palestine to the Base in Egypt. He ran our seven hospital trains without a hitch. There was never any overcrowding. At noon, daily, he knew by phone or telegram the exact number of beds occupied and beds empty in each of our Casualty Clearing Stations, Stationary Hospitals and General Hospitals right down the line; and he could fill or empty them as required. It was an excellent piece of organisation.

To look after the hospital arrangements for the 80,000 Egyptian

Labour Corps in the L. of C., I had Major Treves, R.A.M.C., a nephew of Sir Frederick Treves, as D.A.D.M.S. (Egyptian). With this staff we tackled all the problems of the mixed races we had to deal with as they arose. It was all very stimulating.

Fighting of course was going on all the time We had one brisk side-show on the far side of Jordan in the mountains of Moab which wasn't too successful; and there was constant outpost skirmishing, attacks and counter-attacks all along the front from Jaffa to Jerusalem. In this way the front line was pushed forward twenty miles north of Jerusalem and eleven north of Jaffa.

Two events stand out in my mind. Troops in the Jordan Valley, 1,300 feet below sea level, guarding the bridge over the river, were living in a sub-tropical heat that was very enervating. As long as they remained there, they were listless but not really ill. We had a C.C.S. half-way down the winding road to Jericho at Talaat ed Dumm (the site of the Inn of the Good Samaritan), which took them in when they showed signs of anything more serious. One day it occurred to some-one that it would be a good thing to send a number of these tired men up from Jericho to Jerusalem for a short holiday before returning to duty. So they were bundled into G.S. wagons, complete with rifles and packs, and sent up to one of the rest camps. Now Jerusalem is 2,500 feet above sea level, so the change of 3,800 feet from sub-tropical to temperate was marked but very pleasant.

The men tumbled cheerfully out of the wagons and marched off to the tents allotted to them. Two days later over a hundred of them were dead or dying. It was a tragic catastrophe, totally unexpected, a com-plete mystery until Manson-Bahr came to probe into the matter. Then it was found that the men had died of malignant malaria. As long as they remained in the hot Jordan Valley they were in no great danger. It was the sudden change to the chilly nights in Jerusalem that caused the disaster. Once the cause was discovered we were able to defeat it, and the rest were saved. But it threw a sudden unexpected light on the story of the fate of Sennacherib's army at Jerusalem over 2,600 years earlier which you can read in the Second Book of Kings.

Sennacherib, on his triumphal march to Egypt to fight Taharga, a Pharoah of the 24th Dynasty, in the year 701 B.C., attacked Jerusalem. His men marching down either from Syria through the Valley of

Esdraelon, or possibly also up from the Jordan, got infected with malignant malaria. They could carry on as long as they were marching and fighting in the hot plains or valleys. But when they climbed into the cold Judaean hills and invaded Jerusalem, it was a different story.

For as they surrounded the city "it came to pass that night, that the angel of the Lord went out, and smote in the camp of the Assyrians an hundred fourscore and five thousand: and when they arose early in the morning, behold, they were all dead corpses".

The angel of the Lord was malignant malaria.

*

None of the younger generation will remember the great pandemic of influenza in 1918–19. We in Palestine got it early and very badly. When the epidemic started we used at first to evacuate the sick down to the Base. Then the Base Hospitals in Egypt filled up and I got a 'stand-by' order:

"No more cases to be evacuated over the Suez Canal. Egypt full."

Immediately my Base Hospitals at Kantara, Suez and Port Said also began to fill up; and I had to issue an order:

"Casualty Clearing Stations please hold cases."

It was beautiful sunny weather and the C.C.S.s put the men out in bivvies on stretchers on the sand. There they lay quite happily. We knew that in three or four days their temperatures would drop, and most of them would be all right; and we thought we had solved the problem.

But one day a distinguished General dropped in to visit a sick officer in one of our Clearing Stations. Now this General was a very important person indeed, and what he said went; and the language in which he said it was not always drawing-room language. Behind the Clearing Station he noticed lines and lines of bivvies, each with a prostrate man —all perfectly helpless, all being fed with tinned milk. Altogethe. there was about half a division behind this particular Casualty Clearing Station.

"What the blankety blank are all these blankety blank men doing here. What the blankety blank would happen if the blankety blank Turks attacked! Colonel! Evacuate these men forthwith!" he thundered.

Of course the O.C. of the C.C.S. knew that the General had no legal right to interfere in things medical, and that he could refuse; also he suspected that the Turks were probably suffering more than we were, and not in the least likely to attack. In addition he knew that if he had to pack these poor fellows into ambulance trains and send them down the line, they would be much worse off than where they were, because the desert is sterile, the days were warm, the nights cool and there was no pneumonia about. If, however, he sent them into crowded Egypt, many of them would be sure to get pneumonia, and many of them would die. If he kept them where they were, most of them would probably be all right in a week.

But a red-faced Major-General, all tabs and ribbons, is a fearsome object to tackle. He might claim military safety as against medical opinion and possibly he might win. So the O.C. of the C.C.S. stood to attention and said:

"Yes, sir! Certainly, sir! At once, sir!"

After that he rang me up and we talked it over. Then we shifted the line of bivvies back 200 yards farther away from the Casualty Clearing Station, called the new area 'Convalescent Camp No. 40', and he reported that he had evacuated the lot to this camp, without saying where it was. After that he rang me up again, and we had a good laugh together.

A few days later the General got influenza himself, and promptly refused to be sent down the line. By the time he was well and less truculent the crisis was over.

Years later at a dinner of the E.E.F. Club in London, I told him this story against himself. He said he did not remember a thing about it. Perhaps he had forgotten. Influenza does blot out memory sometimes —or maybe not.

One of the great pleasures in going about in Palestine was seeing the places of biblical interest. I spent days in Jerusalem, motoring up from Ramleh. We had made the Jaffa–Jerusalem road an excellent one by this time, but always at the hairpin bends overlooking the Vale of Ajalon, where Joshua bade the sun stand still, my heart used also to stand still for the few minutes while we tore round, one wheel perched perilously, as it seemed to me, over the edge. I think the A.S.C. drivers used to do it on purpose to take it out of 'brass hats'. Once or twice I thought I noticed a sort of grin on the face of one particular driver who used to take me to the Holy City.

Jerusalem itself always depressed me. Apart from the Dome of the Rock, which obviously was the site of the Temple of Solomon, all the other sites seemed spurious; and the wars of the Christian sects—Greek, Armenian, Syrian, Latin—over the Church of the Holy Sepulchre, and the rowdy scenes on Easter Eve at the Miracle of the Holy Fire, I found most degrading.

Bethlehem and the Church of the Nativity were more soul-satisfying. One felt the Saviour might have been born there.

One day I was told that the broad gauge railway on its way to Jerusalem had reached Artuf, but owing to the steep gradients would stop there for some time. I was to place a C.C.S. therefore at the junction between the two gauges to take the cases evacuated from Jerusalem by the old narrow Turkish railway. I went to inspect the site at Artuf, in a railway lorry, at the point where the Wadi el Surar suddenly begins to rise towards Jerusalem. The site looked rather desolate. But there was a Jewish settlement near-by, where emigrants from Bulgaria had taken over a portion of the Wadi and were making a success of it. The head of the settlement was a charming cultured man who said he would do all he could to help us with fresh vegetables and fruit at the C.C.S., a promise for which I was most grateful.

"Why did you choose this place?" I said.

"Ah," he answered, "it is good soil. But there is more than that. This is Beth-shemesh, where the Philistines brought back the ark of the covenant. To us it is a holy place."

So when I returned to my quarters in the Monastery of Joseph of Arimathea at Ramleh, I took down my Bible and read how the Philistines defeated the Hebrews at Beth-shemesh and captured the ark of the covenant; and how, when they took it to Ashdod, bubonic plague broke out among the citizens; and later when it went to Gath thousands died of the plague. Obviously the ark carried the plague with it. Finally, therefore, when it was brought to Ekron, the inhabitants of that city in fear besought the lords of the Philistines to return it to Israel with a votive offering of golden mice, hoping to appease the wrath of Jahweh, the Jewish God. Terrified by the plague, the priests of Dagon advised the lords of the Philistines to make a new cart of wood and put the ark on it with an offering of jewels of gold in a coffer beside it; and they suggested that the two milch kine who drew it should go their way unguided. If they went direct to Beth-shemesh, they said, then it was really the God of Israel who had smitten them with the plague; but if not it was a chance that happened.

The kine, watched eagerly by the multitude, made straight for Beth-shemesh, the Philistines accepted this as evidence of the power of Jahweh, the plague left the coastal plain, and the ark came to rest at Artuf, the modern name for Beth-shemesh.

I took much more interest in my C.C.S. at Artuf after I read the story again; and I followed the narrative of the later journey to Kirjath Jearim (Karet el Enab), where the ark rested for many years until King David took it from there to Jerusalem after he had captured it from the Jebusites. Enab is on the road from Ramleh to Jerusalem, and we had a Field Ambulance of the 60th Division there commanded by my old friend, Tubby Layton of Guy's.

*

The long summer in Palestine was one of active preparation for the great attack we knew must come before the autumn rains. Everywhere everyone was working. The Indian troops were being trained for active fighting. We of the medical services were perfecting our plans to give the fighting men every possible aid in time of battle. It was hard, constant work. Colonel Henry Wade had been appointed consulting surgeon to the L. of C., and he designed a plan which would allow of expert surgeons working almost in the front line. We had four surgical teams scheduled to work either with Main Dressing Stations or Casualty Clearing Stations. Each team had two operating surgeons, one anæsthetist and four nursing orderlies. Their equipment was carried in two box Fords and two other box cars were used to transport the personnel.

In this way we hoped to have first-class surgical help right behind the front line.

It was an experiment which proved a great success but, like other experiments of the 1914–18 War, was forgotten, to be re-discovered again in 1939–45.

Behind this front line we had three British Casualty Clearing

Stations, two Indian Clearing Hospitals and five Combined British and Indian Casualty Clearing Stations. These provided for our very mixed army of British and Indian infantry, Australian, New Zealand and Indian cavalry. It meant a lot of administrative work; but with the help of Major Munro we learnt what the Indian soldier needed in things medical.

Three linked Stationary Hospitals were placed at Gaza so that the journey from the front line to the Canal could be broken comfortably. On the Canal itself at Kantara we had the original two linked hospitals I had induced the D.M.S. to sanction, so that no one hospital would be as overworked as we had been at the first battle of Gaza.

That, too, was an idea that proved valuable in the Second World War. An anomalous and a much more doubtful idea, which I think was a failure, was establishing two General Hospitals, one of 1,200 and one of 2,400 beds, complete with women nurses, just south of Gaza, and so in advance of my Stationary Hospitals. I thought they were too far forward. They had no *raison d'être*, but weren't they popular with the 'brass hats'! Think of some hundreds of charming girls planted out with little to do on the edge of the desert having a marvellous time, with two distracted matrons trying to prevent brigadiers taking them out for long rides when they ought to have been on duty in the wards. I was sorry for the matrons and very sorry for myself, for I did not want General Hospitals there at all, because I thought it bad policy to hold patients for lengthy treatment in the desert. A General Hospital is for final treatment. Mine, I thought, were completely out of place; and I was at constant loggerheads with their Commanding Officers accordingly, because they wanted to treat the patients, and I wanted to evacuate them out of the way into Egypt.

The two ideas were diametrically opposed. But the nurses were eager to get out from Egypt into Palestine. It gave them a kick to feel they were near the fighting; and to satisfy the numbers who volunteered to go 'up the line' we had to have General Hospitals, and also even had to staff Stationary Hospitals with them. They managed, indeed, to get up everywhere—as far, actually, as the Casualty Clearing Stations. Everyone loved seeing them there, including myself in spite of my opinions on the subject. And how the tommies loved them! To be a woman in the Lines of Communication at that time was to be almost a queen.

One rather charming episode was a visit we had from the late Duke of Connaught. He had been wintering for his health in Upper Egypt; and it had been suggested that it would be a gracious thing if he came to G.H.Q. and presented decorations awarded to those mentioned in despatches after the capture of Jerusalem. So up he came to Bir Salem to Allenby's headquarters, and it was arranged that the presentations should be made at our L. of C. H.Q. in the Monastery of Joseph of Arimathea.

Accordingly we tidied up everything one morning, and the presentations were made in the corridor opposite my office. The Duke looked old, and very tired, but he went through the ceremony of pinning medals and decorations steadily until all was over, in the gracious way that royalty always has.

And then the trouble began. The decorations that had been sent out for the occasion had been lost at sea, and there had therefore been an anxious scurry round to borrow from anyone and everyone who had any. So the same decorations were used two or three times over. That would have been all right if some Australians who had been decorated hadn't promptly disappeared, taking the borrowed decorations with them. There was an almighty shemozzle about it, and I still don't know what happened, but I'm told some fellows never saw their decorations again.

We were sufficiently far behind the front line as a rule to be immune to artillery fire; and unless there was a big attack going on everything around us was normally quiet. But every now and again we would hear a crump and know that a shell had fallen on Jaffa or near Ludd or miles behind the front line near Jerusalem; and it was soon evident that the Turks had a long-distance weapon which they used to pip off at us like 'Big Bertha', the German gun that used to be fired into Paris. We called our gun 'Jericho Jane', and bets were constantly being made as to where she would appear next. The Turks must have used much hard labour carting her backwards and forwards across the wadis. It was a silly sort of thing to do, for its psychological effect was nil.

This went on about once a week for months, and then we noticed that it had stopped, and wondered why. After the great advance we found poor old 'Jericho Jane' lying on her side, abandoned in a ravine in Samaria. Some of our fellows grew quite sentimental over her fate. As an Australian sergeant in one of our C.C.S.s said to me:

"We missed the old bitch."

*

CHAPTER XVI

VICTORY. DAMASCUS

ALL OUR HOPES of a spring offensive in Palestine had been fore-stalled of course by the German attack on the Fifth and Third Armies in Picardy in March, 1918; so we in Palestine spent the spring and summer months preparing instead to attack before the rain.

Allenby had been prevented, you will remember, by water shortage from capturing the Turkish army in front of Gaza at one swoop. He now was determined not to leave anything like this again to chance. The area held by the Turks in front of our line was therefore meticu-lously reconnoitred from the air, and information from spies collected and collated. In addition, at the dark of the moon each month, a mysterious Bedouin appeared at our H.Q., was rowed in a small boat out from Jaffa and dropped on the coast behind the Turkish front. He carried with him a supply of test tubes, and at any well and river, wadi and marsh, behind the enemy's lines he took samples, and also calculated the output of water. The samples came back to our water analysis laboratory at Kantara; and eventually we had a complete record of the physical, chemical and bacteriological content of the enemy water supply as far up as Haifa.

On the other side of Jordan the Arab revolt was making the Turk very uncomfortable. The Hedjaz railway from Damascus to Mecca was constantly being raided and cut by a ubiquitous person named Lawrence. We began to hear about this man. I was told he was not a soldier—"just one of those excavating chaps from the British Museum who worked in the Arab Bureau".

One day, however, I was asked to see a hush-hush patient who had arrived at Allenby's headquarters dressed as an Arab chief, and then had changed into the uniform of a lieutenant-colonel in the British Army. It was Lawrence; and I can't think of anyone less like the mental picture the world now has of him. He was a little man with the delicate frame of a girl, and startlingly intense blue eyes in a thin, very tanned face. He looked about twenty, wore his uniform carelessly— a second-lieutenant's badge on one loose shoulder-strap, a lieutenant-colonel's on the other—and went about in carpet slippers. The condition I treated him for cleared up in two days and he was off again on his mysterious journeys into the unknown. I saw no more of him. But I heard he had described some of the schemes advanced in conference at G.H.Q. for co-operation with the Arabs as "damned nonsense". His reception by the Staff was therefore definitely cool.

We knew practically nothing about Lawrence then; his appearance was quite unimpressive, as I have said; and the legends that have accumulated around him since were only then in the making. His distinction as a writer came of course later. Since reading *The Seven Pillars of Wisdom* I have always wished I had been able to see more of him.

He had impressed Allenby so much, however, that he agreed to collaborate with the Arabs; and I was told to supply Feisal's army with all the medical stores they required, without payment. As a result of this decision to collaborate, two raids were made on Amman, after bridging the Jordan. The raids were not very successful. The Mountains of Moab proved a formidable obstacle, the weather was cold and wet, and delays in reaching objectives allowed the Turks to reinforce Amman. We had to withdraw over the Jordan. The Turks, however, got a fixed impression that we intended to fight our way to Damascus through Transjordania, and this, as it happened, proved most valuable to us later, because they heavily reinforced their army there.

Allenby had studied the history of the previous successful invasions of Palestine. He had noted that in ancient times all of them were fought along the Mediterranean coast, either up from the south from the Egypt of the Pharaohs or down from the north under Sennacherib, Nebuchadnezzar, Cambyses. Turning to modern times, Napoleon had forced his way up from Egypt as far as Acre before malignant malaria decimated his army, and made his dream of emulating Alexander the Great an empty one.

Allenby therefore decided to make his attack also along the maritime plain, and not over Jordan. The problem, then, was to deceive the

Turk, as he did at Gaza, by attacking where least expected. Elaborate schemes to camouflage his intentions were accordingly worked out.

Zero day was fixed for September 19th, and as my part of the camouflage I was instructed to tell the hospitals at Gaza that the Commander-in-Chief would inspect them on September 25th, and the General Hospital at Port Said that he would be there on the 28th. This was for the benefit of the ground spies. I felt sorry at the time for our units wasting spit and polish for a week to get ready for these bogus inspections. But these were my orders.

In Jerusalem I sent a loquacious medical officer to visit all the monasteries and convents, and make a careful investigation of their bed capacity for the reception of the wounded we might expect from an advance over Jordan. This also was sure to get noised around. I put up two dummy hospitals in the Jordan Valley alongside a deserted camp, where all the tentage had been left standing, and 15,000 dummy horses built of canvas had been placed to deceive high-flying enemy planes into thinking the cavalry were still there. I drew the line at erecting Red Cross sky signs at these hospitals; but I ran empty ambulances up and down the Jericho road.

Troops were moved at night from the Judaean hills to the orange groves around Jaffa, where they were hidden during the day. All this was very hush-hush; and in consequence I had querulous enquiries from some of my Casualty Clearing Stations at Ludd, asking why sick and tired men from units as far away as Jerusalem were being dumped direct on them instead of coming through their own Field Ambulances. Why were they not coming through the proper channels? I couldn't tell them that 20,000 men and 12,000 cavalry were being quietly transferred from the Jordan Valley and the Judaean hills to the Plain of Sharon, and Johnny Turk would soon be in for a tremendous surprise.

All our plans for handling our own sick and wounded were well ahead, and arrangements had been made for at least 5,000 sick and wounded prisoners, many of whom we knew would be suffering from dysentery or malaria or both, and would have to be treated by us in our Egyptian hospitals.

I was in daily contact with the D.M.S., Major-General Swan, whose office was at G.H.Q., Bir Salem, two miles away from Ramleh. Everything seemed to be going smoothly. And then one afternoon I had a

message that the D.M.S. and his acting A.D.M.S., Lieutenant-Colonel
Bridges, had gone to Jaffa for a swim, and that Bridges had been
drowned and the D.M.S. rescued with some difficulty.

This was most distressing. Bridges was a first-class officer. He had
taken on the post of A.D.M.S., G.H.Q., temporarily to allow Colonel
Bagshawe, who had held the post without a change since 1916, to have
a holiday before the big advance started. I knew he had been disappointed because he had not been given my job when Allenby took
over from Murray. But he had got over that and we were friends.
The main trouble, however, was the General. The death of Bridges
upset him very much. He just went to pieces for a fortnight. I could
get no orders from him; and the A.D.M.S. divisions were pressing me
for stores and equipment from my Advanced Depots Medical Stores
which I felt they were not entitled to, and over which I turned out to
be right later.

"Let them have them," was all I got out of the General.

Egypt kept asking for information, which I tried to give them; and
Colonel Bagshawe, the actual A.D.M.S., who was on holiday in
Cyprus, had to be recalled hurriedly. I did all I could meanwhile to
shield the D.M.S. because I liked him very much. He was a sound
administrator. He was an old Trinity man like myself. I had been a
Resident to his brother at Steevens' Hospital, Dublin, and I knew his
nephew Jocelyn Swan, one of the surgeons at the Cancer Hospital in
London, very well. But I sensed that there was trouble brewing at
G.H.Q.

One morning I got a message that the C.-in-C. wanted to inspect
one of my Casualty Clearing Stations at Ludd. I had three British
C.C.S.s and one Indian Clearing Hospital there; someone told me,
unfortunately, that Allenby had served in India and I thought he'd like
to see what an Indian Medical Unit was like in war-time with its 120
Sepoy guards in full fighting kit.

Allenby's big car drew up sharp to time, and I met him and introduced the I.M.S. Colonel at the entrance to the Camp. It was beautifully laid out, every tent placed mathematically correct. To the left the
Sepoy guard of fierce turbaned Sikhs with fixed bayonets came
smartly to the salute.

Allenby walked down inspecting the line and shook hands with the Subahdar and each Havildar in turn. This was a great and unexpected honour, something to tell their children's children about years later. Everyone was smiling.

And then the awful thing happened.

To the right as we turned back to go out, 200 men in long, yellow garments stood equally at attention. These were the sweepers, the untouchables. Before we could do anything Allenby suddenly went over and shook the hand of the head sweeper.

"Oh, my God," gasped the I.M.S. Colonel, "I feel sick! Didn't he know?"

My heart also sank, but there was nothing any of us could now do about it. It was just one of those things that shouldn't happen, and when it did it was impossible to do anything. What distressed us particularly was that there was not one of those Sikh soldiers who did not now feel dishonoured. It was a terrible thing to have happened. Obviously the C.-in-C. had never been in India, and was completely unaware of the awful thing he had done.

For the trouble over untouchables is that to touch one makes oneself untouchable. That was the feeling in 1918.

It might have been expected that when India came to govern herself it would be different. But if you look at *The Times* of December 18th, 1953, you will read the following:

"In Madya Prades untouchables are not allowed to use village wells or outer temples. In Madras they are too afraid to use shops, bathing ghats and roads for fear of offending the caste Hindus who employ them. In Sanrashtra they cannot ride horses or eat ghee (butter), and wearing ornaments by their women is frowned on. In the Punjab they walk miles to fetch water and wait hours at wells, paying caste Hindus to draw it for them. In some villages they have tried to draw water themselves under police protection but caste Hindus have stoutly resisted."

If it was as strong as that in 1953 you can imagine what it was like in 1918. I cannot remember much more of what happened on that unfortunate afternoon. I was too unhappy. We went round some of the other units, particularly the chief anti-malarial laboratory of Major Manson-Bahr. I answered dully anything I was asked, feeling I was making a very, very poor impression. At length the ordeal was over.

The Aide-de-Camp said to me:

"Will you ride back to G.H.Q. with the General?"

I felt I could not face it, and I said:

"No, I think not. I shall follow him in my car if he wants me."

The Aide-de-Camp looked curiously at me, but said nothing.

I had a strong suspicion that for some reason the inspection had been arranged to see what I was like. The C.-in-C. was much too busy otherwise. I guessed it had something to do with the trouble over the D.M.S.; and I felt, owing to the contretemps over the sweepers, I had not come well out of it.

I went back to my office very depressed.

Two days later the blow fell.

The D.M.S. was superseded, and the D.D.M.S. of the 20th Corps, Colonel Richard Luce, appointed in his place.

Again I felt quite sick. I had not been able to protect Swan.

Next day the new D.M.S. sent for me, and we went through all the medical arrangements that had been made in the Lines of Communication and in Egypt, for of course I knew them off by heart. I also told him what had been done about the 21st Corps. He knew his own arrangements for the 20th Corps, and thus had a full picture of our plans.

We neither of us mentioned Major-General Swan; but when two years later I was asked by General Macpherson to compile an account of those arrangements for the *Official History of the War. Medical Services. General History*, Vol. III, I wrote this:

> Major-General Swan had by this time organised the Medical Services during the difficult period of reconstructing the Medical Units for British and Indians, and for the coming final operations. After his departure these final medical preparations, made under his administration, underwent no alteration and proved remarkably efficient.

Well. That was that. Poor old Swan was dead by the time this was in print; but the record stands, and I am glad I had the opportunity of writing it.

*

I can still remember vividly the excitement of the great break-through.

Late in the evening of September 18th, far off in the Judaean hills we could hear the distant sound of guns. That meant that the 20th Corps was attacking along the road to Samaria, mainly with the idea of distracting the enemy's attention from the real attack that was coming near Jaffa.

Zero hour was fixed for four-thirty in the morning of September 19th; and a group of us from the H.Q. Staff stood silent on the flat roof of the Monastery of Joseph of Arimathea, waiting, listening. There had been a bright moon but it had set beyond Jaffa about three a.m. and the faint rose tint of dawn was just beginning to show over the Judaean hills.

Promptly to the minute the silence was broken by the roar of 385 heavy guns. It sounded tremendous. This went on without a break for fifteen minutes and then stopped abruptly. We knew that meant our troops were now storming the enemy trenches, and we soon learnt that the attack had been overwhelmingly successful. It was a complete surprise. The enemy were taken totally unawares, and our infantry were through the three miles of front defences by seven o'clock in the morning, opening a gap through which the cavalry poured—nine thousand men and horses thundering through the already broken Turkish army, hooves flying, men yelling, sabres flashing, lances glinting in the morning light. I could see it all in my mind's eye. It must have been a wonderful sight to watch, this the last cavalry charge the British Army will ever make—for cavalry as a fighting arm is no longer possible in modern warfare.

They didn't stop to take prisoners, they brushed aside opposition, they just galloped on, up and up, along the Plain of Sharon, through the gap below Mount Carmel, across the Valley of Esdraelon. They made straight for the headquarters of the enemy Commander-in-Chief at Nazareth; and they arrived there at five-thirty a.m. on the morning of September 20th, to the complete surprise of General Liman von Sanders and the personnel of his Staff. He got away leaving his pyjamas behind, but most of his Staff were caught in their night-shirts.

They had no idea of what had been happening the previous day; for their communications with the Seventh and Eighth Turkish Armies had been severed by Air Force bombing at Afule. They could not believe that it had been possible for our men to advance seventy miles in the time. They thought we must have landed along the coast. They had not had time to destroy the headquarters documents, and these made very interesting reading afterwards. Later in the day a German plane from Damascus came, circled round and landed at the Nazareth aerodrome unaware of its capture. It carried official letters and correspondence for Liman von Sanders—again most interesting.

The cavalry by this time had got behind the Seventh and Eighth Turkish Armies. They had captured the railway which was their only line of supply or retreat. All the enemy communications with Syria had been cut off; and they were caught hopelessly between the exultant cavalry and our infantry divisions pressing ever forward.

It was a débacle. We captured 75,000 men, completely destroying two Turkish armies in forty-eight hours.

It was then our medical troubles began. We had hopelessly underestimated the number of sick and wounded prisoners we were likely to have. We had placed one Egyptian Hospital alongside each of our four C.C.S.s at Ludd, and thought that two thousand beds would be enough. They were quite inadequate. Dysentery, malaria, pellagra claimed thousands, and so did death. We had over ten thousand to deal with.

Another trouble also now overtook us. The troops were moving so quickly onwards, and the Field Ambulances with them, that it was found the latter could not keep up without shedding part of their equipment. So all day, and each day for several days, we of the L. of C. were getting messages by despatch rider like this: "Have had to abandon part of equipment El Tirah (or Tul Keram or Musmus—further and further away each time). Please collect." Just that: "Please collect." No suggestion of how the L. of C., which possessed no wheeled transport of its own, could collect.

Now a Field Ambulance in those days was worth about £20,000, and we did not want valuable equipment to be looted by wandering Bedouin; so with Major Munro I crossed the broken Turkish front to have a look round, and see if we could arrange for empty returning ration lorries to pick up our equipment.

What we came across was most interesting. The trenches were beautifully made, well revetted and loop-holed, and the German engineers had believed them impregnable. There were three lines of them about two miles in depth; and in many places the wire had not been cut completely by the bombardment. Everywhere hundreds of machine-guns and Mauser rifles lay scattered round, abandoned. Boxes and boxes of half-opened and unopened ammunition cluttered the trenches. There were unexpectedly few dead, and such as we saw were mainly Gurkhas, suggesting that the Turks had panicked when we reached them, and the only dead were those of our own men caught in the frontal attack before the enemy fled.

We knew that the headquarters of the Turkish Eighth Army had been at a place called Tul Keram on the Turkish railway about ten miles further north. It had been captured the previous evening, and it was there for the first time I saw the utter destruction that bombing and artillery fire could do. Tul Keram was a shambles, dead men, dead horses, dead donkeys, wrecked enemy transport everywhere. We went into the Turkish hospital. It was horrible. It stank to high heaven; all the patients were suffering either from dysentery or malaria. They were mere living skeletons. When we got back to Ludd we went into the emergency P.O.W. hospitals we had erected. They were already overcrowded, and the hand of death was busy. I noted four G.S. wagons piled high with dead bodies being taken away. That was one day's toll.

Two days later I went again to Tul Keram and took the road east towards Messudieh Junction. I wish I hadn't, for I saw there one of the most horrible examples of the power of air attack I ever wish to forget.

A scouting plane had spotted a long train of guns, transport and troops making for the station hoping to escape north, not knowing that all escape by rail had by then been cut off. They were crowding along a road in a narrow defile; and as soon as the pilot spotted them he flew back to his aerodrome and returned with every machine he could muster. Up and down the defile, backwards and forwards they flew, raining 20 lb. bombs and hand-grenades on the defenceless, disorganised mob on the narrow track confined between cliffs on either side. There was no escape. It was a horrible sight: dead horses, their bellies already blown up with gas, dead mules, donkeys, guns, lorries, wagons, water-carts, field kitchens all smashed, dead mutilated oxen, remnants of human beings; and masses and masses of white army papers scattered for miles on either side, blown out of the wagons trying to carry away the records. I picked up the pay-book of a German N.C.O. It gave, amongst other details, the size he took in boots.

I turned back, sick and depressed. War, when you come up against it like that, is horrible. Yet it had been necessary. This particular bombing finished off the Eighth Turkish Army. A few days later the Seventh Army was caught similarly in a defile trying to escape over the Jordan, and there an even more gruesome destruction took place. In five days Allenby had destroyed two armies. All that was now left between us and Damascus was the Fourth Army on the other side of Jordan; and Chaytor's Force and the Arabs under Feisal and Lawrence disposed of this very soon after.

As the army moved forward we of the L. of C. took over; and my job now was to push Casualty Clearing Stations up into the occupied enemy territory. I established an Indian Clearing Hospital at Haifa a few days after we captured the place, and this proved a great relief, for we could evacuate our sick and wounded and unwanted prisoners of war by ship from there to Port Said and Alexandria.

The Turks carried influenza to our army, and the death-rate was heavy. But in addition we were now in the unprotected area where nothing had been done to kill mosquito larvæ; malaria was rampant; and our men holding the captured towns and the railway began to suffer severely from fever.

The Turks had blown up the bridge over the Jordan near Sâmakh, just below the sea of Galilee, in their retreat. The Bridging Company we sent to rebuild it suffered very heavily. I had to send them four medical officers in succession because each succumbed to malaria after he had been with them a fortnight. When I went to inspect them I found their camp was down by the Jordan where malaria was rife. When I insisted on their moving half a mile up the side of the valley, they were able to carry on again.

One curious episode happening at that time was the complete disappearance of a cavalry squadron. It got lost somewhere on the way to Damascus; and it was the job of the L. of C. to find it. We were searching rather casually when one of our staff, Lieutenant-Colonel McLeod, riding along the ridge over Mount Carmel, spotted what looked like horse lines in the plain below, and thought he'd like to investigate. When he went down he saw at once it was the lost squadron, but then to his surprise he found a German N.C.O. in charge. The N.C.O. explained that he and the other Germans were prisoners of war who had been captured by the squadron, that all the British were down with influenza, and that he and his comrades were looking after them. The Germans, he said, had not attempted to escape. They had no desire to do so and have their throats cut by the Arabs. So they remained.

A fortnight later we were notified that the L. of C. now extended to Damascus and Beirut. That meant I had to take over medical care of both places. Beirut was easy. A Casualty Clearing Station was sent by sea. Damascus was a more difficult problem. It had been captured by Australian cavalry, closely followed by Lawrence and Feisal and his Arab army, and no one seemed to know who was in control.

So Major Blake, our D.A.Q.M.G., and I were instructed to go up to see what we could do about it. The Turkish railway on the far side of Jordan from Damascus to Amman, which Lawrence had been play-fully blowing up for months, had been repaired by our Sappers. It was now in our possession, and the railway from Haifa across the Jordan at Sâmakh connecting up with the Hedjaz railway at Deraa was again running.

I had in the L. of C. Command an R.A.M.C. officer, Captain Mac-kinnon, who had been a medical missionary in Damascus before the war; so I decided to take him with me, to his great delight, in order that he could take over our hospital work there.

Three things stick in my memory still of that journey. One was the wonderful spiral of the railway in the Deran Pass in the hills of Samaria. It circled round in three great loops for about four miles, each loop just about one hundred feet apart on the side of the mountain. Another was the bridge across the Jordan near Sâmakh which the bridge-builders had repaired. And the third was that we cooked our breakfast on the railway station at Deraa sitting on sleepers in the grey morning light, propping up our canteen tins on the railway line. It was all very quiet. There were no signs of the fierce fight for its possession of a few weeks before.

When we got to Damascus Captain Mackinnon took charge of me. We made first of all for his own house, which we found intact except that most of the furniture had gone. He borrowed a screwdriver from somewhere and went up about eight steps on the staircase, unscrewed the under side of one of the steps and drew out with a shout of triumph two beautiful double-barrelled guns.

"I hid them when I left," he said. "Now I've got to find where my piano is."

He did find it. It had been saved for him by one of his old patients.

At Damascus I stopped at the Victoria Hotel. It was most comfortable, run by an old rascal of an Austrian who was quite happy to cater for anyone who paid him. The Turkish G.H.Q. had messed with him, and we had succeeded them a few weeks later. I remember walking across the bridge over the River Barada to the hotel. There was a machine-gun still on the far side covering the approach. Crossing the bridge I met a New Zealand officer coming the other way. He stopped me, smiled, held out his hand and said:

"Hello, sir. D'ye remember me?"

After a moment's hesitation it came back to me.

"So you got out to the front again, did you?" I said in a surprised voice.

"Yes, sir. Thanks to you I was passed fit after eighteen months."

He was one of my first cases at Millbank Hospital in London after I came home from Serbia. I had sutured his median nerve, which had been severed by a piece of shell in France; and I had certainly not expected to get a hundred per cent result like this. It was most gratifying. I had him in for a short drink, for which I was grossly overcharged.

Actually, if I had had the courage, I could have made a lot of money in Damascus that day, as the money-changers there were selling five-pound Bank of England notes for fifty piastres, then worth half a guinea. I thought they were almost certainly forgeries. But I was wrong. They were genuine. They had not been saleable since war began. No doubt they had been bought cheaply by the money-changers, and they were eager to cash in on them when we arrived. Two days later they had risen to par.

My main official job was to take over the Baranke Barracks Hospital and put Captain Mackinnon in charge. We went there and were met by a little German medical officer who had been left in charge. He clicked his heels, stood stiffly to attention and was quite surprised when

I shook hands with him. The place was horrible. It was not his fault, of course. It was in the process of being cleaned up by a horde of Turkish prisoners of war, who were marched back at sunset to a P.O.W. camp run by the Arabs. They complained that they were very hungry, and we found that no food had been issued to them that day, so we had to issue it for them.

When we made enquiries we found that actually there were 20,000 prisoners of war in Damascus, many of them sick or wounded, and the problem of feeding them was a very difficult one. The Arabs had had no experience of this kind of work; and we came to the conclusion perhaps we had been rather too censorious over their refusal to look after our hospital workers.

Next morning, after I had inspected the 66th C.C.S., I left Damascus for Moallaka on the way to Beirut, accompanied by two medical officers, one of whom was a fluent Arabic scholar. At the railway station and *en route* we bought hard-boiled eggs, as there was nothing else to eat. Running round in the station yard we noticed an active little slip of a wide-eyed girl with only one arm. The other had been amputated at the shoulder. She was a real little *gamine*, as sharp as a needle, aged about fourteen. She tacked herself on to us; and spun a yarn to the M.O. who spoke Arabic, saying she wanted to get back home to Moallaka, but she had no money and the railway people wouldn't let her travel without. She persuaded us to hide her in the horse-box behind our carriage, and made us feel we were doing a charitable act.

The train wound its way through the great gorge of the River Barada (the Abana of the Bible), through the Anti-Lebanon, climbing all the time until we reached the Lebanon at Moallaka, where we had a Divisional Hospital Clearing Station. But when we got to Moallaka we had a surprise. The little *gamine* jumped out, cocked a snook at the station-master, yelled derisively at him and us, and disappeared rapidly into the village. The station-master was furious with her and also with us. It seems that even at her age she was already a prostitute; he had got rid of her to Damascus, hoped never to have another sight of her; and here she was back again as bold as brass.

We felt rather foolish when this was brought home to us; and I thought I caught the O.C. of the Clearing Station smiling; but I may

have fancied that. He was most kind, told us he had billeted us in the
hotel near-by, and arranged a bridge party with some ladies after
dinner. This was a surprise. We had not grasped the fact that Moallaka
on the heights of the Lebanon was a holiday resort for the wealthy
merchants of Beirut, and this hotel was equipped with all the amenities
of a Swiss mountain resort. We had an excellent dinner with wine and
liqueurs, found our luxurious beds were furnished with fine linen, and
each room had a bathroom off. The ladies of the bridge party also
startled us a bit. They were in full evening dress. We felt like clumsy
interlopers in their polite society. My French was quite inadequate for
the occasion; and I could not make them out. It seemed they had been
equally polite to Djemal Pasha only a month before.

Next morning we had arranged to go down the forty-mile journey
to Beirut by the rack and pinion railway which descended from the
Lebanon. But the French station-master said the railway was not working. He was almost rude, and we suspected was taking his revenge on
us over the little *gamine* girl. We decided, however, not to make any
fuss about this mainly because we could travel down by the 35th Motor
Ambulance Convoy, which was just as comfortable and probably safer.
So we ended our journey in the hospitable mess of the 32nd Combined
Clearing Hospital that same evening.

This proved to be the end of my area of administration. We had
started fifteen months before with a Line of Communication sixty
miles long, from Kantara on the Suez Canal to El Arish. And in the
interval we had reached and taken on Gaza, Jaffa and Jerusalem, gone
through Palestine to Haifa, crossed the Jordan to Deraa in Transjordania on the railway to Mecca, gone up to Damascus in Syria,
crossed the Anti-Lebanon and the Lebanon and ended up finally in
Beirut, four hundred miles from the Canal where we started. It was a
long, arduous L. of C. journey, looking back on it now. At the time it
came piece by piece, and didn't seem too difficult to manage.

I did not care for Beirut. The French were swanking about in it,
claiming to have captured it before we got there, because they had
threatened to bombard it from the sea and it had surrendered to them.
They totally ignored the fact that it was Allenby's victories that had
made this possible.

Next morning I set off for Haifa in a torpedo-boat. It was a lovely

calm sunny day; we sat on the little narrow deck; and I was violently
seasick. It was a relief to make Haifa, and go to bed in the 33rd C.C.H.
I left in a staff car next day and got home to Ramleh and the
Monastery the same evening.

A few days later we heard that an armistice had been concluded with
the Turks. It was October 31st, 1918. We felt the war was coming to
an end.

When the 11th of November came and we knew the great World
War, which we all thought would be the last, was over, it came almost
as an anticlimax.

There was little rejoicing. We all got a bit wild and had too much
to drink. One Australian battery a few miles south of Ramleh began
to fire recklessly in celebration. But, as it happened, the trajectory
brought the shells down in the almond grove in front of the Monastery
much too close for our comfort. Even then we were too excited to get
really angry. We cursed them violently and sent an urgent message
back by despatch rider:

"Turn your damn guns south! You're shelling us, blast you!"

That was how the First World War ended for me.

And overleaf is a copy of the Daily News Letter, printed in Jerusalem, which I found on my desk on Tuesday, November 12th, 1918.

On Armistice Day David Munro, my D.A.D.M.S. (Indian Troops),
was down in the Canal Zone inspecting Indian Hospitals. In the evening he went to dine with Colonel Powell, the Officer in Command of
the 24th Stationary Hospital under whom I had served as Surgical
Expert before I was made A.D.M.S. The Colonel was one of the old
type of regular R.A.M.C. officers, and at dinner he turned to Munro
feeling sure that he, another regular, would understand.

"Thank God the War's over," he said. "Now we can go back to
real soldiering."

David repeated this to me, and later printed it in his autobiography.

*

There was a noticeable feeling of flatness after the Armistice, but at our
headquarters we were far too busy to be affected by it, trying to arrange
accommodation and treatment for the unexpectedly large number of
sick prisoners of war that we had to handle.

A great camp was established at Kantara, where we had ten thousand of them suffering from every kind of malnutrition, besides malaria. The worst cases of all were those suffering from pellagra, which was then an incurable disease. The poor devils got eczema and diarrhoea. They wasted to skeletons and became paralysed. Sometimes they went completely demented and we could do nothing for them—they just died. Remember this was 1918, and we knew practically nothing then about the vitamins. But a few grains of nicotinic acid or Vitamin B complex would have saved them had we known then what we know now.

Another of our troubles was that everyone wanted to go home. We in Egypt and Palestine had had no home leave like the men in France. Some hadn't seen their wives for years. We heard that the men on the Western Front were getting back in thousands; and as the days went on and nothing happened with us there were grumbles, more grumbles and eventually open mutiny. It was hard to explain to tired, weary men that the shipping was just not there to bring them home.

My job was closing down hospitals one by one as they were no longer required, and closing down stores. I had half a million pounds' worth of instruments, drugs and dressings unopened at the Base Depot Medical Stores at Kantara when the Turks surrendered. Personnel redundant were posted back to 3rd Echelon. Medical officers kept asking to be demobilised, and grumbled.

My own future also gave me food for thought. I had been away from London for three years. What sort of practice would I find when I returned? Would there be any? Should I take a Government job or go back into civil life?

The whole future of Palestine was then in the melting pot. I was offered the post of Principal Medical Officer to O.E.T.A., that is, the Occupied Enemy Territory Administration, the provisional Government of Palestine. I thought this over very carefully. It would mean staying on in Palestine, tackling the problems arising from the sudden pressure of an intense Zionism which the Balfour Declaration had made possible. With a name like mine I felt that I would find it difficult to keep the scales level between Jew and Arab. The Arabs would be suspicious, thinking I was a Jew. The Jews would be disappointed when they discovered to their surprise I was only an Ulster Protestant.

DAILY NEWS LETTER.

THE ARMISTICE.

Reuter (London, Official, Monday, 11.20 a.m.).—The Prime Minister announced that the armistice was signed at five o'clock this morning and that hostilities ceased on all fronts at eleven o'clock this morning.

Foch telegraphed the following order to the Commanders-in-Chief : " Allied troops will not until further orders go beyond the line reached at eleven this morning, November 11th."

Mokattam (11th November, 1918. 6.3 p.m.).—Terms of the armistice include immediate evacuation of invaded territories and Alsace Lorraine within 14 days. Allies to follow up the German troops ; the immediate repatriation of prisoners without reciprocity ; the Germans to surrender 5,000 guns of which 2,500 to be heavies ; 30,000 machine-guns ; the Allies to occupy all the left bank of the Rhine, to hold the crossings and bridgeheads extending to 30 kilometres inland at Mainz, Coblenz, and Cologne ; the handing over of all submarines, of 50 destroyers, 8 light cruisers, and 6 battle cruisers ; the Allies reserve the right to occupy Heligoland ; all Germans in Russia, Roumania, and elsewhere to be withdrawn ; complete abandonment of the Treaties of Bucarest and Brest Litovsk.

(8.10 p.m.).—The Germans are to deliver intact military establishments of stores and food, industrial establishments of railways, waterways, and telegraphs to be delivered unimpaired ; 5,000 locomotives and 50,000 wagons and all railway material for working the left bank of the Rhine to be handed over. The German High Command is to reveal the position of all mines and minefields and to assist in the destruction of all poisoned springs. The cost of all troops occupying the Rhineland is to be a charge on the German Government.

Reparation for all damage ; immediate restitution of all cash to the National Bank of Belgium ; the return of documents, specie, and stock : the restitution of Russian and Roumanian gold ; freedom of access of Allied merchantmen to the Baltic.

Solf bitterly complains to President Wilson of "the fearful terms," saying that the surrender of transport and the maintenance of occupying troops will starve millions of Germans.

GERMAN WIRELESS OFFICIAL (11th November, 1918).—The armistice is to come into force six hours after signature.

Troops remaining in Belgium, France, and Alsace Lorraine after 14 days are to be interned or made prisoner.

5,000 locomotives, 150,000 wagons and 10.000 motor lorries to be surrendered.

In the east all troops to be withdrawn behind the frontier of 1st August, 1914. Period for this not stated.

Unconditional surrender of East Africa.

Return of the reserve of the Belgian Bank, and of Russian and Roumanian gold.

Surrender of 100 U-boats, 8 light cruisers, and 6 dreadnoughts ; remaining ships to be disarmed and supervised by Allies in Neutral or Allied harbours.

P.T.O.

Assurance of the free passage through the Cattegat. Clearance of mine-fields and occupation of all forts and batteries from which this passage might be hindered.

The blockade continues in force; German ships must continue to be interned All restrictions on shipping imposed by Germany on neutrals are to be removed.

Armistice lasts 30 days.

The King, addressing a great crowd from the balcony of Buckingham Palace, said : " With you I rejoice and thank God for the victories which the Allies have won, which have brought hostilities to an end and peace within sight."

British News. Sir Douglas Haig (Monday .—Shortly before dawn this morning the Canadians of the First Army under General Horne captured Mons.

French News. OFFICIAL (Monday).—East of the Forest of Trelon we reached the Belgian frontier. Italian troops entered Rocroy. After severe fighting we forced the passages of the Meuse between Vrigne-aux-Bois and Lumes.

American News. AMERICAN AGENCY (Monday).—Local operations resulted in considerable gains between the Meuse and the Moselle. The Second Army captured Marcheville and St. Hilaire, an advance of 4 kilometres. The enemy is resisting stubbornly in the Woevre, but is being steadily driven back by the Second Army. In the push towards Briey and Conflans the Second Army gained important positions.

The Conflans Metz road is a solid mass of motor transport conveying what the Germans have been able to save from the general wreckage. Booty captured by the Americans is immense.

General News. *Press Bureau.*—Recruiting suspended.

AMSTERDAM (from Berlin, Sunday).—The latest reports state that the revolutionaries in Berlin have won a brilliant and practically bloodless victory. The Naumberg Jaeger regiment was the first to go over!; others followed in quick succession. The telegram adds that everything is orderly. Jubilation prevails throughout the city.

The revolutionary movement is extending throughout Germany with great rapidity ; it is generally led by the Social-Democratic party. Among the latest towns controlled by the revolutionaries are Cassel, Emmerich, Mannheim, Chemnitz, and Frankfurt. The new Government will contain three independent Socialists.

(From Basle, Monday).—Hesse-Darmstadt has proclaimed a republic.

The *Vorwarts* announces that the King of Saxony has been deposed.

COPENHAGEN (from Berlin, Monday).—The ex-Kaiser and his suite are reported to have taken up residence at Count Bentinck's villa at Arnhem.

Havas (Monday).—The British destroyer *Shark* and the French destroyer *Mangin* entered the Dardanelles on Sunday. They will moor before Constantinople, and will be joined later by units of an Allied squadron. Alexandretta was occupied on Saturday.

At the end of a week I declined, and it was then offered to Dr. David Heron (afterwards Sir David Heron), who was A.D.M.S. Egyptian Hospitals, and had previously been the medical officer at the Ophthalmic Hospital of the Order of St. John in Jerusalem. Heron was obviously the man for the post. He was a fluent Arabic scholar and well known both to the Arabs and the Jews. Why they hadn't thought of him first of all I do not know. Anyhow he accepted and made a success of the difficult post.

It was six months after the Armistice before I could get free from my appointment. I had signed on yearly since the war started, each year for another year, as I did not come under the Derby Act and could not be conscripted. In my last year, 1917, this had become something of a joke. I got a notice from the War Office instructing me as a temporary officer to sign on for the duration. This came to me as A.D.M.S. I sent myself a notice to that effect. I then replied to myself pointing out that as an Irishman I did not come under the Conscription Act, and offered instead to serve for another year. As A.D.M.S. I solemnly sent on this offer to the War Office and in a month or so I got a reply saying the War Office would accept my offer of another year. This offer I, as A.D.M.S., sent on to myself, and as a temporary officer I signed on again and sent it to myself as A.D.M.S. for transmission to the War Office. It was just one of those silly things one does in a Government office; but it also meant something more. I could always insist on getting away at the end of the year if I wanted to. So it was of some potential value.

Looking back now, with the experience of two wars in my mind, I think we learnt several things in Palestine which the men in France never learnt, and which were forgotten until the Second World War again thrust them upon us. One was the value of mobility. The Field Ambulances never got bogged down by unwieldy equipment. They moved with the troops.

The Casualty Clearing Stations did not hold up the wounded. They sent them back as speedily as possible. We were the first to use planes to evacuate wounded. I remember that well for very personal reasons. At the first battle of Gaza, a distinguished Australian airman was shot down by the Turks. But by an almost impossible bit of flying he was picked up by a comrade and flown direct to the 24th Stationary

Hospital at Kantara, where he came under me as Surgical Expert. Because he had lain on garden soil I thought I'd better give him an injection of anti-tetanic serum. I had seen such ghastly results from the lack of this in Serbia. So I gave him a prophylactic dose. Within a few minutes he began to swell. His eyelids closed. His face became bloated. His body swelled up. He looked just like the advertisement for Michelin tyres. It was the most rapid case of angioneurotic œdema I have ever seen. Obviously he was allergic to anti-tetanic serum. He recovered after a few days, much to our relief. We did not know then that adrenaline would have reduced the swelling much more rapidly. If we had, it would have saved me a good many hours' anxiety.

The second thing we learnt was the value of expert surgery at the front. We had four surgical mobile units, you may remember, under Colonel Henry Wade (later Sir Henry Wade, C.M.G., D.S.O.), equipped with all the necessary tools for major surgery. They worked at the Main Dressing Stations of the Field Ambulances or at the nearest C.C.S., and were an innovation of immense importance.

The third advance was the establishment of malaria diagnostic centres under Major Manson-Bahr (now Sir Philip Manson-Bahr, C.M.G., D.S.O.), an advance which established a precedent which ought to have been of inestimable value in the Second World War.

Unfortunately this experience was practically forgotten by 1939. Indeed, when the Second World War started, one distinguished Army authority thought it was unnecessary to discuss the matter. Everything possible had been thought of and provided for. And, anyhow, there was not going to be any malaria in this war. What a prophecy, when one remembers the havoc produced by malaria in Burma and Malaya, by malaria in Guadalcanal and New Guinea, by malaria in North Africa, by malaria even in Sicily and Italy! It reminds me of the prophecy made in 1914 that the war would be over by Christmas. We live and never learn.

CHAPTER XVII

COMING HOME

IN MARCH, 1919, I was at length relieved of my post, and instructed to report to Alexandria for embarkation to England. But at the last moment some hitch, of which I cannot now remember the cause, occurred which held me up; and it was two days after the date of embarkation before I could join the ship. Apparently sailing had been postponed for me, much to the annoyance of the Captain. That was a bad start.

Then we found it was a 'dry' ship belonging to the Commonwealth of Australia, and no alcohol could be bought on board. To get over this difficulty, therefore, everyone who felt this might be a deprivation had his cabin stocked with the alcohol he fancied, sufficient, he hoped, for the ten days we should be at sea. But did it last?—of course not! Tongues, especially of the ship's officers, were hanging out when we reached Southampton.

The passengers were mainly nurses returning to England, medical officers and a considerable number of V.A.D.s. I was the Senior Medical Officer aboard, and therefore automatically in medical charge. But I handed over this post to a Territorial Colonel who was a G.P. in peace-time, feeling he could do the job much better than I, and he was happy to carry on.

I cannot remember much of the voyage. The Mediterranean was said to be full of floating mines, and we used to watch the paravanes sweeping from the bows.

England. It was wonderful to be home again. But I felt as a retired Colonial Governor living in Cheltenham must feel—a little debunked. Gone was the deference I had been accustomed to for four years. At Waterloo Station a porter actually bumped into me. For a moment I was surprised and annoyed; and then I had to laugh at myself.

I had nothing to wear except my uniform; and nowhere to sleep except my Club, the Savage, which could put me up for two or three days only. I had no consulting-room, for, as I have said, after paying rent for two and a half years I had given it up, seeing no prospect of the war ever ending. For three more days I slept, rather miserably, at a friend's flat.

And then I went to see her. She had been on my mind all the time, and I had tried not to think of her too much. But it was no good. I went to her father's house in Henrietta Street, Cavendish Square, and sent up my name with the maid.

She came down to the hall to meet me, looking lovely but so frail, for she had been ill. I had a string of amber beads I had brought for her from Jerusalem. She lowered her lovely head while I put them round her neck. Then she looked up at me. That settled it. We both knew it was for always.

That was over thirty years ago, but it is still for always.

*

The next day I paid my third visit to the War Office. The first had been in 1914 when they said they did not need me. The second in 1915 when they decided they did. The third was this one when they had no further need of me. I was issued with what was called a 'Protection Certificate' which said I was 'disembodied' with effect from April 3rd, 1919. It sounded bad, but I felt no ill effects, and decided I could now go home to my family in Ulster.

I had no other clothes and so still wore uniform, quite irregularly, of course, as I had been 'disembodied'; but no one bothered.

My mother looked just the same; but my father had aged. He had had a fractured thigh bone which was badly set in my absence, and it had left its mark on him. It had also made him much milder in manner. I had always been shy with him, and a little afraid as a boy. Even when I grew up I was never quite at ease with him. It was part of the Victorian atmosphere one was brought up in; and it was a surprise to me to find he was really proud of me, and had been seen quietly smiling, and handling the presentation copies I had sent him of the books I had written, when he thought no one was noticing. I understood later what that meant.

I

I had one uncle still alive down in Fermanagh who was older than my father. I went to see him as he had been ill. Everyone was friendly as far as Enniskillen; but when I got out at the station at Lisnaskea a man on the platform looked at my uniform, scowled and spat on the ground. This upset me. I knew nothing much of the Casement rising, the trouble in 1916, and the bitterness that followed; but I was now practically on the border between the warring factions, and obviously feelings were still acute. It gave me a curiously unpleasant jolt. Things were clearly different from the time when, as a boy, I had been stopping with this same uncle on the 12th of July. He was Master of an Orange Lodge then, and all the year round was a peaceful man in a village almost entirely composed of Roman Catholics. But on the 12th he used to erect an Orange banner over his gateway and become very Protestant. Then the villagers would look tolerant, laugh and say:

"Och shure, it's only owl' Alec."

Things obviously were now very different.

Back again in London I was issued with a Ration Book. This was something new to me, and it had to be explained when I was given the temporary loan of a small flat and had to cater for myself.

Renting a consulting-room I next discovered was a very difficult matter. There weren't any available. The men who had been in France, and acquired surgical status there, had got back before me. Men who had dodged the war, and had thus managed to worm their way into positions and practices when we were on active service, had no intention of being pushed out. This was depressing. Perhaps I had been unwise in turning down official posts offered me!

Then when things looked blackest I found a flat at 38 Harley Street and Dr. Swanton, my gynæcological colleague at the Princess Beatrice Hospital, offered me the use of his consulting-room at No. 40 next door on alternate days, until a room became available below my flat.

Just about this time Major Munro, whom we had invalided home shortly after the Armistice, discovered I was back, rang me up and said he wanted to see me.

I could sense he was anxious to talk. He told me that there was a movement on foot to amalgamate the medical services of the Army and Navy, and also take in the Air Force, which up to then had had no medical service of its own.

It was the sort of idea that would appeal to the bureaucratic mind as a neat bit of administrative planning: the officers were all doctors; their training had been on similar lines; the equipment they required for their work must be much the same; and they used the same drugs. Why not then save reduplication and have one medical service for all the fighting forces? After all, an R.A.M.C. officer on board ship would be no more anomalous than a marine.

"Of course it's damned nonsense," said Munro. "The two Services are dead against it; and I'm sure it won't go through. Actually Matthew Fell has been invited to start a service for the R.A.F. He has asked me to join him. We worked together in Mespot. I'd like you to meet him."

So I asked them to lunch at the Savage Club, and we chatted about our past experiences. Nothing was said about the future, but I knew Fell was weighing me up. Munro had been saying nice things about me.

A few days later I saw Munro again. He told me he had definitely taken the plunge and asked the India Office to allow him to transfer to the Air Force. This would mean leaving the I.M.S. and becoming P.M.O. Royal Air Force in India under (Sir) Matthew Fell as D.M.S. He said they were looking for someone to go as P.M.O. Middle East. It would be at least a three-year term.

I congratulated him on the Indian post but made no further comment, and we did not pursue the matter further. I knew what he was hinting at, but I felt in my bones I did not want to go to Persia or Mespot. I had had enough of uniforms to last my life; and I wanted to get married and settle down in London. After all, London was the finest place in the world to live in.

Well, Munro went out again to India. Fell organised the medical service of the Air Force so admirably that it is now by far the best scientific medical corps in Europe; and after he had made a success of it, he went back to the Army Medical Service as Director-General. It is now ancient history also that Munro succeeded to his post as D.M.S., R.A.F. Those who knew Munro know what a success he was in the post. He made an ideal D.M.S.

Dear David. We were friends right up to the end. I still remember his whimsical grin when he was getting round someone; and the way his chin jutted out when he refused to give way to some interfering ass. He suited the R.A.F., and the R.A.F. suited him. He was a good all-round sportsman, a fine shot and an excellent golfer, as a St. Andrews man should be, but a reckless horseman. The one time I was really angry with him was when he lamed my favourite mare at Ramleh. He had a great sense of fun. He could laugh at himself—a God-given gift. I miss him.

But to return to my own affairs. After this somewhat unsettling week I felt I must justify my decision to myself, and forestall any vain regrets, by definitely settling into my pre-war work again. Up to then I had not quite known what I ought to do. It was Munro made me certain of what I really wanted.

The first thing obviously was to get back into professional garments, remember I was a civilian again, and forget to click my heels and salute when I spoke to a lady.

It was then I discovered that the silk hat and morning coat which had been the insignia of the profession had been rendered obsolete by the war. I must confess I regretted this at the time, and sometimes do so still; for one of my proudest moments was when I first donned my topper as a qualified medical practitioner.

In those early days there was an old-fashioned men's hat shop, Harman's, at the top end of Bond Street, on the right-hand side as you go down from Oxford Street. Inside the shop, behind the counter, rows and rows of white cardboard boxes on shelves caught the eye. Each box contained a silk hat, and had the name of the owner of the hat written in large letters on it. These hats belonged to the *élite* of the profession, and were kept beautifully ironed and polished ready for wear. When, therefore, a Harley Street doctor got caught in a shower, or otherwise ruffled his hat, he took it into Harman's, had his duplicate taken down from the shelf and handed over the counter to him. The hat he had been wearing was then ironed straight away and put back in its box on the shelf, ready for the next time. In this way the doctor could always depend on an immaculate top hat. In addition it was a splendid advertisement for Harman.

When I started I had only one topper, and I used to go into Harman's and actually have it ironed on the counter as and when required. It was some years before I could afford two hats. Now, all this, I found, was over, and some of the stateliness of manner that went with it had gone too. Only two doctors as far as I can remember, Sir Frederick Still and Sir Stanley Woodwark, kept up the tradition until their deaths. Still was a little, but much the greater man. Woodwark was tall, handsome and quite conscious that the top hat suited him. Some members of the Savage Club may remember him, smiling and debonair, in the North-East Room.

Obviously I didn't need a new topper on my first return visit to my hospital, where my older colleagues had carried on all through the war. A house-surgeon, whom of course I did not know, greeted me; and I told him I would resume work on the following Monday. I was therefore interested to see what would be the contents of my operation list. Rather to my embarrassment the first case on the list was a cancer of the breast.

'Good Lord,' I thought, 'I haven't operated on a woman for years. Wonder if I'll remember.'

But of course one doesn't forget. It's like swimming or riding a bicycle.

What exercised my mind much more in the following weeks was the question whether or not I should put in an application for a vacancy that I knew was arising on the staff of the Lock Hospital. I had been to see Sir Charles Ryall, the retiring Senior Surgeon, who had sent for me when he heard I was back; and he had said:

"I have been holding on at the hospital, Abe, until you came back, in case you wanted the vacancy."

That touched me. He was a tired old man and I was most grateful to him. But did I want the post? I knew I had a good chance of getting it if I applied. I had always been interested in the subject of venereal disease even from my student days, for, as a Resident, I had had temporary charge of the ward in Steevens' Hospital which had been under the special care of Abraham Colles, famous as the discoverer of Colles' law and Colles' fracture. I had also been Resident Medical Officer at the Lock, and later on had been appointed Registrar. When I had published my M.D. thesis on 'Recent advances in the Treatment of Syphilis', I sent a copy to Jonathan Hutchinson, then one of the greatest living authorities on the subject; and, shortly after, I had asked his advice about specialising in the diseases concerned.

He looked at me with his wise old eyes.

"It depends on what you want," he said slowly. "I was Surgeon to the London Hospital for twenty-five years. I did major surgery there all the time; but I had also what we call a 'concern' about syphilis. I wanted to help those whom no one else cared for. But it killed my private practice in surgery. I had all I wanted of hospital work but not the other. That went to my colleagues. I'm not complaining. My life has been very full."

There was the old Quaker speaking, and I went away very thoughtful, for I did want to stick to my surgery. Sir Jonathan died just before the war, so I could not now take my worry to him. I had to make up my mind for myself.

Well, I took the plunge. I decided to apply. The election date was April 24th, 1919. There were several candidates, but only one dangerous opponent, and I got the appointment. Looking back now over the thirty years that spanned the time between election and retirement from the hospital, it all passed too quickly. I enjoyed every moment of it. It did not kill my surgery as Sir Jonathan had prophesied. I was able to carry on both sides of my practice successfully, because I had worked with Sir Patrick Freyer, Sir John Thomson-Walker and my friend John Swift Joly at St. Peter's Hospital and could thus use urology as a link between general surgery and my specialty. The Dean Street Hospital gave me in addition a deep psychological insight into the darker inner recesses of the human mind; and filled me with an infinite compassion for those who often through innocence, inadvertence, chance, the temptation of the moment or moral weakness had to be rescued from what otherwise would sometimes have been lasting illness, despair or even suicide. When I think of the people I have helped to restore to self-respect I feel that the choice I made in 1919 was the right one. It satisfied the Quaker strain in my blood.

I started work a week after my appointment and with three hospitals using my services I was soon happily busy.

*

The next highlight was a wire dated November 10th:

Your attendance is required at Buckingham Palace on Saturday next the fifteenth inst. at 10.15 o'clock a.m. Service Dress. Please telegraph acknowledgement.

I had an unusual kind of house-surgeon at Dean Street at the time. He was a very tall man almost of my own age who had been awarded a D.S.O. in the war, and intended to specialise in the treatment of venereal disease.

I told him, at the evening clinic on Friday, that I should not have time to change out of service dress before I came to hospital on Saturday after the Investiture: and he said quickly:

"Have you got tan gloves to wear with your uniform?"

"No. I haven't any gloves. I never wanted them in Egypt. But why do you ask?"

"Sir, you must wear gloves. It is essential. People's hands get so clammy with excitement, the Court officials insist on it. I'll lend you a pair. You won't have time tomorrow to get any."

So, accompanied by my future wife and my sister, I arrived at Buckingham Palace, complete with gloves.

The gloves were rather large but I did not think that mattered. To my horror, however, when the King shook hands with me I felt my right hand glove was slipping off. Rapidly I caught the end with my left and looked up at the King. A little twinkle came into his eyes, he said a few gracious words, and the situation was saved.

*

We had decided to get married in the spring of 1920, and so whenever we could manage the time we foraged around looking for some place we could afford. I still had my flat in Harley Street, but it would have been too small for a permanency.

There was a shortage of flats and houses then, as there is after any war, and the prices asked were fantastic. The people we saw seemed all to be harpies battening on those returning. We were almost in despair. And then our luck changed. We saw a little house in what was at that time called Cambridge Terrace, but is now Sussex Gardens. It looked just right. It was just right. The dear old lady who owned it gave us the preference because I had been at the war.

Our parish church was All Souls', Langham Place, but we wanted to be married by the Reverend Dick Sheppard at St. Martin-in-the-Fields. So I went to see him. Everyone loved Dick Sheppard. He had an immense following and St. Martin's was a centre of intense religious activity. But neither I nor my future wife had a residence qualification. Fortunately I discovered that the Savage Club, which was then in the Adelphi, was in his parish; so a few nights there satisfied the law.

We were married at nine-thirty in the morning on April 21st, 1920; and when it was over Dick Sheppard murmured to us kneeling before him:

"May the romance of today ever live in your hearts."

It has.

The day was dull and overcast when we left my wife's old home for Paddington. But as we passed the new home we had taken at 59 Cambridge Terrace (now 118 Sussex Gardens) the sun came out, and suddenly the front of our little house was flooded with light from top to bottom, whereas the houses on either side were still quite dark. It was an odd chance—one in a million probably—that it should have happened at this particular moment just when we were passing; and naturally we looked upon it as a favourable augury.

I suppose one always loves the first house in which one starts a home. We did. We spent twelve sunny years there. I had my consulting-room in Harley Street, and on pleasant days I often walked there. When the great General Strike came in 1926 I was very glad I was near enough to be able to do so until it was over.

Lieut.-Col. J. Johnston Abraham, C.B.E., D.S.O.

The author's wife and baby daughter

CHAPTER XVIII

SETTLING DOWN

LOOKING BACK ON IT NOW I often wonder how any young surgeon got known in the days after the First World War, for one could not advertise in any way, and there was no National Health Service with its paid hospital sessions to make life safe. We did all our hospital work gratuitously, and depended on such private practice as came our way to live.

Naturally at first, apart from this hospital work, I had little to do; but after I came back from the war I found that quite a considerable sum in royalties on my two books, *The Surgeon's Log* and *The Night Nurse*, had accumulated with Chapman & Hall, and Arthur Waugh kept wanting to know when another book was coming.

The war had stopped me thinking of writing, but he knew I had a diary of my experiences with the Serbs in the great typhus epidemic of 1915. I had written this up at Millbank, when it was fresh in my mind, and Waugh had then offered me a royalty of twenty-five per cent if I would turn it into a book. But the work at Millbank seemed more important, and before the manuscript was half finished I was ordered to Egypt. Some of it, of course, was then top secret, and there might have been difficulty in getting permission to publish. But in 1920 this did not matter, and I gave it to him to read. He said it would make an exciting story, for the whole affair had been kept so quiet at the time that very few knew anything about it.

While work was slack I rewrote it. The book came out in 1921 and we called it *My Balkan Log*. It was a bad title because it meant nothing; but it got a front page review in the *Times Literary Supplement*, and a lot of generous notices elsewhere. If it had been published in 1915 it would have been a much greater success. Now, in 1921, everyone was tired of the war; and in spite of its excellent notices it never went beyond a second edition. That to me, who had been singularly fortunate in my previous books, was definitely disappointing. But it didn't depress me. When a writer finishes a book he loses interest in it. It has been born. It must now look after itself. His mind is on his next.

It was years before I looked at the *Balkan Log* again and when I did the horror of the time came back to me with fresh emphasis. I was not surprised people found the book gruesome in 1921. Reading it again I rather wondered how we ever came through, dicing with death daily, as we did.

But writing the book acted like a cathartic on me. I got rid of the memories, and my mind now could concentrate on surgery. I wrote articles for the professional journals and sometimes leaders or leaderettes. I did a couple of technical books. Our little girl was born. It was a joy to watch her blossoming. Doctors sent their panel patients into my hospital for operations, and then discovered me. Work came slowly, and increased gradually. Anxiety for the future receded into the background.

The Savage Club was a great source of pleasure to me then. I lunched there often in the lovely Adam dining-room in the Adelphi looking out on the river. Memories. James Agate in the corner window, obese and conceited. Arthur Morrison, bearded, velvet-coated, smoking his curved amber pipe. C. E. Lawrence of John Murray's. David Hodge of the *Glasgow Herald*, and George Blake of *John o' London's Weekly*. (Sir) David Bone, the sailor, and J. J. Bell, the author of *Wee MacGregor*, one of the funniest books ever written. Alec Waugh starting on his career as a novelist. A. P. Herbert, bubbling over then as now, Charlie Hands of the *Daily Mail*, J. Y. McPeake of *Nash's Magazine* and *Good Housekeeping*, and especially Charles Evans of Heinemann's, who was to alter my life later more than I ever thought possible.

The Club has always been famous for its Saturday night dinners. At these we saw and heard the finest turns coming to London. We listened to Moiseiwitsch at the piano; saw Jack Hassall draw with inimitable ease his cartoons on the blackboard; sang choruses with John Ivimey at the piano, smoked, drank, and went on happily until well after midnight.

Generally I took a guest. They all wanted to see and hear the legendary O'Dell whom I could remember as a striking figure ever since I first joined the Club. He was still wandering round, tall, haggard, incredibly old, turning into the bar in his big sombrero and funereal cloak, ready to accept a drink as if conferring a privilege; going in to dinner, which he also never paid for, and reciting Rabelaisian scenes from what he said was Shakespeare, or still singing in his old cracked voice his one song: 'The Harvest Home'.

Many are the tales told of him. I can remember one example. He was an inveterate borrower. Brandon Thomas, author of *Charley's Aunt*, greatly daring, once said:

"When are you going to pay me back that fiver you borrowed?" O'Dell looked at him in astonishment.

"But I haven't finished with it yet," he said: and that seemed to be the complete answer.

When eventually he was given rooms as one of the Brethren of the Charterhouse, he found attempts to restrict his movements by the Master so irritating that it was with the utmost difficulty he was persuaded to stay.

*

A year before the First World War, and when I was in the full flush of my early literary successes, a friend of mine had said:

"Let me put you up for the Athenæum'.'

"Me?" I answered, in surprise. "Much too solemn for me. Besides they'd never have me."

"Oh, don't worry about that. It'll be fifteen years or so before you come up for election. You'll think differently then."

So my name went on to the candidates' book, someone seconded me and I forgot all about it. No one then had any thought of a war; but in the interval old men died, young men died, others withdrew, the waiting list shortened; and so to my dismay I got a notice in 1921 that my name was up for election, seven years before I had expected it.

I told my wife I couldn't afford the big entrance fee, and after that the subscriptions to two clubs, and I proposed withdrawing my name.

"No," she said, firmly. "You mustn't. If you do you'll regret it bitterly afterwards."

So I allowed my name to go forward, hoping no one would blackball me, for in those days members individually voted at the elections, and one black ball in three excluded.

Luckily no one knew me, so I had no enemies; and when the time came I was elected on my war record. But I was too shy to go near the place for a month.

Then one day I ventured into the great front hall feeling very much a new boy. My proposer now never came near the Club. I knew no one else well enough, and I nearly turned tail and made for the Savage. It was then I saw Sir Arthur Keith.

He guessed how I was feeling, and asked me to come and sit at his table. That broke the ice. In those days he was still Curator of the College of Surgeons Museum, and lunched daily at the Club. So whenever I was there I joined him. There were some six or eight distinguished members who constantly used that table. One was Lord Rutherford, a big, red-faced, hearty man who looked like a prosperous farmer. It was his work at the Cavendish Laboratory that made nuclear fission and the atomic age possible. I wonder what he'd think, if he were alive now, of the developments from his work. Another was Lord Rayleigh, white and ascetic-looking; another, Sir William Bragg, wide-eyed, benevolent. Yet another was Sir Ronald Ross, the discoverer of the mosquito origin of malaria. He was a fierce man with an eternal grievance against everyone—why, I never knew. I believe they taxed his Nobel Prize, or something of that sort. He looked Eurasian and I was sure, probably quite wrongly, had an inferiority complex, which he compensated for by being rude to nearly everyone.

All these famous people were most kind and friendly. I felt quite happy with them. And then one day another member said to me:

"I suppose you know you're the only one not an F.R.S. who dares to sit at the Royal Society table?"

I was flabbergasted. I'd never noticed. I thought everyone in the Club at the other tables at that time was equally distinguished at something else, and so it didn't matter where I sat. It's a fiction that still exists, outside the Club.

For a while after that I was happier at the Savage. One day there I happened to be lunching with Charles Evans of Heinemann's (Charlie to all who knew him). He had just come back from the Isle of Man, completely exhausted by Hall Caine, who for years used to insist on his going over there for a month at a time, tidying up his latest novel.

It was a custom started in Willie Heinemann's time, and Willie had always grudgingly agreed to it because Hall Caine was a best-seller. The one person who wasn't considered by either at the time was Charlie. And now it seemed, though Heinemann was dead, Charlie himself was still carrying on of his own accord.

I remember saying to him:

"You know, Charlie, you should watch that chap, Hall Caine. In one of his novels, *The Christian*, I think, there was a chapter where the nurses held a dance in the operating theatre. Shades of Lister—an operating theatre! What a blah! What you want is a medical adviser to protect you from bloomers like that, now that Willie's gone and you're in the saddle."

It was one of those casual remarks made without any particular intention. Evans looked at me thoughtfully.

A week later he said: "That was an idea of yours, Barney." (I was always Barney to Evans, and the name stuck.) "How would you like to come to the office in Bedford Street, say once a fortnight, and give advice to the Heinemann Medical Company?"

"Love it," I answered.

And in that casual way I made my entry into publishing, and started on something which became eventually a major feature in my life. Of that I had of course no suspicion at the time. It was just an additional job that fitted in with my other activities.

So you can imagine me, very interested, going down to Bedford Street, Strand, next to the Post Office, into the managing director's room with Charlie and the other directors—Theodore Byard, B. F. Oliver and Hugh Elliot—to discuss medical manuscripts and offers of medical books. At first it was once a fortnight for an hour, then later once a week for an hour, then later still one half-day a week, and so on —all started by a casual remark at the Savage Club.

Of course chances of this sort do not come to one as casually as appears on the surface. There must be a previous conditioning preparing one's mind for such a proposal; and printer's ink and the printed page had always had a fascination for me.

Years before, after writing and having had accepted a considerable number of annotations, I had tried to get on the staff of the *Lancet*;

and it had been one of my secret disappointments that I had failed.

(Sir) Squire Sprigge was then the editor. He was a dark, Italian-looking man who told me later, when I came to know him better at the Athenæum, that an ancestor of his came to England as cook to Oliver Cromwell and liked it so much he remained. I think he must have been pulling my leg.

*

In the midst of all this I had a recurring attack of appendicitis. I wasn't surprised. I must have swallowed pounds of sand in my food, and breathed it into my lungs, during my two years in the Sinai Desert. More than once I had had symptoms that indicated all was not well. So as soon as the attack was over I went to see 'Jimmy' Sherren.

Sherren was then at the height of his reputation as a surgeon in London. He was a magnificent technician. When I first saw him operating at the London Hospital, I could see by his bare arms tattooed with anchors and initials that he must have been a sailor; and I found, on enquiring, he actually had served before the mast, was a Master Mariner, held a Captain's ticket and had been for years at sea before he suddenly decided to abandon it all and become a medical student. He had the hard, tanned features of the sailor, still walked with a roll and had no manners whatever; but he was the surgeon other doctors chose to operate on their wives, their children or themselves. It was a testimonial impossible to overlook.

Sherren said I'd better have the appendix out; and on the evening before the operation we left our young baby with her nannie, and my wife and I went to the Nursing Home in Fitzroy Square. She unpacked my things and we chatted quite happily. When it was time for her to leave, I noticed it was foggy.

"I'm going with you as far as the Underground," I said.

To my surprise she suddenly looked pathetic and rather wee.

"No. No!" she protested. "I couldn't bear that."

And I had the greatest difficulty in persuading her. Afterwards she explained that she knew it was wise to have the operation done in a quiet period, when the risk was much less. But the idea of my taking her back to Great Portland Street in the fog made her feel, if I was well enough to do that, why was I being operated on at all? It was illogical but very natural.

The operation took twelve minutes. Sherren was one of those lightning operators then fashionable. In consequence for three days I suffered severely from surgical shock, and after that I was all right. No one then, over thirty years ago, had any real knowledge of surgical shock; but I learnt a lot from this personal experience; and for the rest of my surgical life I never hurried, never dragged on organs, always treated the unconscious body before me as if it had had no anæsthetic. I learnt a lot from Jimmy through my operation that I never told him. We were very close friends. We both loved the sea. He kept my *Log* by his bedside; and sometimes when he came home tired and worried and sleepless, he said, it helped him. That was a compliment I treasured deeply.

He was so brilliant as a student that not only was he appointed to the staff of the London as soon as he got his Fellowship, but also his colleagues guaranteed his expenses for two years.

By the time I knew him he was making a very large income. I thought he was the only surgeon in London who had both a chauffeur and a footman. But Sir Henry Souttar tells me that Sir John Bland-Sutton of the Middlesex Hospital also had a chauffeur and a footman, and Jimmy wasn't going to be beaten by him.

Jimmy was odd. His subsequent conduct proved it. Four years after the time of my operation, whilst still in full practice and at the height of his reputation, he suddenly resigned from the London, and to everyone's astonishment went back to sea as a ship's surgeon. There he made himself a nuisance to the Board of Trade. They had to listen to him about equipment. He discussed things with me; we drew up a list of equipment; and as a result ships' surgeons now have up-to-date tools, and drugs. The Mercantile Marine owe him a lot they don't know about.

Ships' surgeons as a rule are not distinguished London surgeons. Once on a voyage to Australia Jimmy had to put a passenger ashore at Melbourne for an operation. He took him to hospital himself and explained, to the young house-surgeon admitting, how he had been treating him.

The house-surgeon listened, a little superciliously.

"That isn't the way Sherren would have treated the case," he said.

"I am Sherren," replied Jimmy.

And that was that.

I have a very warm place in memory for Jimmy.

*

Shortly after my operation I made the acquaintance of Violet Hunt. She lived at 80 Campden Hill, a house I now pass daily on my way home. At that time she was very well known as an authoress. Her novels were supposed to be improper, though no one now would think so; and there was some doubt about the legal position of her marriage. She said she was the wife of Ford Madox Hueffer, the poet and novelist, who wrote *Romance* in collaboration with Joseph Conrad, and *Zeppelin Nights* with Violet herself. But suddenly just then he changed his name to Ford Maddox Ford, disappeared into Germany, married Violet there, and said he had divorced his wife. It was all very trying. His real wife refused to acknowledge the so-called divorce, and the friends of both found it rather embarrassing.

I cannot remember how I made her acquaintance, but the P.E.N. Club had then just been started by Mrs. Dawson Scott, and Violet proposed me for membership.

It was at one of the dinners of the Club I first met Lloyd Osbourne, Robert Louis Stevenson's stepson. He was there with his charming wife, a pretty woman with a marked American accent in contrast to Lloyd's cultured English. This was a great source of annoyance to her because she was British-born and he was an American. They told me they had been in England for six months, but had been wandering round the world from 1912 to 1922, and never had a latch-key or possessions of their own during that time. America, they said, was impossible since prohibition.

Stevenson had been one of my heroes; and I was therefore very much interested in the Osbournes. Lloyd was then a man of fifty-four, tall, thin with sloping shoulders. He had a mottled complexion, a big Roman nose like the Duke of Wellington's, light blue eyes smiling behind pince-nez, and a crop of abundant grey hair. Both he and his wife talked in a bright American manner, possibly augmented by alcohol.

I liked them but never expected to hear of them again. It was therefore rather a surprise some days later to get a most charming letter from Mrs. Lloyd Osbourne saying they had no idea who I was when we met at the P.E.N., but that thinking it over afterwards it had dawned on them, and she wanted me to know that they had "cherished the *Log* through eleven years of wandering". Statements like that always make me shy. I never know if they're true, but hope they are.

A week later I went to tea with them at 38 Grosvenor Gardens. There was a dense fog, and I nearly got lost though it was only four o'clock in the afternoon. They lived at the top of the building and the rooms were much overheated. I gathered this was because of Mrs. Lloyd Osbourne, who suffered from that prevalent American complaint: sinusitis. Lloyd looked like a benevolent ogre with his huge stooping height, mild whimsical smile and big-nosed face. Mrs. Lloyd was the typical bright American woman, beautifully turned out, well-manicured, hair carefully dressed, complexion well-preserved. They drew me out about Egypt and the war. All I learnt from them was that they were going back to California by a cargo boat to New Orleans.

I used to see them off and on for years afterwards, when they came over to collect royalties on pantomimes based on *Treasure Island*, and on the Stevenson books. Osbourne was an excellent writer but he was so overshadowed by Stevenson that he never got the credit due to him. He told me he wrote practically the whole of *The Wrong Box*. The early part of *The Wrecker*, he said, was also his, and a large portion of *The Ebb-Tide*. I think he often felt aggrieved at the small recognition he received in literary circles. Before the copyright of Stevenson's books ran out he used to come over every year; and every time he came he sold more and more Stevenson relics. I asked him why.

He looked at me shrewdly and said: "I sell them while the going's good."

I thought this rather mercenary at the time; but I can see now what he meant. Stevenson is not read as he was, and Osbourne expected this to happen.

The world owes him one thing, however, which should not be forgotten: Stevenson wrote *Treasure Island* to please him when he was a small boy. And it is probable that *Treasure Island* will still be read and remembered when people have ceased to read Stevenson's other and greater works.

*

It was about this time that one of my sins of omission found me out. Major-General Sir William Macpherson wrote to ask if I had kept any diary whilst I was A.D.M.S., P.L. of C., as he was editing the Medical History of the War and had now come to the Palestine Section. Officially I was supposed to keep such a diary, but I had been warned not to do so in case anything went wrong and it could be used against me. It was the advice of a wily old regular, and I regret to say I had taken it.

So I had to write to Sir William and admit this; but I said if he would get my office files from R.A.M.C. Records at Reading, and give me a room at the War Office, I would do my best to help.

It was curious re-reading memos I had written years ago, coming across names of people I had completely forgotten, noting decisions I had made and sometimes regretted afterwards. But I found it all most interesting, and I delved into details and produced something which I hope satisfied the sort of people who read official histories. To celebrate the end of my labours I asked the old General to a Saturday night at the Savage. We started dinner talking rather stiffly. I filled him up with good Scotch whisky and we ended the evening slapping each other on the shoulder. There's a lot to be said for good Scotch whisky.

The P.E.N. Club's activities in those days were mainly confined to monthly dinners where the members met together and had as their guests distinguished foreign writers who happened to be in London. Mrs. Dawson Scott, a stout little woman of immense vitality, ran these meetings with great gusto. Galsworthy, looking like a successful stock-broker, acted as a distinguished figure-head, and nearly everyone who was of any importance in the literary world belonged.

At one of these dinners I made a very bad break. I was sitting next to Mary Webb, who had become suddenly famous because Baldwin, then Prime Minister, had praised her *Precious Bane*, recently published.

Her best book is *Gone to Earth*, but no one had taken any notice of that until Baldwin discovered her. I had talked to her at a previous dinner, but on my saying so she said she did not remember. Then I explained I was a surgeon and always noticed anything out of the ordinary about anyone. It was a most unfortunate remark, for she suddenly got mad and exclaimed:

"I'm sorry you think I'm odd," and refused to speak to me for the rest of the evening.

What I had noticed was that she suffered from Graves' disease, her eyes popped, and she had a goitre which she partially concealed by wearing a high lace collar. It hadn't occurred to me that she was sensitive about this. To a doctor it was just a fact, not a disfigurement; but I saw at once I had been very stupid and felt most distressed, for she was a beautiful writer and poet with a lovely mind, and I had hurt her.

She died soon after and I never had a chance of making it up.

Apart from this unfortunate contretemps my memory is of a happy sunny year. I was getting more private practice; I was having more interesting operation cases at my hospital; and I was writing a series of articles for J. Y. McPeake in *Good Housekeeping*.

It was the year of the marriage of the Duke of York (afterwards George VI) and Lady Elizabeth Bowes-Lyon, now the Queen Mother. My wife and I watched the procession from a window in Whitehall. It takes very little to make a waiting crowd laugh. The Commissioner of Police on horseback lost his white plumes, and they roared watching a fat policeman rushing to retrieve them opposite the Derby Street entrance to New Scotland Yard. Once the Guards came suddenly to attention, there was a cheer and everyone craned forward; then who should pass but a very seedy civilian in a bowler hat riding a bicycle. That put everyone into kinks of laughter.

I noticed one delicate point of etiquette. When the Duke passed on his way to the Abbey, the Guards gave the Royal Salute. When the Lady Elizabeth passed they did not, for she was not yet Royalty.

It was also the year of the first International Congress of the P.E.N. Part of the programme was a visit to Stratford-on-Avon. We had two Pullman carriages from Marylebone Station and were carefully marshalled into them by the indefatigable Mrs. Dawson Scott. I talked to Charles Dubois, the delegate from Paris, on the way down. He was most illuminating on contemporary French literature. His present god was Proust, recently dead.

It was lovely weather and we saw Stratford and England at its best. We wandered along to Shakespeare's birthplace. The Mayor in his chain, a bit shy of all these queer foreigners, talked to me at New Place.

We lunched at 'The Arden', where I met Bernard Shaw for the first time. He recognised my accent and we started talking about Dublin. He was wearing a badly cut new tweed suit, with knickerbockers and thick woollen grey stockings. He also had on a new pair of bright brown boots, the tabs showing behind, and an awful loud check tweed cap pulled sideways. He looked like a sly elderly satyr. It was a very hot day; his new boots were hurting him as we walked round; and he was very peevish in consequence.

At the theatre the play was *A Midsummer Night's Dream*. Shaw talked to Miss Marie Corelli, very stout in grey silk. We had admired the floral decorations in front of her home on the way up to the theatre. I gathered from Shaw that there was a feud between Marie and the Mayor, a local brewer named Flower. She thought of herself as the Swan of Avon, and wanted to have her way over everything Shakespearean. He was the Mayor and thought his official position should count. She considered him a barbarian. They were at daggers drawn. Few people now read Marie Corelli, but she had an immense following as a novelist in her time. It is probable that Stratford has forgotten her. Flower, however, on the other hand, did much for its amenities. He beautified the place; and Stratford owes a lot to his memory.

On the way back to London I talked to Johan Bojer, the Norwegian novelist. He said we should build churches to Shakespeare instead of Christ. He remarked that Shakespeare must have known many beautiful young girls, and said he could understand that now, for he had been astonished since he came to England at the beauty of English-women; those that went to Norway, he explained, always were so ugly.

I laughed. "Oh, you have been misled by the continental cartoonists who depict all Englishwomen abroad as skinny old maids with buck teeth. You will know better now."

There was a reception at the Suffolk Galleries that evening, after we came back. I introduced Sir William Macpherson to Romain Rolland, a Scots doctor to a French one, but didn't wait to see how they got on. Arnold Bennett, very moist-lipped, was sitting with Willie Rothen-stein, the painter, on a divan; and next them sat Sir William Arbuthnot Lane, the famous surgeon, very handsome but looking rather lost. I spoke to him. He smiled whimsically at me.

"How did I get here?" he said.

"Well, sir, I was asked to supply a list. I sent your name in. I thought we ought to have some distinguished-looking people at the show as well as authors."

*

My memories of those early years after the First World War are very pleasant: surgery during the day, increasing but not as overwhelmingly as later; in the evening music, the theatre, '2 LO' at Savoy Hill when wireless was still a wonder, literary and medical societies, pleasant dinners. It was the sort of life that was possible only in London, Dublin or Edinburgh.

One curious episode at a P.E.N. dinner still sticks in my memory. We were dining at Gatti's and my neighbour was to have been Beatrice Kean Seymour, whom I knew well; but though the cards had not been altered some rearrangement had been made, and instead I found an unknown young woman beside me whose name I never subsequently learnt. I had been operating all the afternoon and was rather tired; so I made no effort to talk. I had no need to. She did all the talking, and in the course of it she said she had been H. G. Wells's mistress and had a daughter by him. Nothing surprises a doctor. I said:

"Oh, yes. How interesting."

She then added that she'd seen him at the last P.E.N. dinner. It was years since they'd met, and she told him he ought to come and see his daughter—she was getting quite a big girl now.

"Did he come?"

"Oh, yes. He came and he talked, and listening to him I could see why I had been so unhappy with him. It was his fault, not mine. He vamped women, sucked them dry, wrote novels about his experiences with them and then discarded them. He has a wonderful brain; but he is a cad."

During the evening Wells actually came in to collect his latest mistress, and my companion tautened up at the sight. I knew then that her story was true.

I used to meet him occasionally at the Reform with Arnold Bennett when I was a guest of T. E. Page of Charterhouse. I had a profound admiration for both at that time. But I have never understood Wells's fascination for women. He was an insignificant-looking, smallish, fat man with a high squeaky voice. You never know, however, what attracts. Somerset Maugham says a woman told him that she loved Wells not for his brain but because his body smelt of honey. One beautiful woman confided to me that she fell in love with her husband because he had a club foot. Another with a very plain husband had two lovers to my knowledge. Both resembled her husband. She was faithful to a certain type of ugliness.

It was at this time I first made the acquaintance of Kipling. He was sitting at the table in the window of the Athenæum nearest the Duke of York's column, having dinner by himself. It was the table Lutyens, Charles Graves and Owen Seaman usually occupied at lunch. I recognised him at once: small, rather bent, with a dark lined face, grey hair thinning at the top, very bushy eyebrows, short-sighted eyes peering through thick gold-rimmed spectacles, a walrus moustache—the kind that went out of fashion after the execution of Crippen—a cleft chin and a jutting jaw. He had just come down from St. Andrews, where he had been giving his Rectorial Address. I had read it in *The Times* that morning; and thought it good but not as good as Barrie's of the year before on 'Courage'. But of course Barrie was on his native heath.

Rectorial Addresses are not always received in silence, and I was not surprised to hear someone say:

"Did you have a rough time at St. Andrews?"

"No. They listened to me," he answered.

I was dining with John Tweed the sculptor that evening, and he said after dinner:

"Let's go and talk to Kipling. He's a bit lonely."

It is not easy to be natural when you are first introduced to a great man whom you have worshipped for years from afar. I had been a Kipling fan from boyhood days. In the town library I had read a story in *Macmillan's Magazine*. It was called 'Tod's Amendment'. It opened a new world to me. I was enthralled. But I forgot then to notice the author's name. I didn't forget the story, however, and when I opened *Plain Tales from the Hills* years later, there it was. I can remember my excitement still—Rudyard Kipling. That was the name. So now I went rather diffidently across the floor of the smoking-room after John.

Tweed was working on his great statue of Rhodes at the time, and they naturally started talking about South Africa. That gave me a lead. My brother had been signalling engineer to the Cape Government Railway, and Kipling had spent an evening travelling with him in his repair van from De Aar to East London. Most of the time he kept asking technical questions, for he had a mania for things engineering which crops up continually in his stories. I reminded him of this journey and the conversation soon went on smoothly—South Africa, Rhodes, Botha, Smuts, Tory politics, the Boers, the British—nothing highbrow.

Kipling pulled at his cigar. I smoked my pipe. Tweed didn't smoke. We had a very pleasant evening. Kipling was an interesting but not a brilliant talker.

This was the first of a number of similar evenings spread over the years that followed, but I cannot recall from those evenings anything that stands out in my memory of his conversation. There was nothing in his manner to show the great man that he was. Sometimes I got the feeling that his visits to the Club were in the nature of an escape. In his home, it was hinted, he was hedged in. In London he could do what he liked. He was hungry for men's talk.

CHAPTER XIX

*

SUNSHINE AND SHADOW

THERE COMES A PERIOD in everyone's life when events run so smoothly they leave few outstanding imprints on memory. In the post-war Georgian decade I reached that period. My wife and I and our little girl were very happy in our home in Cambridge Terrace. We had a cook, a housemaid and a nannie, and we ran it at first on £1,200 a year. But of course eggs were two shillings a dozen and income tax still negligible. The war years were forgotten. I became more and more absorbed in surgery. I wrote two more technical books, one of them in collaboration with an architect and an engineer: *Cottage Hospitals. Construction, Equipment and Use*. My royalties on this came to twelve shillings and sixpence. It did not encourage me to write technical books. But I remembered what Sir Frederick Treves had said to me:

"A young surgeon should publish, or read at some Society, at least three papers a year. It's the only way he can make himself known."

A still earlier mentor of mine, Arthur Vernon Macan, Master of the Rotunda, put it differently.

"Dochtor" (he always called his students 'dochtor')—"Dochtor! D'ye want to be the greatest living authority on something?"

"Well—yes, sir—possibly."

"Right! I'll tell you how. Read up what the greatest living authority says on some subject you're interested in. He's sure to be an elderly man, and he's sure to be a bit out-of-date. Contradict him in print on some point you know he's wrong in. He'll answer you. Answer him back. Keep the correspondence up. He'll retort with the 'club of clinical experience'. They always try to squash the younger man that way, by saying they've proved it in practice."

"Yes, sir. I see. But what would be the good of that to me?"

270

Christmas Day in hospital (1933)

Kipling's funeral

"Dochtor, he'll still be the greatest living authority, but now you'll be second greatest. Presently the old man'll die. Then you'll be the greatest living authority."

The other technical work I wrote confirmed this. It made me the recognised authority on one special aspect of venereal disease.

Every morning after breakfast I took the bus to Bond Street and walked up to 38 Harley Street, read my letters and saw such patients as came to see me.

By now I had almost got used to the miracle of the average. I knew that somewhere every month a number of people I'd never previously heard of would hear of me and come to see me; and there would be enough of them to keep the little house and the family and pay the Harley Street rent. It was a constant wonder to me and I was always grateful for it.

One afternoon a week was devoted to Heinemann's. Four were given to my hospitals. Hospital work was of course still unpaid in those days. Every consultant did voluntary work. But there was no merit about it, for it brought good operation fees, since before the Second World War there were large numbers of wealthy patients whose fees paid for the gratuitous service given to the hospitals.

But the increase in work made it difficult to be always available at Harley Street when wanted. We began to hanker after living 'over the shop'. This, as I have already said, had been the custom of consultants at one time, a custom which my wife had been used to as a girl, when her father lived in Henrietta Street, Cavendish Square.

What made things more difficult also was that just at this time I had let myself in for writing a life of a famous eighteenth-century physician named Lettsom of whom, up to then, I knew nothing except the rhyme:

> When any sick to me apply,
> I physics, bleeds and sweats 'em.
> If after that they choose to die,
> Why, verily!
>
> I. LETTSOM.

It started quite innocently by Hugh Elliot, the managing director of the Heinemann Medical Company, lending me a diary of 1813 written by Lettsom, his great-great-grandfather, and suggesting he would like to publish it, if I would write a short foreword.

"Yes, I'll do it," I said quite happily, and without a thought of what it might involve.

I found on going into the matter that Lettsom was a Quaker, and that roused my interest because of my own Quaker connections. I began to read about the man, and the more I read the more interesting I found him. His personality fascinated me. He seemed to know everyone from George III downwards. He was in every philanthropic movement of the time. He was a friend of Dr. Johnson and of Boswell; of Howard and Neild of prison reform. He championed Jenner and vaccination. He attended the famous Lord George Gordon, of the Gordon riots, in his fatal illness when he died in Newgate prison of typhus fever. He was a protégé of Fothergill; and he founded the Medical Society of London and the Sea-bathing Hospital at Margate. I discovered that to know him and his friends and his enemies—of whom he had many—was to get an inside picture of philanthropy and of medical thought at the end of the eighteenth century.

All this I gradually realised as I was collecting information about him at the British Museum; ransacking the records of the Medical Society of London, his own Society, founded by him in 1773; delving into the records of Friends' House, the Royal College of Surgeons, the Royal College of Physicians and the Royal Society of Medicine.

In addition I found much manuscript material preserved by the Elliot family; and I discovered prints, pictures and engravings in second-hand shops. The idea of a short preface to a diary was completely forgotten. I was collecting, instead, all the things that went to producing a full-length biography. I had embarked, though I didn't know it, on a study that was to last for four years.

Of course what happened then was that some of the references I wanted were at Harley Street, some at Cambridge Terrace, and they never were handy where I needed them. That made us still more keen to have all our activities concentrated under one roof.

And just then one of my fans died. He had read my *Surgeon's Log* and subsequently made our acquaintance. We had dined with him, gone to theatres, been to his house at Ascot as guests for the races. But though we liked him, I was very surprised when his lawyers wrote to say he had left me £1,000 free of tax in his will. It was an unexpected windfall and it helped to smooth the way to what we wanted: a home of our own in the consulting area. So we went house-hunting, and our choice fell finally on 22 Queen Anne Street. It was three doors from Harley Street, half a minute from my old rooms at No. 38. Sir Robert Hutchison, a former President of the College of Physicians, had previously practised from it. The Senior Surgeon at the London Hospital, Russell Howard, lived next door at No. 20, and Mr. Cecil Wakeley, now Sir Cecil and later a President of the Royal College of Surgeons, lived on the other side at No. 24. We were obviously in good company. It was a charming, sunny house facing south. We spent ten happy years there. My daughter went to Queen's College, just round the corner, and so started a close association which has continued ever since.

In Queen Anne Street we were at last able to live 'over the shop' and so appreciated how wise the older-world consultants had been. Instead of being away from home most of the day, I was there all morning seeing patients, or operating in some nursing home close by. I could lunch at home or go to one of my clubs. Afternoons were spent mostly at hospitals; and in the quiet of the evening I could be with my family, my books and my writing. The Harley Street area, though in the heart of London, is at night the quietest place I know.

Wherever I was, my wife could always find me. She was the 'Centre of Intelligence'. I once said to a colleague:

"If you want me, ring up my wife. She always knows where I am."

He looked at me, and retorted with a wicked grin:

"Thank God, mine doesn't!"

Alternate weeks I was on night call for emergencies. When the phone rang in the darkness she would pick it up, gather the details, and tell them to me while I dressed.

Driving in the middle of the night through London, I was constantly struck by the fact that there were always people walking about purposefully, quite ordinary people probably on quite ordinary jobs. The streets of London are never empty. High up in the houses as I passed I would often see one solitary lit window, and wonder what it meant: sorrow, or pleasure or intrigue. London never sleeps.

Life was very full in those days. I was lecturing to students of St.

Mary's Hospital at the Harrow Road Hospital, to Charing Cross Hospital students and postgraduates at Dean Street, operating at the Princess Beatrice, and writing my biography of Lettsom—all in addition to running my private practice.

One valuable find came my way at that time: the diary of a niece of the great John Fothergill, lent me by the Misses Abraham, two charming old Quaker ladies. It gave a graphic almost day-to-day picture of London and the fragrant Quaker world of the period round about 1770.

The biography of Lettsom came out in 1933. The review of it in the *Times Literary Supplement* occupied the two front pages, truly a great Aonour. I think it is the best bit of work I ever did. It took, as I have said, four years to do; but I earned more by writing one short medical story in a Sunday paper which took me only three or four evenings to put together; and my reflection on this is that I am lucky to have been able to do both.

The Savage Club and the Athenæum were my relaxations. At both these places I got away from the constant atmosphere of 'wounds and bruises and putrefying sores' which made up my professional life.

One afternoon at the Athenæum I came across J. M. Levien, who had just retired from being secretary to the London Philharmonic Society. He was talking to Alfred Percival Graves, who wrote the words of 'Father O'Flynn', so I joined them. Graves was then very feeble and grey, slow in speech but mentally as alert as ever. He said in the course of conversation that he had picked up the air of 'Father O'Flynn' from hearing a singer in Kerry, just as Kreisler popularised the Londonderry Air after hearing an itinerant fiddler play it outside his hotel in Derry city. Stanford arranged the air of 'Father O'Flynn', but was not so successful with other songs that Graves gave him. He mentioned that Colles, the music critic of *The Times* and editor of Grove's *Dictionary of Music and Musicians*, was a cousin of his. This intrigued me as Graves, I knew, was a grandson of Dr. Graves of Graves' disease (exophthalmic goitre), and Colles was a grandson of Colles of Colles' Law and Colles' fracture; and both these names are names of international fame known to every doctor through the world.

I had met Colles, the critic, some years previously when dining with my father-in-law's cousin, Sir Edward Troup, then Permanent Under-

Secretary of State in the Home Office; and I'm afraid the fact that he was a grandson of the famous surgeon interested me much more than that he was a distinguished authority on music.

A. P. Graves I met several times later. He was using the Club a good deal at this time, and I always made for him when he was alone, for I did not like his brother Charles, the assistant editor of *Punch*. He told me on one occasion that the Irish bard, O'Callaghan, was the composer of the tune of 'The Star-spangled Banner', the national anthem of the United States, often attributed to an English musician, John Stafford Smith.

*

The items one looks at in one's daily paper have different priorities at different ages. Young people look at the list of engagements and marriages. After fifty, one looks at the deaths and obituary notices of the people who have been one's seniors or even contemporaries. One of the people whose loss I noticed with regret in this way was Major Putnam, the American publisher. He was a very active little man with a high carrying American voice. He used to boast that he had served in the American Civil War and yet was not too old to serve again in that of 1914–18. We made him an honorary member of the Athenæum each year when he came over. I once heard him make an after-dinner speech at a Publishers' Association dinner. It was on Anglo-American friendship, and was extraordinarily good. I was much impressed. At a dinner at the Athenæum a fortnight later, however, he made exactly the same speech word for word—a feat of memory that didn't impress me quite so much at the second hearing.

D. H. Lawrence died a few days later. He was only forty-four. I met him once or twice at the P.E.N. Club. He wore a beard. It is queer how often a beard makes a man look effeminate, or is it that effeminate men take to beards? Lawrence was a very brilliant writer. I read everything he wrote with intense interest. But he was sex-obsessed, like a lot of tuberculous men. I went with John Tweed to the private view of his pictures the year before his death. It was in Maddox Street off St. George's, Hanover Square. The room was full of the most awful-looking ugly women, Eton-cropped, some wearing collars and waistcoats, all heavily rouged, smoking. The pictures were too pitiful. No drawing. No colour. No depth. No vision. Nauseating.

Just genitalia, again and again. Tweed was bored. But they were interesting to me as examples of psychopathic art, of a diseased mind trying to express itself in a medium it was incompetent to use. I was not surprised to learn that the police raided the exhibition next day. Lawrence's novels on the other hand are the work of a master of English, and the censorship over some of them a stupidity totally unworthy of us.

Another and quite a different person who died at this time was Charles Whibley, very pedantic, very accurate, very Rabelaisian in his talk, a most amusing conversationalist. For twenty-five years he wrote 'Musings without Method' in *Blackwood's Magazine*. Wise and witty and extremely Tory in outlook, he took in these causeries the opportunity of paying off scores on his numerous enemies, so that we used to chip him by calling them 'Abusings with Method'. One of his pet aversions was Edmund Gosse. They quarrelled over some inaccuracy perpetrated by Gosse, and for twenty years did not speak.

But Gosse chancing to come to the Club one day as a guest, they met accidentally in the hall, and Whibley, who was not a really malicious man, thought it had gone far enough; so he held out his hand to Gosse and said:

"How are you, Gosse?"

Gosse drew himself up stiffly. "Mr. Whibley, I presume," he said.

"Good God, Gosse," retorted Whibley, "you don't think you're Stanley do you?"

I was seeing a lot of John Tweed at this time. He was a most stimulating companion. Talking of his statue of the Duke of Wellington, he said he had mounted him on a Suffolk punch, because Alfred Stevens told him he must do so, though the Duke never rode on one. The punch was probably the descendant of the Flanders horse used by mailed knights in the Middle Ages.

Now the Clydesdale has taken its place. Tweed said that Cecil Rhodes tried to cross the Suffolk punch with the Basuto pony but found he could not get fertile offspring, whereas with the Waler he could.

The curious position of Tweed's statue of Kitchener on the corner of the Horse Guards Parade has often been commented on. Few people now remember that it was near this very spot that the first recruits for

Kitchener's Army in the 1914–18 War were enrolled; and that is the reason the site was chosen. At one time the head of the statue could be seen from the Prime Minister's official residence, 10 Downing Street, projecting above the garden wall; and to hide it from view a slab of Portland stone was put up behind the statue also projecting above the wall. Mrs. Baldwin objected to this, thinking it was unsightly; and later said to Ramsay MacDonald, when he was Prime Minister:

"What are you going to do about Tweed's tombstone? Why don't you move it?"

Ramsay repeated this to Tweed, and he retorted:

"Tell Mrs. Baldwin that Kitchener will have a longer lease than she had."

He was right. It is still there.

Oddly enough, Sayed Abdel Rahman el Mahdi (son of the old Mahdi defeated by Kitchener at Omdurman) was also critical when he was taken by Mr. N. R. Udal, the Secretary of the Athenæum, to see the statue, and said in surprise:

"Why is he not on horseback? He is on horseback in Khartoum."

To which Udal replied: "Ah, but that is different. This is Kitchener appealing to the people, 'Your King and Country need you!' You couldn't do that on horseback. You must appeal from the ground."

One of the habitués of the Club at that time was Freddy Lowndes, the husband of Mrs. Belloc Lowndes. He was a leader writer on *The Times*, and was generally supposed to do most of the obituary notices. At lunch one day he told me a story of Hall Caine which was characteristic.

After granting an interview to 'Everyman', and knowing how different the result often is from what the person interviewed thinks he has said, Hall Caine insisted on seeing a proof. When it came, he thought it was not laudatory enough, and put in a lot of additional adjectives with his own hand in the 'galley'. To this the editor objected, whereupon he dug in his toes and refused to pass it. The editor then gave in, and agreed to publish the interview as amended, but added he would so do with a photostat of the corrections. That called Hall Caine's bluff. He surrendered.

It is interesting now to read the extracts from reviews of this almost forgotten writer in old Heinemann advertisements. The critics then spoke of him in the awed terms one would apply only to Shakespeare. Little wonder he had a swollen head, and apparently with very good reason, for he was a best-seller. Willie Heinemann, who was a very shrewd business-man, used to complain he never could get the better of him in a bargain, and towards the end came practically to publishing him on commission.

Max Beerbohm, large-eyed, round-faced, very neatly dressed, always exquisitely polite, speaking carefully as if weighing each word, came frequently to lunch at the Club during the winter of 1930-31. I don't think he was ever quite at ease there. I wondered why he was spending the winter in England, where we were having wretched weather, when he might have been at one of his villas at Rapallo. (He had two: a winter and a summer one.)

It was Charles Evans of Heinemann's who suggested a probable reason to me. Max had produced in the previous year a series of caricatures which Charles published. These had been rather tepidly received. The critics said he'd been too long out of the country to reproduce the note of truthful caricature which was his special gift. That, Charles thought, was why he came back to get in touch once more with contemporary life; and it seemed a reasonable explanation at the time. But the actual fact, as he told me later, was that he came over because his sister was very ill, and he returned to his beloved Rapallo as soon after as possible. He adored Italy and he was most unhappy when he had to leave it during the Second World War. Then he would drift into the Club, talk in his gentle, precise English to all and sundry and drift out again. One had a feeling that he felt detached from English life, and no longer was at home in it.

*

I can still remember the excitement of the Election in October, 1931, when Ramsay and Baldwin and the Liberal Party formed the Coalition Government. Kipling came into the Club on October 20th, and I asked him how he was.

"Very ill," he answered, "I shan't be better until the twenty-seventh."

This was said with a twinkle, as the 27th was the date of the General Election, and on it depended whether the country went Socialist or supported the National Government. We had just gone off the Gold Standard, and Kipling was thinking of this when he added:

"I want to go to Aswan, but I don't know if I'll have any money left after the Election's over. Snowden (the Chancellor of the Exchequer) recommends us to stay in England this winter. His object is to kill us off by English cooking so that he can get the death duties."

This was a remark typical of Kipling. He was not a witty man.

We sat up to midnight on the 27th listening to the wireless reports of the election results as they came through. It was a landslide for the Coalition. The Socialist Party was practically wiped out; but I was pleased to see that, all the same, Ramsay had pulled off his gallant gesture by a Socialist majority of 5,000 at Seaham.

Two days later he came into the Club. I was lunching with John Tweed and Llewellyn Llewellyn, and Ramsay joined us. He looked tired about the eyes, but very well. He said he had just been to see the King, and everyone was so kind to him he felt he might get a swollen head. Tweed and I smiled discreetly when he said this.

It is generally believed that it was in the billiard-room of the Athenæum that he and Asquith originally came to the agreement that permitted the first Labour Government to be formed in January, 1924. I am sure Asquith made the agreement in absolute good faith. Constitutionally he was right, but it was a death blow to the great Liberal Party; for nothing was more successful in the Election nine months later than the Conservative slogan:

"EVERY VOTE FOR THE LIBERALS IS A VOTE FOR THE SOCIALISTS."

The Liberal Party has never recovered from this.

*

Lord Moynihan was frequently seen at the Club in the early 1930s, and we wondered what he was after, for he was notoriously a very skilful wirepuller. I suppose he was in some ways the most successful surgeon in England between 1900 and 1925. He was made a K.C.M.G. in 1918, a baronet in 1922, President of the Royal College of Surgeons in 1926 and Baron Moynihan in 1929. One would have thought that was enough for any one man. But there was something else he wanted, and it kept eluding him. He wanted to be a Fellow of the Royal Society; and because certain people were antagonistic to him, he

K

attacked them. He singled out particularly those on the Medical Research Council, accusing them of being detached from practical issues. He said, again and again, that a surgeon who made scientific observations when operating, thus studying the pathology of the living, was a better man than an anatomist making observations on the dead body. The surgeon was, in his opinion, much more worthy of an F.R.S. than an anatomist. In this he was absolutely right, but his methods of gaining his ends alienated people. A good many of the Fellows of the Society were favourably disposed towards him; and amongst them was the President, Sir Charles Sherrington. It is said that Sherrington had actually nominated him at the time Moynihan invited him to a Hunterian dinner at the Royal College of Surgeons. At this dinner Moynihan made one of his characteristic brilliant impromptu speeches. It was so brilliant that Sherrington was deeply impressed, and congratulated Lady Moynihan who was sitting next him.

"Oh," she is reported to have said, "we're tired of that speech. We've heard nothing else for the last month."

That is the story as told me. It may be true. At any rate Moynihan never got his F.R.S.

*

Few people, I think, realise what a tense existence a surgeon leads. He is constantly taking life in his hands; and if he is at all sensitive he has many periods of great anxiety. I had been doing major surgery in London, after my return from the 1914–18 War, for fifteen years; and it now began to tell on me.

I noticed it first on a holiday at Ragaz in Switzerland when pain which started two hours after food was relieved by taking more food. This is typical of duodenitis, and if unchecked develops eventually into a duodenal ulcer.

Early in 1934 I got so worried that I went to a friend and asked him to take a series of X-rays. He told me there was nothing wrong, and to forget it. I was able to do this because about the same time I had an offer for the film rights of my novel *The Night Nurse*. This was most exciting. I was thrilled by the thought of seeing my characters enact before my eyes the story my brain had conceived, and I accepted the terms of the offer. The plot was laid partly in Dublin and partly in County Mayo, so most of the scenes were shot in Ireland. It was actually the first talkie film to be made in Ireland. But a certain amount of interior work, mainly hospital scenes, could be done in London; and at these I was a fascinated observer. Every hour I could spare from my work found me at the Ealing Studios.

Brian Hurst was the producer, and I sat beside him in a camp chair, with the 'continuity' girl squatting in front of us, watching the 'takes', seeing the mechanism working. It was a very hot summer and the temperature in the studios was high. The great lamps which poured down light and heat on the actors added to the intensity.

I learnt a lot about the technique of production at that time, such as the tradition that the heroine should be several inches shorter than the hero so that she could look up adoringly into his eyes, and the simple but important rules that governed the 'take'.

A 'take' was a short scene. Before it was shot the actors got into position, the camera-men got ready, the lights were turned on and a clapper boy crouched in front of the performers with a noticeboard in his hand labelled '143, take 5' or some such numbers. Then there was a call for silence, the director said "O.K. for scene", a voice from somewhere answered "O.K. for sound". The director then said "Take", the cameras turned and the actors began to speak until the director called out "Cut". Then everything stopped. Sometimes one such scene would be repeated, time after time, till the director was satisfied and everyone else was sick of it. Yards and yards of film would be reeled off and examined later by the cutter to pick out the best.

It was interesting to note that often a scene would be shot, and then be followed for convenience by one that came much earlier in the story. That is why the 'takes' were numbered. Also that is where the continuity girl came in, and was so important. She had to make notes of everything the characters wore. If, for instance, the hero wore a bowler hat when he strode across the street in one shot and appeared in a panama in the rest of the same scene, which probably had been shot three or four days later, it was disastrous. The continuity girl's job was to see that a gaffe like this did not happen.

Day by day I watched my story unfold. It fascinated me. I met the actors from the Abbey Theatre who had been engaged to play some of the parts—Sarah Allgood, Maire O'Neill, Katherine Drago, Arthur Sinclair, Joyce Chancellor and the rest. The soft, caressing Irish brogue of the Abbey players was a remembered joy to me. I didn't quite like the songs and dances that the director introduced, though the music had been written by my friend Herbert Hughes, that great authority on Irish folk song. Songs and dances were not in the story, and I thought they didn't fit; but the director said they would help the box office.

All this new world fascinated me so much that I forgot my irritable duodenum. I lived for the picture. And then nemesis struck me. One evening coming back from the studio I was summoned to a case of acute appendicitis. It was quite a straightforward operation, no difficulties, no complications. The patient was all right for two days, and then he got paralytic ileus, a form of intestinal obstruction, and died.

It was an unexpected catastrophe; his people were very upset. They took it very badly, for he was only eighteen. They were sure it was due to incompetence on my part, and immediately I was threatened with an action for malpraxis. They wrote to the Chairman of the Hospital. They sent abusive letters to me. They threatened to write to the General Medical Council. For a week I had a most unhappy time, and my duodenum knew it. I felt all along, however, there must be something wrong, something we did not know. And then it came out. The nurse in charge reluctantly admitted she had caught the patient drinking from the wash-basin in his cubicle. It was so close to his bed he could turn the tap with his left hand, and he had drunk pints and pints of cold water, filling his stomach and small intestine. She had promised not to tell the house-surgeon; but now, terrified by the sequel, she was compelled to admit what she knew; for of course that was what had killed him. He was waterlogged. That stopped the case, and I heard no more about it. But I still felt very distressed.

It was the middle of August, and I was completely exhausted emotionally. For some unknown reason I also got an attack of fibrositis. I left the film to be completed, and went with my wife for a course of treatment to Droitwich, feeling life was very, very grey.

The morning after our arrival I walked up the hill to see Dr. Neligan, to whom I had been recommended. On the way I began to feel 'ghostly'; everything grew hazy; but sitting in his waiting-room until my turn came I recovered.

When I went into his consulting-room he looked at me, took hold of my wrist and after a minute of silence said:

"Is your pulse always one hundred and twenty?"

"No. My average is sixty," I answered. "I'm one of the slow ones."

"You're too ill to take the baths," he said, gravely. "Go back to the hotel. I'll see you in bed tomorrow."

But that afternoon I had a hæmorrhage from a duodenal ulcer, though I didn't realise it at the time; my wife rang him up, and next day on his advice she brought me home. When we arrived at Queen Anne Street my secretary said an old and important patient had just called, found I was expected and insisted on waiting. I said I'd see him and I did see him; though my wife was very angry at my obstinacy, and tried to stop me.

It was a stupid, foolhardy thing to do, and I could not afterwards remember anything about that consultation. He didn't know of course I'd just had a hæmorrhage, but he never came again. So it looks as if this time I hadn't impressed him much; and I am not surprised.

Six weeks passed. I was still in bed, with two physicians and a surgeon looking after me, when the preview of my film was shown in Wardour Street. And so I did not see it. But I heard it had been sold to M.G.M., and the première was to be in New York on October 5th, 1934.

Judging from the press notices, it had a mixed reception both in America and in England. In Ireland, where it was first shown in Dublin on St. Patrick's Day, 1935, it was fairly well received. Actually I never saw it, as I was very ill again when it was released in England. But I was told it had been heavily censored in this country, and the whole story lacked dramatic completeness in consequence.

This annoyed me intensely, so when I was a little better and was allowed to go out, I went to complain to the censor, Mr. Brooke Wilkinson. He had just come back from St. George's Hospital, where he had been operated on successfully by Sir Stewart Duke-Elder. Before that he had suffered from cataract for two years, and had been nearly blind. But when anyone went to see him he used to stand up,

walk forward and shake hands with them. When he was asked how
he saw the visitor's hand, he said:

"I don't. I hold out my hand and he takes it. He has to."

He was still intensely grateful to the medical profession at the time
of my interview.

"My deputy tells me," he said, "that there are scenes about a drunken
doctor in the film. I have the greatest possible respect for the medical
profession, and I will not pass any scene that might bring it into dis-
respect."

"But I am a doctor myself. I wrote the story," I said.

"I don't care. It may be all right in a novel, but I will not pass it for
the films," he answered.

And so the drunken scenes and the seduction episode were cut out,
and the story ruined. I felt very sore about it at the time. Years later
I told James Bridie what had happened.

"Oh," he said, "that's nothing. They bought a story of mine once,
and paid for it. But all they used was the bang the villain made going
out of the back door!"

Considering it all now, however, in the calmness of later years, I
think the censor was absolutely right.

*

Shortly after that I had a relapse. Lying in bed in an enforced quietude,
not able to work, would have been intolerable to me at that time had
I not fortunately had another outlet. I was writing a series of articles in
Nash's Magazine on medical subjects. It was Charles Evans of Heinemann's who suggested to the editor I should do them. But more than
once I nearly gave up. After another relapse I wrote an article on 'The
Fear of Death', and was so ill I could not correct the proofs. My wife
did that. It is the last article in the series published in book form, under
the title of 99 *Wimpole Street*, in 1937.

All the time I was writing these articles I was hoping to get well, to
escape the surgeon. But I didn't get well. Eventually the day came
when I asked Stanley Wyard, my physician, to gather the other experts
I had seen for a decisive consultation with Sir James Walton.

They stood round my bed, the four of them: Dr. Charles Bolton,
Mr. Lawrence Abel, Dr. Stanley Wyard and Sir James Walton;

and I told them I would rather die than go on as I was doing.

After a brief consultation, Sir James came over to the bed, patted me on the shoulder, and said:

"I think I'd better operate on you, old chap."

It was a most generous offer. He was at that time one of the greatest living authorities on duodenal ulcer, and Surgeon to the King. I was very touched. But no, it wasn't what I wanted.

There was a short silence. He smiled encouragingly at me; and then I said:

"That's awfully good of you, Walton. But Lawrence has been looking after me since I had my first hæmorrhage, and if you don't mind I'd like him to do it."

A small man, even some great men, would have been hurt or annoyed at this refusal. Not so Walton.

"Right," he said. "I tell you what. I'll come along and assist if necessary at the operation."

And he did, which showed what a great man he was.

The operation was on March 26th, 1935. That is over twenty years ago. I owe those twenty years of renewed health and vitality to my friend and colleague, Lawrence Abel.

*

Three months after operation I was back at work at my hospitals.

Curious unattached incidents are sometimes sharply remembered at times like these. The Sunday after my first appearance again at the Princess Beatrice Hospital, my wife and I drove out to Hampstead to call on Arthur Waugh, the managing director of my publishers, Chapman & Hall, at his house, Underhill. It was a lovely day; but Arthur was in the doldrums. Someone had left a cigarette burning on a chair a few nights before, and it had started a fire that destroyed four hundred and fifty of his books, many of them autographed. That had upset him. On the other hand he told me that the feud with Sherborne over *The Loom of Youth* had been buried. *The Loom* was Alec Waugh's first book, and the school authorities, much to his surprise, had taken such exception to it that he and his father had had to sever their connections with the Old Boys' Society, and Evelyn went to Lancing instead of following his brother to Sherborne. Now all was forgotten, and both Arthur and Alec were meeting old school friends in amity again.

I had been reading during my convalescence two of Arthur's books: *One Man's Road* and *One Hundred Years of Publishing*. To me they were fascinating. I was able to thank him for the charming things he had said of me in his history of Chapman & Hall, and to tell him how grateful I was for the help he had been to me at the beginning of my writing career. He was a very lovable man; I missed him very much after he retired from the management of the Company. To me, Chapman and Hall was never the same again.

By the autumn I had recovered sufficiently to go to a P.E.N. dinner. H. G. Wells was in the chair. I hadn't seen him for two years and I noted he looked much older; he was fat and grey, but very self-satisfied. He had his latest mistress with him, for there was now no need for concealment since his wife had died. Mrs. Wells must have been a remarkable woman to put up with him, and he must have had some odd twisted kink of affection for her. After she died he wrote a funeral oration which he intended to read over her ashes. But he knew if he read it himself in his little squeaky voice it would fall very flat. So he asked Dr. T. E. Page of Charterhouse to declaim it for him. Dr. Page, who had an effective speaking voice, did so. He told me afterwards the wording was quite beautiful, and some of the people who heard it were in tears.

By this time I was back at work, in full swing. I remember going one afternoon with Edmund Blunden to the unveiling of a bust of Charles Lamb at the Charterhouse Chapel behind St. Bartholomew's Hospital, and the same evening taking my clinic at the Lock Hospital. Life was good again.

*

CHAPTER XX

SOME FAMOUS PEOPLE

IN 1936 the Athenæum was one hundred and twelve years old, and it signalised the occasion by abolishing entrance to the Club by ballot. This method had been getting more and more archaic. It had been found increasingly difficult to whip up enough members to vote, even by offering them free teas on election days. So elections were now left to the General Committee.

Coming out from the first of these Committee meetings we were greeted by the news that Kipling was dangerously ill in the Middlesex Hospital, and had been operated on by Sir Alfred Webb-Johnson and Pearce Gould, junior, for a perforated gastric ulcer.

I had seen him only the week before, when he said he was going to Luxor for the rest of the winter on account of his bronchitis. This and his age and his condition I knew made recovery very doubtful.

Three days later he was dead, and a great Englishman had passed on.

I had known and talked to him at intervals for fifteen years, ever since John Tweed had introduced me one evening after dinner at the Club. I knew of course that during the last ten years or so of his life it had become the fashion of young writers to run him down. That is the normal fate of successful authors after their death. But in Kipling's case it started sooner, for he sprang into fame in his twenties, and had reigned undisputed for over forty years before the decline. I always resented this decline; and I was delighted therefore when a few years ago T. S. Eliot told me he too shared my enthusiasm. The wheel, I think, must now be turning once again.

In the midst of the gloom over Kipling's death we learnt that the King (George V) was ill. When I heard that Sir Maurice Cassidy, the heart specialist, had been summoned to Sandringham by Dawson of Penn, I knew he must be very ill. I can remember how on that bleak

January evening in 1936 we sat round the fire listening to the hourly bulletins on the wireless, hoping for better news, until at nine-thirty p.m. there came the message from Lord Dawson saying:

"The King's life is moving peacefully towards its close."

This announcement was repeated by the B.B.C. every quarter of an hour until one felt it was almost more than one could bear. Obviously the King was unconscious and they were just waiting for the end. It came at five minutes before midnight; and the message to the world went out at twelve-fifteen a.m.; but, wearied by listening to the repetition, I'm ashamed to say I was asleep. My wife woke me and said he had gone. I felt it was the end of an epoch—the same blank feeling I had when Queen Victoria died. King Edward VII's death left me with no such emotion. King George V, I think, came much closer to us. I suppose it was his Christmas broadcasts that made him seem so much more human, brought him so much nearer everyone. Besides I had shaken hands with him myself, and so could shut my eyes and see him in my mind.

Two days later I listened to the proclamation of Edward VIII made from the little balcony overlooking the courtyard at St. James's Palace. The salute of sixty-two guns from the Park started three minutes too soon, and partially drowned the proclamation by Garter King at Arms. People later thought this was an omen.

That morning I had been to the quiet little chapel of the Middlesex Hospital, to pay my last respects to Kipling before the cremation, pausing to gaze at the coffin, draped with the flag he loved so well, with the spray of violets from his widow on the top. On my return to Queen Anne Street I found a ticket admitting me to the funeral service in the Abbey. That set my mind back thinking of the last time I had been to such a famous funeral. It was Lord Lister's, the father of antiseptic surgery, in 1912; and I remembered how moved I had been by the solemn splendour of it all. I remembered also the description which, thrilled with emotion, I had written for a paper called *The Hospital*, and how pleased I was when I sent it in, and how dejected I became when they refused to print it—probably quite rightly.

The funeral service for Kipling was on January 23rd, 1936. I got to the Abbey at eleven-thirty a.m. There was not much congestion as yet in the streets, as the King's body was not due to arrive from Sandringham for the Lying-in-State in Westminster Hall until four p.m.; but people were already collecting in the Strand as I passed through Trafalgar Square.

I had a seat in Poets' Corner in the Abbey within ten feet of the urn. Mrs. Kipling, a tiny pathetic figure in deep black, stood with bowed head while the Dean read the service. Next her was Mrs. Bambridge, her daughter, another tiny, white-faced figure, and towering beyond her Captain Bambridge, Kipling's son-in-law, a huge stooping man. Immediately behind these chief mourners stood a solitary figure, Webb-Johnson, the surgeon who had tried to save Kipling's life. I think very few people at that time knew why he was there or who he was. A little behind him and to the left stood Mr. Baldwin, the Prime Minister and Kipling's cousin.

I watched the urn containing the ashes being placed in the receptacle prepared for it between Thomas Hardy and Charles Dickens. I heard the solemn voice of the Dean as he scattered earth over the marble urn saying "Dust to dust, ashes to ashes". A lump came in my throat.

The Lying-in-State of George V in Westminster Hall started that evening; and for the next few days the long queue of silent people, four deep, from as far away as Vauxhall Bridge to Westminster, moved endlessly through the hall built by William Rufus.

They walked slowly, gazing at the catafalque with the crown and sceptre resting on the rich vestments covering the coffin in which the King's body lay. The catafalque was guarded, four-square, by relays of Gentlemen-at-Arms, Life Guardsmen and Sentinel Yeomen. The Guards in their white plumed helmets bent reverently over their swords; the Yeomen stood rigidly at each corner leaning on their halberds.

The sombre-eyed procession of people moved slowly past, hour by hour, in silent tribute to their dead King, and then passed out into the world and the affairs of the world, filled with a vision of splendid solemnity.

On a dull morning some days later, with streaks of sunshine between the showers, the coffin was borne on a gun-carriage through the densely crowded silent streets to Paddington, on its way to the last resting place of the Kings of England, St. George's Chapel, Windsor.

My wife and I listened to the service on the wireless, and we heard the traditional proclamation over the Royal coffin:

"The King is dead. Long live the King."

George V was dead. Edward VIII was King.

For some days everything after these events seemed very flat. Too much emotion had been concentrated into too short a period.

At the Club, a week later, Ramsay MacDonald arrived back from his election as M.P. for the Scottish Universities. He had previously been defeated in his old constituency at Seaham, by another Labour candidate who had the blessing of the party, and so it was necessary to find him a safe seat without too much electioneering. I was standing with (Sir) Walter Lamb, the Secretary of the Royal Academy, when we saw him in the hall.

"I expect, sir," said Lamb, "you think more of the University vote now than you did before!"

Ramsay was a bit taken aback, for in previous years he had talked glibly of doing away with University seats. But he smiled and passed it off as a joke.

I feel sure Ramsay used the Club as a refuge in the last years of his life; for his treatment by the Labour Party was cruel in the extreme. They never forgave him for joining the Coalition Government with the Conservatives and Liberals. They ostracised him, vituperated him, called him Judas; and this from former friends and colleagues preyed heavily on his mind, for he was an intensely sensitive man.

He was extremely good-looking, and as his hair grew whiter seemed more handsome than ever. I think he loved the pomp and circumstance of office, and he didn't mind Baldwin being the real power while he had the appearance of it. His reputation has risen since he died, just as Asquith's has risen and that of Lloyd George has declined.

Looking back, I think that the end of 1936 saw the beginnings of the political change which made 'Socialism in our time' a distinct possibility. The prestige of the Crown had been shaken by the abdication of Edward VIII. The old order was changing. The menace of Nazi Germany was becoming more obvious. Visions of a grim future were being prophesied in films, plays and novels.

Carter, the publicity man for Korda, came to see me one afternoon. He said he had been working on Wells's film: *The Shape of Things to*

Come. It had cost £280,000 to date, ran for five hours, and would have to be reduced to two and a half. Wells, he said, was very lazy and had to be constantly prodded on by his mistress. He was probably wrong about the laziness, for Wells was a diabetic, and became tired easily when his blood-sugar was low.

It was a jangled world. Things happened to one's family or one's friends. It is tempting fate to have an only son, especially in any of the Services, at such a time. Something untoward seems to happen to people like that, just as rare complications after operation seem to occur, we think, only to doctors, their wives or their children. The death of Sir Humphry Rolleston's only son, murdered by an Arab during a trivial riot in Zanzibar, was what brought this last thought vividly to my mind.

I had known Sir Humphry for many years; and he had been always extremely kind to me. Our first meeting was very characteristic of him. He and my father-in-law, Dr. Francis, were at St. John's, Cambridge, together; and, when Dr. Francis was ill once, I suggested I should call Sir Humphry in to see him, to make sure of my diagnosis.

"He won't make one," said Dr. Francis.

Sir Humphry came, however, and was perfectly charming. The two hadn't met for some years, so they talked about old Cambridge days whilst Sir Humphry examined him. I suppose he was at that time one of the most erudite men in the profession. He read everything. He was editor of *The Practitioner.* He knew so much; he knew so many things; he knew how fallible judgment was that he had got to the stage where he now found it difficult to make a diagnosis. Dr. Francis was right. He didn't make one this time either, and he was equally vague about treatment. I had been warned of this too, so we looked at each other, rather at a loss. Finally I suggested something we might try—I forget what—and he brightened up at once and said:

"Oh, yes. Excellent."

"Will you write the prescription, sir, and I'll take it over to Allen and Hanbury's in Vere Street and get it?"

"You write it," he said, "I'm afraid of the young men there. The other day I went in and asked for something, and a Scotsman behind the counter said to me:

" 'Are you a medical m-a-a-n?' "

"What did you say?" I asked, with some curiosity.

"I said I was," he answered simply.

That was just like Rolleston. He didn't mention he was President of the Royal College of Physicians at the time, Regius Professor of Physic at Cambridge, and Physician-in-Ordinary to George V.

His manner indeed was so mild and diffident that anyone who did not know him might easily have made the same mistake as the raw Scots dispenser.

The death of my old friend the famous actress Mrs. Brown-Potter, also in 1936, brought back many memories to me. She was so utterly lovely. Her beauty took one's breath away, for she was, I think, the most beautiful woman I have ever seen, more beautiful than Lily Langtry, her principal rival in Edwardian days. She once told me she had seventy-six letters from Edward VII locked away in her bank. I sometimes wonder what has become of them. When I came back after the First World War, I found she had retired to live in the Channel Islands, and we lost touch. I did not know her during the height of her fame at the time she was acting with Kyrle Bellew, and later at His Majesty's Theatre with Tree. My memories, as I have said, were of her as Mary, Queen of Scots and Charlotte Corday, with Gilbert Hare, Esmé Percy and Godfrey Tearle.

She was a proud Southern lady from New Orleans, the daughter of a Colonel in the Confederate Army in the American Civil War. Once I saw an unfortunate example of our British ignorance of what that meant. I had gone as her escort to a dinner given by some official society whose title I cannot now remember. She was the star guest; and on our entry the orchestra struck up 'Marching through Georgia' in her honour. This is the famous song of Sherman's ride to the sea which was sung by the victorious Federal Army; and when she heard the first few notes she stopped dead, grew pale, looked at me and said fiercely:

"Take me away. This is an insult I cannot forgive."

I had the greatest difficulty in persuading her that it was just ignorance, pure ignorance, and really intended as a compliment to a distinguished American lady. But it spoilt the evening for her.

The year 1936 saw the publication of the twenty-first edition of my book *The Surgeon's Log*. This work had been selling steadily since 1911 and I was quite satisfied.

But one morning a year before, in 1935, I had had a call from a good-looking young man, Allen Lane, who told me he had been a lover of the book for years, he had just begun to publish a series of paper-backed copyright works at sixpence which he called 'Penguins', and he was anxious to include mine in this series. Although he was charmingly persuasive, I am afraid I displayed no enthusiasm. A sixpenny paper-backed book with a royalty of a halfpenny a copy didn't seem good business to me. Indeed no one, I believe, in the publishing world, and certainly no one like me, thought at that time there was anything in the idea.

But the first four or five books issued went with a bang. The books chosen were good; the covers were attractive; the prices compelling.

I saw I had made a mistake, and when I was again approached some months later, I agreed immediately. The first Penguin *Surgeon's Log* came out therefore in November, 1936, and I have never regretted the day I agreed to its appearance. Very soon it was being used as an English schoolbook in Norway, California and Egypt; and other publishers who had refused it originally now bought chapters to incorporate in text-books of advanced English for schools in this country. That, oddly enough, pleased me a lot.

*

One of my early ambitions had been satisfied when I was elected to the Savage Club. It had been a home and a resting place all during my bachelor days. In its beautiful rooms in the Adelphi looking on to the river I had spent many happy hours. But now, twenty-four years later, the heavy hand of time and big business had fallen on it; we learnt with dismay that the beautiful terrace built by the Adam brothers was to be demolished; and the Club would have to seek elsewhere for another resting place.

Wandering gloomily round from Adam Street, past the *Lancet* offices, to attend the last general meeting of the Club in its old setting, I could see signs of impending change: bills of sale of furniture, empty rooms, vans removing things. Even the sight that morning of my section on Bob Sawyer in the *Pickwick Portrait Gallery* issued by Chapman & Hall to celebrate the centenary of the publication of *The Pickwick Papers* had done little to lighten my gloom, for I loved the old Savage—it had been such a home to me. Two days later we staged a 'Ladies Day' when the wives and daughters and women friends of the members were allowed to view the jealously guarded rooms they had heard so much about but never seen.

Saturday, March 21st, 1936, was the last of our celebrated Saturday night dinners held in the famous old rooms. The programme after dinner was unusual. It consisted mainly of gramophone records of dead Savages: Courtice Pounds, Mostyn Piggott, Bill Barrett, Harry Dearth. Harry's record was a song: 'It's been a beautiful day'. The composer, Sterndale Bennett, was sitting beside me. I glanced sideways at him. There were tears in his eyes. Slowly, reluctantly, we began to disperse. The last member to leave the house officially was Starr Wood, a well-known *Punch* artist who used to issue his own *Starr Wood's Annual* every Christmas. It was the end of forty-five years in the Adelphi.

I never was happy in the new premises at 1 Carlton House Terrace with its memories of Curzon, a cold, remote person compared with his father, Lord Scarsdale, whom I used to attend when I did a locum for my uncle, his doctor.

The family seat was at Kedleston, and in the grounds of the great house was the village church seating possibly a hundred people. Lord Scarsdale had held the family living before he inherited the title; and all round the walls of the little church were mural tablets to former Curzons, none of whom seem to have risen higher than a colonel in the Army or a captain in the Navy. But in the centre of the aisle, taking up much of the space, was one grand catafalque, elaborately carved, dominating everything. Underneath the stone canopy were two recumbent white marble statues lying side by side. One was a woman, the other a man. When my uncle, one day on his rounds, took me in to see the chapel and the tomb, I said:

"Who is the woman?"

"That is the first Lady Curzon. She was a great dear."

"And the man?" I asked.

"That is Nathaniel," he answered, to my surprise.

"But he's not dead yet!" I protested.

"No. But he's making sure," said my uncle.

The general opinion of the world is that Curzon was a proud, unapproachable man, full of conceit, who despised most other men. I'm sure that was wrong. Instead, I believe he was a shy man who over-compensated for his shyness by appearing supercilious and unbending. What Labouchere called his manner of a 'divinity addressing black beetles' was defensive, not offensive. From the age of nineteen he suffered from a tuberculous spine which must have ached continuously. I know. I have seen him in great pain. He had to wear a steel corset most of his life; and a man who is in constant pain may be forgiven for being querulous. His crowning ambition, of course, was to be made Prime Minister; and when George V, on Bonar Law's advice, chose Baldwin instead of him the light went out of his life. I have always had an irrational liking for Curzon. He was a great Englishman with an indomitable spirit. Sir John Thomson-Walker, his surgeon, told me that after his operation he dictated his own bulletins daily, and had the newspapers brought to him to confirm that they had been printed as issued. On the day of his death they came out with a cheerful bulletin, self-composed.

A doctor has many privileges, and not the least of these is the friend-ships he makes with some of his patients. One such friendship I remember with deep affection was with Dr. T. E. Page of Charter-house. We met casually first of all on the staircase of the Heinemann offices in Great Russell Street, years before he became my patient. He was editor of the Loeb Classical Library, and his office was next to mine.

I knew of course who he was, for his appearance was so striking that no one could help, after once seeing him, wanting to find out. Tall, handsome, grey-haired, blue-eyed, and wearing the famous Page trousers, he was a figure impossible to overlook. He once told me that Mrs. Asquith stopped him in Bond Street and asked him to breakfast next day at No. 10 Downing Street. She pretended, when inviting him, that she didn't know his name; and he was innocent enough to believe her, felt flattered and accepted. But of course she recognised him: his tall figure, great leonine head and the famous wide grey-white baggy trousers telling her all she wanted to know. She was quite aware also that he and Asquith knew each other well, for Page was one of the last Asquithian Liberals.

Editing the Loeb Library brought him up from Godalming to Great Russell Street fairly frequently, for most of the work was done by him, his co-editors Dr. Rouse and Dr. Capps recognising that he was probably the finest classical scholar since Porson.

After a morning's work with his secretary, Mrs. Rowan Robinson, he would make for the Reform Club, his spiritual home. Here he was treated almost regally. He sat at a special table to which he invited whom he wished. No one else took it on the days it was known he came to town. The Club did him an honour which I think was unique: they subscribed for a portrait of him while he was still alive. And, in addition, on his eightieth birthday they presented him with a Latin address signed by five hundred members.

Occasionally he would ask me to lunch with him, and afterwards we would sit outside in the gallery and talk. He was a wonderful talker, and he had the most beautiful speaking voice. He loved good food, good wine and good company. He loathed the telephone, and absolutely refused to wear false teeth, though he had only two teeth left when I knew him. He said dentures would spoil his palate for wine, of which he was a connoisseur. He used to send me a dozen vintage port every Christmas.

The famous trousers were made of a dullish white woollen material of which he is said to have bought hundreds of yards at a time. He wore the same kind for years. All sorts of legends grew round those trousers. One was that he bought a mile of the material during a yachting trip to St. Kilda? another that it was surplus war stock left over from the Crimean War. Everybody knew about Page's trousers.

In the evening, after the day's work, he would catch the six-two p.m. back to Godalming, read the three evening papers and then start on a detective story. He used to get through three or four of these a week, and so often outran the supply. They rested his tired mind.

One Friday I met him on the stairs at the Great Russell Street office. He was taking them very slowly; but he smiled his bright blue-eyed smile as usual when I asked him how he was.

"I feel a bit tired," he said.

Four days later he was dead.

I went to his memorial service in the chapel of the old Charterhouse in the City. We had some difficulty in dodging past the vans of meat from Smithfield, but when we did get through the gates it was a sudden quiet joy to park the car in the old square, bright with daffodils and irises. The grey chapel, so silent, so monastic with its low ceiling, its age-old wall tablets and lovely stained-glass windows, was almost filled by those who came to pay their last tribute to his memory. About twenty of the Brothers of the Charterhouse in their black gowns were also present. Someone in a soft, mellow voice read the ninetieth psalm: "Lord, thou hast been our refuge from one generation to another," and Bishop Paget spoke feelingly about Page and his wonderful sweetness and simplicity, so unexpected in such a great classical scholar.

Then followed two hymns, and it was all over.

After this we came away slowly, thoughtfully, out into the ancient square again, and five minutes later emerged through the gates, jumping abruptly from the sixteenth to the twentieth century. I could do no work the rest of that day.

The death of Beatrice Harraden shortly after this brought up once again the perennial problem of the secret of the 'best-seller'. I remembered seeing her years before at the P.E.N. Club. I had read *Ships that Pass in the Night* as an undergrad, so I had been interested in meeting her. She was a small, dark, withered little woman with a snub nose, flat feet, bunions and the kindliest and loveliest brown eyes.

The book is now almost completely forgotten, but when it appeared it was a phenomenal success. It was published by a small unknown firm, Lawrence & Bullen, and the critics took no notice of it. The publishers had paid forty pounds for the copyright, and came to the conclusion they had made a bad bargain.

And then, suddenly, it began to sell. The first edition ran out. It was reprinted. It ran out again; and after that it went through edition after edition. It was translated into every European language, and even into Japanese. The public went crazy about it. The story of how the craze began is that one of the ladies-in-waiting to the late Queen Alexandra, who was then Princess of Wales, saw it on a table in her dentist's waiting-room, dipped into it, got fascinated, borrowed it and showed it to the Princess; and that is how it all started. It may be so. At any rate Beatrice once told me she made nothing out of it. All the money went to her publishers. It was of course just a fragment of autobiography felt intensely, emotionally. It had happened to herself at Davos. She never repeated her first success. None of her later books had any comparable sale; and eventually she had to accept a Civil List pension in 1930. The mystery of the best-seller remained a mystery and still does. One safe thing to say about it is that no one can write a best-seller with his tongue in his cheek. It must have genuine emotion behind it.

CHAPTER XXI

*

FORAY INTO FLEET STREET

WHEN A SURGEON stops doing major operations, and confines himself largely to consultation work, his private practice drops appreciably. This was now happening to me. I found that after my own severe illness I could no longer stand up to the fatigue of long operations. I still could carry on my clinics at my hospitals adequately, but had to leave operating to my younger colleagues.

More and more, therefore, I found myself turning to writing. A collection of essays that I had recently published called 99 *Wimpole Street* had a pleasant moderate success; but what made the book important was not its success but that one of the articles in it attracted the attention of the Kemsley Press, and, though I could not have guessed it at the time, started me on a happy association with Fleet Street, and later with Cassell's, that has lasted steadily for nearly twenty years.

It was the publication of a novel, *The Citadel*, by A. J. Cronin that brought the subjects in which I was interested, and could write about, into sudden prominence.

The Citadel was largely autobiographical. It was an excellent story, extremely well written. Moreover it was written obviously from the inside; and, quite unintentionally, it created in the public mind at that time a suspicion of Harley Street and all its doings, a feeling that the medical profession could not be trusted, that operations were sometimes done deliberately for gain and not to save life. People read it, were worried and began to look at us sideways as if we were criminals. I can remember how intensely it distressed me, for of course it was based on one or two of the black sheep that every profession has. The trouble was that the public got the feeling we were all alike, tarred with the same brush.

And it was at this time, just after the appearance of 99 *Wimpole Street*, and while the feeling was still strong, that I was asked to write a series of articles on doctors, their work, their ideals, the lives they led, the advances that had been made in treatment. I jumped at it. Here was my chance to show the other side of medicine, the feeling of vocation, the light and shade, the frustrations and the triumphs. I had a 'concern', one of my father's expressions, to explain.

I was groping for a plan, a jumping-off point from which I could begin, when one evening, rather tired after hospital, I got home to find that an old patient had rung up and made an appointment for the following day.

"I'm just back from India," he told the parlour-maid. "It's years since the doctor's seen me, but he'll remember."

This was flattering to my memory and intelligence but not helpful, for his name was a rather common one, and the maid in the absence of the secretary had forgotten to get his initials.

I could have waited until next morning, when the secretary would have found out his initials and put the notes before me. But for some reason, I think just because I was tired, I started to look through the card index myself, ranging back to before the First World War. Five years ago. No, not him! Seven years. No, he was dead! Eight years. India. Yes. That was him. And I did remember.

After dinner that evening I looked at my diary. There was a meeting of the Medical Society of London. The subject? Should I go round? No, I wasn't interested. I thought not. Instead I sank into an arm-chair by the fire in my consulting-room. I looked at my twenty-six bulky folio case-books and picked out my man from his volume. He was a misdiagnosed case of malignant malaria that I had spotted, not through any special cleverness but because I'd seen similar ones with Manson-Bahr in the Palestine campaign.

By this time I had become interested, and I began to turn the pages. Names that I had completely forgotten stared at me, and brought back vivid memories.

A faded letter fell out of one page. I opened it. 'Good Lord, that poor soul.' I replaced it gently, for there is something that makes me feel shy re-reading letters of people I have liked but could not help. A mass of newspaper cuttings cluttered up another set of notes. They contained a story that in instalments had flamed across two continents until the inevitable tragic end. Forgetful of time I kept browsing amongst these records of the past, written in the peculiarly illegible handwriting of the doctor, interspersed with scraps of dog Latin and technical abbreviations.

Memories of past years flooded in on me, and suddenly I had an inspiration: why not use these cases, with names and dates and identifying details discreetly and carefully altered, to show the great progress, the immense changes in treatment, that had taken place in the last twenty-five years?

Many of the records contained stories of human tragedy. Many made me wish I'd known then what I know now, for, if I had, I might have saved more. But in retrospect I felt I could indicate how greatly we had advanced, how the horizon of science had expanded, how diseases thought unconquerable when I was a student had been tamed, rendered innocuous, actually suppressed; and I decided I would write it up. That was how I got my pulpit.

So for week after week I told the story of the triumphs of modern medicine in one of the great Sunday papers read by over a million people.

Of course I had to do it under a pseudonym. Of course I had hundreds and hundreds of letters, pathetic letters, from all over the world, sent on by the paper, asking for help, wanting to come and consult me. And of course I had to send out a typed formula from the newspaper office explaining that for reasons of medical etiquette this was not possible. I had tried to build up the idea of the kindliness and humanity of a doctor, and my refusal to see anyone in consultation often seemed heartless, no doubt, to some of these who did not understand; but to do so would have been flagrant advertisement. Often, however, I was able to help by sending the name of a hospital or a consultant who could give the advice they needed. I sometimes wondered what the consultants thought of the patients who thus came to see them, why they came, and who really sent them, since the patients themselves didn't know. Sometimes I did hear, indirectly.

The pseudonym I chose was 'James Harpole' because we lived in Queen Anne Street half-way between Harley Street and Wimpole Street, so I took half of each. I thought I had invented the name, and was much surprised, later, to learn there was a village of that name in Northamptonshire.

There was much speculation on who James Harpole was, and I was frequently asked if I knew. My poker face inherited from my Ulster ancestry then stood me in good stead, as I solemnly considered the matter. One Sunday morning, crossing the corner of Harley Street, I saw a distinguished colleague carrying under his arm six copies of the paper in which my articles were appearing. When I told my wife she said:

"That is fame indeed," and we both laughed.

I used to feel shy and awkward when I saw this pseudonym splashed in big black letters on hoardings or omnibuses describing me as 'The Famous Harley Street Surgeon'. It was blatant nonsense, of course, but it was part of the technique of journalism, and under the cloak of my *nom de plume* I soon ceased to blush. For I felt I was helping to some extent to lessen the fear the average person had of hospitals by explaining how greatly patients could be helped, and how much could now be done in formerly hopeless illnesses.

The success of the series surprised me. I was urged to re-issue the articles in book form, and Cassell's did so for me under the title of *Leaves from a Surgeon's Case-Book*. The book ran rapidly through seven editions in a year. It was published also in the United States, and then it snowballed. It was translated into Dutch, Danish, Swedish, Norwegian, Finnish, German, Italian, Spanish, and finally Portuguese. I was immensely pleased, immensely gratified, and rather embarrassed by the number of author's copies, because each foreign publisher had to send me by his contract three of the first edition and three of each succeeding edition, so in a little over a year I had many more of these books than I had room for, cluttering my shelves.

A second volume, mainly of short medical stories, came out in the following year. We called it *The White-Coated Army*, meaning the men and women working in hospitals in white coats as surgeons, physicians, pathologists, bacteriologists. It wasn't a good title. The Americans, with their flair for publicity, altered it to *Body Menders* in the New York edition.

When it came out in German, in 1938, I had to sign a declaration that the author was of 'pure European descent'. If the Nazis had known my real name they'd never have believed that it was an old Quaker one. Luckily they didn't ask.

By now I had become a regular contributor, turning out copy week by week in each new series, stopping occasionally for a month or two and starting again. Generally the article would be finished and posted off on Thursday for the next Sunday's issue. One Thursday, however, I had sent in a pleasant little story, about animal instinct as distinguished from reason, saying to myself:

'Well, that's done. I can relax.'

But my peace was shattered the same evening by the editor ringing up my wife, and saying violently:

"Good God! What does James Harpole mean! The world is on the brink of the biggest war in history and your husband sends me in a story about a *budgerigar*. Tell him I must have something topical for Sunday."

This was a blow. It was the week of the Munich crisis, and I sat down and thought hard. What could I do? Suddenly I had an idea. The sulphonamides had just been discovered, and at last we had a series of drugs that could combat pneumonia, puerperal fever, septic infection and other deadly diseases formerly capable of treatment only by careful nursing. I used this new discovery to describe how we saved a small boy from death, and called the story 'At the Eleventh Hour'.

They sent a special messenger for it next morning and it appeared in time on the Sunday. Later it came out in the volume entitled *Behind the Surgeon's Mask*, but I kept the story of the budgerigar and the editor had to have it later. It was too good to waste.

The Munich crisis! Looking back on it now, one wonders. Did Chamberlain do the right thing or was it a fatal blunder? I have heard it argued eloquently both ways. But for a time everyone felt easier. And then slowly the tension began to rise again.

In March, 1939, I went on a cruise amongst the Greek Isles. At Rhodes, which was particularly interesting to me as one of the fastnesses of the Knights of St. John, we were told we could not land before a certain time and we could not bring cine-cameras ashore with us.

This surprised us.

Presently a plane was heard and seen approaching. It hovered overhead, circled and finally landed at the aerodrome behind the town. Then we were allowed ashore.

The island was at that time under the flag of Italy, and the Italians certainly had made an excellent job of it. They had repaired and rebuilt the medieval hospital of the Knights of St. John, and on the edge of the seashore there was a first-class hotel with rows of little circular tables under gaily-coloured umbrellas in front of it on the *plage*.

Only one table was occupied. At it were five men, four of them big burly fellows, the fifth a weedy-looking little man.

Strolling innocently down the *plage* thinking of morning coffee, we were hurriedly shepherded back by the *patron*. That was odd. Professor Starkie of Trinity College, Dublin, one of our party, who spoke Italian fluently, questioned the manager, learnt something and persuaded him to go down and talk to the men. When he returned he said that Professor Starkie and one other who could speak German could go along to the group. Starkie and another passenger then went down. I watched fifty yards away with field-glasses, for I was curious and completely mystified. The four big toughs got up, a Mauser pistol bulging in each trouser pocket. They surrounded the little man, who appeared to be a cripple, dressed in a cheap reach-me-down suit. Starkie talked to him earnestly; he talked back rapidly, and then Starkie and the other passenger came away and rejoined me.

"Who is that little squirt and what is it all about?" I asked, feeling puzzled.

"That," said Starkie, "is Goebbels with his bodyguard. He has just landed. I asked him if there'd be a war. He said: 'No, emphatically no,' repeating Hitler's familiar phrase: 'Germany has no further territorial ambitions.' She wanted, he said, to live at peace with the world, and especially England."

That was March, 1939.

A week later, on our way back to England, we landed at Palermo through a double row of grim black-shirts who scowled at us. This was rather surprising. Our wireless had been temporarily dismantled before we were allowed to land; and we did not know that that morning the Italians had invaded Albania.

When we got home we found that our families and friends had been worried about our safety, and everyone was discussing plans for evacuating the big cities. I caught the prevailing emotion and wrote letters to *The Times* about the defenceless state of our hospitals in case of attack.

CHAPTER XXII

THE WORLD AT WAR AGAIN

WHEN WAR ACTUALLY CAME it was almost a relief. My family and I were at our cottage at Frinton, and we had had an air-raid shelter made in the garden with a broad splash of whitewash leading to it from the hall door as a guide to us in the night. We had been told we would have thirty seconds—no more—to get to the shelter and safety when the siren went.

I remember going up to London on the Monday after war was declared. We all thought the train might be bombed on the way, and felt quite heroic on venturing to town. But the Tube at Liverpool Street was carrying its usual load of clerks and little typists from the suburbs to their daily jobs, and I felt deflated.

When, however, I got to my house in Queen Anne Street I found it deserted except for my secretary—the maids had fled home to Wales. I didn't blame them. Everyone who could had been urged to leave London; and all day long train loads of children were being evacuated. In the next few days London was almost deserted—streets and streets of empty houses. Practice for the time being ceased. Most of the hospitals were evacuated, and those which carried on closed their upper floors and saw out-patients when possible in the basements.

After the first shock was over, little by little, however, people began to trickle back. My wife soon had the house running with a skeleton staff, and patients began to come again.

What followed was the period of the phoney war when nothing much happened. Social life was practically non-existent, but a few highlights stand out.

Once my wife and I went to a lunch of the P.E.N. Club in memory of Karel Capek, the Czech author who wrote *R.U.R.*, the Robot play. We sat between (Lord) Pethick Lawrence and Dr. Eduard Beneš.

Madame Beneš and Jan Masaryk were opposite. H. G. Wells cackled. Desmond McCarthy made a beautiful speech. Beneš, a small square-faced man with a long straight nose and close-set eyes, sat silently for the most part. Madame Beneš, very white and pasty, was in deep black. Jan Masaryk, tall, florid, bland, a *bon viveur*, made an excellent reply. He said that Karel Capek died of a broken heart after 'Munich'. I could well believe it, for he was a gentle, shy man, a confirmed pacifist. I had met him some years before his death when he was being lionised in London. No one could have been more unassuming.

Although we were not being directly attacked, as we had expected, there was the uneasy feeling of a lull before a storm. This increased when we heard that Norway had been surprised by invasion and Denmark occupied. But what really shook us was the news that the Germans had violated the neutrality of Holland.

On the day Holland was invaded, I saw on my way to hospital a large flaming notice on a bus announcing a series of articles by James Harpole on 'Six Women'. My first feeling was that I was glad I'd been wise enough to get them written beforehand. My next was shame that such a trivial thought should obtrude at such a time.

On my way back to Queen Anne Street that evening, however, everything felt queerly calm. No sign of war except that I counted thirty-five captive barrage balloons from the flat roof over my con-sulting-room.

We all thought Holland would put up a stern resistance. The news of its unexpectedly sudden collapse was sobering. The further news on May 14th that the Germans had broken through at Sedan was still more serious.

During the awful time before Dunkirk I suffered from persistent nightmares. I had a nephew in the Leicesters, and in my dreams I saw him surrounded by Germans. I found later he had been a Forward Observation Officer, got cut off from his regiment, and, after wander-ing about for ten days, had eventually found his way to Dunkirk; so there may have been something telepathic in my dreams.

The East Coast by now was becoming more and more unrestful owing to the continuous air-raid warnings. The military authorities, too, were anxious to get rid of everyone not officially engaged on war work, so we decided to shut up our seaside house and rent a week-end cottage about an hour's run from London. After the excitement of the East Coast, the sylvan quiet of the new place was delightful. It was a small, white, very conspicuous cottage on the edge of Upper Tewin Green. I liked it. My wife hated it at sight. She felt it was dangerous —unlucky. She wanted to give it up. But her feelings seemed unreasonable to me. It was in the depths of the country, in peaceful rural surroundings far away from the noise of guns and the sight of barrage balloons. So I took no notice. The chief reminder of the war was the occasional drone of heavy bombers in echelon formation hurrying eastwards from the aerodrome twelve miles away. Our official Air-raid Warden lived just across the village green, but there was no First Aid Post in the village and the nearest siren was six miles away.

The local doctor called on us one week-end. He had been in the R.F.C. in the last war.

"Yes," he said, "it is very peaceful here. The people aren't war-conscious. They don't realise that planes travel so fast that we are only nine minutes from the coast."

The Warden, when asked what he did when there was an air-raid warning, said blandly:

"Oh, we go round blowing whistles, but we don't often get one here."

So each week-end we came down from London, and when we got to Tewin the war seemed more and more remote. Early in July, as I was very overworked, I decided to take a short holiday. The perfect weather still continued, and we arranged to put up a tent under the apple trees in the garden, for my daughter to sleep out. But she never did, for the weather suddenly broke.

On July 10th, 1940, as there was nothing much to sit up for after the nine o'clock news, we went to bed. It was a soaking wet night, pitch dark, with low clouds. I remember saying it was not the night for a raid, and we were unlikely to be disturbed by the blowing of whistles in the village.

At twelve-thirty a.m. a high screaming noise woke us, followed by a terrific explosion. The noise was so unexpected that for a second it paralysed every sense and faculty.

I had been through the last war and my first thought was: 'Good God, they're here!'

My second: 'I know I'm still alive because I heard the noise!'

And then my heart missed a beat. 'My wife and Jill—are they all right?'

I shall never forget the agony of that moment, wondering if they were still alive. It seemed an eternity before I heard my wife's anxious voice.

"Are you all right, Jimmo?"

"I think so," I answered dully.

I suppose I was a bit concussed because I only now realised I was still lying on the bed, blood trickling over my face, with mud and plaster falling on me. I had no desire to move. I heard her voice—it seemed a long way off—saying:

"Come on, we must get out of this!"

I was conscious of her half dragging, half pulling me out of bed—only just in time, for as I got to my feet some slates from the roof fell on to my pillow.

Then a curious thing happened. I was aware of something cold and wet dripping on my head and face. It took me a few seconds to realise it was the rain pouring down on me through a great hole in the roof. I think it was the feel of the cold rain that made me pull myself together.

The room was lit up by the weird glare of a burning haystack across the road, and I could see that the windows had been sucked out, glass and frames complete. The floor resembled a ploughed field, mud mixed up with plaster, broken laths and pieces of metal. The electric wires had fused, and as we groped our way downstairs by the light of a torch, I must have been an odd object with my head and face covered with mud. But to our relief, when my wife had washed away the débris it was found I had only a few superficial scalp wounds. She herself had escaped injury as the roof over her bed didn't fall in until later. My daughter's room was quite undamaged.

The people next door gave us a shakedown in their sitting-room for the rest of the night, and in the morning we were able to see what had happened. Nine bombs and a quantity of flares had been dropped around the village. All fell in open fields and did no harm except the one flare that hit the haystack, and the one bomb that fell in our garden, a few feet from the house on the spot where the apple trees had been—the apple trees under which we had planned to put up our tent. If the bomb had been released a split second sooner or later it would have been a direct hit. As it was, it penetrated deep into the soft earth, and the wet mud from the twenty-foot crater was hurled upwards and came down through the roof bringing everything with it. It was certainly an escape.

Of course I was shaken, but I think I suffered more from the officials and the gloating sightseers who flooded in on us. I was interviewed by the police, the local A.R.P., the county A.R.P., the gas and electricity people, the Water Company, the Insurance and the Military. Cars drew up. Charabancs arrived. Strange people who had no right whatever marched through the broken doors, trooped up the stairs in muddy boots, stared at us, peered all over the place calling out to one another. I was very angry. It was hopeless to get any privacy.

We packed into the car and made for home and London. That was the first and only bomb that fell in the area. It was just too bad that we happened to be there. My wife said:

"What did I tell you!" And she was right.

The only explanation suggested worth anything was that the cottage, as I have said, looked on to a large green and probably, on that wet dark night, the place was taken for Hatfield aerodrome ten or twelve miles away.

After our return to London everything was peaceful. We were amused to find ourselves objects of interest to our friends, for to be bombed at that time was a novelty.

The lovely weather returned, and at week-ends, instead of going away, we used to sun ourselves on the flat roof over my consulting-room. We had air-raid warnings, but no one took much notice. The planes bombed the S.E. Coast but did not attack London. Life wasn't too bad.

Copies of the American edition of my latest book, *Behind the Surgeon's Mask*, came along, beautifully printed on lovely paper, such a contrast to the war-restricted editions we had already become accustomed to here. Reviews were good in the *New York Times* and *Saturday Review*.

Shortly after this, however, air-raid warnings became more frequent, mainly during the night. They were bombing the city, and when the

Howard Coster

The Penguin portrait

The author's father and mother (1930)

planes seemed too close we used to go down to the cellar in our 'siren suits', getting back to our bedrooms usually round about four a.m. Daylight warnings we took no notice of.

It was odd how soon we got accustomed to such a life. We thought only of the day itself. There was nothing we could do to minimise the risk of tomorrow, so we accepted it philosophically. The boasted civilisation and security we once considered our heritage had gone, and we simply watched destruction.

The great Blitzkrieg of September, 1940, was now on. Warnings came continuously, night and day. Then one Saturday there was nothing. A lovely quiet day. We wondered what Hitler was up to. Next day we knew. Sunday night was the great fire raid on the City, specially planned because there would be no fire-watchers during the week-end. We could hear the thud of the dropping bombs and the constant drone of circling planes. I stood on my front-door step, about four a.m. The acrid smell of T.N.T. was all-pervasive. I shall never forget that smell. The sky south-east was like daylight. No wonder the Germans could see their work. It was only by a miracle that St. Paul's Cathedral escaped, for the whole area of Paternoster Row was devastated, and several million books, from the warehouses of the publishers around the cathedral, were reduced to ashes.

After that, day by day the bombing became more and more intense, the constant noise more and more irritating. Raids started punctually at sunset. We spent each evening after dark, and half the night, in the shelter.

The night of September 15th was the climax of the Battle of Britain, although we did not know it. Planes continuously overhead. Bombs all round us. Our house was damaged by blast. We felt we had had enough.

Our problem was: how I could carry on my hospitals and what was left of my practice, and at the same time get my family, my furniture and especially my great collection of old and valuable books into a place of safety?

We found refuge for ourselves, but not for our furniture, with relations at Woburn Sands; and from there each day my wife and I came up by car to our house, taking back clothes and kitchen things. It was the possible loss of my library that worried me most. Furniture

I could replace. Some of my books were irreplaceable. Each day as we motored up to London, there was generally a warning near Mill Hill. We called one particular spot 'Siren Corner'. Each day as we came through Hampstead we noticed more and more newly-bombed houses. When we turned the corner into Queen Anne Street we always held our breath. Was our house still standing? It was. We breathed again.

It was almost impossible to get anyone to move furniture out of London; and when at length a firm at Northampton agreed to take ours, the men would not stay in London after three p.m., because bombing started at sundown; but eventually one afternoon we got everything away. Two days later an oil bomb fell on the house opposite, belonging to Sir Alun Rowlands, Senior Physician to the London Hospital. He lost all his instruments, all his books, all his records, all his collection of china. Only the front shell of his house was left. The mews behind was a shambles, and three people had been killed. While I was looking at the wreck I saw Sir Frederick Still standing on his doorstep. He was an odd, shy little man, but a world-famous children's specialist. He never gave up wearing the morning coat and top hat of Edwardian days. It was characteristic of him. He told me he could get no one to move his furniture, so he thought he'd stay where he was. He was a bachelor.

A week later, a stick of bombs fell twenty yards away in Harley Street, and the house where I had had my former consulting-rooms was razed to the ground, killing the caretaker. We were lucky. Oddly enough somehow I expected to be. I thought the one bomb we had suffered from was probably our quota.

It was about this time that Neville Chamberlain died, two months after an operation for cancer. Very divergent opinions were expressed about his policy. Some said if he had been tough with Hitler the war would never have been started. Others maintained that we were hopelessly defenceless at the time of Munich, and he saved us by obtaining breathing space while we rushed the production of Spitfires. No one really knows, except the ghost of Hitler, which opinion is correct.

By now I had settled into a routine. I went to the British Medical Association and got an official pass which was accepted by the police and allowed me to go anywhere in London or the country. I was thus able to attend my hospital clinics, see patients at the new consulting-rooms I had taken in Wimpole Street, and go to Heinemann's in Great Russell Street or the Press at Kingswood in Surrey without let or hindrance. No matter what obstruction might be in the way, it was an Open Sesame everywhere.

I had been a director of the Heinemann Medical Company now for some years, and this began to take up more and more of my time, especially after the managing director was bombed out of his rooms in the Temple and retired for a time to South Wales. This arrangement went on casually for some months until one day I had a long letter from him saying he would not return to London. I ruminated on this but said nothing to Charles Evans, the chairman of William Heinemann Ltd. He had enough worries of his own. His four elder sons had joined up, although two were in reserved occupations, and two had been growing tobacco in Rhodesia and need not have come home. So I just carried on with my hospitals, my practice and the publishing business, waiting for events to shape out, knowing from past experience things have a way of unravelling if you leave them alone long enough.

Wavell's triumphant campaign against the Italians was much in our thoughts early in 1941. Sir Herbert Eason, the President of the General Medical Council, and I had been comrades on Allenby's staff in the First World War, and the desert names stirred old memories. We noted how Wavell kept using again all the Allenby tricks to deceive the enemy which he had learnt in the First World War. Then it had been cavalry; in this war it was tanks. Tactics altered but strategy remained the same. Eason and I were meeting constantly at this time on the Committee of the Athenæum; and one of our uses was to advise on members of our own profession coming up for membership. That was a pleasurable task. Eason's unpleasant task as President of the General Medical Council was pronouncing judgment in penal cases. He hated it. He said the G.M.C. was falling more and more into the hands of Professors of Anatomy and such-like who knew nothing of the perils of practice and the temptations put in the way of medical men. The Roman Catholic Irish and the Presbyterian Scots always voted against a man accused of adultery, even if he had not treated the woman professionally for years—'once a patient, always a patient' was their standard.

*

Wintry weather slows the metabolism of old people. My mother was eighty-five. She died in the heavy snowy weather of 1941, although she was apparently in good health up to a week before. She was always a lovely woman. In death she looked even more lovely. The dead generally look beautiful, for pain and suffering are smoothed out by the fingers of Azrael.

We travelled in cold, dank, misty weather to Tenterden, in Kent, to bury her alongside my father. A policeman stopped us outside Maidstone, as we were in a defence area. He inspected our Identity Cards and waved us on. The service in the beautiful old church at Tenterden was a peaceful interlude; but I hated the burial in the cemetery with rain pouring over the coffin into the open grave; and determined there and then to be cremated when my time came. On the way home we had four air-raid warnings.

*

CHAPTER XXIII

BROADCASTING AND PUBLISHING

BACK AT WOBURN SANDS I found a letter from the B.B.C. asking me to do three broadcasts on scientific subjects under my pseudonym of James Harpole. Naturally I was thrilled; it was my first broadcasting offer, and I started next day to block out the talks.

In the middle of this I had a letter from Charles Evans of Heinemann's offering me the post of Chairman and Managing Director of the Medical Company—one thing piling on another.

Broadcasting I found is not as simple as it appears. I wrote my first script and read it aloud to my wife for timing. It had to be fifteen minutes long, no more no less. I then submitted it to the B.B.C. for vetting. They made some slight alterations, and supplied me with a definitive script which I had to agree to deliver verbatim, a precaution necessary in war-time so that no one could slip in a concealed message to the enemy in code. Two rehearsals for emphasis followed, and we were ready for my broadcast on March 18th, the day after St. Patrick's.

The B.B.C. in 1941 was like a beleaguered city. Everyone was suspect until identified. I was put into a pen until vouched for by the producer, and taken down to one of the studios in the basement. It was a small room with two temporary war-time bunks as well as the normal table, chairs and microphones. The upper studios had been damaged by a direct hit some time before. I tested the microphone for sound, with the controller watching me through a glass window; and after that the producer, Hilton Brown, and I waited quietly, watching the clock hands move round slowly to one-fifteen p.m. A red light then appeared and I was on. To my surprise I found it quite easy. No strain. No nervousness. It was all so quiet. I imagined I was speaking to three people sitting round a fire, not to fourteen million, and it worked. The one thing I did wrong was saying at the end of the broadcast:

"I'm afraid I went too fast."

I said it before the 'mike' was off, and several people who knew my identity chaffed me about it next day.

After that it was easy. I used to do a broadcast from time to time fairly frequently, but none of them gave me the thrill of that first attempt.

The one thing I never could get to like, however, was my voice played back to me on the record. To me it sounded like a pompous ass talking with a rasping twang. But other people said it was just like me. Lawrence Abel, my colleague, sitting in the surgeons' room at the Princess Beatrice Hospital, tuned in on the radio idly one afternoon, heard someone speak, recognised my voice and said:

"Good Lord, so that's who James Harpole is!"

Another time my wife was listening at Woburn, when our cat pricked up her ears and stalked over to the radio looking for me, and was puzzled not to find me. Of course the scientific fact is that no one ever hears his voice as others hear it. For what one hears oneself is a combination of sounds produced by the larynx, tongue and lips conducted through the mouth, conducted through the bones of the skull, conducted through the eustachian tubes and finally conducted through the external auditory meatus to the internal mechanism of the ear. It's quite a different sound from the sound others hear, not nearly so charming, not nearly so mellow—a horrid debunking sound.

*

I came up to town four days a week. During the week-ends I wrote my articles for the *Sunday Graphic*. One morning at Bletchley station I was told there had been a severe blitz on London in the night, and I was rather surprised the train arrived at Euston on time. But that was the end of normality. I got into a No. 30 bus which should have taken me to the top of Harley Street, but when I found myself outside the British Museum, after many turns around craters, I decided to stop at my office at Heinemann's, which was a hundred yards from the Museum. I learnt then that New Oxford Street, Oxford Street and Piccadilly had had most of the blitz and were impassable. The windows of my consulting-room were shattered and there was glass in the streets everywhere. I walked to the Athenæum down Bond Street. Fortnum & Mason's was a wreck. The Linnæan Society, the Royal Academy and the Royal Society had no windows left. At the Athenæum there was no water upstairs and no gas.

After lunch I went to the Annual Court of Governors of the Lock Hospital. Glass fragments everywhere. Doors jammed. I learnt that Paddington, Waterloo and Victoria stations had all been hit. Euston was the lucky one. I got back to Woburn Sands at seven-thirty very tired and depressed. It was a relief next morning to forget everything by writing a new Harpole story.

One of the penalties of advancing years is that one's friends keep dying on one. Two names caught my eye in *The Times* a few days later: Sir Edward Troup and Sir Frederick Still. Troup was a distant relative of my wife, and we used to meet at family parties from time to time. One of his duties as Permanent Under-Secretary of State in the Home Office was to advise the Home Secretary in office at the time whether or not a criminal condemned to death should be executed. I have seen him at a week-end party at a country house lose all the joy of life when called to the phone to give final advice one way or the other. But from long experience he was able to gauge the public feeling in questions of this sort, and so be of great help to any new and inexperienced Home Secretary. Once, however, he told me he found himself being caught out unexpectedly. He had given, as he thought, some sage advice to (Sir) Winston Churchill when he was Home Secretary. Churchill suddenly turned on him.

"Are you Home Secretary or am I, Troup?"

"You are, sir," said Troup.

"Well, remember it!" retorted Churchill.

I was sorry to see the notice of Sir Frederick Still's death. It seemed only a short time since I had talked to him standing on his doorstep at 28 Queen Anne Street. I took my daughter to see him once when she was a little girl, and ever after we used to nod to each other in the street. He loved children and he had a special little examination couch for them. His consulting-room was hung all round with toys to distract the children while he examined them. He was one of the physicians to the Children's Hospital, Great Ormond Street. 'Still's

Disease', named after him, is a form of rheumatoid arthritis occurring in children aged from three to six, with swollen joints, swollen glands, a raised temperature and muscular wasting. It was practically incurable until the discovery of cortisone. Still was a lonely little man. He was a poet and a bibliophile, shy and rather unapproachable. His death gave me a momentary fit of sadness. Although we hardly ever spoke, I felt I should miss his nod and gentle smile in the street.

Now that, in addition to being a surgeon and an author, I had become a publisher, I began to see things from a somewhat different angle. Previously I had felt only the author's grievances. Now I saw the publisher's problems. Charles Evans of Heinemann's was having difficulty with Francis Brett Young at this time. Francis was a friend of us both, but he tended to overwrite. Heinemann's had had a success with his *Portrait of Clare*, a huge novel of 880 pages, in 1927, and Francis was always trying to repeat this success. Evans had published a series of his short stories, *Cotswold Honey*, in 1940; and looking upon this as a mere bagatelle, he was now in the throes of an immense novel about a cathedral which would run to 300,000 words. This, with the shortage and rationing of paper caused by the war, and a first printing calling for at least 40,000 copies, which was the number required for any new Brett Young novel, would mean trouble. So we talked to him, and eventually with the greatest difficulty persuaded him to bring it down to 90,000 words.

Authors, I had now discovered, were a constant headache to their publishers, though luckily neither can get on without the other. One of the greatest obstacles to friendship is the 'sin of after-inspiration', that is, rewriting large chunks of a book when it is in page proof. I was feeling very sore myself at the moment over this. Since I had taken on the managing directorship of the Heinemann Medical Company, one author had run up a bill for corrections of over £600, making his work so expensive that there was a risk it might price itself out of the market. Luckily all authors are not so difficult.

It was while this was bothering me that I ran into my old friend the late Air Vice-Marshal Sir David Munro one day at the Club, and got from him a slant on the way another publisher handled his authors. He had recently given me a presentation copy of his autobiography, *It Passed Too Quickly*; and when I thanked him for the flattering references he had made to me in it, he told me he was sorry he had not been able to say more about our time together in Palestine. What happened, he said, was that he wrote it off quickly, gave it to Bashford's son-in-law to read, and thought it would be returned for revision. He then found it had been set up in page, and when he tried to revise it the publishers, as he put it, "screamed with agony" and said it would cost him £90.

I had to laugh. Actually I think he would have spoiled it by revision. It read so spontaneously as it was.

Authors of course are naturally a touchy lot. If they were not they wouldn't be authors. S. C. Roberts, the Master of Pembroke, once told me a story of J. M. Barrie and A. E. Housman which illustrates this.

Barrie had been stopping with Housman at Cambridge for a few days. But the two men had nothing really in common. Both were unhappy; so, when Barrie wrote his 'bread and butter' letter of thanks, he said he was afraid his visit had "not been a success". To this Housman replied:

DEAR SIR JAMES,
    You are quite right. It was not a success, but that is no reason for spelling my name wrong.

Having known Barrie slightly, and loved all his works intensely, I'm sure the fault was Housman's.

It is generally a good rule, if you like an author's work, not to make his acquaintance. If you do you will probably be disappointed. Once in my younger days, at a Saturday night dinner of the Savage Club, I sat opposite Phillips Oppenheim, whom I used to read with much pleasure. I had innocently pictured him as a romantic, dashing figure. He turned out to be a large, blue-faced, bottle-nosed man suffering from chronic bronchitis, which compelled him to live in the South of France and explained why the Côte d'Azur was the scene of all his later novels.

At the time I felt quite disillusioned. It was foolish, of course, for one should judge an author by his books, not by his appearance or conversation. An author puts his best into his books, not into his conversation. He is seldom a brilliant talker—that is characteristic of the actor, the politician, or the professional raconteur. If you admire an author's work, therefore, it is usually a mistake to meet him socially, unless you are also an author. Then you probably would discuss royalties, not literature, with him. The author seldom has the physical advantages of the actor. His heroes are pipe dreams of what he'd like to have been, but is not.

I had been reading the work of an American writer published by Heinemann's and I said to Charles Evans:

"Charlie, I've never seen this author of yours, but I've a picture of him in my mind. He's a fat, squat man, short-sighted, with big thick glasses. Am I right?"

Evans looked at me. "That's exactly what he is like. But how did you know?"

"Well. It's easy. His heroes are big lean men with fierce flashing blue eyes and aquiline features—the type he most admires."

Similarly with women novelists, their heroines are what they've longed to be. One dumpy little woman I knew and liked couldn't, although a determined virgin, resist writing a love scene every now and then in which one of her characters was seduced on a sofa. I used to watch for this in each new novel as it appeared, and I was seldom disappointed.

*

It is astonishing how people, quite intelligent people, get wrong ideas over things and irritate the other people who really know. I was sitting opposite Lord Woolton at lunch one day. He was Food Minister at the time, and he said he managed to keep the public content by making them think they were leading and he was following their lead. Sometimes, however, he said his advisers were in front of public opinion. There was considerable objection raised, for instance, to adding calcium to bread; and that morning he had had six letters from people saying they could not eat the new bread; and their doctors said this was due to the calcium in it giving them indigestion.

"I can't think how their doctors can have got caught out," he remarked with a twinkle in his eye, "for we haven't put any calcium in yet."

The war, which brought so many restrictions, including shortage of paper, unexpectedly enough benefited publishers of novels enormously. This was something no one had anticipated. But the black-out and the difficulty of getting around kept people at home and encouraged reading. Novels that had been on the shelves, forgotten for years, sold. Publishers found that stock they had written off as unsaleable was again in demand. New books published sold out completely. There was no risk of over-production, no remaindered stock. Everything readable sold.

So although paper was rationed to 37½ per cent of the amount used in 1939, publishers had bumper years—even medical publishers. The one seeming disaster was the bombing of Paternoster Row, when over three million books were destroyed. But even that proved a benefit to some publishers, for, in certain instances, the insurance covered and paid for a lot of otherwise almost unsaleable stock.

Naturally I was happy. I could not have had a more propitious period in which to find my feet as a publisher. And as an author I was equally lucky. The subjects I was interested in were interesting also to the public. I was writing James Harpole articles weekly for the *Sunday Graphic* in company with Paul Gallico and Group Captain Cheshire, V.C.; and I was also broadcasting fairly frequently.

Sometimes it was a short story, and it may be of interest to learn how a short story was broadcast in those days. On one occasion when I was due on the air at ten-fifteen p.m., the producer and I dined pleasantly at the East India Club at seven p.m. The food was good; the burgundy was good; and we left at nine-twenty. I went round to my consulting-room and collected my daughter, who was invited to sit in the 'Dressing Room' at Broadcasting House to hear me. When we arrived we learnt that the programme before us was running slow, and we might have to cut twenty to thirty seconds off our script. That didn't worry me as I knew I could do it in fourteen minutes. Alvar Lidell announced me as soon as the light went red, and I told the story, glancing at the clock at intervals. Twelve—thirteen—fourteen minutes. I finished with twenty seconds to spare, and my daughter, listening upstairs, said it came through with no suspicion of hurry.

Sometimes it was a popular scientific talk; sometimes a feature programme; sometimes a bit of propaganda. I remember two or three scripts in particular, because of the associations.

The first was one I had been asked to write for a broadcast on Sir Ronald Ross, Sir Patrick Manson and malaria, for the European and Empire Service. It was to contain dialogue between these two great men. I had met Sir Patrick Manson and I knew Sir Ronald Ross well from seeing him frequently and hearing him talk. Ross was the son of a Major-General in the Indian Army and had, I think, possibly some Indian blood in him. He was also a diabetic, very bad-tempered, and with a grievance against the world. In addition he was a poet and a dreamer. I was fascinated by him and his contradictions. I admired him very much, and tried to bring all this into the script. It was revised by the B.B.C., some propaganda stuff added to it, produced outside London, and I heard no more of it.

When, however, the recording of it was played back to me I found to my dismay they had given Ross, as well as Manson, a Scottish accent. Ross had a most violent Oxford accent, and I was glad none of my club acquaintances knew I had written the script.

The wonder drug penicillin was just beginning to be talked about by everyone at this time, so one day, in October, 1942, I was not surprised to find a message from Robert Barr of the B.B.C. asking me to do the script for a broadcast on it in a feature called 'Marching On', which came immediately before the nine o'clock news. To make sure I would make no mistakes I went to see (Sir) Alexander Fleming at St. Mary's Hospital, and he showed me the original petri dish on which the fungus 'Pencillium notatum' grew as a contaminant blown through the window. I borrowed his paper describing the incident, took it away, wrote my script, brought it to St. Mary's, and read it out to Fleming to see there was nothing he could object to. It was lucky I did, for quite a lot of people telephoned the B.B.C. after it came through and said I'd got it all wrong. To the flurried officials who rang me about this I said:

"Fleming passed it. Tell them to go to hell." And I meant it.

The third was a script I wrote for Walter Rilla. It was the first of a projected series, 'It Might Happen Here'. The story was a fictitous account of a German landing in the Bristol Channel; and it told how a doctor tried to hide the radium in a West Country hospital from the invaders. I hated doing it, but it was for propaganda purposes. It was written in one of our darkest hours just before Alamein; and was intended to make the public conscious of how grave our position was. But on November 8th, the day before it was due to be broadcast, the secret landing of British and American troops in North Africa took place, and the victory at Alamein was announced. Next morning I heard from Rilla that, on account of the wonderful news from Egypt, Cyrenaica and Algeria, the B.B.C. had decided there was now no point in the broadcast, and the whole series 'It Might Happen Here' had been cancelled. I was overjoyed at the reason, though bang went twenty-five guineas. Or so I thought, though I never was so glad to lose a fee before. But not a bit of it. The B.B.C. paid for it all the same.

*

Life for me was good at the time, except for one worry. Some members of the Library Committee of the Athenæum were very anxious to evacuate all our more valuable books out of London. But the chairman of the Committee, Sir Stephen Gaselee, and some others were stubbornly opposed to anything of the sort. Gaselee dug his toes in, and every time we managed to get a few hundred extra-precious ones sent out of London he was upset. It was not until the Carlton Club was gutted and the Royal College of Physicians damaged that the opposition broke. We got twenty thousand of our more important books away. It was only about one-sixth of the library but it was something. Actually we never were damaged, though six fire bombs fell on the roof of the Club at one time or another; and if it had not been for the devotion of the Secretary, Mr. N. R. Udal, who slept every night on the premises, we would have shared the fate of the Carlton.

But the damage done to our neighbour, the Royal College of Physicians, who had to evacuate their precious library to the cellars of the Royal Society of Medicine in Wimpole Street, made us feel we were justified. This was somewhat of a consolation when we found, after the war, that a lot of the Athenæum books sent out of London had been stored in damp cellars and were the worse for it.

Shortly after the evacuation from the library, Stephen Gaselee died, and then I think we realised what a loss we had sustained. He was the Librarian and Keeper of the Papers of the Foreign Office, a man of immense erudition and a most colourful personality. I didn't know him until he succeeded Sir Denison Ross, the Oriental scholar, as chairman of the Library Committee. But I had dipped into his *Oxford Book of Medieval Verse*. I had read his edition of Monardes's *Joyfull Newes out of the Newe Founde Worlde*, and I had often seen him coming in and out of the Club.

You couldn't miss him. He always dressed in a long grey tail-coat with a high Gladstone collar below a turkey-red face. Generally he wore an Old Etonian bow tie of a flamboyant size over a violently coloured waistcoat. His sponge-bag trousers ended about three inches above his shoes, exposing a pair of scarlet socks partially covered by check spats. Wherever he went he wore a top hat tilted forward. As I have said, you couldn't miss him. There was something of the eighteenth century about him. His knowledge of the classics, medieval literature, and most of the European languages was quite unique. If you wanted a reference to some recondite subject you asked Gaselee— that is, unless it referred to modern science or mathematics. There he was profoundly and joyfully ignorant. His knowledge of wines, his fund of Rabelaisian stories and his powers as an after-dinner speaker were all constantly being drawn upon for our pleasure. No wonder we missed him.

Sir Denison Ross, his predecessor in the Chair, was a much less complex person. His autobiography, *Both Ends of the Candle*, expressed his philosophy of life. He too was a scholar and a *bon viveur*; but he had the puritan conscience of the Scot; and, against my advice on medical grounds, he would go out to Istanbul at the beginning of the war. He liked the Turks. The Turks liked him. He wanted to be where he would be of most use. I knew he would die if he went; and, I think, so did he.

Meanwhile the war went on, but now we felt that we were winning. We never knew until afterwards how near we were to losing.

One unexpected trouble occurred in the autumn of 1942. Charles Evans, the Chairman of William Heinemann Ltd., had his first illness. I took him to see (Sir) Gordon Holmes. It was an unfortunate time to be ill, as A. S. Frere, his co-managing director, was publicity officer to Ernest Bevin and not available, Peter Davies was in the Services and so was Dwye Evans, Charles's eldest son. But Charles improved presently, and things went on much as before.

Early in 1943, we survivors of Allenby's staff in the Palestine

Campaign were feeling angry at the way Sir Archibald Wavell had been treated in recent months. There weren't many of us left. We had started a little dining club after the First World War, the E.E.F. Club, which met yearly; and at our dinner in 1938 I had become so senior I was sitting next to Wavell, his blind eye, which he covered with a glass, on my side. He talked very little. He was a silent man, but one never felt awkward in his company. The Club did not meet during the war, and I had not seen him since 1938; but his reputation in the interval in the Western Desert had become legendary, and we felt very much that he had been blamed unjustly for reverses after the War Office took so many of his seasoned troops to fight a forlorn campaign in Greece.

One Thursday I was passing through the hall of the Athenæum on my way out when I heard the Secretary say:

"Will you sign your autograph here, sir?"

I looked round and was surprised to see Wavell in Field-Marshal's uniform. No one seemed to know he was in England, and I wondered why.

Next day it was announced on the wireless that he was to be the new Viceroy of India in succession to Linlithgow, and the secret was out. Everyone thought it an astonishingly good selection. It was the *amende honorable*, and wiped out the slur on his military career. We gave him a little dinner to celebrate.

Wavell had a quiet charm which grew on one. He was that *rara avis*, a scholar, a poet and a good soldier. It is a combination that probably only Winchester can produce. For some years after 1920 I had played with the idea of writing a history of Allenby's campaign, and had collected all the official despatches and some score of books written round and about it, but never got down really to tackling the problem. I was afraid no one else would do it, and felt guilty. But when I read Wavell's book, *The Palestine Campaigns*, I saw my fears were quite unnecessary. He had written a classic, with which I could never have competed. His anthology of verse, *Other Men's Flowers*, is characteristic of his outlook on life. Years later, when I went to his state funeral in Westminster Abbey, I felt we had lost something almost forgotten since the time of Sir Philip Sidney.

On June 28th, 1943, I was distressed to hear of the passing of my old friend Arthur Waugh. That closed a friendship of over thirty years from the time when I first went up to the Board Room of Chapman & Hall at 11 Henrietta Street, Covent Garden, and there met the short, fat, wheezy man with the big head and pleasant smile whom I shall never forget. I was shy and nervous, for I was seeing him about my first book in response to the letter saying he had accepted it. I liked him at once and I never altered my mind. Not many people remember Arthur Waugh now, though in his time he was recognised as a distinguished critic and biographer; but his two sons, Alec and Evelyn, have made the name famous.

*

I suppose the return in force to Europe, when our troops invaded Sicily in July, 1943, may be considered the first clear evidence we were getting the better of the war. It was lovely weather and my wife and I, during the week-ends, used to lie out in the heather above Woburn Sands and watch the planes flying overhead with the comfortable feeling that they were ours. At night, as we heard the sound of the bombers on their way to Germany, we felt this even more. I can still remember a poem of Noël Coward's that exactly expressed it:

> Lie in the dark and listen,
> City magnates and steel contractors,
> Factory workers and politicians,
> Soft hysterical little actors,
> Ballet dancers, reserved musicians,
> Safe in your warm civilian beds,
> Life is passing above your heads,
> Lie in the dark and listen.

With vivid memories still of the enemy bombers coming over and circling round night after night, dropping bombs on us with apparent immunity, this was indeed a very comfortable feeling.

But one cannot expect unalloyed content or happiness in this life. Two events that month cast a sadness. One was the death of my last surviving brother from coronary thrombosis. It was the end of a long painful struggle. Outside people said it was a blessed relief, but, none the less, to those of the family who were left it was very saddening.

He was my younger brother. I remembered the day he was born. I remembered our nurse taking me out into the garden and showing me the gooseberry bush where, she said, the doctor had found him and brought him into the house. I remembered the many happy days we had had together as boys, long interminably sunny days, and the companionship of later years. All over, all finished.

The second event occurring on the same day was a formal notice that my term of service at the Princess Beatrice Hospital had expired; and the Board had courteously elected me Consulting Surgeon in recognition of my thirty-two years' service to the charity. This reminded me of Sir Walter Langdon-Brown's remark when he was made Consulting Physician to St. Bartholomew's Hospital:

"A Consulting Physician, Abraham, is a post of great distinction but no importance."

Coming on the day of my brother's death it made me feel very old and tired, suddenly.

The business of my pseudonym was giving me considerable trouble also at that time, and I had some difficulty in explaining to Fleet Street what I could do, and what I could not do, without appearing to advertise—the one great sin in medical circles. The *Daily Sketch* was sponsoring an 'Into Battle' exhibition at the time, and they could not see why I should not make a speaking appearance at it. I had to refuse of course, but to help them out I got the names of three doctors not in practice from Dr. Morland, the editor of the *Lancet*, any one of whom would be suitable. I learnt, however, later that they had themselves secured 'Anthony Weymouth' (Dr. Geikie Cobb). This, of course, was an entirely suitable choice as he had retired from practice and so could not be accused of advertising.

Air activity was very intense that summer. Our bombers were going over night and day. We had just captured Messina, the whole of Sicily was in our hands, and we were preparing to invade Italy. In consequence, the Germans were retaliating, and we were getting constant siren warnings. One old lady in a night shelter in London became very irritated by this. She said to the Air-raid Warden, Miss Hannay (George Birmingham's daughter), with much indignation:

"I wish that there Hitler would marry and settle down."

September 3rd, 1943, was the fourth anniversary of the war, and at seven a.m. that morning we heard that British and Canadian troops had landed on the tip of Italy from Messina. W. W. Jacobs, we also heard, had died two days before. I suppose that his name means little today, for the public's memory is very short. But Jacobs was one of the most popular humorists of Edwardian days, and a new Jacobs story in the *Strand Magazine* was almost as much anticipated as a new Sherlock Holmes.

He wrote about the Thames bargees, and his stories were illustrated by Will Owen. The combination was felicitous, and collections of short stories like *Many Cargoes*, *The Skipper's Wooing*, appeared annually for twenty years, to the great delight of a public always hungry for a laugh. I remember him well at the Savage Club, where he used to meet his friend Arthur Morrison. What the affinity between them was is difficult to understand. Morrison was a heavy, squat, paunchy man with a beard; and his stories were always tragic. Jacobs was a quiet, shy, thin, clean-shaven little man, very modest, very retiring. I remember once at a Savage Saturday night dinner we had several American humorists as guests, and a great fat fellow, Irwin Cobb, wearing enormous riding breeches, made what seemed a very fulsome speech about him. I'm sure this was quite genuinely meant, but it proved most embarrassing to Jacobs. For as it went on he grew redder and redder, more and more shy. He shrank into himself, and nothing would induce him to say a single word in response.

All his stories were amusing except one: 'The Monkey's Paw'. It was a horror. It brought cold shivers down every reader's spine. I never could quite understand how or why he came to write it. There must have been a side of him seldom otherwise seen. Perhaps that is where his friendship with Arthur Morrison came in, for Morrison wrote *Tales of Mean Streets*, sordid grim stories of the underworld, completely different from the jolly atmosphere of Jacobs's comic longshoremen. Everyone loved 'W. W.' It is a pleasure to me to remember that Helen Jacobs, his artist daughter, drew the picture of a Chinawoman coming aboard ship at Singapore which graced the dust cover of so many editions of my *Surgeon's Log* for over twenty years.

*

My wife and I were at Buxton, combining a holiday with treatment, during the period when our men were fighting hard to hold the bridge-head at Salerno. This was a name which to doctors had always previously been associated with the celebrated medical school that existed there in the twelfth century. We also linked it up with the 'Regimen Sanitatis Salernitanum', the poem specially written for the guidance of Robert, Duke of Normandy, the son of William the Conqueror, returning wounded from the Holy Land. In it occur the famous lines:

> If you would your health preserve,
> Use three physicians still,
> First Doctor Quiet,
> Next Dr. Merriman,
> And finally Doctor Diet.

These have today a strangely up-to-date modern note.

And it was while we were at Buxton that the following announcement in *The Times* caught my eye:

STIFF. On Sept. 16th, 1943, Harold Henry Stiff, M.B. Cantab, aged 70.

That brought me sharply back to 1901 when I first came to London; and my immediate reaction was a deep regret that I had never made contact with Harold Stiff after that date. Now it was too late. I knew he had practised in Bury St. Edmunds. I had been through it several times by car, and I could quite easily have called to see him. But I thought he probably would not have remembered me, and certainly would not have known what a momentous effect that quarter of an hour's talk with him had had on my life. For if Harold Stiff had not quarrelled with his chief and handed over his house-surgeoncy to me, I should have gone out to the South African War; I should almost certainly have been put in charge of a concentration camp for Boer women and children; and I should probably have died of typhoid, the disease I dreaded most of all in the world at that time. Or I might have survived the war, taken a commission in the R.A.M.C. and spent half my life in India, or settled in South Africa, or the U.S.A., and led a totally different life. Of one thing I am sure: I'd never have gone to Harley Street. All of which makes one realise on what seemingly inconsequential things the whole of one's life may turn. It is a terrifying thought.

When I got back to London I learnt that I was now Senior Surgeon to the London Lock Hospital owing to the death of Mr. Charles Gibbs, Consulting Surgeon to Charing Cross Hospital. Another landmark gone. We had been associated for thirty-six years. He was the most punctual man I ever had to deal with. When I was his house-surgeon, he used to arrive on his visiting day at one-fifty-five p.m. exactly. We started his round at two p.m. and he left punctually at three. I never knew him to be late, and I never knew him to stay for more than an hour. Such punctuality is an uncanny virtue, but I think it belongs to a stereotyped mind. Minds of that type seldom discover anything.

Every now and then, particularly when I was broadcasting, I used to stay in London for the night, and generally the Germans picked such occasions for an air-raid—or so it seemed to me, listening ruefully in bed in the Welbeck Hotel. One dreaded meeting friends at this time or asking about sons, so many splendid boys were being killed. We were winning the war but felt distressed that it was hanging on so long. All sorts of things, trivial things, annoyed. You couldn't get this. There was a shortage of that. Something else was on a quota. If you had to wear glasses or false teeth, you were very careful to keep them at your bedside in case of a raid, for if they were lost it was months before they could be replaced. I remember Sir William Malkin, the Legal Adviser to the Foreign Office, being so pleased he had got a new pair of glasses that he had to stop me in the street to show them to me. He didn't enjoy them for long, however, for a month later, on his way back from a conference in Washington, his plane was lost at sea.

One of the penalties of belonging to a long-lived family is that, as I have said before, you outlive so many of your friends. A few weeks after the announcement of Charles Gibbs's death, I was walking down Wimpole Street, when I was stopped by a colleague and told that John Swift Joly, a distinguished surgeon at St. Peter's Hospital, was dying. This was a shock to me as Joly was one of my oldest friends. I had been best man at his wedding, and I didn't even know he was ill. The war somehow made friendship difficult.

When I went to see him he was lying unconscious, with a ten days' beard, obviously dying. I sat with him for an hour until relieved by another of his friends. Two hours later I heard he had died. Thus ended a friendship of forty-nine years, dating from our undergraduate days. I came to London first, he followed me. I got him his first house-surgeoncy and introduced him to his future wife. He owed a lot to her. It was she who made him a successful surgeon.

I was writing his obituary notice for the *Lancet* when I got an urgent telephone call from the editor of the *Sunday Graphic* saying Mr. Churchill had pneumonia, and would James Harpole please write fifteen hundred words forthwith on the condition, the prognosis and the treatment, to appear on the page opposite the editorial on Sunday December 19th, 1943. A messenger, he said, would come down from London to Bletchley station and collect it at ten a.m. the following morning. So I wrote both the obituary and the article on the same day. That was the first time the sulphonamide 'M & B 693', which saved the Prime Minister's life, became so widely known to the public.

CHAPTER XXIV

*

THE HIGH DRAMA OF 1944–45

THE BEGINNING OF A NEW YEAR is, of course, only an arbitrary point in time, but somehow it doesn't seem so. We are apt to stop, feel the date is important, think, recapitulate and make portentous resolutions. And so, on January 1st, 1944, with the sun shining and the war news cheerful, I felt we were entering on a new era of hope.

I went down the village street shopping for my wife with a satchel ready to carry back things, for tradesmen were not allowed to deliver goods within two miles owing to the shortage of petrol. I tried to get chocolates on my coupons. No chocolates. I tried to get biscuits at the grocer's. No biscuits. I was allowed one box of matches as a favour. I took my daughter's shoes to the cobbler, who was so overwhelmed with work he shut up shop every few days to get time to catch up with arrears. He told me there was such a shortage of cobblers that the Government had to demob men from the Army to serve the public, and that they had had to do the same with miners and chimney sweeps. Nothing, however, could depress me that morning. It was the First of January, 1944, and the war was coming to an end—or at least so we all thought.

My daughter was working at the Foreign Office at Bletchley Park, and to celebrate the New Year the staff put on a revue. We got home at ten-forty-five p.m., pleasantly tired; and then the penalty of being a doctor (or is it the privilege?) overtook me. I was called out by the local G.P. to see someone in great pain, got back home through the darkness of the blackout at twelve o'clock, listened to the midnight broadcast, and so to bed. A satisfactory day.

Signing 1944 on my cheques kept reminding me I was due this year to give the Vicary Lecture, founded in honour of Thomas Vicary, Sergeant-Surgeon to Henry VIII and the first Master of the Barber-

Surgeons of London. This Company was founded in 1540, and its members met and carried on in a somewhat uneasy partnership for over two hundred years. Then in 1744 they parted, and the Barbers and the Surgeons each went their own way.

Nineteen-forty-four was the bicentenary of the parting, and naturally I wanted to deliver something worthy of the occasion. The lecture was endowed by the present Barbers' Company, who, magnanimously forgetting their old quarrel with the Surgeons, had arranged that it should be given alternately in the Barbers' Hall in the City and at the Royal College of Surgeons in Lincoln's Inn Fields. Hitler had disturbed this arrangement by blitzing the Hall of the Barbers, and so it was now given only at the College of Surgeons.

Preparing for the lecture meant delving into records at the Royal Society of Medicine and the Wellcome Historical Library; and, in the intervals of hospital work, Heinemann's and Wimpole Street, I busied myself in one or other of these happy hunting grounds whenever I could until it was time to catch my train at Euston.

One tried to avoid thinking of the war, but it was not possible with thousand-bomber raids on Berlin by night and hundreds of giant four-engined bombers flying south-east in broad daylight as we approached London in the morning.

On one such day I saw in my morning paper that Lord Rutherford had died. This was an almost personal loss, for Rutherford was one of the most lovable of men. With his big body, red face and hearty manner, he would have been taken anywhere for a successful farmer. A man of intense kindliness, it is odd to think that if it had not been for his researches at Cambridge the atom bomb might never have been designed. I am told he was conscious of this responsibility, and definitely troubled in his mind before he died about the advisability of putting such power into men's hands.

I met one of his most intimate friends that day at lunch. We talked about him.

"D'ye know, he shouldn't have died," he said sadly.

"Why?" I asked in surprise.

"Well, a few months ago he got a stiff knee, for which he went to a masseur. The masseur did him good, and later when he got a pain in the groin he went to him again. But now unfortunately it was a strangulated hernia and, when he was operated on, it was too late."

My wife and I at this time were beginning to think of returning to London, so we started house-hunting, with a bias for Hampstead. But just to discourage us there were two heavy raids the week we began to look. The windows of the coffee-room at the Athenæum were damaged by blast; and I found the shutters were up, heavy red curtains drawn and all the lights on at lunch-time. My hospital in Dean Street, Soho, also had been hit, and the back part gutted by fire. We were able, however, to carry on in spite of everything, taking our clinics in the basement.

*

The day on which I was to deliver the Vicary Lecture at the Royal College of Surgeons arrived in April. It was just a year since Sir Alfred, now Lord, Webb-Johnson had asked me to do it, and, conscious of the great honour, I had spent much time preparing the text. The President gave a sherry party beforehand to which he asked a number of distin-guished people. I remember meeting for the first time Sir Alfred Munnings, the new President of the Royal Academy, small, dark with deep-set eyes, a glazed skin, looking like a jockey. Most of his con-versation consisted in running down Gauguin and the other fellows who couldn't paint. My heart warmed to him at once. Another guest was Commander Anthony Kimmins, very tall, very blue-eyed, in Fleet Air Arm uniform. He was much before the public at that time as a broadcaster on the Navy in action; and I remember telling him he was the fastest speaker on record at the B.B.C. There must also have been a lot more people there, but my mind was too occupied to register them.

The lecture was timed for four p.m., so at three-fifteen I went round to the lecture-room to see that everything was in order. I had collected some thirty slides from old prints, drawings and pictures, dating back to A.D. 1500, to illustrate my subject. Judge then of my horror when the attendant told me the lantern, which had been working perfectly, had suddenly failed. This was catastrophic, for I had modelled my lecture entirely round my pictures. At three-thirty people began to arrive and I began to feel very sick. But at three-forty-five the lantern suddenly lit up again, and with a sigh of relief I went back to the President's room to put on my Fellow's gown.

Lectures at the College are conducted with considerable ceremony. Punctual to the minute, the beadle, carrying the great silver mace, advances up the hall, followed by the President and the Council in their robes. Everyone in the audience stands up. The beadle steps on to the rostrum and places the mace on a velvet cushion in front of the President, now seated in his chair. The members of the Council file into the two front rows of chairs, facing him.

Last of all the lecturer appears at the end of the procession, steps on to the rostrum and walks behind the President's chair to the reading desk. The President then stands up, and he and the lecturer bow gravely to each other in silence. The audience then sits down. There is no introductory remark. Nothing. The lecturer starts straight away. When he has finished, the President shakes hands with him solemnly; and now he goes out in the procession immediately after the President, and the whole affair for which he has been preparing probably for months is over.

I, of course, had seen the ritual several times, and the only difference in my case was that the Master and Wardens of the Barbers' Company were also present, as it was their foundation lecture. Sir Stanley Wood-wark happened to be the Master that year; and this was pleasant as we were old friends.

The Vicary Lecture is always on some historical medical subject, and it is the one lecture in the year to which ladies are invited.

Sir John Bland-Sutton, a former President, once said that no lecture should ever last more than an hour. Interest flags if this is exceeded.

"If I'm lecturing, say at four p.m.," he said, "I put my watch to four-fifteen, and I talk until it reads five, so I make myself do it in forty-five minutes. That's the secret of success."

Bland-Sutton was one of our most distinguished orators. It was a wise dictum. I remembered and acted on it.

Apparently the lecture was a success, for in the following week I was approached to deliver the Annual Oration of the Medical Society of London for 1946. This Oration has been given every year since 1774, with only three interruptions. Once in the eighteenth century the orator had an attack of asthma and could not give it; and again in 1915, during the First World War, Sir William Osler, the Regius Professor of Medicine at Oxford, and a figure famous throughout the medical world, was unable through illness to address the Society. Mine, therefore, was to be the 170th Oration, given before the oldest medical society in England. Naturally I was flattered.

All this time the war was still dragging on as a permanent background to our lives; but we were now sure we were winning; and we put up with such discomforts as constant air-raid warnings and shortage of all sorts of things with patient meekness.

One day I went specially to lunch at the Garrick Club with Sir Alfred Webb-Johnson to meet Sir Newman Flower, the Chairman of Cassell's, who had published three of my Harpole books, but whom up to then I had never met. I think he had been attracted to the books because he had been the friend and publisher of Sir Frederick Treves, and he liked medical authors. At lunch he produced a gold visiting-card case which Treves had given him. It had Treves's signature on it; and embedded in the case was the first bullet he had extracted in the South African War. Webb-Johnson, with a twinkle, suggested Sir Newman should give it to the College of Surgeons Museum; but the suggestion produced no result.

After lunch Sir Alfred Munnings joined us. He said he had just been to Buckingham Palace to have his badge of office, as President of the Academy, conferred on him by the King. Sir Walter Lamb, the Secretary of the Academy, went in before him, carrying the badge. It is not worn round the neck, like the ordinary badge of many institutions, but fastened to the lapel.

The King, Munnings said, was in naval uniform, and while he was there he noticed that Millais' picture of 'The Eve of St. Agnes' was in the room. He told the King it was hung too high. This was just like Munnings. He cannot bear to see pictures wrongly placed. He feels for them as one feels for dumb animals when they are being ill-treated.

The same afternoon I had to go back to my office to deal with the recurring difficulties of the shortage of paper for medical books. When war broke out, as I have said, we were all rationed on the tonnage of paper we had used in 1939. This was most unfortunate for our medical company because we had published very few books that year, and our quota, therefore, was quite inadequate for the works we were trying to keep in print. We sold practically every book we issued. That, in peace-time, would have been a great source of satisfaction; but now, knowing we could have sold twice as many if we had had the paper, our satisfaction was tempered with regret. Of course we resorted to the plan everyone else adopted: we used paper of less than half the thickness of pre-war standard whenever we could, for it was not the number of quires of paper that counted but the weight of paper used. That is why war-time books were so thin in bulk compared with pre-war ones. Unfortunately, however, medical books require lots of good illustrations, and good illustrations require good paper, so we were not able to economise on paper to anything like the same extent as the general publisher. Production, therefore, in spite of our sales, was a constant worry.

To meet special cases the Government, in addition to the authorised quota, had a certain amount of extra paper in what was called 'The Moberly Pool', out of which they could allocate supplies to meet special needs. And of course every publisher thought he had 'special needs'.

Ours were for text-books on subjects like bacteriology, war surgery, blood transfusion and things like that. And luckily we had friends at court who really appreciated this. We got nearly all we wanted. No one ever gets all he wants.

*

On June 5th, 1944, we heard that the Germans had evacuated Rome without a fight. This was a relief, as no one but a barbarian would have dared to bombard The Eternal City. My wife and I were stopping at the Welbeck Hotel that night, and on the morning of June 6th we were passing through the hall when we heard a wireless announcement interrupting the programme, blaring suddenly, unexpectedly.

Something exciting was happening.

We stopped.

We could hardly believe our ears. British and American troops had landed between Le Havre and Cherbourg. It was the 'Second Front', the long-expected invasion of Europe.

There was a queer thrilling feeling in London that day. Everyone was holding himself erect. But it was all very quiet. At the Club you wouldn't have guessed anything unusual was happening. It was all so British, this quietude. But there was a brightness in the eye, a spring in the step of everyone. A wonderful thing had happened, a wonderful adventure begun. We were back on the Continent again.

It was ten days later that London once more became a danger centre. We had been hearing vaguely for some months about a dreadful 'secret weapon' that Hitler boasted he would use against us. Sites for this mysterious weapon had been spotted by our planes months previously in and around the Calais area; and they had been bombed consistently. No one therefore paid much attention. It was just another 'Lord Haw-Haw' threat. And then the first V1 fell on London. We called it a 'Radio Bomb'.

I saw my first on June 19th, 1944. I was walking from Great Russell Street to my hospital in Dean Street, Soho, when I watched it passing over Frascati's Restaurant. It exploded behind Whitefield's Tabernacle in Tottenham Court Road, and a great volume of black smoke plumed up.

Soon it was quite clear the bombs were not controlled by radio, but driven by a motor like a torpedo. They were coming over every day now; and Tottenham Court Road seemed to be in the direct line of a lot of them. I could feel the shock of the impact of each in my office in Great Russell Street.

It was odd, however, how soon we got accustomed to these bombs. Hitler thought they would demoralise us. Someone started to call them 'doodle-bugs', and immediately, for some psychological reason, they became much less frightening. But they did make coming up to London somewhat of an ordeal. For they came over at all hours of the day and night. From the steps of the Athenæum I saw one drop behind the Regent Palace Hotel. Once they turned us all out of the Tube at Piccadilly Circus because a bomb had fallen in the river and they were afraid the tunnel to Waterloo under the Thames might have been damaged. So they had closed the emergency flood gates on either side and no trains could run until the 'all clear'.

Another time, whilst waiting at Euston for my train to start, we heard one approaching, whistling overhead. The sound stopped, and we knew that in three seconds the bomb would fall. Would it strike the station, killing hundreds of people? No. It fell in Camden Town, half a mile away, and the train started ten minutes late.

To complaints that the Air Force were doing nothing to stop this strafe, the Prime Minister replied in a broadcast that they had been bombing the V1 sites in the Pas de Calais for nine months. They had smashed over a hundred sites. The enemy, he said, had intended to send over thousands of flying-bombs a day. They actually had sent over only 2,750 in three weeks, and killed about one person and injured three for each bomb. This was consoling, except to the relatives of the people killed and the occupants of the houses destroyed. There was talk of closing the Exhibition of the Royal Academy, but Sir Walter Lamb, the Secretary, was very much opposed to this. He thought it would be a grave political error, even though the attendance was almost nil because the public knew the place was all glass and had no protection. So he resisted the suggestion. Actually Burlington House never was struck, and the Exhibition was kept open all the summer.

A visit to Buxton about this time came as a happy interlude. Here all was quiet, serene—you wouldn't have known there was a war on. We were told they had never had an air-raid warning since the war started. We could almost visualise what life would be like again when there was no more bombing. But the feeling didn't last long. Back in London the doodle-bugs were coming over as frequently as before, and even in Woburn Sands we heard one night the familiar whirring noise overhead. My wife and I looked at each other in surprise.

"Surely they can't have got as far north of London!" she exclaimed.

But this one had. Next day we learnt that a solitary flying-bomb had overshot its target and come down in a remote village in Northamptonshire, killing a number of sleeping people. Truly an unexpected tragedy.

On August 11th, 1944, my father-in-law, Dr. Alexander Francis, celebrated his eighty-first birthday. We both had consulting-rooms in the same house in Wimpole Street; and as he had come up to town to see some patients my wife asked him to a picnic lunch in ours. It was a happy meal, but we didn't think he looked at all well. We wanted to take him back to Victoria Station, but our train left Euston before his, and he insisted that he would go home happier if he knew we were out of London. His station was Three Bridges, and from there he drove himself six miles home. That night he had a coronary thrombosis and died. To be working up to the end, regardless of danger to himself, thinking only of others, was a fitting end to a long and wonderful life of service.

Three months later, on November 24th, 1944, my old friend (Charlie) C. S. Evans, Chairman of William Heinemann Ltd., died. I missed him intensely. We had been friends for thirty years. It was he who introduced me to the hitherto unknown world of publishing, an introduction which led eventually to my becoming managing director of a publishing company myself—a most unlikely thing to happen to a practising surgeon; yet when it did happen it all seemed so natural. It was due to him also, as I have mentioned, that I started writing medical short stories—the beginning, though I little realised it at the time, of a second literary career.

Evans was a superlatively able publisher. He learnt the business under 'Willie' Heinemann, that past master in the art of finding writing talent and new authors. Most of Charlie's authors were his personal friends; and nothing gave him greater pleasure than to act as host at 'The Ivy' or his hospitable home, Bildens at Ewhurst. I had known for a year he was failing. I think he really began to lose ground after the death of his youngest son, David, at the age of nineteen, killed in the great thousand-bomber raid on Bremen. For this brilliant boy was the apple of his eye. All his ambitions for the future centred on him. He was going to be what his father would like to have been, a surgeon; and a copy of every new medical book we published had to go to David. Of course a boy of that age should never have been allowed to go on such a raid. I think his father never really recovered from the shock.

The V2 bombs were now falling on London, and they proved far more nerve-racking than the V1; for with the V1 you heard the bomb approach, you heard the noise of it stop and cut out before it fell; and you knew that if it did not cut out it would pass over you. But with the V2 you had no such consolation. It came over at such a height that you got no warning whatever beforehand, and you were dead or you weren't.

London was a much less happy place during the V2 period. We

wondered if we had been wise to sign the lease of the flat we had taken on Campden Hill, Kensington. One bomb fell in the High Street and was rumoured to have killed a hundred people. One fell near Tavistock Square and shook us badly at Heinemann's. One fell just off Wigmore Street when I was in my consulting-room, and my windows were blown in. At such times fragments of glass scattered by the explosion of these bombs were liable to blind people, and I wrote a warning article on the subject for my Sunday paper.

Just before Christmas there came the news that the Germans, in a last despairing effort, had broken through the American lines in the Ardennes, and were driving on towards Antwerp, where we had immense stores of war material. It reminded me forcibly of the similar set-back in 1918, when we also thought we were winning comfortably and were brought up sharply by the break through at St. Quentin and the drive for Amiens.

Then followed a white Christmas with brilliant sunshine, an Allied recovery in Belgium, a sullen retreat by the defeated Germans, and the New Year of 1945 opened brightly with renewed hope of a speedy end to the war. I went to look at the new flat we had taken with a much less jaundiced eye.

Winter always takes toll of old men. Two well-known medical figures living exactly opposite one another in Wimpole Street, Sir Thomas Barlow and Sir Buckston Browne, died at this time within a week of each other. Sir Thomas was ninety-nine, Sir Buckston ninety-five. When they met, each old gentleman warned the other to be careful not to get run over, and each tried to shepherd the other across Wimpole Street. Sir Thomas, in his prime, had been physician to Queen Victoria. He was the first person to describe Infantile Scurvy. It was called 'Barlow's Disease' after him, and was fatal until it was discovered, many years later, that Vitamin C cured it. That is why babies now have orange juice provided by the State.

Sir Buckston Browne had been assistant to Sir Henry Thompson, the famous surgeon who operated on Napoleon III for stone in 1872; and he specialised in bladder troubles for many years afterwards, amassing a huge fortune. I tried several times to induce him to write his reminiscences of Victorian surgery, but could never persuade him, for by the time I knew him he was very old and very obstinate. In spite of his disabilities he would insist often on walking the streets alone, much to the dismay of his household as he never got used to the speed of motor traffic.

He was always most kind to me. When I sent him one of my articles, he would read it slowly and, when he had finished, write a letter in his characteristic large handwriting and walk round and drop it in my letter-box in Queen Anne Street. His family got him out of London in the worst of the blitz, but he was very unhappy and insisted on coming back to 80 Wimpole Street, where he had his collection of pictures and china. He was nearly blind and very deaf at the end; but he insisted on coming to my Vicary Lecture, sat in the front row and listened, though he can have heard or seen little. That touched me very much. He will be remembered mainly for two things: he founded the Buckston Browne Surgical Experimental Farm at Downe in Kent, Darwin's old home, and he endowed the Buckston Browne Dinner given annually at the College of Surgeons, truly a pleasant way to have one's memory kept green.

In March, 1945, we decided to have a short holiday at Frinton. On a previous visit about a year before we had found the beach a tangle of barbed wire and concrete blocks, and the greensward, which was so peaceful-looking in pre-war days, bristling with A.A. guns artfully concealed in dummy tobacco stalls and little cafés. But except for a few air-raid warnings and an odd bomber coming over there had not been much activity—though broken houses showed there had been considerable damage.

Our house had been commandeered early in the war, and on this visit, as on former ones, we went to a guest-house near the sea—one of the few still open. We arrived in the evening, and after dinner noticed that no one made for a very comfortable-looking armchair in the centre of the lounge, an unusual thing in a guest-house. Presently we saw the reason, for suddenly the guns on the front started firing salvo after salvo. The whole house shook ominously, and everyone gazed anxiously at the ceiling, from which hung a heavy chandelier immediately over the chair. No wonder that chair remained empty.

There were four warnings in the night, and the deafening noise of our barrage drove away all hope of sleep. Towards dawn there was a sound, louder, more terrifying than anything we had ever heard at

'James Harpole'

Charles Seddon Evans

Frinton before. We knew what it was. It was a V2; and in the morning we heard it had come down at Kirby, two miles away.

Once that day when a flight of our bombers was going south-east,
bound for Germany, a number of V1 flying-bombs came over in the
opposite direction at the same time. The A.A. guns were in consequence unable to fire at them and impotently we watched them head-
ing for London unopposed.

The reason of course for this unexpected activity over the East Coast
was that the sites of the 'V' weapons in France and Belgium had been
captured, and the V1's and the V2's were now coming from sites in
Holland. After a couple of days we decided our formerly peaceful
Frinton was now no place for a holiday and returned to work, thankful
to be away from the inferno of the East Coast barrage.

In London we were greatly excited to hear a rumour that the
Americans had crossed the Rhine. Next day it was confirmed. The
First Army got to Remagen, twelve miles south of Bonn, so fast that the
bridge was found intact and they got over practically without a fight.
It took the Germans completely by surprise. The news was extraordinarily exhilarating. I was so elated I went and saw my tailor and
ordered a new suit—the first since 1939.

But of course it was the great crossing at Wesel, where Montgomery
dropped 40,000 paratroops and Churchill insisted on being present,
that was the real highlight. Listening to the wireless reports one almost
felt one was there. The death of Lloyd George in the midst of all this
excitement created merely a ripple. How different it would have been
in 1919!

By this time the danger from the V1's and the V2's was lessening as
we gradually captured their firing sites; and it was cheering to learn
that train-loads of these weapons had been seized *en route* for North
Holland.

*

During the war the three political parties had called a truce and formed
a Coalition Government under Churchill; and it was now noticeable
that with the prospect of victory in sight the Socialists were beginning
to break away. Both Bevin and Morrison were jockeying for position.
That, and the death of Franklin Roosevelt, made one feel that the

M

happy war partnership was rapidly breaking up, and spelt the beginning of the end.

From the war front the news had now turned to what we were discovering in the awful concentration camps we overran as we fought our way to Berlin: starvation, torture, murder. The free world was shocked that such barbarities were possible in a supposedly civilised country. At Buchenwald near Weimar, and at Belsen near Hanover, the advancing army made the local inhabitants march through these camps so that they could not repudiate the stories of atrocities in later years.

*

April 21st, 1945, was the date of our silver wedding. We put a notice in *The Times* and were amused to find that ten other couples had done the same, a most unusually popular date. It was a lovely sunny day. The birds were singing. The lilac, whitethorn and laburnum were all in full bloom. We went for a walk in the woods above Woburn Sands. Life seemed all right.

And yet all the while Berlin was being battered to death, for Hitler was known to be there. Unfortunately we had agreed that the Russians were to have the right to occupy it and the British and Americans were to stop at the Elbe. In retrospect one sees how foolish this was. It seems to have been Roosevelt's fault, mainly; but at the time we were all pro-Russian.

Official records now disclosed the damage done by the V2 rockets. The first fell in Chiswick, September 8th, 1944, the last in Orpington, March 27th, 1945. The number of rockets to reach us was 1,050. The casualties they produced were 2,754 killed and 6,523 seriously wounded. The two worst were one in a Woolworth Store at New Cross in November, 1944, and one in Farringdon Market in March, 1945, when 110 people were killed. I was in my office in Great Russell Street when this latter happened, and we felt the impact very clearly.

All this time we were trying to force the Germans out of Italy, but somehow we had ceased to take much notice of the campaign there. I remember when we captured Rapallo I thought how happy Max Beerbohm would be when he could go back to his beloved Italy again.

Then on April 30th came the ghastly story of Mussolini's body hanging by the feet from a lamp-post in the main square of Milan, and people spitting on it and shooting into it with revolvers—a horrible end.

A week of high drama followed. Hitler committed suicide in his underground shelter in Berlin on May 2nd. The Germans in Italy surrendered unconditionally to Field-Marshal Alexander. Berlin was captured on May 3rd; and, to register an anticlimax, the busmen in London came out on strike against the new summer time-tables.

The next day I went with my daughter to the Private View of the Academy. It was crowded; but no one now wore the conventional silk hat and morning coat customary before the war. Some of the usual figures, however, were still there. I noticed particularly Lady Alexander, the widow of Sir George Alexander, the once famous actor-manager of the St. James's Theatre. She looked incredibly old, raddled, painted, wearing an ermine coat with emerald-green ostrich feathers in her hat—a pathetic sight. With all the war news singing in our ears, portraits of generals were very much in evidence; but it was pleasant to learn from John Lamorna Birch that he had sold five of his six land-scape pictures, showing that people were still conscious of the beauty of our country. The wonderful old man was so elated over this success that later he insisted on demonstrating hand-springs to us on the carpet of his sitting-room at the Park Lane Hotel, although he was well over eighty.

Back in the quiet of Woburn Sands that evening we listened to the nine o'clock news and heard that all the Germans in Holland, Denmark and the Frisian Islands had surrendered to Field-Marshal Montgomery. That, with the German surrender to Alexander in Italy, practically, though not officially, ended the war from the British side. Two million men had surrendered to us, and were safe from the vengeful Russians. But the American Third and Seventh Armies and the Russians were still fighting other Germans in Czechoslovakia, part of Austria and in pockets east of the Elbe.

The danger of air-raids was now over; sirens stopped officially on May 3rd, five days before the German surrender; and church-bells that had been banned during the war, because they were being held in reserve as an invasion warning, were once more free to ring.

Truly a wonderful week of news.

All sorts of consequences followed. It meant that the air-raid shelters could close down. It meant that half a million evacuated children could now return home, if there was a home to return to. It meant that people could take their stored treasures into the light of day again. We found we could have our furniture brought up to London in two months' tin.e. Everywhere the war tension suddenly ceased. Nobody seemed bothering about work. Signs of preparations for V.E. Day (Victory in Europe Day) were everywhere. The papers said it might be announced at any time. The news from Burma of the capture of Rangoon, ten days before the monsoon broke, was an immense military relief and a great triumph for British arms; but it was almost unappreciated at home. To those like me who knew the East, however, it meant that a great port was now open to supply our Army; and that our forward troops need no longer be dependent on supplies dropped almost entirely by transport planes, a method of supply which during the coming monsoon would have been almost hopeless in the howling winds and pelting rain.

On Tuesday, May 8th, 1945, we woke to the realisation that the war in Europe was officially over. At three p.m. Churchill announced the complete unconditional surrender of all the Germans in a very short speech, ending with 'God Save the King'.

It was a lovely hot thunderous day. My wife and I spent a quiet ten minutes alone in the dim-lit empty village church across the way. We then sat in the garden listening to the birds singing, we thought, particularly beautifully. It was wonderful, unbelievably wonderful, to be at peace. We watched the great planes flying overhead, and knew they were either carrying food to the starving people in Holland or bringing home returned prisoners of war, not bombing the enemy.

We heard that the Channel Islanders were freed from the Germans, and that 10,000 German troops had surrendered to twenty-two men of the Royal Artillery. The people, we were told, were half starved. They had eaten all the dogs and cats on the islands and were living on cabbages and potatoes. The German garrison was little better off. They had had no provisions for months owing to our blockade.

The *British Medical Journal* of May 12th, 1945, gave the official total civilian casualties during the war as follows:

KILLED

Men	..	..	..	..	..	..	26,920
Women	..	..	..	..	..	..	25,392
Children	..	..	..	..	..	..	7,736
Unclassified	..	..	..	..	..	537

60,585

INJURED AND RETAINED IN HOSPITAL

Men	..	..	..	..	..	..	40,736
Women	..	..	..	..	..	..	37,816
Children	..	..	..	..	..	..	7,623

86,175

The total number of killed and wounded in the whole country thus amounted to 146,760. Out of these the London area casualties amounted to:

KILLED	..	..	..	..	..	..	29,890
BADLY INJURED AND							
RETAINED IN HOSPITAL	..	..	..	50,497

80,387

From this it appears that London had nearly four-sevenths of the casualties.

CHAPTER XXV

MOMENTOUS EVENTS

NOW THAT THE WAR with Germany was over the Labour Party decided to secede from the Coalition Government. This decision followed upon a letter from Churchill to Attlee suggesting they should carry on together until the end of the war with Japan, or that a referendum should be put to the country on the question, asking 'Yes or No'. Both suggestions were rejected by the Socialists, and it was therefore assumed there would have to be a General Election not later than July.

Meanwhile the net round the War Criminals, as they were called, was tightening. Two of the most hated names after Hitler were Himmler and Joyce. Himmler was the mind behind the Gestapo, the cold-blooded fiend who was responsible for the horrible concentration camps and their lethal chambers. He disappeared when the army surrendered, shaved off his moustache and wore a patch over his left eye. But, as he was being interrogated for the third time at the end of May, because his papers were suspect, he broke down and gave his real name. I think he feared he might be tortured, judging others by his own mentality; and so he committed suicide when being medically examined by biting on an ampule of potassium cyanide.

William Joyce (nicknamed 'Lord Haw-Haw' on account of his supposed Oxford accent) was a renegade Irishman who talked nightly in English over the German wireless throughout the war. His job was to spread 'alarm and despondency', and he often succeeded almost too well. People listened to him, even though he was 'the voice of the enemy', and often believed what he said. He used to prophesy air-raids. He used to read out names of men captured, and consequently thousands of anxious fathers, mothers, wives and children would listen in, hoping to hear that some loved one who had disappeared was not dead but a prisoner. He exaggerated German gains and distorted and denigrated Allied successes. He was a poisonous success.

And so, when he too was discovered and captured in May, one felt a sense of relief, a delivery from something evil.

The sudden cessation of hostilities now made large social meetings again possible without risk; and, taking advantage of this, the Authors Society staged a Sixtieth Anniversary Conversazione at Grosvenor House. Queen Elizabeth (the present Queen Mother) came in turquoise blue which accentuated her china-like beauty. John Masefield, the Poet Laureate, received the guests, and it was a pleasure to me to meet him again, since I always credited him with starting the unexpected popularity of my *Surgeon's Log*. My wife, my daughter and I listened to John Gielgud recite and Masefield read one of his poems. Masefield sat on one side of the Queen; Edith Sitwell, dressed in white with a great white turban, looking like an inspired sibyl, sat on the other. There was much talk and several speeches. The Queen got up to go eventually at six p.m., and so everyone else naturally stood up. Then she got interested in some remark of Masefield's and forgot she was keeping us all standing. No one could leave before Royalty, so there we stood. Suddenly it dawned upon her, and with a smile and a laugh she moved away.

*

A visit we had on July 1st from Sir Raphael Cilento, the Director-General of the Health Department of Queensland, reminded us vividly that, though the war in Europe was over, we were still at war with Japan. He told us that at one time the Japs got within sixty miles of Townsville, in Queensland, and Australia would have been invaded but for the Allied victory in the Battle of the Coral Sea. At that time Australian fighting planes were only half the strength of the Japanese; but, worse than that, this strength was still more depleted by the fact that General MacArthur brought Dengue Fever with him from the Philippines. This broke out at Darwin, spread to the intermediate landing grounds in Queensland, and one only out of all the Australian pilots escaped. The fever lasts as a rule about seven days, but pain in the back and knees is very severe while it lasts; and when the attack is over there is subsequently great mental and physical weakness which may go on for months. So, after the pilots had recovered, it was found that none of them, for the next six months, could fly over 8,000 feet without blacking out. Luckily the Japs never discovered this.

"The risk of invasion is over now," said Sir Raphael with a smile. "There are a million Americans in Queensland, of whom three hundred thousand are in Brisbane alone; and it is a job to feed them as there are more of them than native Australians."

This to us was an unexpected sidelight on the global nature of the war, preoccupied as we were with our own affairs nearer home.

The General Election of 1945 was now being held and, as we were not registered in London, we voted at Woburn Sands. It was a hot, lazy summer day. Lying out in the garden after voting at the local school-house, we noticed the constant flitting of two harassed hedge sparrows, back and forward with full beaks, to one particular spot in the yew hedge beyond the french window on the lawn. I went over to investigate and there found, in the hedge sparrows' nest, a huge disgusting object with a horrible gaping yellow beak and a half-naked gross body partly covered with black and white speckled feathers. It was a young cuckoo which had got rid of the genuine offspring by pushing them out of the nest. As soon as we moved the leaves, it opened its great yellow beak, expecting food. To see the harassed little hedge sparrows frantically flying to and fro trying to satisfy this interloper was a queer sight. We watched this off and on for days. The cuckoo grew its wing and tail feathers in a week and was soon able to leave the nest. It was quite extraordinarily tame, seemed to have no fear, and used to perch in a tree in the garden shrieking with a fine sawlike sound for food. There was something oddly compelling about this shriek, for we noticed that other birds, even sparrows, were fascinated into feeding it, while we sat watching, having tea under the apple trees.

On one of these quiet evenings, sitting out in the garden, we heard on the six o'clock news, coming to us from the sitting-room, that an American cruiser escorted by six British destroyers was steaming up the Channel carrying President Truman en route for Antwerp. From there he was to proceed by car and plane to meet Stalin and, as everyone thought, Churchill, for the Conference at Potsdam which was to settle all our differences for ever. I remember it was July 14th, the date of the Fall of the Bastille; and the French were celebrating both events excitedly. Little we knew on that quiet summer evening how quickly our hopes of the world peace we anticipated from that meeting would evaporate.

It is difficult also now to remember all the inconveniences we still had to put up with, although the war was over. Rationing of milk, rationing of eggs, rationing of clothes still went on. I had been allowed ten pounds to do up my flat. The windows had been blown in twice, and the walls and ceilings of the rooms blackened. Of course, it was a completely inadequate amount. Luckily I had a patient who was an interior decorator. He was of no use to the Government for bomb repairs, and so was not busy. I felt therefore I was not interfering with essential work by employing him. But it took months; materials were scarce; and only one man was working on the job. So throughout the spring and early summer I continued to travel up and down to London from Woburn Sands.

There were of course many compensations for living in the country. One week-end my wife and I went for a walk to what we called 'Lob's Wood'. We found it was being cut down to supply much-needed timber. We watched the lumber-men felling pines and a man cooking dinner for them. There was a resinous smell of burning branches in the air. Sounds of the axe and the sawyers came to us from the valley below. A wood wren was singing. The sun was shining. We walked to Woburn, got our month's quota of chocolate and came home. Life was good again.

The election results in July, delayed for weeks by the Army vote, turned out, to everyone's intense surprise, to be a great triumph for the Socialist Party. The troops voted solidly for Labour. Churchill and the Conservatives were completely routed. Americans and foreigners in general were astounded. They just couldn't understand. One refugee, a woman, familiar with the consequences of a fall from power in other countries, burst into tears.

"I suppose they'll shoot poor Mr. Churchill now," she said.

The result of the election meant that Mr. Attlee replaced Mr. Churchill at Potsdam at the meeting arranged with President Truman and Stalin. I remember that Attlee returned from Potsdam on August 2nd, for I happened to be lunching at the Athenæum that day when he came in with Sir Findlater Stewart and Austin Hopkinson. He was in great form, animated and laughing. He looked happy. It was the first time I had seen him as Prime Minister.

None of us knew then about the one momentous decision that had been made by the principals at the Big Three Conference. Four days later, however, we did. For on Bank Holiday, August 6th, 1945, we heard that the first atomic bomb had fallen on Hiroshima, a city on the Inland Sea of Japan, killing 60,000 people and devastating an area four miles square.

It was the arrival of the Atomic Age.

Few people at the time sensed the enormous change this made in world history. Truman had asked that the Allies should consent to its use in order to shorten the war and save the five hundred thousand American lives it was calculated would be sacrificed in an invasion of Japan. The Japs had behaved so barbarously to our men in Malaya, and they had started the war with America by an act of such treachery, that no one in consequence had any feeling of pity for them. It seemed horrible, but right at the time, that they should suffer; so when we heard they had been bombed at Hiroshima we felt justified: thousands of Allied lives had been saved. The war had been shortened by months, perhaps years.

On August 10th we were told that Japan had surrendered.

I noticed that the girls in the offices opposite the Pall Mall windows of the Club were tearing up letters and snowing them down into the street. There were surging crowds at Piccadilly Circus, mainly American troops on leave. Everyone was very excited.

Presently the news was contradicted. The Japs were trying to save 'face'.

Then came the further news that Nagasaki also had had an atom bomb dropped on it, destroying the whole city. This gave me a pain. It was the first Japanese port I had landed in when I was a ship's surgeon in the Blue Funnel Line, and I had very pleasant recollections of it.

But the bomb on Nagasaki finished the Japs. They surrendered unconditionally on August 14th; and the world war was over. Mr. Attlee, the new Socialist Prime Minister, announced it at midnight, and we heard it repeated at seven and eight a.m. on the 15th. A two days' holiday was proclaimed to celebrate the end of the world war. It was an auspicious moment to start the new Socialist Government policy. The King opened Parliament, and in his speech announced the nationalisation of the mines. The crowds circled round in Piccadilly Circus not caring a rap about nationalisation or anything else. And next day was my birthday.

A great feeling of relief and happiness permeated the minds of everyone, or nearly everyone. For some more sensitive, or more imaginative, did not join in the feeling of general happiness. Sir Herbert Eason, the President of the General Medical Council, told me he couldn't sleep thinking of the horror of the bomb on Hiroshima.

"No man, no nation, should have such awful power. Man isn't fit to be trusted with it," he said.

I thought then he was talking a trifle hysterically. I know better now.

Throughout the war there had been a dearth of medical communications recording new original work; and publishers in consequence had concentrated on keeping the standard text-books in print, not an easy task on account of the great paper shortage. This lack of information concerning recent advances had, moreover, been aggravated by a new and hitherto unknown factor in scientific thought: an official ban on the disclosure of any life-saving discovery that might aid the enemy. Meetings of military medical officers were held at the Royal Society of Medicine to exchange information under a security ban which excluded civilian practitioners. The uses of new synthetic drugs, serums, antibiotics, disinfectants, advanced transfusion techniques, were all shrouded in mystery. This caused much searching of hearts in a profession pledged to save life, whenever possible, in friend or foe. We didn't like it, but we couldn't help it.

With the advent of peace, however, everything altered almost overnight. Doctors released from service had permission and leisure to write. A flood of new original communications appeared in the press of the Allied nations; new techniques were described, old methods found defective were condemned, and suddenly all the standard medical works in print became out-of-date. Books which formerly needed only small alterations for a new edition now had to be entirely rewritten. That meant the standing type was useless and had to be discarded. That meant the new type set up cost three times the old.

owing to the great rise in printers' wages. Binding, too, had risen in price, and paper had gone up four times. All this meant that the cost of medical books soared, to the annoyance of readers who did not understand and the worry of publishers who did. I suffered from this worry. I wanted our books to be up-to-date and naturally was always on the look-out for any new medical material. For this reason I was hoping that we might learn something from the Nazis that they too had been concealing, for German medicine before the Nazi regime had been second to none.

The Germans in the past have been almost pathological in their careful recording of facts; and so whenever we overran one of their hospitals or camps or military establishments, we found minute details of their everyday activity. Even at the horrible concentration camps their records had been kept.

One day an American officer came in to see me with the records of Dachau, describing the vivisection experiments performed there by Dr. Rascher on Poles, Jews and political prisoners. These had been ordered by Himmler ostensibly for the benefit of the Luftwaffe, but they appear to have been mainly sadistic. In them men were immersed in ice-cold water or were frozen naked. They were then resuscitated by various means, and it was found that the best method was to immerse them in water at 40 to 45 degrees Centigrade (104°F to 112°F). This might have been useful knowledge where flying men rescued from the English Channel were concerned. But putting a frozen man into bed with a warm naked woman appeared to me less scientific. At any rate Himmler seemed to think so too, for, when he saw that the game was up, he had Dr. Rascher and Frau Rascher shot in order to hide his collaboration, although Frau Rascher had previously been his mistress. But curiously enough he kept a complete dossier of these experiments, which was found by the Americans in his hide-out hospital. It was this dossier that was offered to me for publication. I read it carefully, decided it had no scientific value and refused it. Actually we learnt nothing from the Nazi regime. The Germans had been cut off for so long from outside scientific thought that they were ten years behind the times.

Knowledge of brutalities and bestialities of this kind made us forget temporarily the other side to the German character: the great contribution made in the past to science in all its branches. This was brought back sharply to my mind a few days later when I went to a meeting at the Royal Society of Medicine called to commemorate the Fiftieth Anniversary of the discovery of X-rays by Röntgen, one of the most epoch-making advances ever made in medicine. It took me back in memory to the first time I ever heard of Röntgen and his rays. It was in the anatomy lecture theatre at Trinity, Dublin. Professor Cunningham produced an X-ray photo of a human hand from a cadaver, showing the bones outlined clearly, with the arteries, which had been injected with red lead, displayed most beautifully, just as if they had been dissected out. The Professor said it was an interesting discovery, it would help anatomists, but he did not think it would be of any practical value in medicine or surgery. If he could have seen in imagination the millions of X-ray plates now used yearly to diagnose fractures, duodenal and gastric ulcers, cancer, stone in the kidney, stone in the gall bladder, tuberculosis of the lungs, tumours of bone and brain and a dozen other things, how differently he would have spoken. Today without X-rays we should be like blind men fumbling in the dark.

Lord Horder at the meeting spoke eloquently of this great gift to healing; and he was followed by the new Socialist Minister of Health, Mr. Aneurin Bevan. It was the first time I had seen this brilliant parliamentarian, tall, pale-faced, heavily built, with his black hair in an old-fashioned quiff such as soldiers used to sport before the South African War when they wore little pill-box hats on the side of their heads. I listened and felt the charm of his soft Welsh voice. It reminded me of Lloyd George, whom I had once attended, and I thought:

'Here is a potential Prime Minister. He has all the gifts. Almost thou persuadest me to be a Bevanite.'

Afterwards I went home and wrote an article on Röntgen for the next week's *Sunday Graphic*.

A fortnight later in the same Sunday paper I read that Charles Coborn had died. It brought a flood of memories, for songs that one hears as a boy, when the mind is wax to receive and marble to retain, strike responsive chords many years later. I remember the first time I saw Charles. It was at the Savage Club, where he sang 'Two Lovely Black Eyes' in six different languages. It is a song that went round the

world in my boyhood, and is perhaps even still better remembered
than his later one, 'The Man Who Broke the Bank at Monte Carlo'.
He must have been over seventy when I heard him first, grey-haired,
square-faced, bushy-browed. Unexpectedly, for one does not associate
it with a *lion comique*, he was a deeply religious man. I don't think in his
later years he liked singing the Monte Carlo song, for each winter, for
two decades after, he used to come at Christmas-time to my hospital
and sing to the patients gathered round the Christmas-tree; and the
only song he would sing, in a surprisingly strong and clear voice, was
'Two Lovely Black Eyes'.

> Two lovely black eyes!
> Oh what a surprise!
> Only for telling a man he was wrong,
> Two lovely black eyes!

The last time he came and sang it he was ninety. We missed him
when he died in 1945.

*

There is a learned body of men which presides over the destinies of the
medical profession called the General Medical Council. I don't suppose
there is any body whose functions are so little understood. Most laymen confuse it with the British Medical Association, and practically
everyone thinks of it merely as a tribunal which deals severely with
doctors who commit adultery with patients. Actually that is happily
the smallest part of its duties, for its main concern is the safety of the
public. It does this, first of all, by insisting on a high standard of
knowledge before anyone can call himself a doctor. This is done by
inspecting the final examinations of the licensing bodies. It publishes
yearly a book called *The Medical Register* which contains the names of
all the people who are entitled to call themselves doctors. This is for
the protection of the public against quacks, for no person whose name
is not on the Register is entitled to call himself doctor or write a
prescription. It publishes at intervals a book called *The British Pharmacopœia* which contains the name, description and dosage of every drug,
old or new, of proved value. Chemists working from this book

dispense the medicines prescribed; and if a doctor, either by inadvertence or because his prescription cannot be read, seems to prescribe a dangerous dose, the chemist's duty is to ring him up and ask why.

Last of all it has to protect the public from anyone unworthy of the trust it should repose in its doctor. A doctor who gets drunk habitually is a fearful menace. He is given one or maybe two chances to reform. Then if he does not, he is struck off the Register. A doctor who dopes himself with cocaine, or opium or any of its derivatives, is deprived of the right to prescribe these drugs. And finally a doctor who abuses the confidence placed in him in family life, or who performs for gain some criminal operation, is deprived of his statutory privileges.

Someone told me that the meeting place of this Council in Hallam Street, which had been blitzed in the war, had now been restored. I had never been into it and, moved by curiosity, I thought I'd like to see its workings. So I went along on Eason's invitation one afternoon to listen to a judicial session.

The Council Chamber, I found, was a fine oblong room with panelled walls and two galleries, one at each of the narrow ends. A cheerful fire burnt under one gallery. Portraits of past Presidents adorned the walls. The President's chair was on a dais, close to the east wall. Behind him were stained-glass windows, six marble busts and side panels with the coats of arms of past Presidents. The reporters' table was just below him on the floor of the chamber. The table for lawyers and legal counsel extended across the floor. The witness-box was on the President's right, the victim's dock across the chamber facing him. The members of the General Council sat on chairs filling the body of the chamber on either side. It was all very formal and impressive.

I listened whilst an unfortunate dentist squirmed in the dock, trying to answer the questions put to him and making a poor job of it. A pathetic dipsomaniac followed. He was very abject. They felt sorry for him and referred him for a year on condition he went into a home. It would be his last chance. He was warned that if he started drinking again he would have no further grace—he would be removed from the Register. When the session was over a messenger came to invite me to tea with the President and Council. They had had a comparatively easy day. There had been no difficult or too distressing cases to adjudicate on, and the atmosphere was one of pleasant relaxation. I went away impressed by the fairness of everything I had seen and heard. I was glad that Eason's task was not always too unpleasant. I knew what a sensitive man he was.

The death of Lang, the Archbishop of Canterbury, at this time revived the gossip over the abdication of Edward VIII. The general feeling I found still was that Baldwin, the Prime Minister, Dawson of *The Times*, and Lang had done the right thing between them when they engineered the abdication. But I used to think Lang still felt the position acutely, for after the trouble he stopped sitting at any of the main tables at the Club. Sometimes he lunched with Canon (now Dean) Don. Usually, however, lonely and tired-looking, he sat by himself. I have learnt since that he was not consulted by Baldwin at any time during the crisis, but he must have taken it very much to heart all the same.

*

It is my habit after breakfast to look through *The Times* before I start the day's work. I read the announcements of births, marriages and deaths to make sure I miss none of my friends or acquaintances. Then I glance through the personal column for anything odd. Many a novelist gravelled for a subject has obtained a complete new plot in this way. Next I look at the obituary notices if they concern anyone I have known. Then come the letters to the editor. I look at these because someone at the Athenæum is sure to be writing about something or somebody, and he may possibly ask me if I've seen it. Then there is the fourth leader—the fourth leader is a joy. I always dodge the other three, unless compelled. And finally I glance through the paper to see if there is anything of general or of medical historical interest.

It was in this way I came across the notice of the bicentenary of the birth of William Curtis, about whom I became interested when I was writing my life of Lettsom—for Lettsom had befriended the eager young apothecary and paid for the production of the first number of his great book, *Flora Londinensis*, which came out in parts over a number of years and was collected finally in two sumptuous folios in 1798. It nearly ruined Curtis, but luckily for him he had also started *The Botanical Magazine* in 1787. This was an immediate success; and, astonishing to relate, it has never ceased publication from that day to this. Curtis said it gave him not only 'meat' but 'pudding'. In 1937 it reached its 150th volume. Every number was illustrated by plates coloured by hand, and this went on until after the 1939–45 War. The plates were drawn and coloured from 1800 onwards at the Royal Botanic Gardens, Kew. There are over ten thousand of them; and until recently they were still coloured by hand by a succession of devoted women artists. The magazine is now published by the Royal Horticultural Society, and as a magazine it is probably unique. When, therefore, I saw a little picture of Curtis in *The Times*, and learnt they were holding a memorial service on the following Sunday at the church in Battersea where he is buried, I felt I must go.

So on a lovely frosty Sunday morning I took the No. 31 bus from High Street, Kensington, to Cheyne Walk and went across the bridge to the old Battersea Parish Church of St. Mary's, overlooking the river on the south side. Curtis's tombstone in the little graveyard, separated from the river by a railing, was a flat, worn, rusty slab with a new white marble block placed over it inscribed 'Wm. Curtis 1746–1799'.

The church of the old village, now swallowed up by London, is beautiful in a restful way. It has some very elaborate stained-glass windows and some fine mural tablets. William Blake, the poet and mystic, was married here, and the Register contains also the signatures of Burke and Wilberforce. The living belonged to the St. John family. Henry St. John, Viscount Bolingbroke, was baptised here. He is remembered now for two things only: the Peace of Utrecht which finished the War of the Spanish Succession, and his nearly successful attempt to bring the Stuarts back, before the death of Queen Anne put finish to the plot. When he died in 1751 he was buried in this church. It is the association of the family with Battersea that suggested the name of the Bolingbroke Hospital founded by the Rev. John Erskine Clarke, the vicar of St. Mary's, in 1901.

I got to the church about ten-fifty a.m., when the old bells were ringing. There was a fair-sized congregation of local people, and a number of botanical enthusiasts brought there, like me, by the Curtis bicentenary. The church has a good choir and a fine organ. The vicar started his service by the well-known lines from Ecclesiasticus, "Let us now praise famous men." The hymns and the lessons were chosen for their allusions to flowers and colour—"Consider the lilies of the field," etc. The sermon was preached by the Bishop of Truro, and the collection was to raise funds to beautify the churchyard and make it a haven of grass and flowers, with seats for old people and casual visitors to sit on and gaze at the passing ships. Turner, it is said, was accustomed to go there frequently to watch and to paint. They keep the chair he used, in the basement of the church tower.

After the service the bishop and the vicar, followed by the choir, went and stood round Curtis's tomb, and finished the last hymn with the rest of us standing on the steps of the church looking on. In the church they had a fine copy of the *Flora Londinensis* and several other works of Curtis's on exhibition. It was to me a most satisfying morning. I found I could go home the whole way on a 49 bus and said to myself I'd go there often again. Of course I never did, but that is life.

I have an impression, probably quite erroneous, that doctors in the eighteenth century who lived in Curtis's time, like Lettsom, Babington and Astley Cooper, had an easier road to success than consultants in the nineteenth and twentieth, especially before the advent of the National Health Service.

I was grousing like this one day to my friend Henry MacCormac, Dermatologist to the Middlesex Hospital.

MacCormac nodded.

"Yes, we did have a hard time. I remember as a young doctor I applied for a job at the Middlesex. It was worth one hundred pounds a year. After I got it I met Sir John Bland-Sutton one day in the corridor. He said to me:

" 'I see you got that post, MacCormac. What age are you?'

" 'Twenty-six, sir,' I answered.

" 'Hm. If you'd been on the Stock Exchange you could almost have retired by now.' "

There spoke the bitterness of an old man who after a long struggle had risen to fame and affluence when he was too old to enjoy either.

One of the men who never had to fight his way was Sir John Broadbent of St. Mary's Hospital. His father, Sir William Broadbent, had been a very famous physician, and the son almost automatically succeeded him on the staff. It made life too easy for him. He never did anything outstanding. He was just a good sound physician. I made his acquaintance after the First World War. His cousin, Sir Edward Broadbent, had been my General in Egypt. I had saved his life by spotting he had typhus fever acquired from his Sudanese servant; and he asked me, when I came home, to see Sir John and tell him all about it. That started a friendship that lasted; and when I heard he was very ill I went to see him. He was lying quietly in bed; he knew he was dying, and he was quite happy about it except for one thing.

"Nobody seems to know what's wrong with me," he said. "I would like to be at my own post-mortem to find out."

There was no post-mortem, so no one does really know, not even the Registrar-General.

*

One of the things that pleased me very much in 1946 was getting royalties due on translations of my books from countries occupied during the war by the Germans. I had never expected this; I had written them off in my mind; but it seems that all through the war, in Holland and in the Scandinavian countries, in Finland and even in Italy, they had been selling my books surreptitiously under the counter. They had kept accurate records of these sales, and now that things were getting back to normal they were paying the royalties to my agent, W. P. Watt.

This unexpected tribute to my work touched me very much. Having some idea what conditions must have been like in occupied territory, and the penalty for disobeying Nazi orders if found out, I felt pleased that people in so many overrun countries should have taken risks to read my books. Preparing these, in addition to all my other occupations, had sometimes been a strain, but this made it seem more than ever worth while.

Writing itself has always come easily to me. Thinking out and doing an article for Fleet Street would as a rule occupy me about three days. Writing an occasional leader or an article for the *Lancet* or one of the other medical journals would take over a week. Rewriting a series of articles three times for a well-known text-book, because of delays in publication and rapid alterations in treatment, once took

several months. All this was easy going in the peaceful atmosphere of
one's study. What took it out of one was publicly delivering an
address before a critical audience of one's fellow-practitioners. It had
to be accurate. It had to be good. It had to be interesting. I was
thinking of all this when I realised that the time had come when I must
prepare the Annual Oration of the Medical Society which I had
promised to deliver in 1946. I knew my Vicary Lecture at the College
of Surgeons in 1944 had been a success. The Oration to be given before
the Society founded by Lettsom in 1773, must, I felt, be made a success
too. So I got down to it.

I have no respect for anyone who boasts of his powers of extempore
speaking; I think it is an insult to any intelligent audience to offer them
one's casual disconnected thoughts; and so I spent a lot of time thinking
out, writing my Oration and then, afterwards, rehearsing it with my
long-suffering wife. I delivered it on May 13th, 1946. The ordeal was
over. Peace fell upon my household.

It was shortly after this lecture that I went to see Sir Almroth Wright,
the inventor of anti-typhoid inoculation, at St. Mary's Hospital, about
a book he wanted me to publish. We were old friends, both Trinity
Dublin men. I had worked under his uncle, Edward Percival Wright,
the Professor of Botany, as an undergraduate, and we had many other
mutual contacts. So it was a great pleasure to see him still active, still
working in the corner of his laboratory at the age of eighty-five. He
sat in his chair, hunched up, his great leonine head bent forward, looking very old but with a mind as sharp as ever.

We discussed the publication of his book *Alethetropic Logic*, which
he had been writing for thirty years. It had been in typescript when he
first gave it to me a year before, but he had asked for it back and kept
on revising until it had become impossible to read. Now, he told me,
it had been retyped. He was full of enthusiasm about it, and was sure
it would be a best-seller. He said it was finished, but, with his passion
for exactitude, I doubted if even now he would be able to leave it
alone.

He took me down to the tea-room where his assistants gathered at
that time of day, and his conversation was as sparkling as ever. I had
a word there with Sir Alexander Fleming, who was succeeding him as
head of the Wright–Fleming Institute. He told me that he was going

over to Dublin in July to receive an honorary Sc.D. from Trinity; and I was able to tell him that I was going over at the same time to get a Litt.D. from my old University.

This to me was a great and unexpected honour, and I was thrilled at the prospect. I had thought no one at Trinity remembered me; and recognition of this kind was therefore all the more welcome. Fleming and I arranged to meet, and go about together in Dublin during the time we were over for the Summer Commencements.

*

CHAPTER XXVI

IRELAND REVISITED

DUBLIN is indelibly associated in my mind with the carefree golden days of undergraduate life. It was years since I'd been across, and I wondered, as we flew over, how I might find it after the interval. I needn't have. It was just the same lovely lazy city of my youth. I might never have been away. The soft familiar brogue hadn't altered.

We were dumped down at 'The Pillar' by the bus from the aerodrome. Nelson's Pillar, I explained to my daughter, who was with me, was the place where all the trams ended and where you made a rendezvous with your 'best girl' of the moment. "Meet me at the Pillar at eight o'clock" was a frequent expression.

The Pillar is a great column like that in Trafalgar Square, without the lions; but I wonder how many Dubliners ever look at Nelson on the top of it. He seems imperturbably, incongruously remote there. No one bothers about him in Dublin. Even during the street fighting all round him in the days of 'The Trouble', he gazed down undisturbed, detached from it all.

There was once, it is true, some talk about blowing him up; for, as a fervid patriot said:

"Why should we have a statue of a one-eyed adulterer in O'Connell Street?"

But the idea was hurriedly dropped when someone else remarked that there were also statues to Daniel O'Connell and Charles Stewart Parnell in the same street, both adulterers, and maybe, therefore, the excuse for blowing up Nelson wasn't such a very good one.

As we passed through College Green I pointed out the statues of Burke and Goldsmith in front of Trinity, and I had a sudden memory of Goldsmith crowned with a 'pot' in one undergrad rag. I noticed that the equestrian statue of 'King Billy' (William of Orange), which used to face the College, was gone. It had actually been blown up by other enthusiastic patriots. I must say I missed King Billy, though his statue was a dreadful piece of bad art—one foreleg of his horse was nine inches longer than the other. But he was a rallying point. We used to march out of Trinity and circle round him to commemorate the Battle of the Boyne. That meant trouble between Town and Gown. King Billy was not neutral like Lord Nelson.

The same kind of little ragged boy selling newspapers as I remembered so well in my day was still in evidence, rather less ragged and selling not papers but coupons. This puzzled me until I found that everyone, rich and poor as in England, had the same amount of coupons, but to the poor in Ireland these were almost of no value. They couldn't afford to use them. So they tried to sell them to unsuspecting strangers—unsuspecting because it was soon quite clear that, as one shopkeeper put it:

"Shure nobody bothers at all, at all, about coupons in the shops. You can buy whativer you like widout thim."

We were staying at the Royal Hibernian Hotel, where I first stopped over forty years before. They had a new restaurant, and there were lifts which I didn't remember. What we found however, rather unexpectedly, was that the food was much too rich and the portions too large for us. We couldn't get through the courses. The waiters seemed to know the symptoms. They called it 'Englishman's Stomach'. This annoyed me, for as an Irishman I objected to having an Englishman's stomach. It was of course the result of the strict rationing we had been subjected to during and since the war. We didn't quite get over it before we left for London again.

I went into the Ulster Bank next morning to make sure my credit from London had arrived. The last time I'd been in the same branch was when I was Treasurer of the Dublin University Experimental Science Association in 1896, just fifty years before. I was living in memories.

It was a lovely summer's day, and I suggested to my daughter we should walk through the College on our way to call on Professor Henry Dixon, F.R.S., at the Botanical School.

I said to her as we turned in through the front gate from College Green:

"College porters pride themselves on remembering faces, but I'm sure no one could possibly remember me."

Inside the lodge there were two of them in the velvet peaked hunting caps that Trinity porters wear.

They looked at us, and, just for fun, I said:

"I don't suppose either of you would remember me."

"No, sir. Sorry, sir," the elder said. Then: "Wait a moment, sir. Yes, yes. I do remember you, sir. You're Colonel Abraham. You haven't changed much, sir."

This took me quite aback. It was so unexpected.

"But how d'ye know me?" I said.

"Well, sir, it's like this. I was in the First Leinsters, and you sent me with half of the battalion back before the third battle of Gaza because we were full of malaria. I remember you because one of our officers said you were a Dublin doctor. But you weren't popular, sir. We missed all the fun. We didn't like it."

I laughed.

"I don't suppose you did," I said, "but you weren't so lurid about me as the Australians I sent back at the same time because they were diphtheria carriers. They cursed me like hell. Their language . . ."

We smiled at one another, and then my daughter and I went on into the College.

"Well, I didn't expect that," I said to her, as we passed through the front quad.

Professor Dixon knew we were coming, and showed us round his magnificent laboratories. How different they were from the two poky little rooms in Regent House where I had worked. There was nothing familiar to me in them—nothing except, oddly enough, one thing: a framed photograph which the Professor had in his private room. I looked at it, somewhat surprised. It was the 1898 Natural Science Moderator group of five men: Sir Arthur Ball, who became Regius Professor of Surgery; William Dinsmore, later a Judge in Malaya; Charles Green, who ended up as Chief Inspector of Fisheries, Eire; Dr. John Laird, who was a distinguished physician in Bolton, Lancashire. I was the fifth, and all of them were dead except me.

Why had the Professor kept it? There must have been nearly fifty such groups since. Suddenly it dawned on me. It was in memory of Charles Green, one of his dearest friends. I made no comment.

While my daughter went with some ladies to Jammets restaurant and had a steak over which she became lyrical, I had lunch in the Senior Common Room with Professor Fearon of the Biochemical School. The Professor is a playwright as well as a scientist—a combination not uncommon in Dublin, where the humanities are still honoured and studied in spite of the pressure of technical education. I found we had many interests in common, outside science. Afterwards he took me to see the War Memorial Reading Room attached to the Library, with the statue of Lecky, the historian, outside. The reading-room had been dedicated to the memory of the Trinity men who fell in the First World War. There were over five hundred names on the marble memorial tablets, many of them of men I had known. What a waste it all seemed after the Second World War had proved the futility of the war-to-end-war!

We dined that night at the Kildare Street Club with Dr. Moorhead, the Regius Professor of Medicine, and Dr. T. P. C. Kirkpatrick, Registrar of the Royal College of Physicians. 'T. P. C.', as everyone called him, was the historian of the Dublin School of Medicine, a very lovable person, and one of the physicians to Steevens' Hospital. Professor Moorhead and I had been surgical dressers under Bennett, of Bennett's Fracture, in our student days. His bandages, I remembered, would never stay on, and Bennett in a moment of exasperation had once said to him:

"Mr. Moorhead, you'll never make a surgeon."

"Sir," replied Moorhead, "I'd hate to be a surgeon."

I reminded him of this, but he had forgotten it. We had a most excellent dinner. The wine was good, the food choice, the conversation interesting.

My daughter and I walked back through the quiet streets to our hotel in the softness of the night, very happy.

The next day was Sunday and we went to Morning Service at St. Patrick's Cathedral. We were taken there by the Principal of Alexandra College, Miss Holloway; and found ourselves rather conspicuously and a little embarrassingly in the pew of the Archbishop of Dublin, the

Most Reverend Arthur William Barton. However, when I discovered later that I had coached the future archbishop for the Boat Club in 1900, I didn't feel so conscious of *lèse majesté*.

After the service Mrs. Wilson, the wife of the Dean, took us through the Deanery and showed us a number of relics of Swift and Stella. Stories, she said, still lingered in the neighbourhood about the 'Ould Dean'. The one that troubled her most was that people said they could hear the Dean "shoutin' and yellin' and chasin' Stella up the back stairs" of the Dean's house. Several maids left on this account. Unfortunately for the authenticity of the story, these particular back stairs and the rooms above are quite recent, having been built by Dean Bernard only forty years ago. But that didn't stop people talking, and maids leaving.

Next morning we went on a tour round the College. The first thing I noticed was the extreme youth of the undergraduates. I remembered that when I was a freshman I thought I was a man. And now it dawned on me that I must have looked just like one of these lads I saw going to lectures. In my time it was the ambition of every junior jib (freshman) not to appear to be such, so he tried to buy an old battered cap and gown instead of the new rig-out that would betray him. I found the jibs in 1946 looked even more dilapidated than we had been—the custom evidently still persisted.

My old rooms were at No. 11 Botany Bay. These are the rooms described in my novel, *The Night Nurse*. We climbed the stairs to the first floor left, and found the outer door open. The 'skip' was inside. (A skip is a college servant in Trinity. He was in my time nearly always a pensioner from one of the Irish regiments.) We knocked on the inner door and he opened it.

"These used to be my rooms many years ago. Could I take my daughter in to see them?" I said, and a coin passed.

"Why, yessir, an' welcome."

So in we stepped into the familiar sitting-room with its old-fashioned grate, side hobs and a blower. The sitting-room had two windows looking on to the square nicknamed 'Botany Bay'. The two bedrooms opened into the sitting-room.

"We had no light except oil lamps or candles in my time," I said to my daughter. "We had no baths in college either. We used the old-fashioned shallow round tin bath-tub of Victorian days, now quite forgotten."

"They do have foine baths now, surr," interrupted the skip.

I nodded.

"I see you have plugged up the dunscope," I said as we were going out.

The skip looked puzzled.

"Dunscope, surr?"

"Yes. It's plugged up with paper," I said, pointing to a small circular hole through the wall from the skippery, so placed as to overlook the outer door. The hole was lined with a foot-length of iron drain-pipe, and it was this that had been plugged. Evidently its use was not known to the skip, nor probably to the present owner of the rooms. This had evidently changed since my time; dunscopes were now no longer required.

The dunscope is an invention of Jacobean days, used originally, as its name would imply, to avoid the unpleasant attention of tradesmen's duns. It had been found so useful for other things that it remained in use until after my time. Practically it is a cylindrical tunnel of about two inches diameter, pierced through one wall of an undergrad's rooms, in such a position as to command a full view of anyone rapping at the outer door. It is usually rather artfully concealed, and the visitor is, therefore, unconscious of the scrutiny to which he is being subjected before admission.

I was naturally very interested to see these old rooms of mine again after nearly fifty years; especially as this dunscope figured largely in an episode in *The Night Nurse*.

When we returned to the hotel we found that Sir Alexander Fleming had called and left a message asking us to dine with him and Lady Fleming at the Shelbourne, where they had just arrived. But we had to answer that we couldn't as we had booked seats for *Professor Tim* at the Abbey Theatre. We suggested instead that Fleming and Lady Fleming should also book for the theatre and that I would take them round Trinity next morning.

Professor Tim is not in the high tradition of the Abbey. I was more interested in the audience and the theatre than the play. The theatre was hallowed by the memory of Synge, Yeats and Lady Gregory; but the play was just a pleasant farcical comedy; and the audience a good-natured one out for a carefree evening. I recognised that I had been foolish to expect anything else. Fleming dropped us at our hotel on the way back; and we agreed to meet next morning in the entrance to Trinity at ten o'clock.

It was a lovely summer morning. We went first of all to the College Chapel; and I commented on the odd fact that three men who had attended as undergraduates there had each become famous afterwards for one poem and one poem only: Toplady for 'Rock of Ages', Lyte for 'Abide With Me', and Wolfe for 'The Burial of Sir John Moore'. Tate who wrote 'While Shepherds Watched their Flocks by Night' worshipped in the old Chapel demolished in 1790.

As we came out of the Chapel into the quad I told them that there was an ancient regulation allowing scholars only to play marbles on the steps. This seemed to amuse them.

We crossed the quad to the Examination Hall opposite the Chapel.

"Tomorrow is Commencements, and it is here you will have your honorary Sc.D. conferred," I said to Fleming, "so you'd better have a look inside."

It is a beautiful building with a fine organ, a lovely gilt chandelier which once graced the Irish House of Commons, a statue of Provost Baldwin and some excellent portraits on the walls: Ussher, Berkeley, Swift, Burke and others, not forgetting one of Queen Elizabeth the First, about which, as I have previously mentioned, there is a curious superstition. It is believed that anyone sitting under it in an examination is sure to fail. There is no rush, therefore, to be near Elizabeth, our Founder.

The Dining Hall is like that of the average Oxford or Cambridge college—a high table, long benches for the undergrads, portraits round the walls, panelling. In my time we used it for dining only, and each table was confined to certain years. There was a 'junior jib' (freshman) table, a 'senior jib' table for men who had passed their Littlego, a junior and a senior sophister table. In my time also we paid 11s. 4½d. English per week for our commons, this curious sum representing 14s. Irish before the Union.

"We'll dine here tomorrow night, complete with robes and decorations," I said to Fleming. "It's a 'gaudy-night'."

In the great Library, which, like the Bodleian and the Cambridge University Library, is entitled to claim a copy of every book published in the United Kingdom, we unexpectedly came upon Sir Herbert Eason, who was over to get an honorary M.D. He was being taken round by Dr. Smyly, the Librarian; and in honour of our two distinguished visitors the Library's unique treasure, the Book of Kells, was taken out of its case. We were allowed reverently to turn some of its lovely vellum leaves with their exquisite lettering and miniatures. This was a great thrill to me, for it is said to be the most beautifully illuminated book in the world; and looking at its loveliness one could well believe it. Someone in the group asked the Librarian what it was insured for.

"Insured!" exclaimed Dr. Smyly, quite shocked. "It isn't insured. How could it be? It is unique. Its value is inestimable. If it were destroyed nothing could replace it. So we do not insure it."

A visit to the Museum followed. This was described by Ruskin in *Sesame and Lilies* as the most lovely modern building in Europe, and by Osbert Lancaster as "one of the greatest masterpieces of the Gothic Revival". After that we went to the Anatomical Museum, where we saw the death masks of Swift and Stella. That completed the morning. Memories, memories, memories. I was full of them going back thirty, forty, fifty years.

*

I wanted to take my daughter to see the hospital I had used as the background for my novel, *The Night Nurse*, and the film *Nora O'Neale* based on it. I had not seen it since 1912, for the anger the novel produced then had made me shy of the staff and the place. Matrons of hospitals had condemned the book as immoral; but now all this was forgotten. The mellowing hand of time had made it seem very harmless. Instead they were just a little proud of it.

So we took a taxi to Steevens' Hospital, going along the quays, past the second-hand bookshops I remembered so well, past Guinness's Brewery, until we turned into Steevens Lane. As we drew up to the hospital I noticed that externally it had altered little, but the door in the wall with its barred peep-hole was gone—the door through which Fitzgerald followed Nora Townsend when he first saw her and fell in love with her. I regretted this change. But the clock in the tower over the arched entrance was still giving the time to the neighbourhood as it had done ever since 1735.

We got out of our taxi and walked under the archway into the quadrangle, and through the cloisters to the matron's room, where we were expected. There we met Dr. T. P. C. Kirkpatrick, the historian of the hospital, and with him we did a tour of the rooms and wards where I had been a Resident forty-six years before.

I wanted my daughter to see the Chapel, the incumbency of which had been endowed by Stella (Hester Johnson) whose name will ever be linked with Swift. She made her will in December, 1727, leaving a thousand pounds towards the chaplain's salary, stipulating that he read prayers every morning and preached every second Sunday in the Chapel.

And further my will is that the said chaplain shall be a person born in Ireland, and educated at the College of Dublin, who has taken the degree of Master of Arts in the said College, and hath received the order of priesthood from a Bishop of the Church of Ireland.

It is likewise my will that the said chaplain shall be an unmarried man at the time of his election, and so continue while he enjoys the office of chaplain of the said hospital; and if he shall happen to marry he shall be immediately removed from the said office and another chosen in his stead by ballot.

The chaplain also had to live in the hospital and not to "lie out of his lodgings above one night a week without the leave of the Governors".

The salary of the first incumbent, the Reverend Peter Cooke, was ten pounds per annum. After six years he asked that it should be augmented, and Swift, who had been present when he was appointed, spoke in his favour. So it was increased to twenty and later by another legacy to sixty pounds. He probably needed the money, for, in spite of the clause in Stella's will, he had married ten years after he became chaplain.

Apparently the Governors had not the same antipathy to married clergymen as the friend of the 'Ould Dean', and Swift himself can have had no objection, for he acquiesced in the recommendation that the salary should be raised. This rise seems to have satisfied the Reverend

Peter, for he held the chaplaincy for fifty-four years until his death in 1787.

I had hoped to show my daughter the quaint little Chapel. It had no architectural pretensions, but the fact that Swift had preached in it fascinated me. Now I learnt for the first time it had been turned into a ward, and the new Chapel, built in 1909, was at the north-east end of the hospital instead of the south-west.

The room I had occupied as Resident, and which Charles Lever, the novelist, had used before me, was now part of the X-ray department, a speciality which was non-existent in my time; and the Residents' mess-room was the Secretary's office.

One room was unchanged—the Library. This is something quite unique in an Irish hospital. It is the collection left by Dr. Edward Worth in 1732, consisting of some 4,500 books, including twenty-one incunabula, on medicine, surgery, botany, mathematics, history and classical literature. They are kept beautifully bound and housed in glass-covered bookcases, just as he left them.

Worth was an undergraduate of Merton College, Oxford; but owing probably to ill-health he never took his Oxford degree. In his will, however, he remembered Merton and left it £2,000 "for the endowment of postmasters of that College", an endowment which it still enjoys. A postmaster at Merton was a poor scholar who paid no fees. He corresponded to the sizars of Cambridge and Dublin. Worth was one of the founders of Steevens' Hospital, appears to have been a man of very delicate health, and died in 1732. The library he left to the hospital narrowly escaped being sold in 1800 when, after the rebellion of 1798, Steevens' was in low financial waters; but it is still there, and Dr. Kirkpatrick took us into the Board Room and displayed some of its rarities with the loving care of the bibliophile. Whether it should remain in the hospital now that its historian is dead is a question. Obviously it ought to be housed somewhere like the Trinity Library, where it would be known and accessible; but it is a part of the history of this quaint old hospital; it is beautifully preserved and its individuality would be lost if it were moved.

Next day, July 3rd, 1946, was the big day, the day for which we had come over specially: 'Commencements', the name given to the degree-conferring day at Trinity. I had to get into evening dress—white waistcoat, medals and decorations—by twelve o'clock, and go down to lunch in the restaurant at twelve-thirty. It was a bit shy-making until I noticed two groups of young men, with adoring relatives up from the country, also in evening dress, obviously going for their degrees, so it was not so bad as I had anticipated. The wife of the Regius Professor of Surgery, Mrs. McConnell, picked us up in her car and took us to the College.

It was a lovely summer's day, and Parliament Square was gay with figures in multi-coloured robes standing round in groups talking animatedly to friends. People were already crowding into the Theatre. My daughter had a special platform ticket, however, so I had not to worry about her. Instead I talked in the sunshine with one or two of my old professors and friends who still remembered me, until I was summoned, together with Sir Herbert Eason, Fleming, Canon Hannay (George Birmingham), Jack Yeats and other recipients of honorary degrees, to the Provost's robing-room. Here our gowns were handed to us. George Birmingham's and mine were scarlet with a deep blue border. Birmingham was wearing the gown that had belonged to Henry Irving, lent to him for the occasion by Laurence Irving, his grandson.

"It is the most beautiful of all the Dublin robes," he said.

Presently we were marshalled in order, and the multi-coloured procession moved across the quad and up the steps into the Theatre. I had forgotten how impressive this was. First came the ancient proctor's book, bound in brass carried by a porter, then the Senior Master Non-Regent, followed by the great silver mace carried aloft by the Steward. After this came the Chancellor, in this case Lord Iveagh, and then the Provost, Dr. Alton. The Masters and Doctors marshalled in order brought up the end of the procession.

We walked in this formation up the central aisle to the dais. The bachelors in arts, medicine and the sciences, awaiting their degrees, were seated in the front chairs. The undergrads, crowded up behind, were not as noisy as I remembered.

The Chancellor in his gold-braided robes rose from his chair and the familiar ceremony in the traditional Latin started. I watched the eager young faces of the newly-made bachelors of medicine, and my mind was full of memories.

The Library of Trinity College, Dublin

Sir Almroth Wright, aged 70. A drawing made for the Medical Research
Club by Mr. Francis Dodd, R.A.

Only two doctors were up for their M.D. It happened that one was a woman; and the undergrads, quick to notice this, started humming the 'Wedding March' as the two went forward together. Name after name followed monotonously, and I woke up with quite a start when someone behind me, looking at his programme, said:

"You're next."

In a sort of half-dream I remember shaking hands with the Chancellor, bowing to the audience and returning to my chair again. I had been admitted a Doctor of Literature. The ceremony ended with the traditional announcement by the Chancellor:

"Comitia solvuntur in nomine Patris et Filii et Spiritus Sancti. Amen."

Afterwards the Provost gave a sherry party in his house. I had never been there before, and was entranced with its beauty—the eighteenth century at its best. People in the grand salon said flattering things to me. It was all very pleasant. I almost believed them.

We dined in Hall that evening. The Regius Professor of Surgery and I met in the Senior Common Room, donned our robes and proceeded down to the Hall. I sat between my old Professor of Botany, Dr. Dixon, and Dr. Kirkpatrick of Steeven's, opposite Jack Yeats, the painter brother of W. B. Yeats.

It was a simple, beautifully cooked dinner, and the wines were superb. That is what one would expect, because the College had been buying its wines from the same firm of wine merchants in Bordeaux since the time of Charles II. We had some excellent music sung by the chapel choir augmented by the choir of St. Patrick's Cathedral. Speeches were short. The Provost said some pleasant things about my literary work. Between that and the wine I felt glowing all over.

Next day we spent calling on people to thank them for their kindness, and in the evening we went to the Gaiety Theatre to hear Sean O'Casey's new play, *Red Roses for Me*. It was an odd, difficult, beautiful play, a queer affair about a strike and Orangemen and Catholics, a Protestant clergyman, modelled I think on Dean Swift, and a strange old fiddler. I felt I should have to see it three or four times before I understood what the playwright meant.

*

N

The following morning we took the nine a.m. train from Amiens Street for Belfast and the North. How often I had taken that train at the end of term in the old days!

I wanted my daughter to see the historic country where her ancestors had lived for over three hundred years, and to meet some of her relatives still living there. She had seen the beauty of Dublin, felt the charm of the South. I wanted her now to sense the Ulster tradition, feel the loveliness of the Ulster scenery, visit the historic sites which her forebears had helped to defend, and understand the depths of emotion and the feeling behind the word 'Partition'. Just as Highlanders and Lowlanders are both Scots, so Ulstermen and Southerners are both Irish. But there is the same difference in temperament in Ireland as there is in Scotland, and unfortunately this is deepened in Ireland by the difference in religion. Living out of Ulster I try to be balanced in my cerebral cortex, but I often find to my surprise my hereditary emotional centres in the hypothalamus unexpectedly strong. So, as we passed over the Boyne on our way north, I reminded her of the story of William of Orange and the battle of 1690 which drove the Stuarts out of Ireland: and when we walked around on the ramparts of Derry, the 'Maiden City', I recounted again the story of the grim siege and the heroic defence that has held the imagination of historians ever since.

I showed her 'Roaring Meg', a silver model of which was presented to Sir Winston Churchill when he was made a Freeman of Derry. 'Roaring Meg' is the big gun still on the city wall which hurled defiance at the army of James II. In the Cathedral we handled the cannon-ball carrying the summons to surrender so contemptuously ignored.

The English have short memories. They forgive the people to whom they have been cruel. The Irish never forget, and I think my daughter understood this when I took her to Coleraine to see the Orangemen parade on the 12th of July to celebrate the anniversary of 'The Boyne'. The 'Lodges' were due to entrain at ten-thirty a.m. for Garvagh, where there was to be a gathering of 20,000 men, so we got to the station early.

The Lodges were already assembled at the railway gates, the men with their orange or purple sashes, each Lodge with a silken banner carried by two men in front, with two boys behind them holding the side ropes. Most of the Lodges had a fife-and-drum band. The drums were the main feature, especially the big drum which was often beaten with rattans so violently, and so enthusiastically, that the wrists of the drummers and the parchment of the drums became blood-stained before the day was done. There was a pipe band in kilts, for, of course, we're sib to the Scot. Some of the bands had a sort of uniform, but many of the Lodge members walking behind the bands wore hard hats or caps or even top hats.

The bands played 'Lillibullero' or 'The Boyne Water', 'The Girl I Left Behind Me', 'Croppies Lie Down', or some other tune associated with the occasion.

There was a religious fervour about it all that I had almost forgotten. I should have remembered this, for when the Ulster Division advanced to their almost total destruction on the Somme in the First World War they charged to the old Orange tunes.

Motoring round that afternoon, whenever we passed through a village we generally found the orange garlands strung across the road, and the big wooden frames covered with bright orange shavings—just as I remembered them from my boyhood. There, as before, were the panel paintings of William of Orange on his charger, the mottoes and the proudly displayed names of places famous for their historic associations. Only Queen Victoria had gone—replaced by a portrait of George VI. Brought up in the Harley Street area, my daughter found all this most intriguing. She was learning to be an Ulster-woman.

Before we left for London of course we had to see The Giant's Causeway, that extraordinary eruption of lava which solidified into thousands of columns of basalt on the North Antrim coast forty million years ago, and is now found projecting for some hundreds of feet into the sea before it disappears. The other end of the eruption is at Fingal's Cave on the Island of Staffa; and the legend is that Finn McCoul, the Irish giant, father of Ossian, challenged the Scottish giant, Ben-a-donner, to combat, built the causeway between the two places, defeated the Scot and then, to prevent a surprise attack after he'd won, destroyed the portion between Ireland and Scotland. Hence the name 'Giant's Causeway'. The columns of basalt are mainly irregular pentagons and hexagons interdigitating, made up of segments of one to four feet. There is, however, one perfect octagon, known as the 'wishing chair', which is supposed to be lucky. You sit on it and drink a little water from the 'wishing well' in front of it.

A charming young bride was there just before us. The old woman with a shawl over her head who had charge of the well offered her a cup of water.

"Drink it," she said, "and have your wish."

The girl gazed up with starry eyes at her newly-wed husband.

"I'm so happy," she said, "I've nothing to wish for."

The old woman looked at her slowly with her wise old eyes.

"Weel, ma dear. Can ye na wish it'll aye be so?" she said gently.

The girl's face suddenly became solemn and she drank, said nothing and moved away.

*

CHAPTER XXVII

MORE FAMOUS PEOPLE

THE WORST OF A HOLIDAY is the slackness afterwards and the mass of work that has piled up during one's absence. I had promised to write six articles for the *Sunday Graphic*, and needed to get down to this. There were decisions to be made for Heinemann's, there were patients filling up my appointment-book, there was trouble at the hospital. In addition, one of the articles I was doing would not come right. I revised it three times at the editor's request and had it retyped. Then in despair I refused to do any more to it. The result seemed awful to me, but, after it appeared, I met Lakin of the *Sunday Times* on the following Monday.

"I read your article yesterday," he said. "It was excellent."

So, obviously, the revision had been successful. I felt happy. I wished I could have felt equally happy about Sir Almroth Wright's *magnum opus*. After I came back from Ireland I spent a morning with him at St. Mary's, again discussing the book.

I found him, hunched up as usual in his chair, bending over a cup of coffee on the laboratory bench. He looked tired and weak. I knew he had just passed his eighty-fifth birthday, and I was afraid for him. I knew he couldn't last much longer, and I did want to get the book out before he died.

My difficulty was that if I gave him an estimate for publishing it and we began to set on that assumption, as soon as he had the galleys he would start rewriting; and, if it ever got to page proofs, he would rewrite again. He had the itch for perfection. Like every great artist he was never satisfied with his work and suffered heavily from after-inspiration.

There had been a broadcast about him a few days before; and various paragraphs like the one in the *Evening Standard* reminded the world that he was the discoverer of anti-typhoid inoculation as well as the original of Sir Colenso Ridgeon in Bernard Shaw's play *The Doctor's Dilemma*.

Shaw and he were friends, both Irishmen, both fighters. They scrapped continuously, but understood each other.

Coming back from interviewing the Professor, I saw in the early evening papers an announcement of the death of H. G. Wells. Heinemann's had published his last book, a most depressing picture of the future of humanity, coloured by his disappointment with life. This had distressed me, for his works had given me many happy, pleasurable hours in the past, before he ceased to be a novelist and began to think of himself as a major prophet.

*

The Kemsley Press has a pleasant custom of giving occasional lunches at which contributors to its papers can meet and get to know one another. I was at one of these lunches at Claridge's, in honour of Paul Gallico, the exuberant American whose *Snow Goose* had had such a great success. Large, rotund and jolly, he made a clever after-lunch speech, watched with rapt admiration by his tiny little wife. The technique was perfect. It is one in which Americans are much more successful than we are.

I sat between Frances Pitt and Marguerite Steen. It was an intense pleasure to me to meet Frances Pitt, for every Monday, for years during the war, I used to buy the *Evening News* specially to read her nature article in the train on the way to Bletchley. At the lunch I found she was just recovering from a fracture and had to go about on crutches, but nothing could daunt her cheerful outlook.

Marguerite Steen's work as a novelist I did not know, but I had read her masterly life of William Nicholson and I possessed copies of some of his colour work, so we had points of contact. The Reverend W. H. Elliott, whose weekly sermons were such a great source of comfort during the war, was of course well known to me. He had been my patient. Another guest, C. B. Fry, was a hero of my youth. It was strange to feel almost of his own age at this meeting. But the person who interested me most of all was Group Captain G. L. Cheshire, V.C. He was so different from the hearty R.A.F. bigmoustached type one associates with the Service. I watched his beautiful sensitive face with intense interest. It was obvious he was one of those highly-strung, quick-reacting persons whose body responds automatically more rapidly than one can reason. He knew what to do before he had time to consider how to do it. He was sure before he knew he was sure. I remembered that he had been a spectator when Nagasaki was devastated by the second atomic bomb, and I wondered if that was why he had resigned from the R.A.F. to work for the broken men of the Services. I knew he felt he had a mission and I hoped he would succeed in his quixotic action. But I wondered, watching him with the eyes of a doctor, if his body was not over-engined by his mind.

To grace the party came the young and beautiful Marchioness of Huntly, a daughter of Lord Kemsley. I was interested to meet her, as her husband had succeeded that wonderful old man, Charles Gordon, 11th Marquess, 'The Cock of the North', who used occasionally to call in of a morning at Queen Anne Street to consult me, and then walk on down to the House of Lords. He was at that time well over seventy. His idea of a fee was to pay me one Scots pound note, which my bank credited to me at 19s. 6d. As there was nothing ever the matter with him, I was quite satisfied. His physique for an old man was remarkable.

*

Nineteen-forty-six was the centenary of the discovery of ether anæsthesia by Dr. Morton of Boston, Mass., and consequently there were numerous meetings and articles to celebrate it in London. It is remarkable how quickly the discovery became known all over the world. It was something desperately desired and eagerly grasped when it arrived. Three weeks after Morton demonstrated its use at the Massachusetts General Hospital, Robert Liston, the Professor of Clinical Surgery at University College Hospital, had a patient on whom he proposed doing an amputation of the thigh, and he decided to use the astonishing new drug.

The patient, however, panicked on the operating-table, broke loose from the surrounding restraining students, fled down the corridor and barricaded himself in a lavatory. Here he was pursued by Liston, who was a big burly Scot. Liston burst open the door, seized the patient, carried him back to the theatre, had him anæsthetised by force and amputated the thigh in one minute. The man woke up later and refused to believe he had been operated on until they showed him the bandaged stump.

Towards the end of 1946, two matters of special literary interest to me occupied my mind. One was that my *Surgeon's Log* had gone out of print and a thirtieth edition was therefore called for. But publishers were painfully short of paper in England, and printing wages had been climbing steeply since the end of the war. A way had to be found to produce the work at a price that would be reasonable, and happily it was discovered that this could be done in Australia. I promised my publishers, Chapman and Hall, that I would write a new preface, revise the text and add an additional chapter at the end, bringing the ship home to Liverpool instead of leaving her in the middle of the Indian Ocean. So I re-read the book after an interval of twenty years; and then found that I should have to rewrite and tone down some of my impressions of the Japanese if I was to sell the work in Australia, where it had been popular as a prize book for schools for many years. Australians had no love for the Japanese. They had painful memories of the shocking brutalities perpetrated on them during the war.

The second was my decision to publish a life of the famous German scientist, Ehrlich, the man who invented '606'. There was now living in London a lady, Fräulein Martha Marquardt, who had been his secretary for the last fifteen years of his life, and she had written a biography of the great man in English. I felt that it was a unique book and should be published. Her style, however, was so Germanic that I knew the text would have to be thoroughly revised before it could go to press. I asked my daughter to undertake the task and Sir Henry Dale, then President of the Royal Society, who had worked in Ehrlich's laboratory as a young man, offered to write an introduction to the book. He also read it for technical accuracy, and we published it in this country and America. It was well received.

Success in publishing technical books depends largely on a flair for what the public wants on the part of the publisher, but still more on production and afterwards on salesmanship. A good technical book does not always sell itself. There may be more than one rival just as good. It is not like a novel—anything may happen there; for something quite unlikely may turn out to be a best-seller without any assistance from the publisher.

When I took over the Heinemann Medical Company, I was given an excellent production manager, Leslie Cavender. He really knew that side of the work. Several times before the end of the war he was called up for the Army; but each time, to my relief, he was turned down by the examining board. They never gave any reason, and I thought it was his eyesight, for he had nystagmus and was very myopic. Otherwise he seemed extremely fit. He was pink-cheeked, cheerful, bursting with energy. He ran up and down the stairs without effort, daily.

One Monday morning in March, 1947, when I arrived at the office I was told he was not well. He looked white. I suggested he might go home for the day, but he said he was feeling better; and after we had gone through the mail, he went to the outer office and started working at his desk. Two hours later I was called hurriedly. They said he was lying on the floor, unconscious. I found to my horror that he was dead.

I telephoned for an ambulance; and later the police interviewed me. I said I was sure that it was a coronary embolus. This was confirmed at the post-mortem, so there was no inquest. Even though I am a doctor and have seen this happen twice before, once at a public dinner, once at a meeting of a Medical Society, I was badly shaken. He was my friend.

I had to give a postgraduate lecture that afternoon to candidates working for the Diploma in Public Health (D.P.H.). I got through that. What had been much more difficult, I had to break it to his wife. Poor thing, at first she refused to believe me.

"But he was so well this morning!" she exclaimed increduously.

It was hard for her to grasp the fact that since the morning, when she had said good-bye to him on the doorstep, she had become a widow with four children.

Of course we saw that neither she nor they suffered financially.

A few days later I was watching Sir Geoffrey Keynes operating on a patient of mine. I have always had a great admiration for Keynes. He does two things supremely well: he is a brilliant surgeon, and his

N*

reputation as a bibliographer is world-wide. It is a most unusual combination.

We were talking casually while he was getting ready for the operation and this point came up.

"I love both my professional and my literary work. I wouldn't have had it otherwise," he said.

And to this I nodded in complete agreement.

I, too, had found my literary work added to the pleasure of my professional life, and also to the enjoyment of my rôle as a publisher. This latter part of my activities indeed was now exercising my mind very considerably. For the problem of whom to get to replace our production manager had become acute. Various names were suggested, none quite satisfactory. And then someone had an inspiration.

"What about Owen Evans? If there's anything in heredity, a son of Charles Evans should be just the right person."

I mentioned this to A. S. Frere, now Chairman of William Heinemann Ltd. He had been co-Managing Director with C. S. Evans and had been released from his war work with Ernest Bevin when Evans died suddenly. He jumped at the idea.

"Of course," he said. "Just the man. Why did we ever think of anyone else?"

So that was that. Thus commenced a happy association and a deep friendship which has lasted ever since. We settled down to a smooth collaboration; and my intuition proved correct. In March, 1950, Owen Evans, Charles's son, became a Director of the Heinemann Medical Company.

When he joined us in 1947, medical politics were much on my mind. We were in the throes of negotiating with the Socialist Government over the terms of the National Health Act; and I noticed one day that Baldwin was in the Club on one of his now infrequent visits to London He was sitting in his usual place in the gallery, under the picture of Sir Humphry Davy, talking to Sir Frank Smith, F.R.S. We had a Pilgrims' dinner that night, and I thought he was probably up for this, but found when I got there that he wasn't. I wondered then if it had anything to do with the proposed Health Service. So next day at the Club I asked one of his friends.

"No," he said. "He came up to dine with Attlee. They are old friends. Attlee was a bit lonely and wanted advice. For, as Baldwin said sardonically: 'When a man's been Prime Minister for a year, he hears his friends sharpening their knives behind his back.'

"Baldwin," he added, "is a great Englishman. He told me that his main reason for forming the Coalition Government in 1932 was that he was sure Labour was bound to come into office soon, and their best men needed to be trained before being allowed power."

That conversation pleased me, for I'd always admired Baldwin from the time he made his quixotic gift of £200,000 to reduce the National Debt, and was surprised that no one followed his example. There was something charmingly idealistic about the action that appealed to me intensely. Yet, in spite of his *naiveté*, he had his feet firmly planted on the ground. He thoroughly understood the psychological outlook of the man in the street. He once said:

"When the working man, lying comfortably in bed on a Sunday morning reading the *News of the World*, hears the church-bells ringing, he likes to think of the King going to church at Sandringham. It's the sort of king he feels confidence in. That's why Edward VIII had no real hold, and there was so little public opposition to his abdication."

There was nothing of mockery in this remark. Baldwin was a man whom most of his critics, and even his biographers, failed to understand because they were unfamiliar with his Methodist background. When that is taken into account it is easy to read his mind in his actions; for Baldwin had a deep religious sense of mission, and in everything he did he followed the dictates of his conscience and his belief in Divine Guidance. It is not an attitude of mind one generally associates with the politician; it puzzled many of his contemporaries; and it has puzzled most of those who have written about him since. But, if it is once appreciated, everything he did falls into line, and his complete honesty shines out.

A week later we had a shock. My wife and I had been to the St. James's Theatre to see a play by Clemence Dane, *Call Home the Heart*, one evening. When we got back to our flat we turned on the wireless and then, to our surprise and distress, heard that Sir Almroth Wright had died (April 30th, 1947). The morning before, his secretary, Mr. Dare, had been in to see me about his book, *The Principles of Alethe-*

tropic Logic, which I had at last arranged to publish. He brought me a letter written by the old man, saying he had been ill but was better, and asking me to go down to Southernwood, Farnham Common, Bucks, to see him about publication. In a postscript he added "They say I am better, but I doubt it". It seems he was right, for this was the last letter he wrote, and I have always felt honoured that he wrote it to me.

I went to the Royal Institution next day because I had been nominated a 'Visitor' for the following year, but I wasn't really interested. I kept thinking of the wonderful old man.

We had a memorial service for him at Holy Trinity, Prince Consort Road. It was taken by Canon Hannay, better known as George Birmingham, author of *Spanish Gold*, *General John Regan* and other books. They had been at Trinity, Dublin, together, and Wright had asked that the Canon should conduct his funeral service when his time came.

I sat with Sir Alexander Fleming, and in the church I saw Lord Iveagh, his old friend, and Lord Moran, the President of the Royal College of Physicians. The choir sang the Trinity hymn 'Abide With Me', and Canon Hannay read the lesson from Ecclesiasticus, "Let us now praise famous men." I felt happier after it.

Wright took his degree in Modern Literature when he was at Dublin. He had an enormous memory for verse—he could quote poems in German, French, Italian as well as in English; but he could not write simple English; and in his work he was constantly inventing neologisms, made up from Greek, which he said were necessary for clear understanding.

I was talking to Charles Singer, the historian, about this at lunch one day and asking him his opinion of Basic English, the method by which it was claimed one needed only 800 words to make oneself perfectly intelligible.

"You *can* manage to write in English using only eight hundred words," said Singer. "The New Testament has been rewritten in Basic English, but the eight hundred words do not include scientific terms. There's Ogden, the originator, over there. Let's talk to him."

Mr. C. K. Ogden, I found, was a medium-sized man in the early fifties, dressed carelessly in brown tweeds with a smooth oval face, a quiet voice, light blue eyes and thinning hair. He suggested we should dine together one evening, and then go to his house in Gordon Square to see his linguistic library.

So Singer, Ogden, Mr. Malcolm Letts the historian, Sir Arthur MacNalty of the Ministry of Health and I took two taxis, between us, to Gordon Square after dinner a few weeks later.

It had been a bright sunny day and the evening air was soft and pleasant in the quiet interval after the theatres open. Piccadilly Circus was just beginning to be a blaze of shooting colours. Gordon Square was quiet, deserted. Ogden said he owned two of the tall houses side by side. In these houses there were thirty rooms full of the most amazing collection of junk of every description I've ever seen. And when I say 'junk' I do not mean it in any derogatory way. The word was suggested by the extraordinary collection of objects we found in the rooms. There were books in thousands, books in every known language, and of all ages. They were in glass cases or piled on tables, piled on chairs and safes, piled up the staircases. Then there were musical boxes of all shapes and sizes, several large enough to play complete operas. In addition there were musical stuffed birds in cages. They sang when a button was pressed. There were dozens of antique clocks with moving figures that rang bells, clockwork statuettes, photos, engravings, china, marble-topped inlaid tables, cupboards full of all sorts of odds and ends, a picture said to be an early portrait of Shakespeare. I stayed to midnight and then tore myself away. Ogden seemed oblivious of time.

Some days later I had lunch with him and he explained the basis of his collecting. All the books, he said, represented something in acoustics or linguistics—even the musical boxes were part of the scheme to study sound. He said it was *accentuation* that made it difficult to understand foreigners.

I think there is something very important in that statement.

*

The death of the 6th Earl of Harewood in 1947 brought back memories to me—memories of his great-uncle, the 2nd Marquess of Clanricarde, probably in my time the most hated absentee landlord in Ireland, where he had an immense estate. It was said his life was not safe in

Connaught on account of his exactions; so he never went there. His agents were constantly shot at by 'Moonlighters'; life for them became intolerable; and eventually towards the end of the Victorian period the whole great estate had to be sold to the Congested Districts Board.

As it happened, when he got ill some time in 1912, Dr. Macnaughton, his usual physician, was away in Iceland, where he went annually for two months' fishing with Hall Caine, and he had asked me to look after his practice. I had heard lurid stories about the Marquess when I was a boy, so I was very interested to see the old man professionally.

He was living in a cold, miserable little flat in Harewood Place, Hanover Square; and when I saw him, he was huddled up in bed with obvious bronchitis—no fire and no amenities.

He asked me to write a prescription for his chest, and told me to use an old envelope, lying on the bureau, to save notepaper. He looked at the prescription. He then asked what it would cost, and wanted to know would it really help him. He said he could afford to see me only once at 10s. 6d.

I listened to all this, knowing he was an extremely wealthy man, wrote my prescription and left. I never saw him again; but I learnt from Macnaughton that he was a miser, that he was an expert of international repute on *objets d'art*, that he bought and sold china, miniatures, etc., and made quite a lot of money in so doing. It was a queer, macabre episode and stuck in my memory. None of his relatives would have anything to do with him.

But it seems that young Lascelles, coming home from the war in 1915, felt sorry for the old man and asked him to lunch at his club one day.

Hubert George de Burgh Canning, 2nd Marquess of Clanricarde, remembered this, and when he died he left his entire fortune, said to be over two million, to Lascelles.

There is a moral in this somewhere.

*

People saddled with Victorian furniture nearly always suffered from steel engravings of Landseer's 'The Monarch of the Glen' and Luke Fildes's 'The Doctor'. When my uncle got married three of his patients sent him framed copies of 'The Doctor' as wedding presents.

The centenary of the American Medical Association was in 1947. It was founded fifteen years after the British Medical Association (1832), and to celebrate the occasion they issued a postage stamp which had on it an engraving of Luke Fildes's famous picture. I asked his son, Sir Paul Fildes, about the original. He said it belonged to the Tate Gallery but it was hardly ever there. Sir John Rothenstein sent it round the country on exhibition and one could seldom see it in London. The copyright in the picture, he said, had lapsed. Agnews bought the tail end of it for five pounds. There never was any copyright of course in the U.S.A.; they could use it without fee; and his permission consequently had not been needed before they issued the stamp.

I asked Fildes who was his father's model. He said: "No one. It was a composite portrait."

Lots of doctors who knew his father used to sit in the chair. Sir Richard Quain, an ugly old man, thought he was the original. Some people said it was Sir William Broadbent. I had heard Sir Clifford Allbutt credited with it. Fildes told me his father built the room shown in the picture up to full scale in his studio; and he used to get up early in the morning to paint the faint daylight coming in as he actually saw it. The Victorians took a lot of trouble when they wanted verisimilitude.

"My father knew all the distinguished Victorian surgeons and physicians, especially Sir Frederick Treves," said Fildes, "so when, as a boy, I got an attack of appendicitis, Victor Horsley did the operation because Treves was away in South Africa at the time. Later, in 1901, the pain returned, for Horsley had only partially removed my appendix at the first operation, leaving the stump. I remember Treves standing at one side of my bed and Sir Thomas Barlow at the other. Treves said peevishly:

" 'I do wish Horsley would stick to his bloody skulls and leave bellies to me.'

"Old Tommy Barlow was a bit shocked at Treves's language.

" 'I hope, my boy,' he said to me, 'that you will keep to yourself any expressions of opinion of this kind made by Sir Frederick Treves.' "

Sir Victor Horsley, of course, was a magnificent brain surgeon, but he had specialised so much in this that he was lost in the surgery of the abdomen. I met him once only professionally. It was over his father,

John C. Horsley, R.A., the artist, who was then living at Tunbridge Wells, where as a young doctor I was doing a locum. He was very old, very stubborn and would have nothing except homœopathic drugs, of which I was completely ignorant.

Horsley telephoned that he was coming down to see him, and I was very worried because there was so little I could do or suggest.

I knew of Horsley's belligerency. He was always fighting something or somebody. He maintained long before anyone else that smoking caused cancer of the lung, and that alcohol in any form was a poison. He championed the suffragettes. He fought the anti-vivisectionists, who slandered him continually. He used to go to the annual meeting of the Fellows and Members of the College of Surgeons and violently attack the Council for not allowing the members any voting rights.

I remembered seeing him at one of these meetings: thin, pale-faced, restless, with tousled hair and the eyes of a fanatic. Carelessly dressed, he was totally unlike the picture one visualises of the bland, polished man of the world associated in the mind of the public with the name of a Harley Street consultant.

So when he came to see his father, I expected to be sharply cross-examined. Instead he was charming, very quiet. He thanked me for all the trouble I was taking.

"There's nothing really anyone can do for my father," he said. "Let him have his homoeopathic drugs. They can't do any harm. He will just fade away. Come and see me in London when you get back."

I said I would, but I was too shy. I never did. It is one of my regrets. The First World War started soon afterwards. He went out to Egypt and then to Mesopotamia. He insisted on walking about there without a helmet, and he died of heat stroke. It was only later when I started to read up the history of neurosurgery that I came to realise what a pioneering genius he was.

*

After the horrible winter of 1946–47 with its snow, frost and rain, its coal shortage, its gas and electricity breaks, we had a lovely summer. Our little house at Frinton, which we had been able to reoccupy the previous year when requisitioning was over, therefore proved a joy.

Week-ends were possible and one glorious month of sunshine made life seem all right again.

It was in the autumn of this year I first met St. John Philby, the European adviser of King Abdul Aziz Ibn Sa'ud of Saudi Arabia, a sturdy bearded figure with a legendary history of travel and adventure in the Near East comparable to T. E. Lawrence. We had mutual contacts, such as Allenby, Arnold Wilson, Clayton and Lawrence himself. We were familiar also with some of the same ground in Egypt and Palestine, and he knew some of my books. Every year or so he turned up in London for a month or two before returning to his palace in Mecca where, as a convert to Islam in 1930, he had his spiritual home. It is due to him that the great oil industry of Saudi Arabia now exists. The Arabian Government's revenue previously came largely from the Mecca pilgrimage. This averaged five million a year, but in the great world slump of 1931 it dropped disastrously, and the King was in despair over revenue. In this state of mind he consulted Philby, who replied:

"You are like a man sleeping over a buried treasure and complaining of poverty."

"What do you mean?" said the King.

"Your country is full of buried treasure. You are sitting on a gold mine," answered Philby.

He meant, of course, that oil was known almost certainly to be present in the King's territory. Ibn Sa'ud was aware of this, and it was only the fear of exploitation by Americans that had held back the wily old man, for the Arabs were then much opposed to any sort of European infiltration. They had seen, however, the wealth that had poured into Persia as the result of the revenues from oil, and they were tempted.

It was therefore largely on Philby's advice that permission was given eventually to explore. Whether this has been to the advantage of Saudi Arabia or not is very problematical. But there is no doubt of the oil being a gold mine. Saudi Arabia is now one of the richest countries in the world.

Talking quietly one evening after dinner, Philby told me this fascinating story. Later he published it in extenso under the title of *Arabian Days*.

*

CHAPTER XXVIII

DEATH OF A HOSPITAL

THE PERIOD OF AUSTERITY prescribed by the Chancellor of the Exchequer, Sir Stafford Cripps, to reduce the dollar deficit was now on us. Enamel ware disappeared from the shops. Coffee became scarce. The points system was extended. Potatoes were rationed. We groaned but endured.

There was a feeling that our Islands were overpopulated and that more and more people ought to emigrate to the Dominions. Many ex-Service men who had been caught up in the war before they had had time to think of a career were too restless to settle down; and many, including one of my nephews, with brilliant war records behind them, decided to emigrate to Canada. There, in the New World, they found opportunities awaiting them which they had tried unsuccessfully to discover in the old.

It was in fact a time when some of the younger generation seemed to lose faith in the future of Britain, and many of their elders, disillusioned by irritating restrictions which they thought peace would have done away with, talked pessimistically. My own fears about the future of medicine at that time did not help.

And then one day quite illogically, since it had nothing to do with the future of Britain or medicine, my spirits recovered—all because the thirtieth edition of my *Surgeon's Log* was issued, bringing the number printed to nearly half a million, and starting in me the itch to write again. It was a figure that made me regret I had not had time to write more than a dozen books in my lifetime. For, like many doctors, I have often toyed with the idea of writing detective stories round some Holmesian figure, based on one's medical knowledge of how to perpetrate a crime not too easily detected.

Crime has always fascinated me. I have known two murderers in my time, neither of whom a jury would have convicted; and, years ago, when Charles Evans suggested I should approach Sir Bernard Spilsbury and offer to collaborate with him in writing up his criminal cases, I was delighted.

Spilsbury interested me intensely. He was the most talked-of personality associated with Scotland Yard for over a quarter of a century. Whenever a murder or a suspected murder was being investigated, Spilsbury was the pathologist who did the post-mortem and gave evidence in the criminal court afterwards. He first became famous over the case of Dr. Crippen, and after that he was never out of the public eye. He gave his evidence quietly, marshalling the facts so clearly that whatever he said carried conviction to both judge and jury. He acquired the reputation of unshakable certitude. Counsel for the defence could not move him. Juries were hypnotised into accepting his conclusions as unanswerable. It was a very dangerous eminence. There is an uneasy feeling in the profession that he was sometimes too sure, that he erred on more than one occasion. I think he was wrong twice.

Charles Evans and I tried our best at intervals for years to get a text-book of Forensic Medicine, or at least an account of his criminal cases, out of him. Time and again we approached him, but each time he was adamant. He would not agree. And then one day I learnt that he had died suddenly in the solitude of his laboratory at University College. It was an unexpected end to a great career.

I think he must have been a lonely man in spite of his great fame; for the elder son to whom he was devoted had met with a violent end. It was in the middle of an air-raid, and some twenty of the Residents at St. Thomas's Hospital had just finished dinner. All had left the dining-room except two: young Spilsbury and a friend. They were lingering over their coffee when the bomb fell, killing both. Spilsbury never quite recovered from this; and when he developed angina pectoris I suppose he felt he had had enough. I knew then that I should never do that book on his cases I wanted to do so much. Someone else did it, I believe, later.

*

We were now in 1948; and the shadow of the coming National Health Service was falling across the hospitals. The era of the voluntary system which had worked for centuries was drawing to a close. That was inevitable. The hospitals were nearly all bankrupt. The cost of treatment, owing to the advances in technique and the elaborate scientific investigations now required to satisfy modern methods of diagnosis, had vastly increased. Repairs which had been urgent had been postponed owing to the war. Salaries had risen. The cost of food, drugs and equipment of all sorts had rocketed. Crippling income tax, surtax and death duties had dried up donations. The hospitals therefore could no longer carry on without Government subsidies; and that meant Government control.

Only the great teaching hospitals seemed to have any hope of surviving without the constant irritation of bureaucratic restrictions. And so, many of the smaller non-teaching hospitals began trying to creep under the wings of the teaching hospitals, by becoming attached to them in one way or another.

I had retired from the active staff of the Princess Beatrice Hospital in 1943, so no longer had any say in its future. But there was no age limit at the Lock Hospitals; I was still on the staff; and I was very much concerned about their future. The major hospital of two hundred beds was in Harrow Road. The smaller one, and the better known, was in Dean Street, Soho. The Harrow Road hospital had been requisitioned by the Army in 1940, but was now empty again.

The work of the Dean Street hospital had been carried on all through the war, though it was struck twice. It was in good working order and a great number of patients attended its clinics. With the acquiescence of my colleagues on the staff and the concurrence of the Board, I decided to approach the Middlesex Hospital to take it over. The two hospitals were within five minutes of each other. The Dean Street hospital was modern and beautifully fitted. It seemed an ideal combination. I discussed it with Lord Webb-Johnson, then President of the Royal College of Surgeons and Consulting Surgeon to the Middlesex. He warmly supported the idea; but the negotiations failed, to the loss, as it turned out eventually, of both hospitals, now involved in the political warfare going on.

Doctors are not as a rule much interested in politics. They are naturally conservative-minded. They have little faith in panaceas. They have seen too much of life to be affected by slogans. But they have also seen how poverty, low wages, bad sanitation, illiteracy, often accompany disease and crime; and they have none of the complacency of the Tory mind. At this time, however, we were all politicians, for we were in the throes of the controversy over the proposed National Health Service. Aneurin Bevan was accusing us of trying to sabotage the Act then before Parliament; and, in spite of ourselves, we had to become politically minded.

Nationalisation was in the air. March 5th, 1948, was the date on which the railways of the country passed from private to public owner-ship. *The Times* was full of regretful obituary notices from the chair-men of the great national railways; the Socialist press on the other hand dilated rosily on the dawn of a new golden age of which nationalisation was the god—two contrasting views neither of which has survived the test of time.

I was interested to read them, but such are the limitations of one's mind that, though I was worrying about my hospitals, I was tem-porarily distracted by memories of my early years in London produced by a much smaller notice in the *Daily Graphic*. This was an obituary of Jack Hassall, the originator of the pictorial poster.

Some readers may remember the famous picture of a jolly old salt, arms akimbo, prancing along the sands, and, underneath, the legend: "Skegness is so Bracing."

That was Hassall's first; it made his reputation, it made Skegness and it started a new art in Britain—the art of the picture poster. Dear old Jack Hassall, casual, careless, good-natured, just a boy who never grew up. No Saturday night dinner at the Savage was complete without Jack and his rapid drawings on sheets of paper pinned on the black-board. It was nearly always a Red Indian with great crow feathers that he drew, for Jack had been a farmer in Canada before he discovered he was an artist. He was a fine painter, none the less, apart from his poster work. 'Agincourt' and 'The Return of the Raiders' were shown at the Academy.

I can see him still in my mind, square-built, fair-haired, handsome, with bright blue laughing eyes. Generous to a fault, he was preyed on constantly by soakers, and had to live on a Civil List pension at the end. He had outlived his fame.

*

Temporary distraction of one's thoughts, however, does not last. I was deeply conscious, all through 1948, of the apprehension many of us felt over the form the National Health Service appeared to be assuming. We feared we were being dragooned into becoming civil servants, our liberty was being threatened, the personal relationship that existed between doctor and patient was being destroyed. I myself, after over forty years of voluntary service to my hospitals, felt very, very depressed about the future of the profession to which I had given most of my working life.

It was then that my love for the drama came partly to my rescue. The Mercury Theatre at Notting Hill Gate was a short walking distance from us, and we became interested in the work that Martin Browne was doing at this charming little theatre, producing mainly plays by poets. There we saw a revival of T. S. Eliot's *Murder in the Cathedral*, the play which started the happy association between the author and the producer of *The Cocktail Party* and *The Confidential Clerk*. There we saw that fascinating Irish play, *Happy as Larry*, by Donagh McDonagh, which included an obvious caricature of Sir William Wilde, the father of Oscar Wilde. It was there we also saw Martin Browne's production of James Bridie's play *Tobias and the Angel*. This reminded me of how much, years previously, I had loved *The Sleeping Clergyman*, with its pathological background, now so curiously up-to-date, about the discovery of a cure for poliomyelitis.

When, therefore, the Martin Brownes asked us to meet Bridie at their flat in Portland Court, we were delighted. James Bridie (O. H. Mavor, M.D., LL.D., in private life), was a big, square, blue-eyed, clumsily-built, stooping man with a shrewd Scottish face and a humorous mouth. He was quiet until he warmed up, and then he just let himself rip. After dinner he talked for the rest of the evening, telling funny stories about Glasgow doctors.

During the war he had rejoined the R.A.M.C., and was stationed at Purdytown, near Belfast, as a medical officer. He seems to have enjoyed himself there, for he said that the two people who really thought Belfast was a wonderful place were St. John Ervine and himself. This, I told him, was an astonishing understatement, since every man, woman and child in Belfast thought the same. When my wife and daughter and I left before midnight he was still talking.

That was the beginning of a friendship which lasted from that day until his death. I don't know anyone to whom I took such an instant liking as O. H. There was something unexpectedly affectionate about him which was quite out of keeping with his appearance.

He was elected to the Athenæum in 1940; but he told me, with humorous exaggeration, that he had always been afraid to go there. What he thought of doing was to get very drunk one evening and scandalise the place. I suggested we should go together, get tight and so break his hoodoo.

But I never saw him there. We used to meet often at the Garrick Club; and when he was rehearsing a new play I would walk round with him after lunch and sit in the wings of some deserted theatre, watching Alastair Sim go through the business with the company.

His plays always ended a little vaguely. Critics said he got tired before he finished them. I think that was not so. He admired Bernard Shaw immensely, and was much influenced by Shaw's dislike of the machine-made, neatly rounded-off plays of Pinero, Sutro, Galsworthy and Somerset Maugham. That, I think, was why he did not care over-much for *The Sleeping Clergyman*.

Felix Aylmer told me once that after Bridie finished *Daphne Laureola*, Edith Evans complained that he did not explain why, in the play, she left her husband for the chauffeur. On the way down from Scotland he rewrote the final speech, which she delivered with great effect.

"It sounds good, but I don't know what it means," she said.

"Neither do I," said Bridie.

He had a habit of buying houses, disliking them, selling them and going elsewhere, for no apparent reason. Once, however, he bought a house outside Stirling and found that the neighbouring farmer had a right of way across his front lawn. So, this time, he had a real reason for leaving. Actually he made money by his constant sales, as property steadily appreciated yearly after the war, and when he sold he always got more than he gave.

*

Gratitude for American aid to this country during the war, aid which was personified by Franklin D. Roosevelt, was given visual expression by the statue in Grosvenor Square unveiled to his memory one lovely morning in April, 1948. The 'Pilgrims' had a special stand allotted to them at the north-west corner of the Square close to the statue, and from this we were able to watch the whole ceremony. The statue showed Roosevelt standing erect. This, we were told, was by Mrs. Roosevelt's special request. The band of the Royal Marines was posted on one side of the draped figure, the band of the American Marines on the other. There was a special stand for Members of Parliament in the centre of the Square facing the statue. They looked a motley lot, some members wearing caps and short coats in an otherwise tall-hat and morning-coat assembly.

The King (George VI), the Queen and Queen Mary, the two beautiful young Princesses and the tall Duke of Edinburgh were on a special stand. Mrs. Roosevelt in deep black, looking very pathetic, unveiled the statue. The King laid a wreath and made a short speech which was relayed by loudspeaker. The American Ambassador followed, and made a long one. After this we were able to walk around freely, seeing at close quarters people whose names were much in the public mind at the time. I felt I was living history.

One of the outstanding figures of the time was Wavell. I had always had an intense admiration for him since the Palestine days; and I had watched, with pleasure, his successes at the beginning of the Second World War in the Libyan desert, felt sorry for his ungenerous treatment after the débacle in Greece, pleased when he was given the Vice-royalty of India and again distressed at the way he had been bundled out. He was now back in London as Governor of the Tower, and we were seeing him once more at the Club. He looked old and tired, however, and was very quiet. It was obvious to me that his real life's work was over, he was just living on; and I was not surprised to hear on the wireless one evening, two years later, that he had died peacefully at the Tower.

My wife and I had special tickets for the funeral service at Westminster Abbey, and, though I had an attack of my old enemy lumbago, I insisted on going, strapped up. There was a great crowd outside the Abbey watching the troops lining the route from Westminster Bridge, where the coffin coming by barge from the Tower was due to be landed.

The main aisle of the Abbey was packed with people, including many old soldiers of both wars. I noticed a few faces I thought I remembered dimly as we passed up. We had seats in the Poets' Corner, to which we were ushered by officers of the Black Watch, Wavell's old regiment.

Sitting in the quiet of the Abbey, we could hear in the distance the pipers playing 'The Flowers of the Forest' as the procession, moving slowly and solemnly, approached the West Door. The great congregation watched silently as the cortège moved up the aisle, six men of the regiment carrying the coffin on their shoulders.

It was a beautiful service. Outside, the bugles sounded the 'Last Post' when it ended; and then followed 'Reveille'. A very great soldier had been laid to rest.

*

In spite of all my other interests in 1948 my mind kept harking back to the National Health Service and its effect on the quality of the work we were doing. In retrospect I think now that perhaps I took everything too much to heart. Things are never as bad as one fears. At the time, however, I felt that doctors were not good, fundamentally, at defending themselves against possible aggression. Their origin in the Middle Ages from the priesthood, and their connection with the Church down to the time of Queen Elizabeth the First, fostered the feeling that their work was a vocation and haggling over terms of payment was almost unworthy of their calling. The doctor's hood, which is now an ornament, was once the receptacle for alms of thanksgiving to the monk who relieved suffering. The doctor's gown is a relic of his monastic origin. A monk skilled in the healing art was sometimes permitted by the bishop of his diocese to break his vows, leave his cell and go out into the world to heal the sick. It was a privilege which could be granted, refused, or rescinded. That is why the Archbishop of Canterbury can still give the Lambeth Degree in Medicine, and why the Dean of St. Paul's claimed the right to license or refuse to license doctors in the City until the time of the early Georges.

The monk charged nothing for his services; and down through the centuries the staffs of the voluntary hospitals did likewise. Now suddenly, by an Act of Parliament, this long tradition of voluntary

service disappeared in a night; and we all, or nearly all, became paid
servants of the State. It was a wrench.

Many of the older men resigned; but I felt I could not. The future
of my surgical hospital, the Princess Beatrice, was in the safe hands
of my colleague, Mr. Lawrence Abel. But the Lock Hospital was a
different matter. I had been associated with the place for over forty
years, and I felt I could not desert it at this critical time. The hospital
had a long historical tradition behind it. It stemmed from the old
lazar-houses of the Middle Ages, when Lock Hospitals sheltered lepers,
and not only lepers but all those derelicts covered with the foul ulcers
of untreated scabies, then an incurable disease, as well as other outcasts,
their faces mutilated by ravages of lupus or the cancerous spread of
rodent ulcer—all loosely diagnosed as leprosy.

Outside each lazar-house were two large wicker baskets filled with
rags, tow, wool, etc.; and with the contents of these baskets the patients
wiped their sores clean before admission. The baskets in France were
called 'Les Loques'—the rags—and in Norman England came to be
known as 'Les Lock' in consequence. The old 'Les Lock' chapel for
lepers with this inscription on it was still in existence in Southwark
until comparatively recent times. Towards the middle of the fifteenth
century leprosy was rapidly declining in Europe; and when the great
pandemic of syphilis started in 1495, after the return of Columbus from
America, the lazar-houses were transferred to the use of venereal disease.
It was in this way the name 'Lock' became associated with venereal
disease.

There were eleven Locks in London when this happened. These
had been reduced to two in 1720, one in Kingsland, North London,
for women, one in Southwark for men. Both of these were under the
care of the Governors of St. Bartholomew's Hospital; and there is a
tradition that Percivall Pott got his fractured leg returning from the
Lock Hospital in Southwark to St. Bartholomew's.

Both hospitals were old and costly to maintain, and St. Bartholomew's wanted to get rid of them. They were closed down therefore
in the reign of George II; and patients were admitted instead into
Bart's. There were in consequence no Lock Hospitals left in London.
This was particularly felt in the West End, which was now growing
rapidly. St. George's Hospital at Hyde Park Corner had been opened

in 1733 for the treatment of patients, but there were no facilities for the cure of venereal disease anywhere outside the Royal Hospitals of St. Bartholomew's and St. Thomas's.

It was this deplorable state of affairs that induced William Blomfeild, one of the surgeons at St. George's, to think of starting a Lock Hospital in the West End. He was Surgeon to Frederick, Prince of Wales, the son of George II, and he was thus able to collect around him a number of philanthropic peers and wealthy commoners, and so start a hospital in Chapel Street, close to St. George's, just off Grosvenor Place.

In this way the London Lock Hospital was founded in 1746.

The area around was then largely waste land infested with footpads; but when the ninety-nine-year lease was nearly finished the whole nature of the district had changed. So, when the Governors of the hospital asked for a renewal of this lease, it was refused by the Grosvenor Estate.

The Governors, mortified at the refusal, determined never again to take a lease. They looked around and finally chose a freehold site of four acres on Westbourne Green, where the famous actress Mrs. Siddons had had a cottage. This they bought from her executors, and on this they built the new Lock Hospital which was opened in 1842.

Later, finding out-patients would not go so far from the centre of London, they bought another site in Dean Street, Soho, in 1869. There were thus two hospitals with the same title under the same management, and that was how things stood when war was declared in 1939.

The hospital in Harrow Road was commandeered by the Military during the war, as I have previously mentioned, and the work of the Lock concentrated in Dean Street, Soho.

This was the state of affairs when the National Health Service came into being, and the two hospitals came under the administration of the North-West Metropolitan Regional Hospital Board, over two hundred years after their foundation. That turned out to be a fatal day for the Lock Hospitals. The Harrow Road buildings were in bad repair, the necessity for a large number of beds for the treatment of women was much less acute, and accordingly the site, worth anything up to £200,000, was turned into offices for a section of the Board.

To me this brought a sadness, for it terminated many associations. I had been house-surgeon there; I had been registrar; I had worked with Fleming on the pathology of the diseases there. Later I had been appointed surgeon, and I remembered the children's wards we had started, the maternity department we had been so keen about, the babies we had delivered free from disease, the jolly Christmas parties we used to have. I missed all that. But I was satisfied it was necessary, and had no grievance. We carried on at Dean Street, busy, doing excellent work.

For the time being, therefore, all seemed well. We were allowed to treat patients exactly as before, except that we were now paid for the work the medical staff had been doing voluntarily for over two centuries.

I was pleased and happy that it had all been arranged so smoothly; I was pleased that I had been allowed to stay on as Senior Surgeon until the hospital was securely on its new course; I was contented, able to relax and pursue some of my other interests with a quiet mind.

But there was an undercurrent. Many people thought that a hospital known to treat nothing but venereal disease labelled patients, and made them disinclined to go there for treatment. They thought that this could be done better at a general hospital, where no one would know what was wrong with them, and that the Lock Hospital, therefore, was not only non-essential but a hindrance to successful treatment. It was a logical view and appealed particularly to the tidy bureaucratic mind. The obvious corollary therefore was: the Lock Hospital should be closed down. So in their wisdom the North-West Metropolitan Regional Hospital Board decided they would close it down.

But they had overlooked many things, and they had misjudged human nature.

The hospital in Soho was situated in the midst of a foreign population which had looked upon it as their hospital, when they were in trouble, for generations. As the *Lancet* pointed out:

The particular area which the Lock Hospital serves happens also to be a hotbed of venereal infection, and so is the surrounding district. It is an area where foreigners predominate . . . it is the heart of the region frequented by the prostitutes of the West End. Few of these people will travel for treatment even if they will attend at all, and there is no similar treatment centre within easy reach. This neighbourhood is a very special problem.

To the argument that patients would much prefer admission to wards in a general hospital not labelled V.D. the *Lancet* replied:

This argument, however, appears to be more convincing in theory than in practice. Actually the patient will be a great deal happier in a special hospital than in one where the nurses and other patients regard him as unclean.

Finally the *Lancet* suggested that the hospital should be turned into a postgraduate training school for venereology. Following this leader, a former Inspector of Venereal Disease Centres to the Ministry of Health weighed in, condemning the closure. Then the *British Medical Journal* came out with the statement that "To remove the London Lock Hospital from Dean Street would be an act of medical vandalism". *The Times* and other papers next took the matter up. The fat was in the fire. The Regional Board, alarmed by the outcry, drew in its horns and the hospital was saved.

But the bureaucrats were just waiting. They waited for a year, and then politely retired me from the staff, a thing they were perfectly entitled to do since I was nearly ten years over age under the new regulations.

They waited a little longer. And then they struck again—in the following summer. They said there was no need any longer for a special V.D. hospital. Patients with venereal disease, owing to the rapid cures produced by penicillin, were now adequately looked after by the general hospitals; and the Lock Hospital's building could be much more usefully employed to house the West End Hospital for Nervous Diseases, which had been bombed out during the war.

It sounded convincing. I saw that to fight it would be just a repetition of the former struggle. I felt that the press would not again give the same publicity to the defence as they had previously done. We were no longer 'hot news'. I was tired. So I did not again attempt to rescue the place.

Perhaps I was wrong. Perhaps I might have been able to organise a

Postgraduate School in this historic hospital for students from the Empire and Commonwealth, as suggested by Sir Wilson Jameson, then Principal Medical Officer to the Ministry of Health. Perhaps if I had been younger I might have saved it for a second time. Perhaps.

Anyhow it died after over two centuries of voluntary, almost thankless, service to those unfortunates whom the world generally passes by on the other side.

The records of the hospital, complete from 1746 to 1948, were of course of priceless historical medical interest. They carried in their pages much history of contemporary charitable endeavour during the eighteenth and nineteenth centuries. Great names appeared in their pages as patrons—princes, peers, painters, poets. Handel gave the hospital the proceeds of oratorios, Garrick and Rich of plays, Van Der Gucht of pictures. Miss Linley, the future wife of Sheridan, arranged concerts. Famous surgeons gave their services voluntarily: three generations of Lanes, to whom St. Mary's Hospital owes so much, two Colsons and many others.

I was afraid these records might be lost or sold as waste paper, by a Board devoid of any historical feeling; so with the help of Sir John Charles of the Ministry of Health I rescued them; and they, with a portrait of the founder, William Blomfeild, are now in the safe keeping of the Royal College of Surgeons in Lincoln's Inn Fields. Some day I hope the history of this unique hospital will be compiled from the yellow, faded Minute Books written in the careful copperplate handwriting of former forgotten secretaries.

*

CHAPTER XXIX

DOCTORS AND WRITERS

TIME MOLLIFIES MEMORIES. We as a nation have a great gift for compromise. The National Health Service has proved itself on the whole. By a process of trial and error we have found out some of its weak spots. Defects have been remedied and will continue to be remedied. For the Health Service is now part of our rapidly developing social conscience. It has separated need from charity or direct payment.

The old voluntary hospitals did wonderful work in their day; but many people were ineligible for treatment except as private or semi-private patients. The family doctor also had to charge for his attendance, and often in the past the fear of crippling bills prevented patients getting early and adequate treatment. The National Health Service has ended this fear. It was the only way also in which Exchequer funds could be made available to meet the enormously increased expenses of running hospitals, with all the advantages of the latest discoveries in medical science.

I can see this clearly now in retrospect. But at the time I did not see it; I did not think so; I was sore and angry at the closure of my hospital. And as a relief I threw myself into writing again.

I was talking to George Birmingham casually one day on these lines, telling him how I had once had ambitions of becoming a playwright; and, as a novelist and dramatist himself, he naturally understood and sympathised with this.

"It's only a pipe dream now," I said. "It will never happen. But I've still got my dream."

George Birmingham must have thought I meant something more than I said, for he suggested later that I should have myself put up for the Garrick Club, the meeting ground of so many dramatists and actors.

I have been grateful ever since for the suggestion, because there I have met some of the most charming people in the world. Though it did not stimulate me to try playwriting again, it made me many new friends and gave me the opportunity of meeting Bridie when he came to London.

At the Edinburgh Festival, then in its second year, my daughter and I saw a lot of him. He was stopping at the North British Hotel, and Eric Linklater came in one morning while we were calling on him. They chaffed each other unmercifully. It was obvious they were great friends.

A few days later I was Linklater's guest at the Scottish P.E.N. luncheon. Dylan Thomas and Richard Church were the lions. Linklater was in the chair and made a charming speech of welcome to us. Thomas, unfortunately, was in one of his peevish moods, and complained bitterly of the neglect of poetry in Britain. I murmured a few words of thanks. Bridie said nothing most successfully.

Bridie always fascinated me. I don't know why. He was no beauty. He could be very rude. But he had the heart of a child; and all the wonder of a child would sometimes creep into his blue eyes. Then he would stare through you, oblivious, seeing visions. Something of this suffused all his plays. His friends called him O. H., and O. H. he was to me until his sudden death at the age of sixty-three. I still feel sad when I think I could have made his acquaintance so much sooner. Bridie just walked straight into my heart. There are people like that. I miss him.

Another friend that I miss is Sir Alexander Fleming, the discoverer of penicillin. I was Surgical Registrar at the Lock Hospital, Harrow Road, a few years after the Wassermann Reaction became an essential part of the diagnosis of syphilis; and Ernest Lane, who was then Surgeon to St. Mary's Hospital and Senior Surgeon at Harrow Road, had Fleming appointed pathologist to do the blood tests.

Fleming was a Lowland Scot, I was an Ulsterman and we understood each other. We used to do a modification of the Wassermann which we called Fleming's Reaction. It was simpler but not as reliable as the standard Wassermann; and Fleming, with his love of accuracy, discarded it during the First World War. He resigned from the Lock in 1919 before I came back from Egypt, and I saw less of him in

'James Bridie' (Dr. O. H. Mavor)

Sir Alexander Fleming

consequence; but when we met it didn't seem to matter how long or how short the interval, 'Flem' was just the same. He was working then under Sir Almroth Wright; and when I went to call on the 'Old Man' there was 'Flem' in his laboratory, bending over his microscope working away patiently, unobtrusively. No one took much notice of him, or indeed of anyone else, when the 'Old Man' was about, talking brilliant sense, and sometimes brilliant nonsense; for every light paled in the area surrounding Wright, and everyone, including Fleming, felt that it should be so.

"Discovery comes to the mind prepared" was one of Pasteur's dictums. Fleming used to say, half in earnest, that his discovery of penicillin was accidental. It was not. He was working on naturally occurring antiseptics when he discovered Lysozyme, a substance dissolving bacteria, which he found in tears and in nasal secretions. And it was noticing dissolved colonies of staphylococci on a Petri dish, one day, that drew his attention to the fungus which had accidentally contaminated the culture he was growing. Anyone else would have thrown this contaminated culture away. Fleming, because he had been working on Lysozyme, did not. His curiosity was aroused by the fact that the fungus also dissolved away colonies of bacteria; and he wanted to find out why. In other words, his mind was prepared.

So he subcultured the fungus, a blue mould named Penicillium Notatum, again and again, and made fluid extracts from these cultures which he called 'Penicillin'. But he could not concentrate the substance, and his solutions were too weak, too impure and too easily destroyed by alkalis to be of much use. As he said to me a little plaintively:

"I am a bacteriologist, not a biochemist."

He wrote a paper for the Royal Society on the subject, which attracted no attention at the time; but, with the stolid obstinacy of the Scot, he would not give up. He never allowed the cultures to die out; and it was from these cultures that, ten years later, Florey and Chain were able to produce the concentrated penicillin which revolutionised the treatment of so many diseases, and gave a new therapeutic agent, the first antibiotic, to the world.

Of course, after the greatness of the discovery had been grasped, Fleming was overwhelmed with honours. He was knighted, he shared the Nobel Prize with Florey and Chain, he was elected F.R.S.,

o

and Universities all over the world vied with each other to do him honour.

At the Athenæum there is a regulation known as Rule 2, by which candidates can be elected, without the usual long years of waiting, if they are "persons of distinguished eminence in Science, Literature or the Arts, or for their Public Services". For them, if elected, there is no waiting.

When Fleming's name was suggested for this honour, I had the great but easy privilege of proposing him before the General Committee. And under this rule he was elected in 1948.

To celebrate, he suggested he should give a small dinner and I should choose the menu. We had that dinner and I made sure it would be an excellent one. The guests were Sir Ernest Rock Carling, Consulting Surgeon to the Westminster Hospital, Dr. Thomas F. Cotton, the heart specialist, and myself. We four had a very happy evening. Fleming was his usual charming diffident self. No side. No ballyhoo. Just 'Flem'.

That is how I like to remember him.

*

It is a common belief that people whose interests in life are scientific can have little appreciation of the arts, of literature or of music. This may be so to some extent in pure science, but it certainly is not so in medicine, where the human touch is so vastly important.

Many of my medical friends are devotees of music and the ballet, some are painters, some, usually surgeons, are sculptors. I for my part have always been fascinated by the drama and enjoyed the company of dramatists and novelists. One dramatist in whom I have taken a personal interest for years is Denis Johnston. His grandfather, James Johnston, was my godfather and a second cousin of my grandmother, Sarah Johnston; and Denis was a small boy in Dublin when I was an undergrad. It was the ambition of his father, Mr. Justice Johnston, that he should follow him in the law, and he was called accordingly to both the Irish and the English Bar. But he did not love the law enough. I remember one luncheon party at the old Grand Hotel, Trafalgar Square, when his father and I tried hard to persuade him to stick to it. This must have been about 1920. He had just come down from

Cambridge, where he had been President of the Union, and his father had visions of his becoming another Edward Carson. But he refused. He said he wanted to be a writer. I felt with his father at the time that he was making a mistake: writing is such a chancy job. But the success of *The Moon in the Yellow River* made me see that he was right and we were wrong. Writing was his *métier*. I learnt from this never again to attempt to thwart some inborn instinct, even if it seems foolish. For if you love what you have chosen to do in life nothing else matters. And if you are a writer the joy you get out of it is the greatest possible inducement to continue at it.

One of the most prolific authors of recent years was Edgar Wallace. Many people believed it was impossible for him to have produced the amount of work he did. They said he must have had 'ghosts' writing for him. His very charming daughter, Pat Wallace, the wife of A. S. Frere, the Chairman of the Heinemann Companies, was dining with us one evening, and when I mentioned this persistent rumour she was rightly most indignant. She told us then exactly how he did his work.

He woke at seven a.m., she said, and read all the morning papers in bed. Then he got up, donned an elaborate Turnbull braided dressing-gown, and pulled on a pair of mosquito boots which he said prevented him feeling draughts. He hated draughts. Breakfast was at nine a.m. sharp; and everyone in the family had to be punctual. Shortly after nine his secretary, Graves, who was reported to be the fastest typist in London, arrived; and they discussed the racing news and made their bets with 'Duggie'. Then Wallace, very reluctantly, did his letters and dictated articles.

Lunch was at one o'clock, and all sorts of people used to blow in; for he kept open house for actors, editors and his friends. In the afternoon he dictated his stories to a dictaphone. He had two of these, and he often ran two stories at one time. Over each dictaphone he had a large sheet of cardboard with a list of the characters in each separate story, so as not to confuse the names.

His secretary would bet against the number of cylinders he could use in a day. The secretary would say he could do eight. Wallace would maintain he could do twelve. That kept him at it.

He usually went to a theatre in the evening; and after the play was

o*

over people dropped in until about two a.m. He kept a night foot-man from eight p.m. to seven a.m. This man's duty was to prepare tea at any time for Wallace and his guests. He did the ordering by pushing a bell concealed under his table. He slept from two a.m. to seven a.m., and then the routine started all over again. He wrote *On the Spot* in three days, after ruminating over the details for six days crossing the Atlantic. He was of course a phenomenon unequalled by anyone except perhaps Dumas *père*. Dumas claimed to have written twelve hundred works, and really did employ 'ghosts', probably because dictaphones had not been invented in his day.

*

Medical societies where doctors meet to discuss matters of mutual interest date from the middle of the eighteenth century. The oldest in England is the Medical Society of London, founded, as I have mentioned before, by the Quaker physician, Lettsom, in 1773. Because I had written a life of this famous doctor, the Society some years later made me a Vice-President. This was an honour I much appreciated. On April 29th, 1948, my wife and I had been to the private view of the Academy, where the ladies were wearing what was then called 'The New Look'. When we got home, to my surprise, I found a message from the President asking me if I would deliver the Lettsomian Lectures for 1949. These Lectures were founded in honour of Lettsom, and it is a definite distinction to be asked to give them. I was immensely pleased. I almost replied 'Yes'; and then I began to think. It meant giving three lectures on some subject of growing importance in surgery. Could I do it? I had been forced to give up my active surgical life after my operation some years before. Could I therefore do anything original for the Society worthy of the honour? No! I thought not. So I declined. But I felt a warm glow of satisfaction that I had been asked for days afterwards. Actually the lectures were given by Sir Horace Evans that year, and so the Medical Society of London scored.

Instead, I agreed to deliver the Lloyd Roberts Lecture for 1948, following Field-Marshal Montgomery, who gave it in 1946, and Sir Harold Nicolson, who gave it in 1947. This was an annual affair in memory of a Manchester doctor, Lloyd Roberts, but no one in

London seemed to know much about him. I saw Sir Robert Hutchison one day at the Athenæum, told him I was giving the lecture, and asked did he know anything of the man.

"Yes," he said, "a little. I gave the lecture once. I thought at the time that Lloyd Roberts was a very conceited man to found two lectures, one in London and one in Manchester, in his memory. Nobody in these lectures takes the slightest notice of him or his memory—so you needn't."

This seemed to me rather rough on Lloyd Roberts. After all it was his money that endowed the two lectures; there must be something curious about a man who would do this; and so I decided to burrow into his history. And the more I did the more amused and interested I became. For Lloyd Roberts was an eccentric, a 'card', a character straight out of the pages of Samuel Smiles and *Self Help*. So much so that I made up my mind that my lecture, at any rate, would be about the man himself, and the times he lived in.

He was, in fact, a grand subject, for he practised medicine from the end of the Crimean War in 1857 till 1920, two years after the end of the First World War. And when you think of the enormous difference in the outlook and in the practice of medicine between these periods you will see what a really magnificent platform I had to talk from.

Lloyd Roberts started life as an errand boy in a chemist's shop. He ended it as a consultant who had an immense practice, made a great fortune, was an expert on art, a connoisseur of silver and a very knowledgeable bibliophile. He was born in 1835 at Stockport, two years before Queen Victoria came to the throne, and one year before Dickens drew his inimitable picture of the medical student of the day, Bob Sawyer, in the *Pickwick Papers*. Anæsthesia was new when he was a student. He heard of a man named Lister when he was thirty-five. He was forty-seven when Koch discovered the tubercle bacillus. He heard of Röntgen Rays when he was sixty, the spirochaete of syphilis when he was seventy; and he was seventy-four when Ehrlich gave chemotherapy to the world by inventing '606'. When he was eighty he probably heard of hormones and vitamins, but I doubt if he understood their significance. He practised up to a month before his death at the age of eighty-five.

Many were the stories told of him. He described himself as "a general specialist with a leaning towards women". He was, in fact, a gynæcologist. When asked once by Sir John Bland-Sutton to define gynæcology, he said:

"Anything in a woman that is operable or lucrative."

That sounds cynical, but patients said it did them good merely to see him. They loved him, and no one loves a cynic. He was a born healer. He had an instinctive insight into human frailties.

"There are two ways of getting on," he used to say to his students. "You can be clever or you can be kind. Well, you can always be kind."

Another of his remarks to the general practitioner was:

"Be sure and take off your overcoat in a patient's house. If you're only there a few minutes they will feel you're not in a hurry."

He never walked a step if he could help it. He went about in an old-fashioned single-horse brougham, sitting stock upright, top hat perched jauntily on the back of his head and with a plaid shawl over his shoulders on cold days.

One story about him got eventually into *Punch*.

Coming back by train to Manchester after a country consultation he found a brother physician in the same carriage.

"How did ye get on, laad?" he said in his broad Lancashire accent.

"Very badly," replied the physician gloomily. "Very badly. Spent all the day going to see my case, and all I finish with is eleven guineas. How did *you* do?"

"Oh, I got seventeen pounds, fourteen shillings and threepence-ha'penny," said Lloyd Roberts.

The physician stared at him.

"What a queer fee!" he exclaimed. "Why did you charge that?"

"It was all they had, laad. All they had," replied Lloyd Roberts.

Of course that was a leg-pull, but you can see what a lovely subject he was for a lecture. I revelled in it. I called it 'Victorian Doctor', and when I had finished I felt I had done something to revive the memory of a very delightful personality.

Going round to my consulting-room after the lecture I heard a disturbing rumour which rather damped my satisfaction. It was that there was something wrong with the health of the King, George VI. The rumour turned out, unfortunately, to be true, for four days later it was officially announced that the circulation in his right leg had become so impaired by atherosclerosis that he might develop gangrene. I looked at the signatures to the bulletin, that Tuesday morning, and knew from one on it that an operation to increase the circulation was being considered.

"That means," I said to my wife, "that the visit to Australia and New Zealand they have been arranging for months is off. How very disappointing!"

It will be in the memory of most that an operation was done, that it was successful, that the King recovered and the Australian proposal was revived, only to be abandoned through the later fatal outcome.

The death of kings is always of dramatic interest. I can remember the stunned feeling that came over the Empire when Queen Victoria died. Everyone felt it was the end of an era. Edward VII left no such feeling. He was a popular but distant figure. George V came much nearer to us. We heard his voice on the wireless. We could think of him as a man not unlike ourselves, although he was a king. The message from Dawson of Penn coming over the wireless, punctuating the last few hours at Sandringham, iterating and reiterating "The King's life is moving peacefully towards its close", made him seem almost painfully near to us.

George VI came even nearer. Television brought him into our homes. His reluctance to take over the burden of kingship; his devotion to duty; all produced a deep affection which is still an active memory.

But at the time of his first illness no one anticipated a fatal issue, and the world went on happily.

Easing the last days of the dying is one of the privileges Medicine shares with the Church. Two of my friends died at the end of 1948: Hugh Elliot and D. S. MacColl. No two people could have been more dissimilar. Elliot was the great-great-grandson of the famous Quaker physician, Lettsom, and he had all the quiet sweetness of his Quaker ancestry. He was a barrister of the Middle Temple, lived there, but never practised. Instead he became a publisher; and it was as the Chairman of the Heinemann Medical Company that I met him first, became his friend and adviser, and later his successor in the Chair.

We worked together for over twenty years without a single disagreement. I knew for some time after he retired that he was dying, and he knew it too, but we never mentioned it. We just talked about his books, his pictures and the future of the Company. One afternoon when I went to see him he looked very frail, and I was not surprised when the little Irish nurse who was looking after him rang me up the same evening to say he had died at nine-forty-five p.m. I saw him the morning after. He had the calm white sculptured beauty of death. Acting according to his wishes, I cut his radial artery to make sure he was dead.

Douglas Sutherland MacColl was a completely different sort of person. He spent his life fighting. He was never happy unless he was attacking someone or something. Tall, lean, grey, with a faint Scottish accent, 'a bonnie fechter', he was a holy terror. At Oxford he won the Newdigate and never allowed you to forget it. He was a friend of Ruskin. He knew Matthew Arnold, Andrew Lang, Mark Pattison, Walter Pater. He attacked the Royal Academy consistently throughout his life, was contemptuous of the Chantrey Bequest, at one time was Keeper of the Tate Gallery, and afterwards of the Wallace Collection. He started the 'Friends of the National Gallery'. Everyone recognised his great ability and his integrity; but everyone was afraid of him, except maybe John Tweed, who was also a rebel himself. At the Club, painters and architects avoided him. They kept him off the Arts Committee for the sake of peace and quiet. At the end he was very lonely. He had two sons living, but his wife was dead. Nearly all his contemporaries were dead. His tongue had been so blistering he had almost no friends left.

I had a curious affection for him. I never knew quite why. I went to see him in Hampstead, a gaunt skeleton of a man, all alone except for a devoted old family nurse. He was very tired and, at the age of eighty-nine, I think he was more than ready to die.

The death of my old friend Robert Lynd, in 1949, left another blank. Robert was literary editor of the *Daily News* and later of the *News Chronicle*. I knew him first as a boy coming down to Portrush in the summer holidays, diving off the rocks at the famous 'Blue Pool' or racing along the sands with my brother and myself.

Our paths took different directions, and we did not meet again until 1913, when he came to see me in Wimpole Street, very tall, very bent, looking like a benevolent stage bishop, with just the same charming smile that I remembered.

He said he was worried about his heart. He suffered from a fear that he would die suddenly. I examined him, could find nothing wrong and told him so. I heard later he had had this dread for years; but, as he lived another thirty-six, I think his fear must have been groundless, and my prognosis correct. During all that time he was turning out book reviews and charming little whimsical essays in the English tradition like 'The Art of Letters', 'The Pleasures of Ignorance' and 'Life's little Oddities', all immensely readable—worthy of Charles Lamb himself, I used to think.

I felt a sudden loneliness when I heard of his death. It was another link with my boyhood broken.

*

I have often wondered what makes people prefer one doctor to another, for I have frequently been struck by the inconsequential choice that patients have shown when I meet their family doctors in consultation. And I have come to believe that it isn't so much knowledge as kindliness and understanding that determines their choice. Possibly that is one reason why Irish doctors are often so popular in this country.

There have been periods, however, when for political reasons Irishmen have not been popular; and young doctors have then found difficulty in obtaining hospital and other appointments. This from time to time becomes very important because Ireland, like Scotland, produces more doctors and more whisky than she needs, and she has to export. So, to further the interests of young doctors, there has existed for many years in London 'The Irish Medical Schools and Graduates Association'. I was President of this Association when war broke out in 1939, but during the war years it ceased to function. After peace came, however, we revived it, and I was again elected President in 1949.

In the gift of the Association is the Arnott Memorial Gold Medal, founded in memory of Sir John Arnott, the proprietor of the *Irish Times*. This magnificent medal is awarded at intervals to some Irish doctor "for gallantry in the field, or some achievement in medicine, surgery or medical research". Twice it has been presented to Irish doctors who have won two of the thirty-seven V.C.s awarded to the R.A.M.C., but generally owing to a shortage of V.C.s it has gone to medical research. And the list of recipients is graced by such names as Sir Almroth Wright for his work on typhoid inoculation, Sir Peter Freyer for inventing the operation of prostatectomy, Sir Havelock Charles, a distinguished surgeon in the Boer War, Sir Berkeley Moynihan (Lord Moynihan), the famous Leeds surgeon, Sir Gordon Holmes, F.R.S., the neurologist, Sir Robert McCarrison, formerly Director of Nutrition, India, and Sir William MacArthur, a Director-General of the Army Medical Service and a distinguished Gaelic scholar.

I was therefore very gratified when the Council of the Association voted to present me with this medal in 1949, in recognition, they said, of my work as a medical historian.

When I told my wife the date of the presentation, she said:

"But how lovely! That will be the twenty-ninth anniversary of our wedding day!"

Women have a knack of remembering dates like this.

One of the privileges of being President of the Association is presiding at the luncheon of Irish doctors at the Annual Meeting of the British Medical Association.

This was held at Harrogate in 1949, and there I met several men I had not seen for many years. It was an eye-opener. They all seemed so old. I looked at one man in some doubt, and said to myself:

'Who is that fellow

> Standing with reluctant feet,
> Where waistcoat buttons
> Almost fail to meet?

Surely not George Dinsmore who used to play three-quarter for Lansdowne?'

It was. And I have no doubt George was wondering if I was the same man he used to know. But, over the wine and our reminiscences of the golden days of youth, we forgave each other for being surprised at the results of Time's handiwork.

*

CHAPTER XXX

THEN AND NOW

ON DECEMBER 21ST, 1950, I had been a doctor for fifty years, and that started me looking back on my life and thinking of the changes I had seen and experienced in surgery and medicine in the previous half-century.

When I qualified Queen Victoria was still on the throne. People were singing 'Soldiers of the Queen' and 'Good-bye Dolly Gray'. The Boer War was petering out; Lord Roberts had come home in triumph, leaving Kitchener to finish the campaign; and there was a general feeling of relief in the air. We boasted that the sun never set on the Great British Empire. I was twenty-four years old, wide-eyed, hopeful, with all the world before me. Life was intensely exhilarating. There were so many things I could do, so many openings.

One of the first places I went to look at when I came to London was Harley Street, the Mecca towards which the eyes of every aspirant to success and fame in our profession naturally turn.

Harley Street was then an exclusively doctors' street, apart from a bank at each end to capture the guineas, Queen's College in the middle to educate the children of the consultants, and a Home for Decayed Governesses next to Queen's, for no reason whatever.

Wimpole Street was not so strictly professional. Where Queen Anne Street crossed it, there was a baker's shop that sold Sir Henry Thompson's bread on one side, and a public-house on the other. Sir Frederick Treves, however, practised there and gave it distinction. But because nearly everyone lived over his consulting-rooms the so-called 'Harley Street area' was much more extensive then than it is now. The side-streets, Queen Anne, Welbeck, Weymouth and Devonshire, were mainly medical. Every house in Cavendish Square harboured a doctor. Henrietta Street (now Henrietta Place) was almost entirely medical.

Hanover Square and George Street had consultants. So had Manchester Square. Brook Street had its quota. My old chief, Keetley, lived in Grosvenor Street. Even in the City there were still consulting surgeons

Bart's and London men in Finsbury Square, Guy's men in St. Thomas's Street—for the day of the motor was not yet, and an assistant surgeon or physician had to live within two miles' cab distance of his hospital to be readily available for emergencies. Jonathan Hutchinson told me he got on the staff of the London Hospital because Mr. Wordsworth, a nephew of the poet, refused to live near; and Arbuthnot Lane, greatly daring, said he moved to Cavendish Square without permission of Guy's.

The position of the consulting surgeon and the consulting physician in the profession was then still supreme. The specialist had not yet really arrived. There were of course ophthalmic surgeons and obstetric physicians, one or two throat surgeons and, oddly enough, a number of dermatologists whose main source of income, I was told, was treating unacknowledged or unrecognised syphilis; but by and large the consulting surgeon took on anything surgical and the consulting physician everything medical.

Naturally there were far fewer consultants then, and everyone knew everyone else. Most of them, as I have said, lived over the brass plate; it was not customary to see more than one name on each door; and when a consultant took a house his neighbour's wife called on his wife soon after. Today it is not unusual to see six to ten plates on a door. No one knows who anyone is, and nobody cares—the specialist has swamped the consultant. Dental surgery is now a recognised specialty; but the idea of a dentist daring to aspire to a plate in the sacred Harley Street area was then almost unthinkable. A dentist was hardly considered a gentleman in 1900. There was no dental register until 1922, and any unqualified person could call himself a dentist until that date.

It was not possible to see a consultant in 1900 without a letter of introduction from the family doctor—a very good rule, now nearly dead, which had much to commend it. Appointments were not made for any definite time. Patients arrived, waited in the waiting-room and were ushered in turn into the presence by the butler. It is said that those who knew the ropes tipped the butler in order to be seen sooner.

Consultants wrote their own reports to the family doctors by hand, and posted them in the evening. The idea of having a young woman secretary typing out confidential letters would have been unthinkable in 1900.

The fees for consultants were two guineas for the first visit, and one guinea for each subsequent one. With income tax about a shilling in the pound, real golden sovereigns in circulation, and prices what they then were, these were far better fees than are customary today.

*

The type of surgery fifty years ago was very different from what we see today. Thinking of the operations we did I can remember long lists of 'glands in the neck'. Excisions of tuberculous elbows, hips and knees were next in frequency. This was an indication of how prevalent in those days was infection from tuberculous milk. Hernias and hæmorrhoids came next. Removal of the appendix was just coming in. Keetley was very pleased and excited, I remember, when I once collected six cases for him in a fortnight; and he operated on them all successfully.

Appendicitis was then considered a comparatively new disease. Of course it wasn't really new. It had been with us always, only it just wasn't recognised. Formerly, when a patient got it he either survived or died, for he was never operated upon. But if a post-mortem was done, it was found he had died of inflammation of the bowels. Sometimes instead of dying he got an abscess low down on the right side; and this abscess, if left alone, used occasionally to burst and discharge externally. Accidents of this sort suggested to surgeons that they should operate and drain the abscess instead of allowing it to burst. It was when operating on such cases that J. B. Murphy, a famous surgeon in Chicago, discovered the whole trouble started from inflammation of a small wormlike tube of the bowel, the appendix, which lies low down in the right side of the abdomen. When it got inflamed the disease would sometimes spread to the surrounding parts of the intestine, and peritonitis and death were liable to follow. So, when Murphy discovered this, he began to remove the appendix as soon as painful symptoms appeared, and thus often saved the life of his patient. This was a mile-stone in the history of abdominal surgery.

Sir Frederick Treves was probably the first surgeon in England to remove a diseased appendix; and Keetley was certainly one of the earliest to follow in his footsteps.

It was the sudden illness of King Edward VII in 1902 which made the great British public conscious that there was such a disease and such an operation. They have been increasingly conscious of it ever since. Years later, I asked Treves how he felt when he was called in to see King Edward and knew that all the Court physicians and surgeons were against his operating.

"I told them," he said, grimly, "that there was no difference between a king's abdomen and that of one of his gardeners; and if he were a gardener I'd operate. That got 'em. Actually, I didn't do an appendicectomy on him. I opened the abscess. The appendix had sloughed off, and I couldn't find it. I was on tenterhooks for a week, but he recovered, and all was well."

That shows how we have progressed. Everyone now would think it criminal to hesitate for a moment about operating on such a condition.

In 1900, gastric ulcer with severe hæmorrhage in young women was common; but duodenal ulcer, on the other hand, was only beginning to be recognised. We treated it by using a metal contraption called a Murphy's Button. The results were very uncertain. If the operation was successful the Button passed on down the intestine. If it didn't, it fell back into the stomach and had to be removed by a second operation. I feel sure if I showed a Murphy's Button to a medical student today he would not have the faintest idea what it had been used for.

Stone in the kidney was still mostly diagnosed, when I was a house-surgeon, by the typical pain of renal colic, for X-rays were not good enough to show definitely the shadow of stone until about 1904. In cases of renal colic, therefore, we used to cut down on the kidney, take a long needle and push it into the kidney substance. If a stone was present it gritted. We were nearly always right in our diagnosis, but if not we put the kidney back and sewed up the incision in the loin, generally without any ill effect to the patient.

Operations on the gall-bladder were still looked upon as dangerous, in spite of the pioneer work of that bumptious little man, Mayo Robson. If we operated at all, it was to drain it directly through the abdominal wall, letting it go on discharging bile till the wound dried up.

We were good at crushing stone in the bladder. We learnt that from surgeons of the Indian Medical Service. Cancer in the abdomen or rectum was treated as a rule by colotomy. There was nearly always a colotomy or two in our surgical wards. And of course we had lots of fractures. Chest surgery simply meant operating for empyema or fractured ribs. Ideas of removing a lung or doing plastic operations on the heart were still in the womb of time. No one dreamt of such things. Indeed, twenty-five years later, when Sir Henry Souttar first put his finger into a heart to stretch the mitral valve, he was warned that if the patient died he might have to resign from the London Hospital. Now they do a hundred a year there.

Brain surgery in 1900 was as yet confined to treating fractures of the skull and abscesses of the brain. Horsley was just beginning his pioneer work at University College Hospital, removing tumours from the spine, trephining for growths in the brain, starting a new specialty: neurosurgery.

After I came to London I went once to see Sir William Watson Cheyne operating at King's College Hospital, which was then just behind Lincoln's Inn Fields. The operating theatre was a huge lecture room with tiers and tiers of seats in ascending semicircular rows, and the operations were done in the narrow space on the ground floor, surrounded on three sides by these tiers of seats. The case, wheeled in, was first demonstrated to the students, then anæsthetised, then operated on. How impossible that would be today; but no one thought it out of the ordinary in those days.

At the West London Hospital the one theatre was a bare room with a north-lit window, a linoleum-covered floor, and a big open coal fire in the winter. Why we never had an explosion when we used ether I cannot understand. There was a Lister's carbolic spray on a shelf in one corner. I was just a bit too late to see it in use. Surgeons had long since stopped operating in old greasy frock coats. Instead, we wore waterproof aprons that had been sterilised with carbolic acid, for the white operating gowns with long sleeves and rubber gloves, now customary, had not been invented. Masks had not been thought of. We operated with our bare hands, which used to get very raw and painful from frequent dipping into carbolic lotion, or corrosive sublimate, or both when we were extra busy.

The operating-table was of wood. It had no tilting mechanism. Metal instruments were boiled, but knives still had black or white bone handles and so were put into one-in-twenty carbolic lotion to be sterilised. Private operations were done in the patients' homes. A room, cleared of furniture, was made into an improvised theatre; and bowls and basins from the kitchen were commandeered. Sometimes the patients' relatives hired an enamelled iron operating-table, but often only a kitchen one was available. The general practitioner in charge of the case usually gave the anæsthetic; for the professional anæsthetist was only just beginning to be recognised.

Years later I saw the table King Edward VII had been operated upon by Sir Frederick Treves. It was a beautiful mahogany brass-bound affair, flat and without accessories, very unlike the streamlined chromium-plated table of the present day, with its heating arrangements, head rests, method of raising and lowering, and complete tilting mechanism such as every hospital now uses for the poorest patient.

*

When I decided I wanted to be a consultant I had to make up my mind between medicine and surgery. If I had been able to foresee the enormous strides in medicine that were coming in the next thirty years, I think I might have preferred to be a physician rather than a surgeon.

But I had always wanted to be a surgeon and in 1900 there seemed to be no future in medicine, for, apart from six or seven real drugs that really cured, the pharmacopœia was cluttered with hundreds of useless placebos.

People died of pneumonia, they died of typhoid, they died of scarlet fever. Tuberculosis claimed its thousands yearly. Children died of measles, marasmus, enteritis. There was little one could do for such patients except nurse them and hope for the best. The outlook of many physicians, therefore, at that time was one of therapeutic nihilism. When patients recovered we talked of the *vis medicatrix naturae*. When they died the fact was accepted as inevitable. Everything had been done that could be done, was the comforting formula.

Surgery, on the other hand, was forging ahead. Surgeons were doing things that seemed worth while. They got results. They cured people. The only rival to surgery, in my mind, was gynæcology. Dublin is famous for its school of midwifery and diseases of women. I liked treating women; but I had the impression that the day of the woman doctor, then beginning to dawn, would gradually drive out the mere man. I didn't know much about women in those days or I'd never have thought that. So I decided to be a surgeon.

I do not regret the choice I made over fifty years ago. But with an ambivalence of this nature ever present in my mind I have never lost interest in medical progress or in conditions peculiar to women. In my practice I have found this of the greatest benefit to my outlook on the whole world of medicine; and I have always looked on myself as a physician practising surgery. I have watched and been thrilled, therefore, by all the advances in every department of medical research and practice throughout this half-century; and I have seen how often advances in surgery have been dependent on something in medicine or one of the 'ologies' apparently unconnected, for science is increasingly interdependent, and nearly every new discovery somehow or other eventually dovetails into, modifies or supersedes surgical practice.

Diphtheria, for instance, was always with us when I was a young house-surgeon. Practically every week I would be called down to the Reception Room, generally in the middle of the night when I was on emergency duty, to save the life of some tiny mite with croup, struggling for breath, carried in wrapped in a shawl by its distracted mother. This was a condition requiring rapid treatment. I had to do a tracheotomy, that is, cut down on the larynx, open it wide, and put in a silver tube to get past the stoppage in the windpipe and so enable the child to breathe again. If this was not done quickly the child died. Nowadays, a house-surgeon might go all through his term of office and never see a case; but in those days it was so common we became very expert at it.

Von Behring, however, in his laboratory had already devised something that was going speedily to make our skill at doing a tracheotomy unnecessary. This was antidiphtheritic serum, which, given in time, aborts the disease. Now we go further still. By inoculating children beforehand we prevent them even acquiring the disease.

In the First World War, when I was in Serbia, I used to look on helplessly at wounded men dying in awful agony from tetanus (lock-jaw), because I had no serum. In the Second World War, tetanus toxoid protected against infection by tetanus so much that we hardly ever saw it.

In the Boer War more men died of typhoid than of wounds. Now a vaccine of dead typhoid germs protects against typhoid. So when you travel by plane to certain countries you are compelled to have an injection of T.A.B. vaccine and yellow fever vaccine. The T.A.B. is to protect you from getting typhoid or paratyphoid by drinking water or milk contaminated by the typhoid or paratyphoid bacillus. The yellow fever vaccine is to prevent you carrying the fever from Africa or South America, where it is common and you could catch it, to Asia or Australia, where it does not occur and you could introduce it.

Up to 1900, drugs to cure disease were largely the result of chance discovery—digitalis for heart trouble, opium for pain, quinine for malaria, mercury for syphilis. But by 1910 the biochemist had come to the help of the physician. He had begun to *invent* drugs to cure disease, and his method was to infect some laboratory animal, like a guinea-pig or a white rat, with a known disease and then try the effect of the drug he had invented on it. If it failed to cure or was dangerous to life he discarded it. If it cured the laboratory animal he tried it next very carefully on man. That was how Ehrlich discovered that '606' would cure syphilis, and, in so doing, thus became the father of chemotherapy.

There is a disease called puerperal fever which attacks women in childbirth. It is very deadly. Yearly it killed thousands of mothers. We knew the germ that caused it. We knew that it could be carried by the nurse or the doctor or a visitor or even by the patient's own hands. It occurred when every precaution was taken, and the tragedy of the young mother dying, leaving motherless children, was ever in our minds. And then came a drug called 'prontosil' which had been found to cure swine fever. It was tried on puerperal fever. The year was 1935, and suddenly puerperal fever ceased to be a menace.

A whole new series of drugs based on sulphanilamide, the active principle of prontosil, then rapidly began to appear. The biochemists vied with one another to invent them. Diseases like pneumonia, spotted fever, meningitis and the like, which were often so fatal, became almost innocuous. Sir Winston Churchill owed his life, for instance, to one of these drugs when he got pneumonia in the middle of the Second World War.

The revolution in medical treatment was almost comparable to that of Lister and antiseptics. Medicine was now getting powerful weapons to fight infection. The dead period was vanishing. No longer was it necessary to stand by with folded arms waiting for disease to kill or nature to cure.

But even as early as 1929 another great advance was being worked out by Fleming, based on his discovery that the blue mould, Penicillium Notatum, had the power of destroying bacteria. It was the war that saved this from being looked upon as an interesting scientific curiosity of no practical value, for the discovery was then taken up by the Medical Research Council.

It is an odd thought that but for the war, and the need to search for anything likely to be helpful to the wounded, Fleming's work might never have been followed up. Luckily it was. Since then more and more antibiotics have been discovered almost yearly, and are coming into use. A new source of power against disease has thus been put into our hands. Fleming built for humanity a bridge to health greater than he or anyone else ever could have anticipated.

When Starling and Bayliss discovered 'Secretin' in 1902 in the laboratory of University College and called it a 'Hormone', I am sure they had no idea of the future of the word and the immense new field in science they had opened. Today everyone knows about hormones, for they control growth, they can make a giant or a dwarf, their presence can produce a genius, their absence an imbecile. The sex hormones are responsible for the beauty of woman, the virility of man, all the romance of life, love and passion. No one knew anything about hormones when I qualified in 1900; and I was in practice for twenty years before I heard the word 'Vitamin'. Now every morning my letter-box is cluttered with so-called 'literature' extolling the virtue of this or that vitamin or combination of vitamins.

Whilst all these fundamental discoveries were being made, there had also been so much progress in surgery that the idea has become prevalent that surgeons are now many more times more skilful with their hands than they were fifty years ago. That is not correct. Surgery has advanced enormously. Areas of the body, 'silent areas' in 1900, are now being actively investigated; but this is largely due to the help surgery has obtained in diagnosis and treatment from physiology, radiology, biochemistry, anæsthetics and other scientific aids. Arterial grafts, intricate operations on the brain, eye and heart requiring great skill, are now possible because of these aids. The surgeons of fifty years ago had equal manual dexterity and an even more delicate sense of touch. But without the modern aids to diagnosis and treatment they could not have attempted, or even envisaged the possibility of attempting, many of the operations we do today.

When X-rays were discovered we thought they would be useful only for fractures. Exposures of half to three minutes were needed to get a picture then, and the rays showed up only dense objects, bone or foreign bodies like bullets. The abdomen was a 'silent area'. It showed up nothing under the X-rays. Then an American physiologist, Cannon, had an inspiration. He fed cats with porridge mixed with bismuth, an opaque substance that showed up with X-rays. The bismuth coated the intestinal tract of the cats, and he was able with the aid of X-rays to photograph the outline of the cats' stomachs and the small and large intestines, and trace the movement of food through their bodies.

Surgeons were quick to seize on this. Why not try it on man! And so we were able to see for the first time the outlines of the ulcer in a stomach or duodenum, or the narrowing produced by a cancerous growth in the gullet or large intestine.

Injections of certain opaque materials intravenously were found under the X-ray to outline the kidney or gall-bladder and tell us definitely if stones were present in either organ. We no longer had to cut down on them blindly. Arteries were injected and we could trace tumours in the brain. It was thus a matter of skilful carpentry to operate on a certainty; but if we had had this knowledge in 1900 we could have done the same.

Very beautifully planned operations were carried out in Edward VII's reign, and it was a well-known gibe: "The operation was successful but the patient died." Today we operate no more skilfully on the same conditions; but the patients do not die, because the pathologist has taught us the supreme value of blood transfusion during operation;

and we prevent them from dying after operation by continuing, if necessary, these transfusions, and watching the water and electrolyte balance so that our patients do not get dehydrated—words that meant nothing in 1900 to a surgeon, but conditions which caused more deaths after operation, especially in children, at that time than anything else.

Instruments have been perfected since 1900 which were then in their infancy. We can see into the lung with a bronchoscope; we can see into the bladder with a cystoscope; we can use a sigmoidoscope; and often we can treat by means of direct vision some of the things we see with these instruments.

*

In 1900 we had two main anæsthetics: chloroform and ether, both merciful helps to the surgeon, but each potentially dangerous to life. Now we have intravenous anæsthetics, spinal anæsthesia and a number of general anæsthetics from which to choose, most of them much safer than the two we depended on in 1900. Formerly one had to push the dosage of these anæsthetics to get the patient so relaxed that the surgeon could operate. Now we have relaxants which take all resistance out of muscle and permit one to use much smaller amounts of any anæsthetic. We can operate on the heart with safety and do prolonged operations on the brain without risk.

On the other hand whole fields of surgery that once existed have now almost disappeared. Tuberculous glands and joints are examples. We seldom see a typhoid ulcer now. Many of the grosser deformities of Victorian days have disappeared. We used to do elaborate operations for rickets because we hadn't discovered the vitamins. Now a rickety child is a rarity, thanks to Vitamin D. Children used to die in thousands every summer of what we called scurvy rickets (Barlow's disease), simply because we did not know that Vitamin C (ascorbic acid) was a complete cure for the condition.

Even in recent years, in spite of all our care, patients died of septic infections after operations, and if possible we avoided operating on certain organs or areas because we feared such infection. Now, thanks to the sulphonamides and the antibiotics, which we use as figurative 'umbrellas' to protect the patient from infection, we are able to take risks in these areas and save life, knowing we can control infection should it arise.

Surgery has been fortunate in that it has been able to take advantage of the work of the immunologists like Sir Almroth Wright with his vaccines, the organic chemists like Ehrlich with his '606' and Domagk with his sulphonamides. The physiologists, Starling and Bayliss, started the work that gave us hormones such as insulin. Biochemists like Gowland Hopkins gave us the vitamins. From the bacteriologists like Fleming we got the antibiotics.

All this we owe to that side of our profession we associate with medicine. I am glad I am a surgeon; but I always have the feeling that many of the fine feathers we assume, and the public allows many of us to assume, should really bedeck the 'backroom boys', many of whom the public never hears of.

*

I resigned my last hospital appointment about the time of the death of George VI. This death seemed somehow to mark the end of another epoch. We had been used to kings for fifty years, and now a beautiful young queen found herself unexpectedly early on the throne. The similarity to the story of the young Queen Victoria was in everyone's mind; and just as the death of Queen Victoria seemed to us who remembered it to be the end of an era, so the accession of Elizabeth II brought a feeling of a new and brighter reign, a sudden hope to a world weary of international fear.

We felt that another Elizabethan age was about to begin. We felt we might again see the light and fire, the same boldness and enterprise that symbolised the age of Elizabeth I. We hoped the new reign was going to rejuvenate our tired post-war world.

It was a heartening feeling, but maybe we were hoping for too much. A wave of pessimism succeeded the first glad surge of optimism. Old men, as you know, have always said: "The country is going to the dogs." Their blood runs cold. It distresses me, however, to hear young men echoing this pessimism. I remember their saying it before the First World War, and I remember how gloriously they proved themselves wrong. I remember it being said before the Second World War, and again the pessimists were confounded. So now, in spite of wars and rumours of war and the threat of mass destruction, I am still a confirmed optimist; and I believe the pessimists will once more be proved wrong and we shall see the sun coming up over the horizon of a peaceful world.

*

L'ENVOI

LOOKING BACK OVER MY LIFE I feel I must often have given a wrong impression of myself. Some people may have thought me bored and superior, for I have a poker face. But I have never been bored in my life; I do not know what boredom means; and I have never felt superior. Instead, all my life I have had to force myself to meet people and do things. Essentially I am a looker-on at life, and every responsibility I have undertaken has been thrust upon me. I have never tried hard to get anything.

But I have been fortunate.

Everything I have done seems as if it were inevitable. I haven't had to fight for it. It just happened. I am lucky in that I come from tough, long-lived Ulster stock. Ulstermen have a fine conceit of themselves. It is a sign of provincialism we share with the Scots; and it is our natural reaction against the preponderance of the English. But it is the quality that has supplied five recent Field-Marshals to the British Army, and fourteen Presidents of Ulster stock to the United States. So I hope it may be forgiven.

I was fortunate in that I came, an impressionable youth, into the cultured atmosphere of Trinity at a time when Dublin had such scholars as Bury, Mahaffy, Palmer and Tyrrell in classics, Salmon in mathematics, Dowden in English, and such scientists as Cunningham in anatomy, Fitzgerald in physics, Joly in geology.

I was lucky in that the medical curriculum had not yet become so crowded that the classics had been driven out, and I could study Aristotle in the morning and pathology in the afternoon with the same professor, Tully O' Sullivan. The atmosphere in Trinity at that time was, as Dean Inge noticed, eighteenth-century, and to me the eighteenth century is still my spiritual home.

At Steevens' Hospital with its memories of Swift and Stella, Colles and McDonnell, and its unique library, carefully guarded by that great bibliophile T.C.P. Kirkpatrick, I acquired the love of medical history which has been such a guide and pleasure to me all my life.

I cannot think also it was an accident that at Steeven's I had charge as a Resident of Colles's ward, learnt of 'Colles's Law', read his great classic, and thereby laid the foundation of my life-long interest in the study of venereal disease which he so greatly advanced. I feel that it was a memory of those student days, and an intense desire to help and succour the derelict and despised sufferers from the consequences of their infections, that turned the scales when Jonathan Hutchinson advised me against taking up the subject, saying it would kill my surgery. It is a decision I have never regretted. It did not kill my surgery—I had twenty-five happy years of it. But it did enable me to rescue several poor souls from despair and suicide, and to restore self-respect to many others. Through it I was often able to preserve family life, make deep and lasting friendships, and gain an insight into human nature which has made me more charitable towards all men.

The failure of my health from overwork in 1906 was a blessing in disguise. It drove me to sea as a doctor and resulted in my writing *The Surgeon's Log*, thus opening a second equally fascinating career to me.

When the First World War broke out I was crippled with sciatica. If I had been fit I should have been almost certainly in the R.N.V.R., since I love the sea and the men who sail in ships. But instead I had the experience of the great typhus epidemic in Serbia, joined the R.A.M.C. and ended up on Allenby's Staff in Palestine. Perhaps if I had been in the Navy I might have been fortunate in some other way. I do not know.

I have seen so much of the seamy side of family life that I hold myself singularly fortunate my own has been such a happy one.

I have had to undergo two major operations. They taught me much of how a patient feels; and made me, I hope, gentler, more understanding and more considerate of the doubts and fears of others who have been under my care.

My professional life has also been a happy one. My colleagues have honoured me sometimes beyond my deserts. In my work I have tried always to keep before my mind the maxims of that great doyen of our profession, Sir Robert Hutchison, who prayed:

> *From inability to let well alone;*
> *from too much zeal for the new,*
> *and contempt for what is old;*
> *from putting knowledge before wisdom,*
> *science before art, cleverness before*
> *common sense; from treating patients*
> *as cases; and from making the cure*
> *of the disease more grievous than the*
> *endurance of the same,*
> *Good Lord deliver us.*

Literature has been my second love, and I have valued immensely the friendship of other writers. Much that I have written has been from the heart; and it has been a great pleasure to me during and since the war, when writing under my pseudonym as 'James Harpole', to get hundreds of letters from all over the world from people whom I have helped or whose fears I have allayed.

I can truly say, therefore, that "the lines are fallen unto me in pleasant places; yea, I have a goodly heritage".

FINIS

*

INDEX